Praise for Glen David Gold's

I WILL BE COMPLETE

"Equally subtle and shocking, as clear-eyed about how the sins of the parent are visited on the child as it is generous and loving. . . . You cannot read it and remain unchanged."　　　　　　　—*The Irish Times*

"Brilliant. . . . Dazzlingly insightful. . . . Moving."
　　　　　　　　　　　　　　　　　　　—*The Spectator* (London)

"Remarkable. . . . Gold's book is funnier and more hopeful than any story about a child's abandonment and a parent's descent into terrifying chaos has a right to be."　　　　　—*The Sunday Times* (London)

"Compelling. . . . Both funny and profoundly moving."
　　　　　　　　　　　　　　　　　　　—*Sunday Express* (London)

"Smart, generous and gripping until the very last pages. It's one of the best books I've read [this year]."　　　　　　—Johanna Thomas-Corr,
　　　　　　　　　　　　　　　　　　　　New Statesman (London)

"So well told, with such lucidity and honesty, it's almost frightening to read. . . . But Gold wears his wisdom and novelist's powers of observation lightly, remaining beguilingly modest and likeable to the end."
　　　　　　　　　　　　　　　　　　　—*The Big Issue* (London)

"A searching memoir."　　　　　　　　　—*O, The Oprah Magazine*

"Engaging. . . . A strong memoir that oozes with the excitement of a life well-lived—and well-analyzed."　　　　　　　—*Kirkus Reviews*

Glen David Gold

I WILL BE COMPLETE

Glen David Gold is the author of *Sunnyside* and *Carter Beats the Devil*, which has been translated into fourteen languages. His short stories and essays have appeared in *McSweeney's*, *Playboy*, and *The New York Times Magazine*. He lives in Los Angeles.

www.glendavidgold.com

ALSO BY GLEN DAVID GOLD

Sunnyside

Carter Beats the Devil

I WILL BE COMPLETE

I WILL
BE
COMPLETE

A Memoir

Glen David Gold

VINTAGE BOOKS
A Division of Penguin Random House LLC
New York

Portions of this work first appeared, in slightly different form, in the following
publications: *East Bay Express*: "One Man's Family" (January 13, 1995) and
"War of the Gargantuas" (March 6, 1998); *North County Reader*: "Baby, with
Me, Every Day Is Christmas" (May 22, 1997); *Zyzzyva*: "The Plush Cocoon"
(No. 100, Spring 2014) and "Operator, Information" (No. 108, Winter 2016);
"Anatomy Lesson" first appeared in *DUST-UP Anthology*, No. 1, originally
published by Bookcount, Los Angeles, California, in 2004.

The Library of Congress has cataloged the Knopf edition as follows:
Name: Gold, Glen David, 1964– author.
Title: I will be complete : a memoir / by Glen David Gold.
Description: First edition. | New York : Alfred A. Knopf, 2018.
Identifiers: LCCN 2017060203 (print) | LCCN 2017049131 (ebook)
Subjects: LCSH: Gold, Glen David, 1964—Biography. | Authors—United
States—Biography. | Parents—United States. | BISAC: BIOGRAPHY
& AUTOBIOGRAPHY / Personal Memoirs. | BIOGRAPHY &
AUTOBIOGRAPHY / Literary. | BIOGRAPHY & AUTOBIOGRAPHY /
Artists, Architects, Photographers.
Classification: LCC PS3607.O43 (print)|
LCC PS3607.O43 Z46 2018 (ebook) |DDC 818/.603 B—dc23
LC record available at https://lccn.loc.gov/2017060203

Vintage Books Trade Paperback ISBN: 978-1-101-91245-4
eBook ISBN: 978-1-101-94640-4

Book design by Maggie Hinders

www.vintagebooks.com

Printed in the United States of America
10 9 8 7 6 5 4 3 2 1

for Sara Shay

My mother assures me none of this happened.

1

THE
LAST KINGS
OF
SAN FRANCISCO

---

for Jennifer Leung

ADDRESS UNKNOWN

I THINK YOU'RE AN ADULT when you can no longer tell your life story over the course of a first date. I might have gotten this idea from my parents, because they reinvented themselves so often. Their stories have odd turns which speak not of one life, but of many that don't seem to match up, and of choices you'd think no one would actually make.

When I was twelve years old, I lived by myself for a while. This was the mid-1970s in San Francisco, so the rules were a little different then—and yet not so different that me living alone made much sense. When I describe what happened, people tend to ask, "But how did you end up so—" They dance around the word "normal," then realize it doesn't apply, and instead they say, "So *nice*?" I'm not nice. I'm polite. *Nice* is a quality and *polite* is a strategy. But I have ended up happy. Also, I've ended up something more unusual than that: autonomous.

I have a good memory but lately I've been looking for people who might know more, and I come up empty. Life in the 1970s led to a lot of bad luck and unexpected consequences. Perversely, I'm relieved when I learn some people I wanted to talk to are dead. But then I find one man I don't actually want to: Peter Charming. He's almost invisible, but I'm good at research.

He has no business licenses. He doesn't own property in his name.

The house he lived in when I knew him turns out to have belonged to somebody else, and even his 1970s phone number is assigned to a different person in old directories. I can't find any criminal records, though those are difficult to get to the bottom of. The San Francisco Superior Court, however, provides some sheet music in a way and it's up to me to imagine the score. There are civil lawsuits. In some, he's the defendant and in others the plaintiff. One of them went on for seven years and struggled all the way to trial twice.

There are ways the mind pushes back against knowing too much. You research too long. You obsess over irrelevant details. Your memories tend to come in snapshots without context. You amaze the world by how unfazed, how *nice* you seem. You discount cruelties as if they're anecdotes best brought out in a barroom competition. You also tend to say "you" when you mean "I."

When I was a kid, Peter was bad to my mom. She managed to escape eventually, but at a cost. I don't know if the damage he inflicted upon her was worse financially or emotionally. In our family, money is a convenient cipher for the wounds that are harder to qualify. Accounting for his charisma and promises, you could reduce him to an elemental force that moved my mother and me forward, then backward, then apart. My mother is much more important, but when I think of looking directly at her I reflexively retreat into research. I would rather look into Peter's life again.

People leave San Francisco but something always gets left behind. Usually it's gossip. I've mentioned his name to people who were in that social circle and it's like he never existed. I'm sure they met him and I don't think they're lying when they say they don't remember. He was of a time and a place that are gone. It's like asking about a statue in a park now the site of a high rise. *What happened to that old bronze bust? Didn't you see it?*

His picture is in the society column of the *San Francisco Chronicle* in the late 1960s, and he looks young. He hasn't learned arrogance yet. Instead, he looks just shy of self-confident, asking the camera to confirm it sees him as handsome. He's an escort for women who are older. They have their own money, and my hunch is that when they stopped seeing Peter, they still had all of it, minus what they'd given him knowingly. That was before the 1970s, the time that was made for him.

. . . .

One person reacted to his name, once. At a party sometime in the 1980s, I met a novelist whom I knew by reputation—a happy bullshit artist in the way of those Beats who made careers and academic posts by riding out the ambiguity of whether they'd actually had Kerouac sleep on their couch.

I was twenty-two and the novelist was in his sixties. He was talking to a beautiful woman who held her drink with both hands and who regarded him with suspicion, like he was about to offer her candy. As I was walking by, he brought me into the conversation, which I recognized as a gambit to make her reduce her grip on her glass to one hand, to let the other settle to her hip.

"Excuse me," he said to me. "You look part English."

"That's true."

"Is the other part—Jewish? I ask that as a full Jew myself."

"It is."

"I've often thought the combination of English and Ashkenazi makes the most handsome man in the room. Don't you think so?" he asked the girl, who was noncommittal. "This fine woman," he said a moment later, "still hasn't decided to leave her husband for me, but I can't blame her."

"The question is whether she's going to expand her horizons or let them stay as they are," I said.

He started to say something he'd prepared but faltered. The conversation continued the way he was driving it as before, but his interest in her—obligatory as it already was—was complicated by this: I wasn't a chump. I'd been moderately funny but I hadn't tried to compete. I was staying in the conversation to make him look good. That's a set of skills that develops in unusual circumstances. After the woman left for better prospects, he wanted to know about me.

"How did you come to San Francisco?" he asked.

"My mother met a man at the Mark Hopkins Hotel."

When that was all I said, he laughed. "What is it about the Mark Hopkins?"

"She met a man who said he wanted to buy her a balloon and take her to Paris."

I have to stop short my writer's memory, the desire to underline. I can't claim that he froze his wrist just as the drink was about to meet his lips. "I think I knew that man," he said.

"You knew Peter Charming?"

When he spoke again, it was with caution. "Do you know where he is, still? Are you friends with his people?"

"No, not anymore."

It was unnerving to see a man like the novelist, whose identity pivoted on tall tales, sweep my eyes with conviction to see if I was telling the truth. How would he know if I was sincere? He asked my mother's name, I told him, he squinted—vaguely, he thought he remembered her, but he wasn't sure.

"Is your mother all right?"

"No."

"I'm sorry."

I'm never sure what to say when people have to say that about her.

Finally, he said, "Charming was doing terrible things."

"I know."

"You knew?" He looked alarmed. It was as if I were aware of atrocities but had done nothing.

No, maybe not, I realized.

"It was the seventies," he said, "and some of us fell victim to improving ourselves in ways that turned out *silly*. It was a *silly* decade. People took advantage of that. Charming was bad. I heard bad things."

"Like what?"

"White slavery."

I'd seen some things but no, I hadn't seen that. I wanted the conversation to last longer, but another woman walked by, as pretty as the last, and in mid-sentence the novelist waved her down, introducing us. He told her I was his son.

As I shook hands with her, he made up a biography for me, the spawn of his second marriage, I was out from Cleveland, I was on the crew team at my college, didn't I look just like him? As he spun the story I went along with it. He said my mother, his ex-wife, was English, and he felt that the combination of English and Ashkenazi Jew was the most handsome on earth. Hadn't he done right by me? Wasn't I a wonder?

· · ·

Later, I phoned my mother to tell her much of this conversation. I treated our talks back then like trips down hallways with certain rooms under lock and key, but I didn't think about why I was so careful. I told her about the novelist introducing me as his son, which she found delightful. I didn't say he'd asked if she was okay, or that I'd said she wasn't.

"What did he say about Peter?" she asked.

"He said Peter was involved in white slavery?" I rarely speak with that uptick. But I was asking a question as subtly as I knew how, not very subtly at all. What exactly were Peter's limits?

She answered in a way that I would have said I felt nothing about. "Oh, Peter. You know, it was so hard to stay mad at him. He was like a big kid."

And there it was, that statement I felt nothing about, remembered for decades when I have long forgotten the details of birthdays and first kisses. How did I really feel? I felt a dry, hot, constricting tension that I did not allow dominion over me. I felt like I wanted the conversation to be over so I could tell people about it and read from their faces how I should feel too. Might it be disturbing that my mother had suggested human trafficking was forgivable, if not childlike? I'm not asking that rhetorically; I'm looking for confirmation. I look to you, you nod, I nod back.

"How do you feel, Glen, about a man you knew well perhaps being the worst sort of human being?"

With pride in my voice at my own detachment, I would say, "Nothing," and upon your suggestion—probably unspoken, probably just a puzzled squint that I'm trained to look for—that someone more fully aware might feel *something*, I would think, "No, I'm too strong for that. Nothing can touch me."

That reaction is what this story is about. For much of my life there has been a circuitous pathway between when something happens and when I react. This gives the illusion of stillness, when in fact it's about trying to accommodate too much at once. I do not have feelings so much as I gauge what a loved one would want me to feel, and then I tell myself about that.

Perhaps that's familiar to you. Have you ever used a key on the lock of an old mountain cabin, felt it stick, and tried to imagine its teeth engaging tumblers? Have you tried making friends with its unknowable history, coaxing it into unfreezing, and have you promised you will not give in to a burst of anger that could snap it in half? Then you know what it is like to be my mother's son. It's exhausting and it's where art forms are born. I think Baroque draftsmen who made etchings of labyrinths were men raised by shattered women.

Peter Charming is a part of the story, but really, I'm looking for my mother, or what remains of her. There is not going to be redemption here; nor am I going to indict her as a monster. There is another way to go for those of us who can no longer love our mothers. I have learned compassion for her, what an old friend calls "compassion from a distance." My mother's life has been a tragedy but mine has not. And let's be honest here. My mother isn't the story, either.

I'd like to tell you about myself, which makes me want to apologize, the way my needing anything always does. I place a high value on autonomy. When I was so young that my memories were hardly even meant to be permanent, three or four years old, my parents and I were watching television. I saw actors talking to camera. It impressed my parents. They said there was something sophisticated in admitting that the scene had an audience. So, while I was hammering the flippers of my pinball machine, or sinking shampoo bottles in the bathtub as if they were my great-grandfather's U-boat, I began talking to camera myself. I knew it wasn't real, but it was also as vivid as the adventures I gave my stuffed kangaroo.

When I was alone in a room, I was never alone, for there was an audience I was meant to entertain, and after I was put to bed, time and again my mother or father had to come into the room to tell me to be quiet, because I was still telling the events of the day to my invisible confederates, whom I loved for giving me a purpose.

There was a rule I hewed to like it was superstition. In bed, lights out, I only had to talk until I'd described my day well enough that it felt true. There was a comforting assurance that if I told the story right, I could finally go to sleep. This feeling has never left me. Now, I tell myself that if what I say here is true, I will be complete and that is what I'm looking for, too.

2709 SETTING SUN DRIVE
CORONA DEL MAR, CALIFORNIA
92625

I KNOW SOME FACTS, but they don't make my mother any less of a mystery. She grew up in London during the war. She told me that bombs sometimes fell on her playground. She married an American GI, moved to Hollywood, divorced him, and met my father.

When I was little, she talked about her first husband as if he'd been a tree branch fallen on a path, something she'd gotten around so she could be free to meet my dad. She told the stories of more recent times with leisure and nuance. It was as if everything that had happened in England was marked by fog and switchback trails overgrown with nettles. Everything in America was easily mapped—obstacles met and overcome, culminating, she wanted me to know, in my birth. "You were wanted," she said often, emphasizing the first and last words of the sentence.

I grew up in Corona del Mar, south of Los Angeles, in a house that faced the sunsets. I can't imagine how different it was for my mother from her childhood.

She didn't fit in. She looked like she should—long blond hair, slender body, kind blue eyes, skin that tanned easily—but she was German blond, European stock, a stranger here, something her body knew well. She was a little deaf, and when she didn't understand what someone said, she looked at them with curiosity that made her seem alien. She had a modest two-piece swimsuit of pale blue, insulated with many layers of material between its exterior and where it touched her body. Its bottom piece reached above her navel, the better to cover a mysterious curved scar on her back that, when I was very young, I would touch with my fingertips to try to understand the different ways skin could feel. When she herself was four years old, she'd been in the hospital for many months. No one had told her why. When she came to the United States, a doctor saw the scar and asked her why she'd had a kidney removed.

She didn't know she was missing a kidney.

How disconcerting it must have been to hold in her mind both her gothic childhood and her present life of coastal breezes, sunglasses, money in the bank, her own swimming pool, going barefoot at cocktail parties, how even in wintertime her friends would pick fruit from their backyards, make bowls of sangria, and greet her at their front doors with a happy *Mi casa es su casa*.

Because it was Southern California we took long drives almost every day. I learned that when we went by a pasture, if you relaxed your eyes and let the fence posts rush by, the tiny flickers of the sights beyond would resolve into glimpses of the farm. That's what it was like with my mother's past life.

She sewed clothing for me. She made me tuna melts for lunch. When I couldn't sleep, she sat on my bed and sang "Moon River." She read up on ESP and decided she and I had it. I used to lie on my bed and try to send out brain waves to my mother. SOS! Sometimes, on a different day, she would come into my room and ask if I'd just been "calling" her, and I always said yes, and she would nod, significantly, admitting to a seasonal wind only she and I knew about.

I was hers then. I loved my father but I belonged to my mother. She was very funny and knew how to be silly when I was little, and witty when I was a little older. But I knew a look on her face, an expression that needed to be *solved,* because it wasn't anything like ease. Under big canvas reflective hats, zinc oxide on our noses, sunscreen on our shoulders, we hiked at the beach in our swimsuits, exploring the tide pools, tipping our big toes into sea anemones for the thrill of feeling them latch on, and something was wrong. When I learned how to swim beneath an approaching swell, I popped up safely, and yet my mother's concerned eye fell on me with a weight I didn't understand. Back onshore, she reached for my hand as if there were a border crossing only she could see, and there were armed guards whose graces she would have to court with politeness and fear. Her silent gaze, if it could be translated, said, *You don't know what you escaped*. And, because her worry lingered, *It might come back*.

I can see why she liked my father. His family was a block of Russian Jews, a solid, basalt-steady heredity. They were simply Russian Jews as far back as there had been deer in that particular forest. Then the Jews moved to Chicago and opened a hardware store and things got better and there was the sense that everyone was spreading out in similar directions—upward, onward. My great-grandfather had been a rabbi in a shtetl overrun by Cossacks. My grandfather ran G&M Hardware on 58th and Calumet. My uncles were lawyers. My father was an engineer. He traveled much of the year because he was making money for our future. That was a new, matching pair of gifts for her, his easy confidence that there would be both money *and* a future. His family's trajectory of abundance was easier to hang on to than whatever hydra's head of worry was on my mother's side. It must have been seductive for a while.

When I was six, I asked my mother to explain the world map. What country fit where? It was hard to comprehend where England was in relationship to, say, Israel. When my mother pointed out their great distances both from us and from each other, I felt desolate. I had so wanted Israel and England to be next door. I couldn't explain why.

"It's normal," she said. "When you're young, you think the world revolves around you. You'll start expanding outward. A young person thinks the world revolves around his country. When you're grown up, you'll see how the whole world fits together."

"What about now?" I asked.

"You're self-centered."

I thought about that. "Is that good?"

"Only someone who was self-centered would ask that."

She said this with love, I should mention. Around the same time,

I'd added up a column of numbers faster than she had, then I'd said to her, "It's okay. Mommy's brain is slow." So that's what she was up against.

Our development was called Harbor View Hills. When we drove its gentle curves, it was in a new Mercedes 300 SEL on freshly poured streets that fanned out like the veins in palm fronds. When a road stubbed out in a cul-de-sac, its edges touched emptiness, scrub and raw earth. History only extended back five years or so.

In the early 1960s, in Corona del Mar, Orange County, California, the landscape was all fields and open, rolling hills, and as the seasons turned, it was like money rained down upon the earth. Ranch houses and shopping centers for people like my family grew, and the more the money rained down, the larger the houses got. There was a middle school dropped into a local dirt field before the rest of the neighborhood had grown enough to be attached to it. One afternoon, the crew poured the school a sidewalk, and the next morning they found mountain lion tracks in the concrete. This was the end for the lions. No one saw a mountain lion in Corona del Mar again.

I looked, every day. I wanted there to be a mountain lion. I loved lions.

We owned a vacant lot, the last lot in the neighborhood. I explored it for dandelions to blow apart, reeds to make whistles from. I imagined finding sacks of Morgan silver dollars smuggled from Carson City. I loved to stand on the lot and know we were holding on to it as an *investment*. My father told me we *invested*. When kids from the neighborhood tackled each other in the grass, I would find a reason to stand near them and say, "Well, you know, this lot is just an investment."

I was an anxious kid. I was born with a job. My parents told me they wanted to be parents so they could avoid the mistakes their own parents had made. I think they said this to let me know I was loved, but it made me feel pressure. I was going to have a *better* childhood. I wasn't sure what that entailed, but it suggested responsibilities.

I had insomnia. I was weaker and more fragile than the other kids, but my brain was enormous and my mother asked me to be kinder to my playmates than to keep letting them know that. I might have had allergies—they seemed to come and go. But I really loved lions. I had a pin-back button of Frasier, the lion who had fathered two dozen cubs at a local theme park. When I was too old for stuffed animals, I still had three of them, Gopa, Jespah, and little Elsa, lions named for the cubs in the *Born Free* sequels.

My mother and father decided to get me a kitten. He was going to be my friend. He was a Siamese seal point from our local pet store. He was just a white dot with brown tips on his nose, ears, and tail and I cried when I met him because he was so tiny and frail. He grew up lush and heavy, with blue eyes that followed me wherever I went. When I left the room, he came with me, to see what I was doing. I named him Leo.

I learned from Leo how to pet a cat. I became the best petter-of-cats anyone knew. It was a slow process, and I ended up with lots of scratches, but I never minded. Leo was teaching me how to listen. My mother was ill with migraines that lasted three days and I had to be quiet for long hours. So I played with Leo. I learned how to read the signs of changing atmosphere before he even gave them. When he fell asleep on my bed, I figured out how to curl myself around his body so that I could touch him.

On those nights, I thought as I fell asleep, "I'll be what you need me to be," which felt like a perfect relationship.

I asked my father what the happiest day of his life was.

He said, "The day you were born," and I knew he had to say that.

I should mention that he was teetering toward raising a monster. Everything about me was reported to relatives as special, down to my birthday. I'd been born on both Easter and Passover, making me in their mythology a Matzo Bunny. The family legend was that I was smarter than either one of my parents, all of our relatives, and, just maybe, any other child yet born. They regarded my intelligence, whatever it actually was, like a pile of fissionable material that needed velvet ropes around it. My father wanted to send me to a gifted school. My mother, who had seen the worst of elitism in England, thought I should learn to fend for myself in public school.

My father talked her out of this. Clearly at a public school I would make other children feel bad about being idiots. They would beat me up. I would probably get into drugs, a view confirmed by the headmistress of the Eldorado School, which had an intelligence test to get in. Public schools, the headmistress explained, were dens of violence and race war and—as she'd already mentioned—drugs. My father didn't need to be convinced, but then again he was a happy elitist. I went to Eldorado, where we taunted each other on the playground in limericks and foreign insults, the bullies being not just tough but smart.

My father truly enjoyed my brain. So of course my birth was something he would say was the happiest day of his life.

I asked, "What was the second happiest day of your life?"

"The day I met your mother."

I was pretty sure he had to say that, too. My mother was a prize. My father had been a teenager with thick glasses, a passion for engineering, and an unashamed interest in the accordion, and there are photos to prove it. He used to make jokes about the millihelen, the amount of beauty it takes to launch one ship.

He was a smart Jewish boy who'd had enough therapy to know he should get away from his family. He'd selected a college by using a protractor to draw a circle the size of a one-day car trip around Chicago, and then he only looked at schools outside that circle. It worked—his family didn't visit him.

He married young and divorced young, and psychoanalysis lasted exactly long enough for him to decide he would never feel guilt again. He would be amoral, cheerfully so. If something gave him pleasure, he did it. He chased women. He got contact lenses. He became a Republican. He was a unicorn, the only Jewish Republican ever born between 1910 and 1960 in the city of Chicago.

He moved to California with a Porsche like James Dean's and got his hair cut a little like James Dean's, which would have been effective had this not brought out his jug ears and Russian bear-baiter nose. The rest of his daily outfit—lab coat and bow tie, not quite right for a Porsche driver—showed him to be an egghead, passionate but inept, maybe a little adorable. On the second happiest day of his life, he introduced himself to my mother by shyly putting two tickets to the Hollywood Bowl and his phone number under her car's windshield wiper. She accepted. On their second date, he brought his laundry over and he never left.

With the love of repetition that only a seven-year-old has, I plowed on: third, fourth, fifth, sixth, seventh happiest. And that's when it started to get interesting. "The day I left home to go to college ... the day I got out of the Air Force ... the day I became a millionaire ..."

I don't recall how far down the list this was, but I made him go back to it. When had he become a millionaire? Recently. His company Certron made cassette tapes. Herb Alpert and the Tijuana Brass was Certron's client. They were the biggest recording stars in the country. I danced around my room to "Tijuana Taxi" and "Casino Royale" and "A Taste of Honey." I lay on the floor to feel how sad "This Guy's in Love with You" sounded. If I hadn't felt sad enough, I played it again until I got the feeling of desolation right.

When Herb Alpert signed his contract with Certron, my father became a millionaire.

"Really, a millionaire? Not just a hundred thousandaire?" I asked. Was he still a millionaire? Were we rich?

Yes. When I think of that moment, I see my father smiling behind his sunglasses. What a trajectory, from accordion-playing dork to a man with money and a gorgeous wife and, probably, so much more to come. We were driving in his 1969 Rolls-Royce Corniche and he was happy to let me know we were rich.

I remember coming home from that discussion. Spinning back from the garage, arms pumping and me skidding to a halt in the kitchen. "Mom! Mom! Did you know we're *millionaires*?"

This went badly. I released those words and I instantly had the same feeling as when I'd pet Leo for one second too long. I wanted to unsay them, then I wanted to add something that would let my mother know I didn't actually care about it in whatever way she disapproved of. I think she worried that even hearing the word "rich" was like being exposed to a virus. Being rich unnerved her. I can hear her voice saying, definitively, "You have to understand, money cannot ... money cannot ..." and then trailing off.

My father only smiled, in a way that seemed to annoy her. And the angrier she got, the more smug he seemed. All my mother could tell me was that the world was more of a problem than my father believed. She had a rule: she did not read me fairy tales. She said she didn't want me to think that anyone would rescue me. The world I lived in, she told me, wasn't real. "You're in a plush cocoon," she said.

My father thought my mother worried too much. Money delighted him the way his woodworking tools did, only more so. "There's no substitute for information, except money," he said, and only someone who loved both would have said that. He thought it was inelegant to own an object without knowing its value—not in dollars, but why it was worth having. Otherwise, it was like looking at *Playboy* without reading the articles. My father read the articles in *Playboy*. He allowed me to read his *Playboy*s as long as I could pass the quiz he gave me every month. What had Roman Polanski said in his interview about fate?

My mother said, "You can't let your possessions possess you," which I thought sounded smart. She said that when she wrote her novel, it would be called *Money Matters,* and the title, she said, looking at my father, would be *sardonic.*

My father appreciated my mother for double-checking him that way. She was the one with the conscience. Once in a Beverly Hills restaurant, my mother was mistaken for the actress Linda Evans, and then she spoke, and it turned out that *Oh,* this beautiful woman was from *England.* Which in my father's universe made her a woman with value added.

For a while, my father's worldview won. We spent money. My parents went to an auction once. My mother came back alone that night, saying my father had stayed behind to bid on something spectacular. Her tone was reserved, in that she loved his enthusiasm and shuddered at its consequences. Around five in the morning, he came home, unshaven and triumphant as a woodsman, carrying a heavy velvet-draped case in both arms. It was a chess set.

Now it seems one part real, one part dream. You could stage a Russian aristocratic tragedy on its gold and onyx squares that were surrounded by tiny silver posts and chains as if the game within took place in palace chambers. The four-inch-thick base presented a Baroque overload of cloisonné tableaux—medieval courtship scenes taken from Flemish tapestries. The pawns were soldiers, the bishops carried torches with a flame made of real gold, the castles were crowned with filigree of crenelated silver. The capes on the kings and queens were smooth with crushed semiprecious stones.

The three of us stared at it. It was bigger than we were. My father said it was a Fabergé, or a contemporary studio's work. We called it the Fabergé chess set. We never used it. It was too precious to do anything with except admire it. We brought friends over so we could all admire it.

We lived in a house with such fine things around us. *Let me show you this,* my father might say, opening up a curio cabinet, a bottle of brandy, a jewelry box. *Note the maker's mark.* He had a tiny Lucite cube in which a miniature of the Certron prospectus floated, the idea being that *all this*—the house, the lifestyle, the future—*came from what I did here.*

Imagine it's 1969 and we're in a five-thousand-square-foot ranch house, a freshly remodeled rectangle around a courtyard of fuchsias that attracted, to Leo's delight, hummingbirds. We had a swimming pool and a Jacuzzi. Floodlights outside, track lighting inside to show off the nail sculptures and Chinese scrollwork and the contemporary pop art and op art. The designer kitchen, with appliances in avocado green and an Amana Radarange microwave that cooked with science. The living room conversation pit with hidden television cabinet, executed by contractors who'd worked on the Haunted Mansion at Disneyland. The darkroom where my father developed and printed the color photographs he took on weekends at the local salt marshes and Japanese tea gardens.

In the recreation room is the Derby Day pinball machine rescued from a penny arcade. And the Hammond "Follow the Piper" organ with twenty-two synthesized instruments, including the twin mallet marimba, on which I would play for our guests all eight verses of "In the Year 2525" without encouragement. And here is a gift from cousin Howard, who worked at Mattel: a wildebeest head mounted like a trophy. When you pull the nylon string coming out of its neck, a tiny mechanical voice box implant within is activated and the same voice as the Ken doll murmurs risqué phrases. *In sixty-nine do unto others as they do unto you. Pull that string again, buster, and we're engaged.*

And this is my bedroom, with Danish modern furniture and a collage of black light posters and psychedelic wall paints my mother had assembled during brave trips to the head shops on Balboa Island, where there were actual hippies. One whole wall was a Dennison's Chili billboard, studded with visual puns like Op Art bull's-eyes. Dennis Hopper and Peter Fonda rode their motorcycles with a trail of balloons behind them that my mother had inserted herself. The walls told a story that leapt from place to place and hewed to its own magical logic.

Now look from the window down the hillside, past a thicket of ice plant, to see our vacant lot, the last one in the neighborhood, our investment, planed flat, with a lawn whose surface bears the architecturally perfect diagonal lines of a rider-mower that every week managed to avoid my hand-painted wooden croquet equipment.

At the other end of the house, my father's office is all about the future. This tall plastic podium, sterile as an X-ray technician's station, is a computer terminal. You ease the phone receiver into a soft headphone-like umbilicus and a gigantic mainframe computer downtown, a DEC-10, whistles and shrieks information stored on rolls of yellow punch tape that makes confetti in a clear plastic box jumpy with static electricity. My father works here so much, so late into the night, the maid refers to the computer as his mistress.

Linger at a side table in the dining room. My father gives a tilt of the head. "Here's our chess set. It's a Fabergé," and then on to the artwork.

Here's the mock-up of a submarine the L.A. Fine Arts Squad floated in Newport Harbor. Here's a Frank Stella lithograph we picked up at the Jack Glenn Gallery. No, we didn't buy any of the Peter Max paintings; they were too popular, and clearly overpriced. My father would say something like that, or I would, which either drew laughter or confused stares.

I couldn't tell you what our guests thought. I had a tin ear for response. I did not know how to impress anyone. Sometimes, if Leo walked by, I would pick him up and announce he was a rare seal point Siamese and he had a very unusual voice.

Mostly I was excited because of the surprise at the end of the tour. Standing barefoot in the shag wool conversation pit, I would give visitors a presentation about our coin collection.

My father and I went to so many auctions at Bowers and Ruddy the auctioneer would wink at me when Dad let me raise the paddle. We had a 1794 variant cent and an 1808 described as unique in Sheldon's

Penny Whimsy. "Thomas Jefferson himself might have carried these pennies in his pocket." I presented the half-cents, the two-cent pieces, the three-cent pieces, the proof Barber dime, the doomed twenty-cent pieces. In 1916 the Standing Liberty quarter (and here, an aside on the importance of Art Nouveau) was bare-breasted, and in 1917 America demanded a breastplate. We hadn't even gotten to the gold pieces yet.

I read Yeoman's *Red Book* by flashlight, memorizing coinage runs, mint marks, Colonial patterns, the relative values of double die errors. I was so overwhelmed by the love of knowledge I wanted to crawl inside the coins and live their histories with them. My father's version of a fishing trip was to bring me rolls of nickels from the bank for investigation, seeding one with an AU-55 three-legged buffalo, whose discovery made me jump off my bed in shock. The story of catching that particular trout became part of my presentation.

Now I can hear my voice becoming shrill as the sun goes down and the moon comes up. I see, superimposed over my features, a cloth monkey with a key in his back, banging cymbals together until there are nothing but cheese rinds and empty Chablis bottles and the final spark and thud coming from the fireplace as the last of the logs is consumed. Our visitors watch with embarrassment a child juggling plates, counting out how much of his time playing with tiny metal cars has been appropriated by pursuing the love of his parents. The end of the tour isn't the coins, but me—I am the big finish, the most curious gem in the collection. I tell my history stories, I actually bow for applause at the end. My father approves, my mother begins to get a migraine, I'm just a kid, I don't understand cause and effect.

I'm sad to end that house tour. We were there so briefly. When it was already too late, my mother didn't know. She said, "When your father cashes his Certron stock in, he can retire." She said, "When my therapy is finished, I'll have more time to work on my novel." Something about how well she enunciated made me pay attention. None of that "when" was going to happen. It turned out we didn't have money, just Certron stock.

One day, Herb Alpert would be driving down the Pacific Coast Highway in his convertible, listening to a Certron tape. It would break.

He would put another tape in, and it would break, too. He would pull out of my father's company and the stock—the basis of our fortune—would plummet. Certron would blame my father publicly for the problems, and fire him, and no audio firm in the country would hire him.

I've mentioned that my mother was prepared for loss. My father was not. He didn't know how to fail. He didn't know he *could* fail. That wasn't part of his family story. Nor could he cope with how readily my mother would say it was okay that he'd lost. For her, that acknowledgment was a kindness, a pushing back of a chair at a certain sad feast familiar to her, and for him it was betrayal.

What happened to my father after that is something I can explain. What happened to my mother is different. She wanted to be a writer, and all the novel fragments and memoir fragments she showed me in the years since were kaleidoscopic attempts to explain what she saw. They are heavy with momentum, yet somehow lack direction. It's as if she is simultaneously defending herself from an invisible judge, and yet also daring herself to make certain assertions that she can't quite spell out, hoping someone will read between the lines and understand her.

She was going to lose everything, slowly, beginning with the material things she cared little about. Then she was going to lose her sense that anywhere in the world was safe.

Ultimately she, my father, and I rescued ourselves, but we did it at a cost, and we did it separately. I don't think anyone would call what we managed a success.

Before all that unraveled, my mother called her family one night. It couldn't have been her only phone call home, but it was a *production,* as my father would say. Mom made the call at midnight our time, eight in the morning there. Many of her siblings didn't have phones and I imagined them all packed into a single room somewhere in a damp flat in Uxbridge to hear the voice from California. Since my mother had trouble hearing and she worried she would miss something important, my father set up a reel-to-reel tape to record the conversation on both ends.

He was always organizing things for her like that. I recently found a chart he'd made, and from its details I'd date it to when he was courting her. It's a precisely rendered map of my mother's family for three generations. I can imagine my father drawing it, and showing it to her and saying, "See, it's not so terrible. It's not so mysterious." And her giving him that smile that understood how kind life was, sometimes.

That was what marrying my father had meant. He had promised her that by living in the sort of world that had him in it, things would make sense for her. Of course, his chart couldn't encompass all the emotions in the single blueprint-like line that linked, for instance, my grandfather George and his wife, Elsie. There were no dotted lines for abandonment. There weren't lines leading to suicide. The link between one box and another didn't indicate a union made in joy versus one made under the obliteration of hope. There were no diagrams that explained how people felt, and, as was his tendency, my father stumbled, all knees and elbows, when it came to the complexities of the heart.

His chart also turned out to be wrong. My father didn't know about the secret lovers or the bigamous husbands. He didn't know about my mother's missing twin. For instance.

On her side of that transatlantic phone call, her voice was slow, each phrase separated by unnatural space so she would be heard. Gradually, something else happened, something bizarre that made my skin ripple with goose bumps. As she spoke, years peeled away and she sounded much younger. Thousands of miles vanished, and she was sucked back into that room of family, where her accent returned. She sounded like a teenage girl, and she sounded helpless. Her siblings were Rosemary, Anna, Elizabeth, Ursula, Georgina, and Jonathan, and my cousins were Angela, Maria, Gary, Jimmy, Simon, Isabelle, Amanda, Christina, Peter, Paul, John, Debbie, Nicola, and Marc. I name them here not in the spirit of my dad's chart, but the opposite. Naming them doesn't begin to bring them under control any more than naming the elements of the northern lights allows you to guide them.

After my mother hung up, the American had shed from her, and she was weeping. Something in the call had wrecked her. She left, and closed the door to the bedroom, and a migraine began. I wouldn't see her for days.

My father wanted to understand. But his mind organized the more difficult emotions as if they were equations in chemistry or geology, fields to which he'd never been that attuned. Before the phone call to England, what he had been the most proud of recording had been the *Bob & Ray* comedy show. He never really stood a chance. Whatever my father brought my mother was not going to rescue her.

Three little dots in that huge house that night: my mother in her bed, my father in his office, and me in my room. I was talking to myself, of course, as there was so much to say.

I gave up on trying to sleep. I walked quietly in my cotton pajamas the full range of the house, giving myself the tour. I mouthed the words without speaking so I wouldn't wake my parents. In the dark, I noted the Fred Eversley Lucite sculpture, and explained to no one how it was placed so that the setting sun would illuminate its many colors.

I was aiming at one piece of art that carried its own gravity. It wasn't part of the tour. It was hidden from easy view. I stopped just outside their bedroom. I pressed myself into a small alcove. On the wall above me was the painting, a portrait. The spotlight shined on my grandfather George.

It was unlike anything else in the house. It was hardly art as I understood it. Its background browns were oppressive, Teutonic murk meant to be folds of drapery, so dense with shadow George could have posed by gaslight. He might have been any age from twenty to forty. He wore a dark suit and a red tie. He held a cigarette loosely, as if it were natural to his class, a riding crop.

He had been the most handsome man in Germany. He was the first-born, he spoke seven languages, he died terribly at forty-three. Since George had died so young, he would never be a success or a failure. He would always stare out at you with potential. His gaze knew everything about you, it held out a little hope, it evaluated, sympathized, and found you wanting.

When you moved, the light played over the canvas, showing restoration marks. My mother told me she'd had it repaired because it had been torn. Much later, I learned the truth, that someone had stabbed the portrait right through George's face.

My parents' end would be awful, but nothing to have shocked George. It was not like the nature of fate had changed since slapping him down. It's just that it was happening so far away from him, in such a sunny place, to people with such good humor about life, that it seemed unlikely. But it turns out that no matter what you free yourself from—your family, your past, your disasters, your belief in God—you aren't really *that* free. George would have known that. I used to imagine his hand reaching out of the painting to offer the cigarette, a comfort and a way of passing the baton. *Here, old chap,* he would say. *I know what you escaped. So sorry it came back.*

333 EAST ONTARIO STREET

APT. 2206

CHICAGO, ILLINOIS

60611

TOWARD THE END, when I was nine, my mother ordered my father a 3.5-inch telescope so he could see the Comet Kohoutek. Kohoutek, which appeared every 150,000 years, was theorized to be the largest comet Earth had ever seen. Its tail would take up a quarter of the nighttime sky.

Every night for a week, my father unbuckled the leather case of his new Questar and took me onto the deck that wrapped around our house so we could prepare our observations. With the December winds whipping up our hillside, and the lights of Newport Harbor making a modest interruption of our sightings, we started with the naked eye. My father told me that the only way to see the faintest stars was to avert your eyes from them. It had something to do with how visual purple worked with the eye's rods and cones, but the important thing was to just notice how it worked. Look north, look south, just look a few degrees away, and the dimmest, farthest, quietest objects in the sky revealed themselves.

"Look at the Big Dipper," he said. "There are seven stars, but you can only see the seventh if you aren't looking straight at it." He was right.

The telescope was polished aluminum. I made sure I didn't let my finger near the lens, which I respected as my father had rhapsodized over the necessity of retaining its perfect smudgeless clarity. I loved what he knew and the care he took. He never talked down to me. I tried to honor that. We had an instrument worthy of viewing the night-time sky in this era that we were lucky to live in. *Time* magazine had put Kohoutek, "the comet of the century," on its cover that week. It was larger than Halley's Comet. It weighed a trillion tons. Planetariums were sponsoring parties. 747s would streak across the skies, festive with guests making champagne toasts alongside the comet at apogee.

But Kohoutek turned out to be a smudge. Even with our telescope, Kohoutek was a fleck you could brush out of the night without feeling a loss.

"I'm sorry," my father said the first evening. This wasn't him accepting responsibility so much as his acknowledgment that sometimes what you were promised ended up disappointing you.

And I *was* disappointed. But nonetheless, the skies gave you what they gave you. My parents' marriage was suffering then, and my dad and I spent more time in our heavy coats outside, together, than we would have otherwise, as this was a chance not to return inside the house. While the comet was with us, he and I looked through the telescope, averting our eyes and hoping that playing with the focus knobs would let us see things more clearly. Sometimes one or the other of us would say, "Yeah, this is pretty crummy." And then the comet was gone.

It turns out the most obscure things in your life are invisible when you try to look at them directly. For instance, the end of the marriage. I tend to look away.

My mother was writing a new novel then. It was narrated by a woman married to a character named Ron, who was distant and controlling. They'd become rich recently and it was ruining their marriage. The narrator was frightened by the child she and Ron had. The child was super-naturally intelligent and foresaw the problems in their marriage before they did. She showed it to me to see what I thought.

I wondered if, when it was published, people would—because people weren't clever—think it was about her and Dad. She would have to let them know it was just fiction.

It's probably as hard to describe any parent as it is to catch your own profile in a mirror. In my mother's case it's even more complicated. She had been born Cockney, within the sound of Bow Bells, but she wasn't *a* Cockney, she hastened to add. "I had to take care of the boardinghouse when I was seven because Mummy . . ." Her mother drank. Her mother drank because she was schizophrenic. My mother had an older sister, Rosemary, but the truth was, I was old enough to know now, Rosemary was a half-sister. There had been an Italian man, a semi-Mafioso, before her father. In fact, her father and mother hadn't been married when my mother was conceived, so she felt terribly guilty, as if it were her fault that two people so ill-matched were forced together. She felt guilty until the day her father died, and then she felt so much worse.

She was alert to other people trying to control her. My father, for instance. He was hapless when it came to emotions—he said "I love you" because he knew he should, but it came out like the Pledge of Allegiance. He was stiffening more since things were getting difficult financially. He was traveling to Chicago, sometimes for months at a time, for our futures. And when he was back, he was frosty to her.

The local consciousness-raising groups were appealing, but they were also angry, and close-minded. She tried to have a civil conversation with Judy Chicago, and came away feeling Chicago was just as bad as the society she was critiquing. What if she took another writing class? Volunteered at a women's clinic? Made friends who weren't so rich? What if I had a younger brother or sister?

She would say this and then, wherever we were, look at me for an answer. It was like those moments where we shared our ESP. Only now it made me nervous. And then it hit me, *I was the child in her novel*. I knew more than she knew about what she should do. It made me feel an electric kind of horror, like dreams in which I was supposed to be flying an airplane.

Once, fooling around with a cousin, I got my hand slammed in a car door. Within a minute it started to swell and by the time my mother had driven me to the emergency room, it looked like an apple was trying to force its way out of my palm. The technicians brought out an X-ray machine, which panicked me. "It won't hurt," they said, but that wasn't what bothered me. The pain in my hand had shaken loose something primal. My life had already been asterisks and strange circumstances, and nothing about me was ordinary. I thought, "Don't you know I'm in *gifted school?*" Looking inside my body had to be an awful idea. What terrible structures would they find in there?

When the X-rays however showed the normal anatomy—granted, some of it smashed—I felt relief. There were bones in my hand. Just like what anyone else had. I was not special. Thank God. This set up a little island for me to visit when I felt circumstances had gotten too strange. The island where everything was normal. I would visit often as my mother realized what she wanted her life to be like.

On a Sunday morning my parents told me they were separating, maybe they were divorcing, they weren't sure, it was hard to know. They were going to play it by ear, my mother said. We were in the sunken conversation pit in the living room. Spread across the couch was the Sunday paper. I could see Prince Valiant's primary colors and unwelcoming dense text. It felt unbalanced, like its weight would cause the page to fold over. I realized I was weeping and that embarrassed me, so I stopped.

I have letters between my parents from that time. My father wrote that he couldn't believe how maturely I was handling it. My mother replied they didn't have a child, but a thirty-six-year-old midget. The idea was that I was so smart I had placed out of having the reactions a normal kid would. None of us believed that, but it was convenient. In a crisis, you need to say and hear optimistic things when there isn't any real hope.

I was a mouthy kid, not that pleasant, and I didn't have many friends to talk to. There were many days where I would take the croquet set alone onto the field and play by myself in the afternoon breeze.

But the threat of divorce was a leveling influence. Classmates were one by one having family meetings on Sunday mornings, being told they were still loved just as much by each parent separately, and that nothing was their fault. Mondays at school, one gifted child or another showed up red-eyed and in a wrinkled shirt, not wanting to talk about it, getting picked up at three o'clock by a parent with a youthful haircut in a new sports car, usually a tobacco-brown Mercedes.

I witnessed these developments with a sense of awe and adventure, a line of children being forced to cross rope bridges. One weekend I stayed with Richard Lewis, whose father had the Newport Porsche dealership. They were living in the family beach house, along with a new coltish girlfriend who was some unknowable age older than us and younger than the dad. Richard's mom had not worn bikini bottoms around the house, nor baked brownies that were explicitly not for us, nor had she made Richard's father look so happy. I was ten years old, and my appreciation of the sights and sounds around me was starting to deepen, so the girlfriend's presence was as magnificent to me as a mermaid's.

In the morning, Richard and I sat in his dinghy a hundred yards offshore, fishing with bait he'd bought with quarters from a trawler in the harbor. I saw his father's girlfriend walking from the house and diving into the ocean, and even though I'd grown up near the beach, it was like I'd never seen a woman before. Divorce could be exciting. I didn't say this to Richard, who regarded her with dull and disgusted eyes.

Look what my dad wants, he muttered. No one can condemn an adult with so few words as a ten-year-old. I didn't say much in return, maybe affirmed how much everything sucked—we were at the dawn of the age when everything sucked. But secretly I wondered if things could get interesting if you woke up each morning without knowing whom you might meet that day.

My father started living in Chicago. My hair was becoming greasy and I was entering the age of clothes that didn't look right on my body, and no matter how much I showered, I smelled like stale cereal.

I stayed with Mom in Corona del Mar. She started dating. She brought a man to the house and I explained to myself she was allowed to do that. Still, when her date met me, he asked if I wanted to go hunting with him and I asked him if killing animals made him less insecure about his masculinity.

See, he wasn't nearly as magical to me as the mermaid had been. If Mom was allowed to date men, and they were allowed to talk to me, they should be at least as smart as I was. My mother was embarrassed but not the way I thought she should be—later that night I walked past her bedroom and saw her hugging him in the doorway. I stepped back, barefoot, telling myself dating was a normal, natural, and healthy thing for her even if she was doing it with an insecure idiot.

I lay down with microwaved pizza in the recreation room, which was as far away as possible from my mother's bedroom. KTTV was showing a marathon of Japanese monster movies like *War of the Gargantuas, Godzilla vs. Monster Zero, Mothra.* In one of these was a scene in which a secret agent's boat capsizes in a storm. The next morning he washes up on a lonely beach, almost dead. And yet he's perfectly manicured, suit dry, hair combed so well that scientists could calibrate their instruments by the line of his part.

On the floor, I pretended I'd washed up like driftwood, pummeled by the storm, skin a contour map of bruises and scrapes. I was about to be patched up for one final mission. I didn't imagine what that mission was—just that it was final. I imagined the agony and exhaustion of being rehabilitated. There would be such terrible setbacks on my final mission. Almost extinguished but not quite. It felt good.

There was a cliché about divorcées, and my mother embraced it, telling friends she was "finding herself," even as she made fun of the phrase. She wanted to move us from the plush cocoon into a real neighborhood. That might mean Seattle or Portland or New York. She was in touch with her sisters—maybe we would all live together somewhere. San Francisco? She was investigating it, so she put me on a plane to see my father in Chicago.

When Dad picked me up at the airport, I saw his hair was longer. He had new designer glasses. He was wearing a Steve McQueen–style turtleneck, apparel that was young and in fashion. There was a woman with him.

"This is Ann," he said.

She nodded. I nodded back as if this were normal, meeting my father with an unannounced woman.

We walked down the concourse, toward Baggage Claim. I was hyperaware of Ann, looking for clues. I wasn't sure why he had come to the airport with her, nor why she was still with us. My father spoke again. "I met her at the commissary at the Board of Trade. She was trying to change a two dollar bill." A long pause. "Into a three dollar bill."

"Uh-huh," I said, to acknowledge that a joke had been told.

My father was forty-four years old. Ann was twenty-seven. We drove in what I remember as a Sunday-heft-of-cathedral-tunes-like silence to a downtown high-rise, McClurg Court. I didn't know what we were doing there. Was I staying there? Was Dad? Where did Ann live?

Recently, I asked my father about his stiffness when it came to difficult moments. He told me he'd concluded he was bad at explaining awkward things and much better at just presenting them without comment. Which is why he stopped explaining things. This apparently worked better for him than it did for anyone related to him.

It turned out my father lived with Ann in her apartment. It was ultramodern and efficient in the way young, single, well-off professionals lived. I thought, "My father has the right to start his life over."

White walls, one bedroom, a kitchenette, a living room with a foldout couch. He did not give me a house tour. It was neither warm nor cold, but airless. The windows didn't open. There was wall-to-wall carpeting. I sensed the dull pulse of the building's climate control, which managed to ride tensely between sound and sensation.

My father and I still had the same sense of humor, but that was now like a valve that had rusted shut. If I happened to laugh at something, he looked at Ann to say with his eyes, "See, this isn't so bad." What I know now is that my father was trying to prove to himself that he wasn't feeling guilty, and that made things uncomfortable, the way it always does when you tell yourself that you aren't feeling what you're feeling.

He made lists of things to do. There were foreign movies to see. We would visit museums. We would visit the Sara Lee factory. And then we did that. When there was nothing left to do, the three of us played gin rummy. Ann made butterscotch brownies, and then made them again, because we ate through the first batch in the place of conversation.

I can't imagine what Ann thought as she opened up her one-bedroom to a ten-year-old who was paying attention to every movement she made. I doubt my father had prepared her for my arrival any more than he had prepared me. I couldn't have told you a single personality trait of hers. She was, I now understand, nervous and far too young to know what she was doing. She read for hours at a time, mainstream fiction from the library, and she and my father did the *New York Times* crossword puzzle together on the couch, quietly, and I wondered sometimes if the silent occupation was a way to not volunteer anything I might use against her.

At night I lay awake on the fold-out couch in the living room. There was a clock on a bookshelf. It was silver metal, a three-dimensional, cylindrical T, like the tip of a periscope. Its round plastic face was marked with crosshairs around which a black pupil revolved, once per minute. As it moved, the face changed colors. I watched it for hours.

We saw every movie in town, from *The Phantom of Liberty* to *And Now My Love*. It was a season for difficult movies, so we saw Werner Herzog's *The Enigma of Kaspar Hauser* and something with Liv Ullman that was so slow it had the rare effect of making me wish I were back in the apartment.

I wanted brownies in the afternoon, but I felt I couldn't have one until my father did. Happily, every afternoon, and every day a little earlier than the last, my dad cut himself a brownie. I would follow. He would eat it, not looking at me. I would stare out the window. And so the week passed.

The truth was—and I can't blame her for this—Ann didn't want me around. This is why my dad felt guilty. It was nothing personal, just atavism, a lioness defending against the litter of a previous mate. I was certainly not charming, or plucky enough in any way I can remember.

But Ann loved him. He was in love with her, and I can see why. They had a kind of level-headedness together that he couldn't have found with my mother. Beyond the art and movies and books, they had every section of the *Wall Street Journal* in common. They discussed capital the way other couples might discuss baseball, with the same passion and knowledge and humor and faith that it made the world a better place. Also, Ann was rich. That was a new kind of added value for my dad. It must have been very different than being with my mother, who so feared being rich.

I linger here because I need to explain what was going to happen. When I was in my thirties and my father in his sixties, he said with the same voice that he had used to explain George Carlin routines to me, "I sold you out."

He added that he wasn't sorry. He said it was just one choice among many he'd made. "I'm amoral," he said. "You wouldn't believe some of the things I've done." He said, "It was too bad you got caught in the middle."

I can't say that my father's late-life dabbling in explaining himself felt any better than him acting and having me guess why he'd done things. I want to credit him for taking some responsibility, but I also have to call bullshit. My father wanted to be amoral the same way I would like to be the Hulk. Cheerful amorality was his unattainable superpower.

He loved Ann. And he loved me. And he loved being rich. And those things couldn't work together. He already wanted to marry her. A shadow would skim across a conversation, a comment about my future, a glance from Ann, and his face would show a pang of that thing he said he no longer felt: guilt.

When I returned to Corona del Mar, my mother picked me up impatiently—she had a story. She'd arrived in San Francisco and within minutes of sitting at the Mark Hopkins bar, met a man with the most unlikely name. Peter Charming. Of the Rhode Island Charmings. He had shown her his American Express card to prove it. "He had the most ridiculous pickup line," she laughed. "'May I buy you a balloon and take you to Paris?'"

She had stayed in San Francisco instead of visiting Portland and Seattle. She said Peter had a Victorian mansion and drove the car Steve McQueen did in *Bullitt*. This was a step up over my dad wearing a sweater like McQueen did. Peter didn't just have the *type* of car, he had the *actual* car used in the movie. He played chess, and he had a café circle of interesting friends. Peter wanted to meet me.

"Is he your boyfriend?" I was ready for a new boyfriend.

He was a friend, but relationships were more organic and loose than how society defined them traditionally, she said. People didn't really belong to each other, she said, which was news to me. Just a week in San Francisco had alerted her to how our culture put a lot of pressure to fit us into molds we didn't naturally fit into, like "boyfriend," or "wife." By nature, she explained, we were actually much more complex than that.

It sounded like a paragraph of an article someone had given her that she strongly agreed with. It also sounded so sophisticated I felt the urge to already know all of this.

Besides, my mother continued, Peter had a girlfriend who lived with him, Sue, and my mother liked her. "He can be aggravating and irresponsible. And funny. He's like a big kid."

Still, I was pretty sure I could destroy him, if we met. I said he sounded more fun than Ann had been.

"Who's Ann?" my mother asked.

My mother had me write letters to Peter Charming saying I was going to beat him at chess. "Go ahead and taunt him," she said. "I'd like to see what he's going to really do."

My role was apparently gatekeeper now, something combining son and disapproving, pipe-smoking father. I was fine with this. Sometimes Mom dictated specific insults.

"Tell him he lacks dignity," she said. "Tell him he's immature."

As I wrote him, I thought, "Peter, you can't court me. I will impress you and I will make you want to impress me. And then I'm going to sink your ass at chess."

I should mention I wasn't actually good at chess. My mother assumed I was. So I assumed it, too.

On Halloween 1974, Peter visited our house in Corona del Mar. After thinking about it for a while I decided to greet him wearing a rubber Creature from the Black Lagoon mask and offering him a glass of Chablis.

He said to my mom, "You didn't lie—you don't have a kid, you have a thirty-six-year-old midget."

He didn't ask me about school or whether I liked Disneyland. Instead, he put me to work uncorking the next bottle of Chablis. As his arm moved over mine, I was awestruck by a heavy square of gold on his wrist that flashed under the candlelight. His watch! He wore a Pulsar, a *digital* watch. I'd heard about digital watches. They were supposed to cost two thousand dollars. When he tapped a button on the side, the time appeared in ruby digits that illuminated the hints of mind-boggling Jack Kirby–like circuitry behind them.

He was a clotheshorse, which meant expensive bell-bottom jeans faded perfectly to a sky blue, a huge brass belt buckle, Pierre Cardin patterned polyester shirt with two buttons undone, and a collar the size of a paper airplane. He smelled of just enough cologne, was fastidious about his fingernails, and wore a tiny Star of David on a chain around his neck. He had a money clip but no wallet. He wore a tight afro that he attended to with a cake cutter that jutted up from his rear pocket.

I thought he was a lawyer, or he let me think that. He didn't mention what he did or how he'd come to have a mansion in Pacific Heights. He told me obvious lies, knowing I knew he was bullshitting me: he was a spy; he knew Groucho Marx; he was a grand master chess champion.

"You are *not* a grand master."

"You're right. When you're right, you're right. But I'm still going to beat you, kid. And after I beat you, you'll wish I *was* a grand master, because at least then you'd have an excuse for losing." He'd outthought me. He put his hand on my shoulder. "Now, where's the cheese and crackers?"

I took him to the kitchen. He rummaged through the pantry as if it had been waiting for him. By now I had a comeback and was waiting to drop it into the conversation, but he was already on to something else. On his way to the crackers, he'd found a can of something. He held it behind his back.

"Kid, would you eat shit?"

I forgot what I was going to say. "What? No."

"Even if they perfumed it and said it was nutritious? I think you would."

I was suspicious. "What's in your hand?"

"How do we get outside?" I took Peter to the screen door by the kitchen and he led me, hand on the back of my neck, to the deck that overlooked the street far below. It was after dark. He was looking at the view.

"What are you doing?" I asked.

He adjusted his trousers, smoothed down his shirt, and raised his arms. "Look at this. Kid, I bet you don't even see it, do you? Corona del Mar, the Pacific Ocean, that Ferris wheel down there, all the lights. It's fucking gorgeous. Every day of your life you should be grateful for this view. Your father, who is a genius by the way, invented cassette tapes and his hard work got you this. You are part of the charmed elite." He showed off what he'd pilfered, a can of Spam. "You are too intelligent for this. This? This is shit."

"Mom only got that because—"

"You're going to blame your mom for this? That's bullshit. What do you like to eat?"

"Macaroni and cheese."

"Macaroni and cheese? You ever been to North Beach? The Washington Square Bar & Grill has the best macaroni and cheese in North America."

I wasn't sure about that. I really liked Morton's frozen macaroni and cheese. But I knew what he probably meant, the restaurant food was more sophisticated. I wasn't ready for that. Also, why were we outside?

"Kid, I want you to throw this Spam away, now."

"Okay." I didn't move.

With a sigh, Peter took it back from me. Then, arcing his arm in a clean overhand pitch, he threw the Spam as far as he could. A few seconds later, in the darkness, there was the sound of metal tumbling over pavement far below. I couldn't believe he'd done that.

"Do you have other cans of that?"

We did! We had a couple. I fetched them. This was fantastic.

"Now—throw them the fuck away, kid."

There was no one around to tell me not to, and so with my throwing arm, I tossed the two cans down the hillside. They calved the ice plant.

"Are you ever going to have Spam in your house again?"

"I don't know—Mom buys—"

"That is bullshit. Don't let your mom take the heat. You love her, right? You want the best for her and for you. Fuck Spam. No more Spam. Now let's go inside and eat cheese and crackers until we can't see straight."

When I remember Peter's voice, I can hear his monologues as if they play on a loop somewhere independent of time or space, like there's a station eternally broadcasting him and it's just a matter of what's playing when you happen to tune in.

"Do you know about lateral thinking?" he asked. "You aren't the kind of kid who gets trapped by boundaries." It was later, and my mother was watching, in what had been my father's office, something unprecedented. We'd been building toward it not just that night but for the weeks since my mother had mentioned Peter was a chess master. Three chairs around a small white porcelain table, that second bottle of Chablis to the side. My father's stereo playing something I didn't even know we had, Joni Mitchell. She was a friend of Peter's. Mom had bought her albums, apparently.

Peter couldn't figure out how to adjust the volume, so he directed me to the pre-amp. He made us wait, his finger tapping empty air, until he could talk-sing along to my mother. "You know they love you when they're there. Am I right, baby?"

Peter saw my expression. I knew immediately that he'd said something about my father. "Your mother is an amazing woman. And you're a good kid. Tell me if this makes sense."

I said sharply, "If what makes sense?"

"Easy there. Don't get mad at me for talking. See, there's rational thinking, which is about going from step A to step B, and that's where the guys in suits, the squares so straight they step out of the shower to pee, that's where those guys stop, endgame." He was talking over the music, but the beat and the bass line made it seem like he was providing lyrics. "Those guys, they never get further than figuring out the easiest path that everyone sees. Then there's where you're at, a better place, the imagination. You, you're reading funny books and your mom says you draw and write, and you're in that fancy school for smart kids, right? What you need to study is lateral thinking. What looks like a boundary to some poor schmuck who follows the rules turns out to be exactly the stepping-stone you need to move ahead. Abstract thinking goes from A to Q to Z and gives B and C and D the finger. Fuck 'em if they can't take a joke."

So many Charming-isms. My mother must have contributed to the conversation but Peter was like a lightbulb throwing her part into shadows. No man, be he Texan or Eskimo, can stand a kick in the balls. Don't shit where you eat. Don't get distracted and keep your eye on what you want, kid, and don't let someone else dictate your life.

Why all this attention from him? That's easy—my mother was a beautiful woman. Even better, she was soon to get a divorce settlement. With a plate of cheese and crackers next to us, Peter and I were setting up our mutual future, through a game of chess.

I can't count the number of rules that were being broken. Playing chess in my father's study, with Peter, who that night—even I knew it, and somehow I didn't care—was going to sleep with my mother. And he had put Joni Mitchell, an artist my father *never* could sign to Certron, on my father's stereo equipment.

We were going to use the Fabergé chess set. It was like breaking into a temple to drink the wine. Peter kept turning the pieces around in his hand, asking me which was the knight, which was the bishop, claiming they were too ornate—too "bullshit"—to tell the difference between them.

"You can't tell how exquisite this set is?" I asked.

"It's exquisite. And it's bullshit."

It was a long game. My mother started remembering that there was a James Bond film on, and maybe I wanted to watch it. But Peter said he wanted to finish our match. I kept thinking about his rap on lateral thinking. If I tried too hard to beat him at chess it might mean something other than what I'd thought, like I was missing a larger point.

I checkmated him. Or he let me checkmate him.

"I'd have won," Peter laughed, "if I wasn't so stoned."

He must mean drunk, I thought, even though I knew he didn't. He was treating me like a grown-up. Not just a grown-up, but a compatriot. This was him exercising lateral thinking. Making me question whether something was or wasn't what it sounded like was a subtle invitation to take just a tiny step further. Further where? There was only one way to find out. Come here, let me show you.

M Y MOTHER was blessed with the ability to launch new adventures with little fear. She had been the child born out of wedlock, then the resourceful girl who ran the household, then the wife of an American soldier, a divorced secretary in Los Angeles, a middle-class mother, and a rich divorcée. I don't think she would have pointed to any of those roles to say, "That's it, that's when I was most like myself."

Except now. She was fond of saying to friends that when she turned thirty-nine in 1974, she realized what she wanted to be when she grew up. "It's so ironic," she said, about everything in general and each circumstance specifically. She used the word "ironic" so often I started to make a little sigh every time. "Ironic" might as well have been the Latin on our family crest.

Mom explained: there was an exam in Britain, the 11+, dreaded by all eleven-year-old working-class kids because it separated the wheat from the chaff. If you passed—no one in her family did—you were elevated from the crushing life of your ancestors. You were allowed into schools that prepared you to handle the levers that made the world turn. Otherwise, upon your failure you were condemned to an education of a grayscale life, the assembly line, no better future than the occasional rueful laugh on a Saturday night at the pub. It was a cruel test, promising a rare bit of class penetration, and then dashing hopes as soon as they were raised.

And yet my mother passed. Brilliantly.

She got a scholarship to Bishopshalt, the type of school with badges and uniforms and students who would later know the catacombs of Parliament. Her sisters were jealous. She was accused of having a big head, of thinking herself above her station. And then, a family crisis prevented her from following through. For one moment she'd had a vision through a door cut into a brick garden wall, of gaiety, power, and improvement. Now she was stuck again.

What was worse, in a way, was that her crushed, guilt-inducing, poverty-stricken father had been a child of German military aristocracy, complete with summers in Calais and motorcycle trips across the continent. What that must have been like, father and daughter together, almost living up to their potential, then fate striking them both down. But they had a role model for how the family could turn out: Aunt Ingrid.

Aunt Ingrid was a journalist. She flew around the world writing articles for important magazines. She befriended movie stars and politicians. She was a member of the jet set, a passport and toothbrush and a pack of Gitanes in her overcoat and drinking dictators and publicists under the table in search of a groundbreaking interview. When she visited Uxbridge, she brought with her breezes of sophistication and kindness, but not promise. Once that scholarship was gone, there was no longer promise in my mother's life.

And then at the age of thirty-nine, promise magically reappeared. My mother could join the smart set. She was not ignorant of how that class lived. She was never flashy or indiscreet—those were adjectives she deployed when describing how an otherwise intelligent person could be déclassé. But when she looked at herself in the mirror at I. Magnin, trying on a crème-colored Burberry trench coat, she did say it looked smashing on her. Her dream was to wake up and drive to the airport and on impulse jump aboard a flight. Unlike so many other things, she would get a chance to do that, soon enough.

My mother was in the habit then of explaining what she knew of the world, and I would say something, and she wouldn't hear it. I would say it again, and she would fall silent, blue eyes still for one extra moment, then she would say, "Mmm?" for me to repeat myself. Sometimes she couldn't hear me but other times she could.

Terms of the settlement were kept from me but she did have assets, as one might say discreetly. My mother claimed she got very little and my father claimed she got an enormous amount—hundreds of thousands of dollars—meant to keep her stable for the rest of her life. I've seen the numbers since and I think these views were clouded by their anger at each other. There weren't hundreds of thousands of dollars. There was some cash, some corporate paper, and some property—like the art— that could be sold to get more cash, or managed as an investment. In a stern letter, my father drew a chart for her, with much more brittle penmanship than the chart he'd once done of her family tree. It showed how bonds earmarked for my college education would, though their face value was small, be bountiful when I needed them. All she had to do was leave them alone.

My mother rolled her eyes at this. How well had *he* done with money, exactly? He had never yet understood her needs or her desires. I think this is when I learned the word "élan," as my mother used it with a quiet smile and a way of spreading her hands, like she was smoothing out problems by sheer force of style. Peter Charming, she said, had a kind of élan, for instance, but she said she saw through it—he had it the way someone who practiced piano long enough could almost sound born to the keyboard. Peter liked having us around because she had the real thing.

Her mother and father, and her ancestors before them, didn't have a chance like this, but that was in the old countries, England, Germany. Here, you could make your own luck if you tried. She and I were going to show Dad what she could do. She had a story in mind, with a young Cockney girl who'd been pushed too far by a man who wanted to mold her without taking in who she really was. "Just you wait, 'enry 'iggins, just you wait," she was fond of saying. She meant my father, or all men, or an invisible enemy force that was more amorphous than just one person.

.   .   .

One Friday in November, around six o'clock, our phone on Setting Sun Drive rang. My mother came into my room, eyes awake with mischief. "We're going to San Francisco." As in: right away. Turn off the TV. Peter Charming had bought us two tickets on the last flight PSA had that night. He was throwing a party that wouldn't be complete without us there. We didn't need to pack. We would stay at Peter's Pacific Heights mansion.

I had some new comic books I wanted to read and old ones to reread, so I didn't want to go. My mom started packing anyway. Peter called again, and my mother, deep in her walk-in closet, put me on the phone. He wanted to know what she was doing.

"She's packing."

"Make her stop. Go in there and get her the fuck out of her closet. Tell her to just get her purse and you and get on the plane. We'll buy clothes tomorrow. Tell her to fucking quit the closet shit. We'll buy her a whole new wardrobe."

I did that, exactly, letting Peter listen in. I was laughing as I tugged my mother away from her suitcases, and she was laughing, too. I'd forgotten I didn't want to go.

Three hours later, we were getting out of the cab in front of Peter's house on Broadway and Laguna. It was two stories, flat-fronted and plain blue outside, nothing ornate. There were a lot of stairs involved. We could see through the front windows that the living room was packed with people. Peter was there with a glass of wine in his hand, which he handed to my mother. "You made it! You made it! You're incredible. I can't believe you and the midget just got on the plane. Suzie Blue will show you the place. Sue Blue! Sue Blue!"

He had more to say but it was hard for me to listen, for many reasons. For instance there were two men kissing in the hallway. They had perfect hair, Ryan O'Neal hair, tousled without being shaggy. *Oh,* I thought, *those men must be gay.*

Sue embraced my mother and kissed me on the cheek.

I had never seen anyone like Sue in person. She was a figure out of a Truffaut film. She was tall, willowy, platinum blond, with blue eyes and red lipstick that made her skin look white as plaster. I'd previously thought "skin white as plaster" was a silly exaggeration. Her voice was tranquil, as if she had been born in the middle of this party and had taken in stride everything that had happened since. She wore jeans and a silk blouse and tiny button pearl earrings, and she breezed over to hand Peter a new glass of wine, then floated back to us. She *floated*. I realized during the long time I stared that this was an effect—effortlessness. I'd never seen effortlessness.

As she took us upstairs, I noticed people smoking pot. The bad kids in my neighborhood smoked pot on the beach or the public stairways by the high school. Weren't the adults here worried about the cops? No one here seemed worried about anything. In fact, that seemed to be a feature of the party. So I decided, without this being effective, that I wasn't worried.

Upstairs was the master bedroom, with bookshelves from floor to ceiling and piles of books by Peter's bed. The hallway was narrow, with a kind of floor I didn't recognize (it was hardwood) and the doors had dinged-up complicated moldings that didn't match from one room to the next. Here was Peter's office, where someone was stretched out on the leather couch with electrodes on his head.

"Biofeedback," Sue explained, pitching the unfamiliar words as my mom and I trailed behind. It was like acupuncture, or massage. My mother was fascinated. She wondered if it could help her migraines. I wanted her to try it. I wanted her to try everything. I was also afraid of everything, but I'd picked up on the atmosphere. If something was strange, it was new, and embracing it meant you were breaking free from something old.

Sue led me to my room, where there was a brass bed and some old white shelves overstuffed with books. The guests' coats were piled on the bed, which Sue patted. The bed rippled. *It was a water bed.* Even the most spoiled of my classmates didn't sleep on water beds. "And these are for you if you get bored," she said, handing me some underground comic books I'd never heard of. I would never admit to being bored here. I wanted to move in and live here until I was no longer terrified by everything I saw.

A little while later, I stood in the living room, halfway behind the fronds of a potted fern, sipping a Coke, nodding to the music, and pretending I'd been to parties before. The hors d'oeuvres smelled of roasted garlic and the burgers were dressed with aioli and capers. I realized I didn't even know what a hamburger meant on this planet.

Peter swept by with a girl on his arm, stopping at the stereo. He ignored me. The Rolling Stones' *Aftermath* was playing, and Peter was explaining to her that while they were in the studio, groupies were actually blowing them. Then he took off the record and put on Joni Mitchell. "You should hear her do it in person. She's in town later, you should come by, her voice is best around five a.m.," and then he was gone again. I took more sips of my Coke. I pretended I wasn't waiting for the police to arrest us all.

Sue found me. "I was looking for you. You're the only person here who will appreciate this. Do you play pinball?"

I was amazed she was looking for me. I wasn't sure I wanted her to find me, afraid she might take me someplace even further beyond what I knew how to deal with. *Glen, here's the harem. Glen, here's the rifle range. Glen, let's rob a liquor store and turn over some cars and set them on fire together.* I would have done any of that with Sue. And pinball was something I knew from my old life of several hours ago.

I followed her through the kitchen—so many open bottles of wine!— how strange to have a hulking refrigerator from the 1950s, a stove from the 1920s, who had ever thought of stuffing olives with blue cheese, was that a braid of garlic hanging from the ceiling?—to a mud room, where there was a pinball machine not too different from my own.

The room's walls were peeling so that paint chips feathered the nests of newspaper and cordwood. There were faded Art Nouveau posters tacked to the walls. Sue said the house had been built in the 1870s and that after the earthquake it had been a makeshift hospital. Survivors had brought the owners gift baskets she'd found in the attic. She was pretty sure it was haunted. My home in Corona del Mar felt inadequate.

Sue turned on the pinball machine so she could play with me. She asked if I'd read any books by Tom Robbins. Or *Grapefruit* by Yoko Ono? Had I heard of a comic strip called *Odd Bodkins*? She asked all this while rolling a joint.

I didn't know how to talk to her. I lunged for the only thing I thought I knew. "You can play as hard as you want," I said.

"What do you mean 'play hard'?" she asked.

"I mean, don't be nice or anything."

"I'm never nice," she said. I flushed with embarrassment. And within a few minutes she was massacring me. The joint went to embers on the edge of the pinball machine. Her long, polished fingernails were atop the flipper buttons, not so much banging on the machine as massaging it to do her bidding. "I do this for hours," she said.

She was a potter and her kiln was behind the house in a little studio that was her private space. When she was blocked, she came in to play pinball. Her work was all over the house, thick-walled vases and tiny hanging mirrors set into subtle, color-shifting glazes. I couldn't say whether I liked them, but they spoke of artistic confidence. She had an affinity for when to smooth the clay out and when to leave a thumb-print so it looked rustic.

When it was my turn, my eyes darted back and forth from the machine to Sue, who was pulling on her joint. "Your mom has pretty eyes. So do you."

I didn't know what to say about that.

"Do you like girls?" She came across as much as she could like another kid asking the question, but still I couldn't think how to answer. "I don't mean to embarrass you. Do girls like you?"

"I don't think so." It was my turn again. Flip, flip, plunk. Without warning, she laughed. I could feel my throat hurting. "You don't have to laugh at me."

"I'm sorry. I just realized that when you get older, girls are going to like you. Hey, look at me."

Her eyes were huge.

"Do you believe in ESP?"

I didn't want to sound stupid. But it wasn't a trick question. "My mom and I have this psychic link."

There was shuffling all around us. Hors d'oeuvres moving into the kitchen, platters moving out. Laughter. Music. Sue licked her finger and tapped at the joint to extinguish it. "Some people think I'm a witch because I can see the future. You're going to end up very handsome. You'll have lots of girlfriends." I imagine being hypnotized would feel like this did. "Not yet, but when they do they'll all be very pretty women who love you. You're a lucky kid."

Somewhere out there, my mother was drinking her glass of wine and having a conversation with someone. Was it like this? Did everyone in San Francisco have conversations like this? Was that what being here meant? It would be like living in a Tarot card.

Sue was calm. I finally asked, "Are you really a witch?"

"Well." She shrugged. "I *am* from Wichita."

The doorbell rang. It was now my job to answer it, as Peter thought it would be great, "decadent," he said, to have a kid greet people and hand them glasses of Zinfandel.

When I opened the door there were two cops on the porch.

They asked for Peter, and as I remember it he was already on his way to the door. He winked at me.

I was so traumatized I have no idea how the next hour or so passed. What I remember was sitting on the stairs and looking through the wooden posts like jail bars at one of the cops. The party was still going. The cop asked how old I was. I told him I was twelve, which sounded better to my ears than ten.

I asked, "Do you care that people here are smoking pot?"

He wriggled a finger at me in a "come here" gesture. I pressed against the railing to get closer. He exhaled pot smoke into my face.

The next morning Peter, Sue, my mother, and I took a walk down to Aquatic Park, where Peter pointed out the Italian widowers playing bocce ball. My mother had a cappuccino in North Beach and the four of us sat at a café table. I didn't know air could feel cold in the mornings. The light was sharp and crisp. That my mother ordered cappuccino so easily reminded me that she had been missing Europe since coming to California.

She struggled to explain how wonderful this all was, and Peter said San Francisco was enchanting, but not as great as it had once been. He and some friends had co-owned a nightclub by the Cannery called Arthur. Up all night, coffee in the morning on Broadway at Enrico's, watching secretaries pass by, seeing if they could make them stop and say hello, new girls every day. His friend Ron was an opera singer with the Met, Trevor was a fashion designer, and maybe they dabbled at actually doing that stuff, but mostly they owned a nightclub.

Mom asked, "Do people have jobs here?" because it didn't seem like anyone took anything seriously. It wasn't frivolous. San Francisco ran on melancholy. People here knew San Francisco wasn't what it had been. If only you'd been here a little while ago, that era when things were more festive. The attitude was, *We'll play, we'll make life a game, but that other time we can't quite put our finger on, that's when you should have been here.* Every boutique owner, every bearded street artisan with a booth of hammered silver rings, every cab driver loved it here, but the love came with sadness. San Francisco forgave that feeling. *I know you're sad, let's all be sad together.*

Mom and I went home.

I stood on our vacant lot in Corona del Mar as the winter sun was going down. It was just me, a boy who'd been told he was a thirty-six-year-old midget, and his croquet set. Listlessly I hammered balls through wickets, not feeling committed, instead making panoramic circles to take in every bit of the scenery. My croquet set was no longer enough. My house and my street and my view were no longer enough. It felt like there should be sad music playing for me as I for the last time gathered up my mallets and posts and said goodbye.

My mother explained to me that the plush cocoon was over. The stars were lining up. Everything she knew suggested that with a little effort, luck, élan, a prosperous life would be ours. Which is of course the crux of a good con game.

*A*LICE DOESN'T LIVE HERE ANYMORE was the first movie my mother and I saw in San Francisco. It played at the Alhambra, a 1920s Moorish theater that was exotic, with stamped tin chandeliers and heavy velvet curtains trimmed with arabesques.

The movie was about Alice, played by Ellen Burstyn, widowed, starting her life over again in a new town. She tries to be a singer but ends up a waitress, and meets terrible men before finding a handsome rancher, Kris Kristofferson, who takes care of her. In one scene, on a long drive from one town to the next, Burstyn is trying to figure out the roads while Alfred Lutter, playing her son, my age, tells her an annoying and dirty joke. "Shoot the dog! Shoot the dog!" was the punch line.

I knew that joke. Further, my mom and I had *just* driven from Corona del Mar to San Francisco, staying overnight in a motel that was seedy enough to allow Leo in our room. Like Alice, we had our belongings in the car, and I told jokes, but mine were funnier than Alfred Lutter's, even if my mother couldn't hear that. I also kept letting Leo out of his cage because I felt sorry for him. That turned out to be a mistake every time.

When we left the theater, Mom and I felt exhilarated. We'd just seen a movie about us! Except instead of singing, my mother was going to be an investor. And she wasn't going to fail.

"We'll live frugally," my mother said, "within our means." We had a flat on the second floor of a 1920s apartment building with twenty-year-old appliances to which we added the Amana Radarange microwave. The Persian rugs overlapped in the living room and dining room. My coins were in a safety deposit box. I was in public school. Sixth grade at Winfield Scott was 70 percent Chinese, 29 percent black, and me. The Chinese and black kids hated each other. But I was looked at as a kind of an albino buffalo, something so strange bumbling through the hallways that they preferred to ignore me. It was all right.

Sometimes I sat on the end of my mom's bed while she rolled a joint. She didn't want to hide anything from me. I liked her smoking pot—she became silly when stoned, and more talkative about her past. Also, I wasn't positive about this, but she seemed less deaf when she was high. I wondered if marijuana helped deafness.

Her, waving the joint. "Don't you do this."

"I'm not interested. Adults are boring."

"Ha. Good." She took a hit. "You realize I'm only doing this for my second childhood, right?"

"Your first."

"You're a good kid, Charlie Brown. My first childhood."

In September 1939, a few days after war was declared, my grandfather was taken away in the dead of night to an internment camp on the Isle of Man. This was supposed to be temporary, but none of his British relatives would vouch for him. As the war wound down, and people in his circle were returned home, George remained in the camp for months and then years longer than anyone else he knew. My mother had letters between her parents outlining the hardships and deprivations that each of them faced—him, a prisoner, and her, a single woman with a boardinghouse filled with children and soldiers. There were so many milestones he missed, and so many hopes raised then dashed that he might return. This was how my mother learned the concept of "when," as in "when your father comes back, we'll finally make a go of being happy."

The family was never sure, but he seemed to be the very last man released, late in the war. My mother had missed him terribly and had simultaneously known almost nothing about him. When he was taken away, she was four years old. When he was back, she was almost ten.

His return was difficult. No one would hire a prisoner from the Isle

of Man. Regardless of his polyglot background (he had been a transla-
tor before the war) and his intellectual backbone, he could only find
jobs in manual labor. And then, more children, more mouths to feed.
He took out his frustrations on my mother, lecturing her in French
when he was angry.

"He knew I didn't speak French," she said. The burden of being
daughter to a genius was huge. Worse, a genius whose potential wouldn't
be fulfilled. "I never felt like I could give back anything, it was never
enough. I'd disappointed him by being born. It's been a slow process,
my son, slow but steady, letting go of those hang-ups."

"Why did they stay together?"

"My parents?" She exhaled a hit of pot. "It must have been the sex."
And then she laughed, and I laughed, too.

Like my father, my mother had started dressing more in fashion,
but it looked good on her. Cream-colored linen bell-bottom trousers
that trembled with the winds, with knit blouses, buttoned at the line
between discreet and otherwise. For high-fashion evenings, she had a
vest made of feathers, which she once wore with no shirt underneath to
an art opening. She was noticed.

She hadn't moved us so she could date Peter. I'm not sure their physical relationship continued after the move. I remember Peter throwing
his arm around her at a party and whispering, loud enough that I could
hear it, "You and I are both more sophisticated than the people we sleep
with."

It was beautifully said. My mother got to feel smart and independent
and yet part of the club. Peter continued not to shit where he ate.

"There are no limits," she said. "Not for you, either. You can do anything." She said I didn't have to think the way other people did. I could
go to boarding school, she said, I could go to Switzerland.

That last part made me feel a little dizzy, excited but terrified, and she
said she was only suggesting it to get me to think how much potential I
had. I could be an artist.

"I was a model when I was seventeen. Did I tell you that already? Did
you know I used to sing? I used to sing when I was seventeen. I sang
'Moon River' to you when you had ear infections and couldn't sleep. I
always used to wonder if I could sing in a nightclub. Maybe I can now."
But not like *Alice Doesn't Live Here Anymore*.

. . . .

My mother was right—she was about to launch into a great adventure. She was smart, determined, had money, and lived in a town that took pride in supporting even crazier dreams. But there was an obstacle to her getting the life she wanted.

Maybe it was one of those joint-smoking moments, maybe another time. My mother told me the story of the last day she saw my father before the move to San Francisco. She told it so vividly that I remember it as if I'd been there. She said she and my father had met in the house on Setting Sun Drive. Five thousand square feet echoing now, as boxes were half-packed, parcels stacked in the terra-cotta-tiled hallways, "Fragile" stickers from Bekins Movers on the crystal. Discolorations on the wall where sunlight had fallen around the framed things that had been a sign of prosperity, then prosperity fleeing. My mother with a handkerchief on her head, dusting, was having my father over to sell him back some things she'd gotten in the settlement. This would buy her some breathing room.

My father showed up with Ann. This was how my mother met her. Ann and my father walked through the house, Ann pointing out the things she wanted to buy. Some artwork. Some jewelry my father had given my mother. It wasn't a long visit, less than an hour, and in that hour, the younger woman my father was sleeping with bought my mother's possessions at a bargain price.

Sometimes I imagined my father writing a check in what must have been a silent room. I imagined the three of them standing in the kitchen, empty counters, gashes in the walls where the artwork used to be, and him making a futile joke as he handed the check over.

As she needed that check, my mother would hold her tongue about all the ways she felt. My father didn't see what was wrong, she told me. It was a financial arrangement to him.

My mother told me my father had chosen Ann for her money. She said this with sympathy. She told me the story to better narrate the end of our old lives. My father valued things, not people, because he was afraid. She felt sad for him. "Your father and I were in love. He doesn't want to risk that again."

She didn't want me to grow up like him, cold and remote. Walling off your heart, she explained, was worse than being willing to risk it again.

This was a beautiful lesson. I still believe in it even if that meeting in the house never happened.

Since I started working on a memoir my father has been answering my questions like he's giving the instructions to defuse an especially tricky bomb. He's been explaining what happened, but he doesn't justify his behavior. He sees justifying things as caving to guilt. When I ask what he'd been thinking that day, he laughs. "Are you kidding? Me, taking Ann to that house? We didn't do that. I can't imagine doing that. I mean, think about it."

I have. For a man who claims he has no conscience, he still tends to misremember his more hurtful decisions. My parents both would like to believe themselves the wronged party here.

So I asked Ann. She says that my father did indeed take her to the house. It was during the divorce, before my mother and I had moved out. It wasn't to buy anything—Dad wanted to *show off*. Specifically, he drove her to Corona del Mar to indicate he was still rich. He was going to pretend the accumulation of objects with such good stories behind them meant he could still afford them. He was going to give Ann the house tour of his life.

I was prepared to hear that my mother's version was correct, and that's how she met Ann. But Ann says that when my father opened the door to the house, it was empty. There wasn't a thing there except a closet of my father's suits.

My mother hadn't left a note. Neither my father nor Ann knew where we'd gone. My father told me the same story, down to the suits in the closet. He said he panicked because he had no idea where I was. He had to ask a neighbor what had happened, and he heard that a thirty-foot moving van had pulled away earlier. My mom had moved us without telling him.

So when my mother told me about that upsetting encounter with Dad and Ann, it's not just that it never happened, it's that something else, entirely of her own making, had happened instead.

And yet my mother wasn't lying to me. She had a strong backbone, a moral compass. But at the same time she was forging an identity, a plucky survivor who'd been victimized in the past by people like my father. I don't think it was too far from my own fantasy of washing up on a beach after a storm, battered and bruised and just barely surviving. However, she saw a storm no one else could see. It was one made just for her.

My mother talked a lot. She narrated what she was doing, why she was doing it, what she was going to do next. In San Francisco, she was beginning to tell the story of her own life.

She was, by fate or irony or collision of time and circumstance, in a city populated with other folks whose histories were self-generated, too. She and San Francisco were a perfectly ill-fated match.

I loved Peter. Even at the time, I wouldn't have said he loved me back, but he enjoyed grandstanding. He woke each morning by throwing open the windows of his bedroom and yelling, "I love you, my beautiful San Francisco." If he had change nearby, and there were tourists, he would scatter pennies out the window.

After showering and doing his nails (he was obsessive about his cuticles) he would put on a leather coat, grab his leather satchel, and, after a leisurely morning coffee, drive to appointments at boardrooms or cafés or warehouses around the Bay. His *Bullitt* car didn't run—it was parked up the block but it never got ticketed because Peter had an arrangement. Instead he drove a corporate car, a new Buick someone had given him to pay off a debt, and which he'd customized so the license plates said 007 LTK. He drove it impatiently and when I rode with him, he sometimes, just to upset my mother, drove on the sidewalk.

One night he came over for a dinner party and when he and I checked on the spaghetti, he introduced me to the method of throwing it upward to see if it stuck to the ceiling. This led to him throwing it directly at me, and within a minute, we'd covered the whole kitchen in spaghetti and sauce. The walls, the floor, us, covered in dinner.

Even he was surprised I'd participated in that. With sauce dripping off his face, he whispered, "There's people ready to eat and we just fucked it up. What are we going to do?"

I said, "What do you mean 'we'? I'm just a kid—you're the one in trouble."

That became a staple story for him. "This kid here, he pulled a Peter Charming on me. He's treacherous." Which thrilled me. Peter was grooming me to behave badly, and I was an excellent apprentice.

I stayed over at his house once and when he left for work, I hid cans of Spam in his pantry, his linen closet, the box he kept his dope in, and the pocket of one of his business suits. He retaliated by ambushing me after a dinner party with a cream pie. I felt like if I studied long enough I'd be his equal.

It was sometimes hard to tell when he was actually doing business, but that ambiguity suited him. He used the phone constantly, and he hated the phone. One night, someone put him on hold and in exasperation, Peter yanked the phone out of the wall and threw it in the fire. It exploded.

"Boom, it was like shrapnel, you have to see it," Peter was explaining as he ripped my mother's phone out of our wall. He bundled the cord around it and then threw it into the fireplace. My mother was trying to stop him, as he was talking over her. "Watch. Ready? Watch. No, watch watch watch."

As promised, a wall of flames shot out of the fireplace. My mother wasn't impressed. She was mad. She had to rent another phone now.

Peter announced that he had safety concerns. "Did you know," he would say when visiting people's parties, "how hazardous your phone is?" And then he would throw the nearest phone into the fire.

Once a week, my mother, Peter, Sue, and I went to the Washington Square Bar & Grill, a gossipy North Beach hangout, where we sat at a large round table with an ever-changing group. Margo St. James, who was organizing a prostitutes union, seemed moderately amused to discuss her job with an eleven-year-old. I met columnists for the *Chronicle*—Art Hoppe and Stanton Delaplane—and a couple of times Herb Caen waved but didn't slow down as he crossed the room.

The restaurant was up the street from Comics & Comix, so if things got slow, Peter would hand me a ten dollar bill. When I came back, I would read the latest *Avengers* while waiting for my spaghetti. It turned out the Vision was actually the original Human Torch, a fact that I couldn't get anyone at the table interested in, as the adults were flirting over me.

San Francisco, 1975, was built for dating. There was no activity, from shopping to exercising to taking the bus, that didn't have quotation marks around it, as if everyone knew that whatever motions you were making toward working or eating or buying clothes were only cover stories.

My mother couldn't go to Safeway without men ramming their carts into hers and asking how long to cook a chicken breast. Peter had his own routine. Every morning he walked downhill three blocks and sat in the front window of the Café Cantata with the paper folded back next to a café au lait. He spent his afternoons talking to women as they passed by. Drinks were at Perry's and dinners at the Balboa Cafe, all within walking distance not just of each other but also his house. Mac-Arthur Park, a bar with brass rails and ferns, was his most distant outpost, but Henry Africa's would do as well. This is how he met what he called his *newies*. Sometimes he sent Sue in his place to bring newies back to the house for him.

Sometimes I met him at Café Cantata and he expounded to me about the world.

"Kid, when I turn forty I want to be known as the Silver Fox, so I'm going to pay my friends a thousand dollars each to remember that." Or "Kid, stop cracking your knuckles and stop slouching, Jesus; the way you moan about your life, it's like you know nothing about your people's history. Have you ever read *The Painted Bird*? No? *That* kid had something to complain about."

Whenever I stayed at the café long enough he gave me ten bucks to pretend I was his son. "See that girl there, with the black hair? Tell her your father wants to buy her a balloon and take her to Paris."

Our apartment was four doors up from the Egyptian consulate. One day a boy and girl who lived there, roughly my age, were waiting outside. They'd just come back from Egypt and while they'd been gone their house had been vandalized.

"You know who did that?" the girl asked.

"No, who?" I asked.

The boy said, "Wait, wait." And he looked around the bus stop for eavesdroppers. "Are you Jewish?"

I told a half-truth. "No."

"Jews." He nodded at me meaningfully.

I asked what he meant. Jews had wrecked his house?

"My father told me."

"Which Jews?"

"How should I know? The ones who were in the house, of course."

There hadn't been Jews in their house. It had been drug addicts that a halfway house had boarded there—I'd read an article about it in the *Chronicle*. That night at the Washington Square Bar & Grill, I knew I had a story to tell.

"Hold on," Peter interrupted. I hadn't even gotten to the good part. "What did he say when you told him you were Jewish?"

I was confused. "I didn't—"

"Fuck that. If a guy like that asks if you're Jewish, tell him, 'Fuck yeah, I'm Jewish.' And if he doesn't like it he can go fuck himself. You have to be proud."

"I am proud. But I'm also not really Jewish."

This made him apoplectic. Now another front in the argument had opened up. I was half-Jewish, and according to Orthodoxy, it was the wrong half. But Peter was having none of it—I was making excuses for not standing up for myself. He talked over me so that I could hardly make my point. If I'd told the Egyptian kid I was Jewish, I would never have heard his story.

"Why the fuck do you care what he has to say?"

I couldn't explain. I kept trying to rephrase it. I wanted to know people's secret lives; I wanted to hear contrary views; I wanted to be a fly on the wall. I knew two things were true: I wanted to be a writer, so I said writers interviewed people. Also, I didn't want to piss people off. I didn't actually say that part to Peter because I didn't want to piss him off.

My mother was driving me somewhere and she said, "I have to get my watch back."

I asked where it was. She'd left it at a man's house.

"What's next? Your underwear?" It came out too quickly. It was like I'd hit her in the face. My mind was going in circles. Was there any legitimate reason an adult woman would take her watch off at a man's place? I wanted to scramble backward, tell her I'd just been bantering.

Later, Peter pulled me aside. I'd really hurt my mother's feelings with that "underwear" wisecrack.

"If it hurts her feelings, she needs to stop leaving her jewelry at men's houses." I was still puzzled by how the watch had ended up there, as I wanted all the evidence to add up to her only *pretending* to have sex.

Peter said, "Your mother respects you. She's treating you like an adult. You have to react like an adult and respect her back. No judgments. Endgame."

Soon after, my mother and I went to a party at Peter's house. He didn't bother leaving his throne—an overstuffed chair by the fireplace—to say hello. He seemed self-contained and impatient with me. "You should go read the new *Odd Bodkins* book Sue Blue has upstairs—check it out."

"There's a new one?"

"It's great."

When I collapsed on the couch in his office, I saw it was the same book as last time. He'd just told me it was new to get rid of me for the evening, which was fine—I reminded myself I didn't like seeing him either, sometimes.

A minute later, my mother was upstairs. "We're leaving."

I protested, but she was already stepping down the stairs with outsized caution, her shoulders stiff as she shuffled through her purse for her car keys.

Then we were in the Mercedes and she was sitting upright. She gave off a furnacelike heat, and it was hard to look straight at her. I think she'd stopped blinking.

We were going to visit Peter, then we were leaving. I was good at finessing through reversals like that. I'm okay either way, what do you want, we'll do it that way.

The way home was a straight line along Pacific Avenue. Every street corner had a stop sign that seemed to take my mom by surprise. I held on to my seat belt and looked out the window. I'd started learning when things were built because when I walked to school and saw a house that looked embarrassingly out of place, it always turned out to be from the 1950s, when nubby stucco and aluminum windows struck people as a good idea. I felt sorry for those houses.

We parked in front of our apartment building, where there were marble columns flanking the entrance, and the columns had acanthus leaves on them. My mother curbed the wheels. She turned off the engine. There were jets of fog rolling toward us. Looking straight ahead, she hissed, "Peter and his precious fellatio."

·   ·   ·

Years later, my mother got stoned and started writing her life story. She told it from my point of view. It was called *My Mother's Lovers— and Other Reasons I'm Valedictorian!* My character was a jaded eleven-year-old who can't be bothered to remember his mother's boyfriends' names, and so he gives them nicknames like the Mad Italian Professor. When she read it aloud to me, I felt the same queasiness I did when she described an article she'd seen about mother-son incest taboos. In some tribes, sexual experiences like that were part of the growing-up process, she said, and wasn't that interesting?

The real Mad Italian Professor, Cesare, was a graduate student. My mother had promoted him. I remember whenever he got angry, he absently twisted the hair of his eyebrows into Satanic peaks. Once he said Schopenhauer would have hated me. "Schopenhauer was a fool," I said, though I'd never even heard of him.

That I was eleven years old didn't matter; me saying that sent Cesare into a fit. This was okay. I was impressed he had no intention of being my friend.

My mother was frequently out most of the night. You couldn't say she was at a party or on a date—she might start out in one direction and end up in another. I used to stay up, talking to myself and listening to the sounds of the San Francisco night. There were foghorns that struck me as mournful and a strange ticking I eventually realized was conden-sation dripping from a gutter onto a ledge. I watched *The Tonight Show* on a portable black-and-white set that I kept switching off in case what I'd just heard was my mom coming home.

Leo had a cat door. Sometimes I heard him scurrying in with a mouse, and I would get up and watch him spar with it until it was dead. One night, Leo jumped out his door, then back in. He meowed. He had that Siamese nuclear wail of a voice. I went to the kitchen in time to see him jump out the door again.

"You want me to follow you, boy?"

I opened the kitchen door. I was in my pajamas. Outside was a set of wooden stairs painted a pistachio color twenty years ago, now flaking and weather-beaten. Leo was on the flight leading up. He seemed to be waiting for me. I carefully left the door on its latch. As I went up the stairs, Leo paused on every landing for me.

He led me to the roof. I hadn't known you could get to the roof. It was flat, with flashing around the vents and chimneys that poked through the surface. There was mist sweeping past us, little grains illuminated by the brilliant streetlights in front of our apartment building. But I wasn't cold. The nearest foghorn let out a moan and a few distant ones seemed to answer. Leo walked along the edge of the roof, tail straight up, his kingdom four stories below.

There was no one else here. No one on the street, no cars, no pedestrians. I could see lights in the windows of houses near us, but no one was moving. I pretended it was just me and Leo in the empty city, two pulses attuned to the mysteries of the foghorns. If you were in this town, they weren't exotic, they were part of your brain, and I understood why San Franciscans had an innate melancholy. It was why they liked jazz. Born to foghorns.

I felt a calling. I had to notice all the world's wonders and sadness, and to report to someone somewhere how much there was left to lose. I felt extended beyond myself. Though I couldn't say why, I didn't want to leave this. I tried to trick myself into remembering it. *I am remembering this moment now so it's not lost,* I thought, *and if I remember myself remembering, it's a moment that will never really disappear.* Nothing is empty, nothing is really lonely, if someone is there to share it, even if the sharing was with my cat. I said, "Thank you, Leo," like he had orchestrated it for me.

As I walked back to the apartment, the telephone was ringing. I answered it. I heard a quick voice—my mother's? someone else's?—and then confused noises. I was terrified.

"Are you there? Listen. Listen to this. Just hold on."

Mom. I held the phone. Four-part harmony came up, a cappella. I'd heard it on the radio before—it was a song called "Operator" and it had a gospel insistence that was catchy. People on the other end of the phone were clapping along in a scattered, Pacific Heights white-person attempt at keeping time. Mom was breaking some kind of contract by calling me. She was supposed to enjoy herself without letting me know. I was supposed to be home, perfecting my loneliness.

When the song was over, Mom got back on the phone. "Did you hear that, darling? You know who that was?"

"No." Annoyed.

"The Manhattan Transfer. They're in Peter's living room. Lots of love, Mommy has to go now."

She hung up. She had called herself "Mommy." This was to make herself feel young, at the expense of making me feel about four years old. I got back into bed.

I managed to be half-asleep when the party arrived at the apartment. Soon the liquor and music and laughter had reignited.

I shuffled out of my bedroom. Sometimes an eleven-year-old smartass lent an exotic presence to my mother's parties. But I had a sense for atmosphere, and this one struck me as off-kilter. The lights were low. I didn't recognize anyone. People were locking themselves into our bathroom in pairs, and coming out exceedingly alert.

In the living room, my mother was sitting on a man's lap. When she saw me, her face went livid. "Out!" she yelled.

I made it to my bedroom door, then realized that meant ceding my territory. I returned to the living room, where my mother was still in the man's lap. Me standing there didn't make much of an impact on him. He was blond, with a mustache and a half-smirk. If I meant to seem like a cop, he looked at me like he knew I didn't have a warrant.

I extended my hand. "Hi, I'm Glen. I'm her son."

"Georgio," he said, but not as if I'd shaken him up.

"I told you to go to bed," my mother said.

"Mom, I'm plagued by feelings of unreality."

She stood, grabbed me by the wrist, and led me back to my room. "Go. To. Bed."

"But I'm plagued by—"

"No, you're not." She swept me into my room and slammed the door.

I listened to the mysterious party sounds and I felt sorry for myself. Eventually, regardless of the noise, I fell asleep.

I woke up when I felt the weight of my bed shift.

There was a man sitting at the end of my bed. He wore a black leather jacket and a leather cap. "Sorry." He stood. "I was trying to be quiet."

There is every reason, when looking at this with contemporary eyes, to fear for my safety. It was 1975 and San Francisco, however, and expressing fear at the unfamiliar or threatening would have been inelegant. So I behaved as if this were normal. This didn't mean I was safe, as terrible men have always taken advantage of those who attempt bohemian life.

"Sorry. Go back to sleep." He looked apologetic, like the full weirdness of being in my room had just hit him. "I can go back to the party." He looked at the door grimly. Finally, he said, "It's only that your mother said you had the new issue of the *Fantastic Four*."

"I do," I said brightly. "It's on the spinner rack."

I had a spinner rack, one of those displays from drugstores with "Hey Kids, Comics!" on a panel at the top.

"Whoa. You do have comics," the guy said.

"It's terrible for condition. You can read whatever you want, but be careful taking them out."

"Cool! Thanks." When he looked over the comic book covers, his face fell. "What happened to Captain America?"

"I know, he looks dead. The government let him down, so Cap stopped wearing his old costume and he's Nomad now."

There was an especially loud burst of laughter from the party, through the closed door. He tossed up a dismissive hand as if apologizing for all things adult. "I'm in the, I'm in the, you know, the group."

"Group?"

"The Manhattan Transfer."

"Oh. Are you going to sing?"

"I hope not. Is the Hulk still Bob Banner?"

I corrected him: Bruce Banner, and then filled him in on the latest. Glenn Talbot, the Hulk's rival for Betty Ross, was replaced by a Russian spy. He found a seat at my desk, under my task lamp. He checked his fingers for dirt before he started reading. "I'll turn off the light when I go," he said.

I got back into bed. I thought of questions to ask him, but he seemed to like the silence. This was a type of adult I met more often than you'd think—kind enough to wipe his hands before looking at my comics. It felt good to know there were adults who could be at the party who didn't want to be at the party.

When I woke up later, he was gone, my comics were in a neat, squared-off stack, and the task lamp was off.

The next morning I found a sandwich my mother had made for me on the counter, in a brown bag, with a can of soda. This meant she'd made it before going to bed, and she was still asleep. I went off to school.

When I came back that afternoon, she was sitting in the living room, weeping. She held a crumpled-up Kleenex in her fist. The telephone was at her feet.

I asked her what was wrong, and, between sobs, she answered. Her man from last night, Georgio, had just been arrested. He'd been trying to pawn her jewelry.

I put my arms around her shoulders. But I was awkward. I didn't know if I should say anything.

She pulled away. She looked at me with watering eyes. "He could have just asked me for the money, damnit. I can't believe he was so intimidated by me having nice things that he couldn't even ask. I can't believe it. I can't believe it."

Then she stood, got her purse and her keys together, reapplied her lipstick, and walked to the car, alone. She drove to the police station and bailed him out.

———

Peter lectured Mom. Didn't she understand there were men who meant her harm? He knew she wanted to believe the best of people, but not everyone deserved that. My mother reacted by turning polite. Still, he wouldn't let it alone, digging at a scab he should have let heal. Which makes sense, because he had trouble believing she would be so naive. Also he was protecting his territory.

Georgio said he loved my mother. Lots of men said that to her. She was lovable, but also it was an era where "I love you" was as common as "Hello." It felt good to say and to hear and it cost nothing. Peter said, "You know how you know they love you? They love you when they're there."

He was saying this about himself. He was being "there" for my mother by lecturing her. He was also pointing out that my mother's lovers tended to say "I love you" on the phone, in whispers, so that someone nearby wouldn't hear them.

My mother didn't like any of this. There were phone calls. Across the apartment, I could hear her voice rising, and then the impact of receiver against cradle as she hung up on him. Her, flying across the house in her bathrobe, face red with anger. *Goddamn him,* she hissed. *Trying to control me.*

It might have been because of that infraction or another, but one day Peter showed up at our door unannounced, stooped and straining with the gift of an enormous rubber plant. My mother recognized it as one of the two rubber plants that had stood in the sentries' box in front of the Presidio. She refused to take it, and shut the door on him, and Peter yelled from the street, "History will show that I tried to make up with you and you turned me down!"

She ran into him at Macy's, where he pretended she was a clerk and said, "Miss, I'd like to see something in black lace panties."

She said to me, "It's hard to stay mad at him."

We were back at his house soon enough. And Peter had a plan that he took his time unveiling. Like many of his plans, it would accomplish several things at once, but at first it seemed like it was about me, terrifyingly.

We had missed his birthday, he said, the one where, very late, Joni Mitchell had come over and sung for the few guests, and later he and Sue and a newie had screwed blue until the sun had come up.

I asked him if he really knew Joni Mitchell, as his star had diminished in our house so much I felt like challenging him.

"Didn't I say I knew her? Didn't I say that?"

"You say a lot of things."

"You're doing me a disservice, you're calling me a liar and that's uncalled for. Stand up. Get the fuck up, come on."

My mother was already objecting to whatever he was about to say. Peter put his hands on my shoulders.

"Kid, your mom just went through a bad situation with a man who was not straight with her. I want her to know there are father figures who you can look up to. I also think it's time to launch you in this social world as a decent young man." Eye contact with my mom for a moment, then back to me. "So listen. This is about trust. If I tell you something, it's true. I do not lie to you. I'm not two-faced, and I don't lie. If I say that in three hours you're going to have a date with a beautiful blond twelve-year-old, you will. If I say a big black man will come up to you on the street and hand you a deck of cards and the joker will come out of that deck and spit prune juice in your eye, it will happen. Do you trust me?"

I didn't follow the part about the prune juice and the deck of cards.

Mostly I wanted to know what he meant about the twelve-year-old girl. Peter and Sue shared some kind of look.

"Think he's ready?"

"Ready for what?" I asked.

"Kid, how would you like a date with a beautiful blonde named Miriam this afternoon?" Then he was off on a roll. "I got laid the first time when I was thirteen. It was terrible. I had to stand in line. Summer camp, some girl on a mattress, and we stood *in line*." He repeated the phrase "in line" a few times as if to emphasize the horror of it for him in particular. I'd like to think someone thought to ask about the girl, but I'm not sure. I was trying to understand what this had to do with me dating. He said, "I didn't want it, I didn't have to have it, and I hadn't even been out on a date before. I should have gone out on a few sweetie dates before, gone through the sweaty palms thing. Just go out for coffee with this girl and don't worry about it. Have a chance to be a gentleman before your hormones pressure you to make stupid decisions."

As he was talking, it was like his words got tinnier and more menacing, the buzzing of bees in my ears. It seemed like a terrible idea to me.

My mother approved of it. Somehow this melted things between her and Peter—they had a project together that she saw the merits of. She said the phrase "sweaty palms" a few times as she and Sue talked over how they should prepare me. Peter ordered me to take a shower.

I was soaping up when the bathroom door opened. "The first question is what color flowers you're bringing her," Sue yelled at me, her eyes averted.

"Purple?"

"I should have guessed purple," Sue said.

"Miriam is really pretty but don't let that intimidate you," Peter said while driving me down the hill to Cow Hollow. It was just him and me in the car. "Beautiful women never know they're beautiful," he said. "Only tell them how pretty they are when you're ready to give them that power over you. Whoever needs the relationship less controls it. Let me see your nails."

"She's going to notice if my nails are clean?"

"Yeah, she is."

My mind was blank. I yawned a lot. We stopped at a flower stand, where Peter paid for a spray of purple flowers by rolling a twenty off his Star of David billfold. He explained to the flower girl, who was pretty but not pretty enough for him to hit on, that this was for my first date, and she was easily brought into the conspiracy, smiling at me while I forced what I hoped was an adult smile in return.

Back in the car, Peter continued: "Now, this is the beginning of your dating history, kid. You gotta decide what kind of person you're going to be—you come at this with wealth and privilege, and don't be a schmuck about it. Be yourself, but also ask yourself what kind of man you want to be around women."

I didn't understand.

"Like are you going to be the kind of jerk who steals a woman's jewelry?"

That, I understood. As we pulled up to an apartment building on Octavia, Peter told me the plan. It was four o'clock. He would be back at six-thirty. He told me to take her around the corner to his morning hangout, Café Cantata. "They serve Cokes and desserts, that sort of stuff." He handed me ten dollars. "That should cover it."

We paused outside the apartment door.

"Two things," he said. "First, women's liberation is important, but always open a door for a lady. If you come to an open doorway, let her go through first. That's not sexism, it's respect. Got it? I said, 'Got it'?"

"Got it."

"Second, you're my son."

"What?"

"Fix your shirt. It's tucked into your underwear."

Miriam's mother opened the door. She was beautiful and blond and young, with a small, turned-up nose and warm brown eyes. She wore a tight peach-colored T-shirt and a peasant skirt and she smelled good. She was so attractive I was terrified of meeting Miriam. "Hel*lo*, Glen," she said, making it sound like my name had several syllables. "Peter, your son is *so handsome*. Miriam is *so excited* to meet you. Are those flowers for *her*? Purple! She *loves* purple."

She was talking down to me. I never let that kind of thing stand. But I was having trouble containing my nervousness about the date alongside how I wanted to crush that singsong condescension, so I was just quiet and red, which made my rage look like sweetness to Miriam's mom.

"You look a*dor*able," she said. "She'll be back in a second, she's at the *drugstore* buying *special lipstick* for this afternoon." She sang out, *"This is so ex-ci-ting."*

She brought us into the apartment, which was overheated and narrow, with shag carpet and a lot of brass fittings. "The big date! This is a thrill for me, too, Glen, my baby is eleven, but I've never even hired a sitter since the divorce. I'm always with her, and I get so overprotective. So I'm entrusting her to you, young man. Will you take care of her?"

I knew how to answer that one. "Yes."

A key turned in the lock. Miriam was coming in.

Her mother announced, "Here she is! Miriam, it's Peter and his son, *Glen*. Come and meet *Glen*, Miriam."

Miriam smiled at us all. She was an inch taller than I was, with long black hair parted down the middle. Her face was unusually flat, with a pug of a nose, and she had a nice smile. *"Hi, Glen,"* she said with the same emphasis her mother had, and her eyes shifted from me to her mother and back. "And you're right, Mother, he's *so handsome.*" She smiled as if we were all people of the world here, and we all knew what a date meant.

"I, flowers," I said, my throat dry.

"Purple!"

Her mother bent down over us. "Okay, kids, the adults are leaving now. Are you ready to go on your big date?"

"I've got to get my purse."

"We'll be back later. You stay out of trouble with Mr. Charming's son, okay?"

She kissed Miriam on the nose. I tried to make eye contact with Peter one last time, but he was already talking to Miriam's mother as they left. The door shut behind them. Miriam and I were alone in her apartment.

"This is a nice place," I said.

"Really? I fucking hate it." Miriam hunched over a bed in the living room and threw the covers back and forth until she found her purse. "Let's go. But don't slam the door or my fucking bitch of a landlady will scream her fucking head off."

I liked swearing, but I'd never loaded so much into one sentence. Suddenly, Peter's instructions to me seemed prudish, but nonetheless I let Miriam through the door first, which left me holding the doorknob. I closed it, but it didn't catch. She took the doorknob from me and slammed the door, good and hard. She looked up at the front of the building, as if at her landlady, and gave her building the finger.

"Where are you taking me?" she asked.

"Café Cantata."

"I know where that is. That's a fucking expensive place. You and your dad are rich, aren't you? You can admit it. My mother already told me."

"We aren't that rich."

We were on Union Street now. I had no idea how to behave, and I was thankful Miriam talked. "You bought me purple flowers. The lipstick I got for our date? See? Purple. Mom says purple is immature but she's immature so she should fucking know. Here's my bank. I have fifty-three dollars in my savings account. You know what pisses me off? Adults who think kids don't know anything."

"Yeah. Like adults who ask you, 'How's school?'"

"Or like guys who make comments to you and think you don't understand them. I mean, give me a fucking break, I'm only eleven."

I had been preparing to say something else but I didn't. I wasn't expecting her to say that, and it gave me an uncomfortable glimpse of a world I couldn't take in. I tripped over something not actually that important. "Peter said you were twelve."

She lit up. "What else did he tell you about me?"

He had said she was a beautiful blonde. I had a hunch repeating that would be bad. "He likes your mom."

"Oh," she said, disappointed.

Peter had suggested we sit at his regular table at the Café Cantata, so we could people watch, but it was taken. The waitress led us into a back room. I hadn't known there was a back room. She gave us a food menu. I hadn't known there was one of those, either.

"Do you think those people know we're on a date?" Miriam waved at the next table.

I hadn't thought about it. I was too self-conscious about my every word. I had to remember I was Peter's son, for instance. We were in the geographic center of the San Francisco pickup world, and at tables all around us were mysterious social cues as men and women sized each other up using measurements as precise as the rules of cotillion. Miriam's voice, its volume, her confronting the world with a big, brash stick, made me nervous. I was stiff, feeling like a banker in a British comedy meeting a life-embracing mod chick. Those bankers never ended well. I said, "Do you like movies?"

"Yeah. Like horror movies?" she asked. "Does your dad let you see stuff like that?"

My real dad did. Peter would have, too. "Yeah." I was going to do what I did at Peter's parties: act. I'd always been on dates. I'd breathe deep and feel relaxed in this, the best of all possible worlds. "And you know, Miriam," I added, "I just saw a movie by a director named Ingmar Bergman."

"Really?"

"She's Swedish."

"Really. With, like, subtitles."

"Lots of subtitles."

"You must be fucking smart."

"We're all smart, Miriam. Me, Peter, you, your mom. The movie was about a woman who was depressed. Strangely, I walked out of the theater more glad to be alive."

She nodded. "Huh. Yeah. When actors feel bad in a movie or on TV, you feel like you aren't in such shit yourself. That's why I like *Gilligan's Island*. Every week, they're still stranded on that island. It makes me feel better about sleeping in the living room."

I wasn't sure what to say. There was a distance between where I slept and where she slept that I couldn't gap just by sounding smart. "Well, at least you're in San Francisco. There are a hundred million people who would give up their legs to trade places with you."

She narrowed her eyes at me. "Who the fuck would want to sleep in the living room?"

When the waitress came, Miriam opened up her menu. I hadn't known it had an inside. I opened up mine and ran my eye down the entrées, which were arranged in ascending price, and my eye got to the bottom, the Seafood Special, just as she was saying, "I'll have the Seafood Special."

The waitress wrote it down. It was twelve dollars. I had ten. "And you, sir?" She was young and pretty, and waiting on kids seemed to amuse rather than annoy her. My mind closed up. I couldn't order anything. In fact, I couldn't even afford Miriam's meal.

"Coke," I whispered, but she couldn't quite hear me. I'd been shocked into being a kid. But—if it were Peter, he would go out on a high note. "There's a drink Peter orders all the time. It's a coffee drink, and it sounds like a bullfighter."

The waitress laughed. "Do you mean a café au lait? For the young mister, a café au lait." She wrote it down. But then, a small cloud in the sky, she looked at me. "You know someone named Peter who orders café au laits here?"

"His father, Peter Charming," Miriam said.

The waitress evaluated me for a moment. "All right, then," she said, and left.

"You know what my favorite movie is?" Miriam said. I wasn't paying much attention. Having no money was compounded by a new problem. The waitress knew Peter. She didn't like him. It wasn't hard to figure out why. I would have to wash dishes. I knew that wasn't a real option, only something that happened in movies. I had no idea how to get out of this. "My favorite movie," Miriam said, "is *Alice Doesn't Live Here Anymore*."

That brought me out of it. "Really?"

"Uh-huh. I love it."

For a moment, the problems retreated. I started to tell her how the story in the movie was just like me and my mother. Leaving the old home together and starting a new one.

"I thought you lived with your dad." Then, when I fumbled, she said, "You know why that's my favorite movie? Because of the scene in the beginning, when she's little, and when she sings off-key and then she says, 'If anyone doesn't like it, they can blow it out their ass.' That's great."

I excused myself to use the bathroom. A moment later, I found our waitress at the register. "Excuse me?"

"Master Charming," she said.

"I'm not—"

"That girl Sue isn't your mother, is she?"

"Peter isn't my dad. My mom is a friend of his. He told that girl I'm eating with that I'm his son. My real dad lives in Chicago."

She said slowly, "The sad thing is I believe you."

"I have a problem. Peter gave me ten dollars to take this girl to lunch."

"Ahhh."

"So I was wondering."

She put her pencil behind her ear. "Here it comes."

"Maybe you could get the chef to put about seven dollars' worth of food on her plate. That way, I could have my café au lait and there would still be about a dollar fifty for a tip."

A new look crossed her face, a reappraisal. "You aren't Peter's kid, are you?"

"No."

"Yeah, you couldn't be. I like the part about you still tipping me. I'll talk to the chef."

"And if anyone doesn't like it, they can blow it out their ass," Miriam was saying as we walked back up Union Street. I wanted the date to be over so it could be a story I told.

We went inside. Miriam turned the lights on. "You want a tour?"

"Okay." I liked house tours.

She pointed. "This is the hallway. That's the kitchen. That's my mother's bedroom, there. I sleep in the living room. Sometimes I wake up and I can hear her *making connections*." She ground her knuckles together.

I didn't have a response. It was quiet.

"Oh my God, *Bewitched* is on! Let's watch *Bewitched*!" She fell on her bed. I sat next to her, at a distance, and I thought about my mother's bedroom and mine. As *Bewitched* unfolded, I decided that in San Francisco, among the elite, where every man was a prince and every woman a princess, we didn't let such things affect us.

When the show was over, Miriam kissed me on the mouth. I tried to push her away. She was stronger than I was. She held me down and tried to kiss me again.

"I need to kiss you, Glen. I'm in love with you. You're going to be my boyfriend."

"I don't want to kiss you."

"We have to kiss. Hold still."

We were wrestling around when the key jangled in the lock. It seemed to take forever, as if someone were deliberately making noise. I threw Miriam off me, but she grabbed my arm and tugged me toward her bed. "Please don't. Please start kissing me. You have to start kissing me. Please."

I pried loose. I was sweaty and breathless, but standing alone in the hallway when her mother came in. Then I realized there was a smear of purple lipstick on my face. I was not a gentleman. I'd been caught mauling an eleven-year-old. Miriam stood behind me, eyes on the carpet.

Her mother called out to Peter, who was just coming up the stairs, "Oh, *Peter*. I wonder what they were *doing*. Peter? I said I wonder what they were *doing*?"

When she turned toward me again, she had a smile on her face that was the pride of ownership.

There was a dinner party that night. Peter had called friends and told them I would tell the story of my first date.

"I don't understand women," I said. "She ordered the most expensive thing on the menu and she didn't eat it."

"You understand women," Peter said.

"You said she was a beautiful blonde. She wasn't pretty, and she had black hair."

Now Sue glided in. "Glen David Gold, you don't have to be beautiful or blond to be a beautiful blonde." She kissed my forehead like a punctuation point and then she left again while the adults laughed for what felt like the rest of the evening.

It was a good line. We create our own realities, make our own beauty, that was the landscape she meant. But saying Miriam was a beautiful blonde didn't explain her bed in the living room. Or her dodging her mother's boyfriends. Or the metal-against-metal feeling of her hopelessly trying to kiss me.

My story was deemed a great success, and the date an experience, a perennial the adults would want to hear about again and again. Except my mother.

I saw her seeing me standing next to Peter in front of the roaring fire, and the way he and I ceded parts of the story to each other. As when I used to do presentations about the coins, my mother was narrowing her eyes at how I soaked up the attention. She had worried about me becoming cold like my father, but now she was concluding I would become like Peter. In her eyes, had I known how to read them, there really was no good pathway for me, in that I was starting to become a man.

Someone finally asked Peter: During my date, what was *he* doing? You know, after he left with Miriam's mother.

Ah, of course. The real reason for the date. He'd wanted to fuck her for ages, but she kept saying she couldn't with her daughter around. I heard that and I took it in—Peter had used me—and when it was my turn to speak again, instead of hitting the laugh lines, I was thinking, "I can hear her making connections," and I faltered.

My first date had meant I was in charge of an afternoon. How to behave with a girl. I knew some small ways now I could finish the phrase, "I am the type of man who . . ."

Who tells stories about the sad life of someone less fortunate than himself, apparently. I did not feel good. Some people were not beautiful or blondes and Peter's world didn't have room for that.

———

Something shifted a little bit after Miriam. I was unsure of Peter. My mother was unsure of me. Moreover this was when Peter was helping my mother invest her money, a situation I know little about to this day. But if you look at the date with Miriam as a template, you could reasonably assume there were always lateral and tangential plans unfolding without explanation of who was going to benefit.

I do know the investment results were not as straightforward as you'd think. To reel your mark in, you have to let her win a few hands first. So my mother was about to win a few. But then Peter would fatally overreach. It had to do with the part of her Peter could never control, the part she refused to cordon off, her ready and resourceful heart.

I am proud of my mother's ability to love, particularly after two marriages. And I'm impressed by her simultaneous desire for autonomy. Only a strong person knows how to ride two horses going such different directions. Amazingly she was about to get all her contradictory dreams fulfilled. But it's hard to write this next part because I know what's coming.

My mother is made of traits and characteristics that don't seem to add up. I have sometimes mistaken the way she lived for being inexplicable. But that's not quite right. Her desires are like the raw pieces of brightly colored glass you'd insert in a kaleidoscope. The horizon line viewed through a specific eyepiece, accounting for the interruption and tumble of strange and jagged emeralds and lapis, ends up being a world-view. It's a metaphor I've often considered in opposition to my father's worldview, the one seen through the telescope.

Imagine the hands of a clock at midnight, the beginning of the day. When I was born, my point of view was my mother's. As I grew up, I separated and yet I was connected—like the hands of a clock—until all I believed was in complete opposition to her worldview. And then I began to see things from her perspective, which felt like being dragged backward into defending her, but which wasn't. That's not the way clocks work. I have empathy for her without having to defend her. I can account for my mother the way I do the passage of time. You can describe time. But you can't be so arrogant to think you can explain it. It's like that with my mom's need to maneuver her way past some obstacles toward the bright and confusing future she wanted.

The immediate obstacle in her path? That would be me.

———

My mother was antsy. I wasn't the public school sort. "Remember, there are boarding schools," she said, again, which wasn't what I'd been think-ing. I felt nervousness in my chest, the same way I had when she pre-sented me with a key to let myself into the apartment, or when Peter had given me ten dollars for the date with Miriam. Mom reminded me she had heard about places in Switzerland where the children of diplo-mats went. I could learn French. It would be an experience.

I wasn't ready for that, but the truth was, she wasn't looking for my permission. She had already entered a crafty letter exchange with Dad—first she mentioned how well I was doing, and then how mature I was. She said I seemed to judge her social life badly. She didn't men-tion my crack about her missing underwear, but she used the phrase "Glen is always underfoot." Further, she said, I seemed to get along very well with him and Ann, and in a return letter my father blocked that with a careful description of how small the apartment was, and in the following letter my mother suggested boarding school.

My father wrote back that he wasn't going to pay for that. (My father wasn't going to frighten Ann off with a monthly payroll in Swiss francs.)

Soon after, my mother enrolled me in a local day school, the Town

School for Boys. It was walking distance from our flat. We went to Young Man's Fancy, a store in Presidio Heights that the school had recommended I purchase seventh grade clothes from. Not that Town had an official uniform, but they had noticed that when a boy came to Town late—that is, after first grade—he might have trouble fitting in. They suggested that dressing like my peers would reduce the culture shock.

With an adult's idea that it would make me blend in, my mother bought me corduroy trousers cut for my husky frame and a deep blue sweater with a spectrum of thin colorful lines that clung to my belly, under pectorals that were now unnervingly growing into breasts.

"You're just going through a puffy phase," my mother said. "You'll grow out of it before the fall."

I decided that I would exercise more and eat less, probably, and that maybe I would have a growth spurt so that when I met my new friends—I would have friends—I wouldn't be fat, just smart. And funny.

When I visited Chicago that summer my father took me and Ann to visit my grandparents, where the living room couches were encased in plastic to preserve them. There was some cross section of family there, as if Grandma Frieda had dug her palm into a bin of mixed relatives, to encourage some cousins and great-aunts to come mourn the child of divorce. No one else in the family had divorced, not even Harry the Horse Thief, who had to be dragged out of the brothels on Friday before dusk. My father continued to concern them.

On the wall, directly in front of me, were three photographs. One was of my uncle Nortie marrying his lovely bride, who twenty years later sat with all of us now; one was of my uncle Jerry marrying Barbara, who was hilarious and smart and who was with him now in Westchester County, close enough to New York for Jerry to take the train every day to his job as a successful attorney. In between, there had once been a photo of my father and mother marrying, and there had, before that, been a photo of my father and his first wife marrying. Now there was a photograph of me, age five, in a sort of one-piece with shorts that my mother had sewn. I have a triumphant smile, as if I am acknowledging that I am just as marvelous as the audience expected.

It was strange to see that photo, given how indistinct and awful I felt now. Clearly no one wanted to talk about the photograph. Grandma Frieda had had no good options. Keep the photo of my mother up, even though Ann was coming? Impossible. Blank space on the wall? That would call attention to itself. Just a photo of Dad? That would be almost comically terrible. The photo of me was the best choice, or it was until a lull in conversation, when I asked why there was a photo of me on the wall.

I felt something acrid and hot. My father shrank, saying, "Glen David . . ." as he only does when exasperated with me. Simultaneously, all the old people in the room fought to come up with an explanation. They talked over each other.

I thought that at any given moment there had to be a comment that would make a whole room laugh. I had no idea what this was, but I was sure that if I considered it enough, it would come to me. When there was a new pause, I said, "Another awkward silence," which turned out not to be the thing that would make everyone laugh.

Instead, Uncle Nortie and my father asked if I felt awkward, and as I was answering that, Aunt Rhoda asked me the same thing, while the more distant relatives said they weren't feeling awkward, there was nothing to feel awkward about. They transparently ignored Ann, as if by not looking at her, she would be a part of the family. Of course that meant that she stood out as clearly as if my father had taken a photograph of her and put it on the wall over mine.

My dad asked me how things were with my mom. I knew Dad loved a good story, so I told him about the time Peter Charming met me at the airport with a custard pie. My father liked cars, so I told him how Peter once had a Jaguar that had broken down too many times, so he'd taken out a classified ad: a Jaguar will be parked in the Marin Headlands this Sunday. There will be a sledge hammer. Five dollars buys you one swing of the hammer. Ten dollars buys you three swings. He made thousands. (Not much of a response to this story, either.) A guy once welshed on a business debt and Peter forgave him but bought his soul. The guy couldn't pay the money back fast enough—he paid Peter in the middle of the night.

We were driving somewhere, my father and Ann in front, me in the back. I announced, "Peter says the twenty-dollar bill is the most common bill in circulation, so counterfeiters—"

"What?" My father shouted. "That's ridiculous."

"No, it's true. The twenty-dollar bill is the most common bill in circulation."

"No, it's not. How can you say that?"

Then Ann jumped in. "The one dollar bill is more common."

"How often do you see one dollar bills, Glen? Often! Twenty-dollar bills, much less so," my dad continued.

"Plus, there are more fives and tens than twenties," Ann said.

That made sense. I tried to reason out where I'd gone wrong, but it was suddenly hard to think. "But the twenty—"

"I mean, if there were more twenties than ones, ones would be more valuable," my dad interrupted. "If Peter Charming said the moon was made of green cheese, would you believe that? When you say things like that, I can't believe anyone is ever paying attention to you," my father said. "Your mother is a flake and she surrounds you with her flaky friends."

I recalled, even though I couldn't express it, that what I'd meant to say was that the twenty-dollar bill was the most commonly *counterfeited* bill in circulation, but it didn't matter anymore. My father and Ann were verbally elbowing each other aside to yell at me. Once upon a time, back when we were still happy, coins and currency had been a friendly topic for me and my father. That was gone.

"It's like the argument about the catalytic converter," my dad continued. "Uninformed people like you make decisions and it hurts the rest of us."

I didn't know what a catalytic converter was. But I knew, suddenly, that I wasn't smart. I cried.

Was it that night? On some night, I started crying and I couldn't stop. After trying to hush me for a while, my father and Ann went quiet.

The apartment had a design flaw, a support pillar that belled out where the wall met the window, leaving a couple of feet for me to stand in the corner, unseen. I squeezed in there to press against the wall while the adults sat quietly somewhere else, reading, doing crossword puzzles.

I watched the weather over Lake Michigan. I repeated to myself, moving my lips but not even whispering, "This isn't so bad."

I walked down Michigan Avenue with my father. It was cold enough that my ears hurt. He finally said, "If you have any questions . . . if there's anything confusing you about sex, sexual issues . . . you can ask me."

I fished for that response, the one that would make him laugh. I couldn't figure it out. I knew that all I had to do was wait till I got back to San Francisco and tell Peter what my father had just said, and that would make Peter laugh. Because Peter had made the same offer just weeks beforehand.

When I flew back, the pilot told the passengers with a chuckle that we really shouldn't worry about it, but there had been a little hitch with the landing gear and regulations required that there be "trucks with red lights" on the ground meeting us, but again, really, don't worry.

I might have been the only person on the plane not worried. If he'd meant "ambulances and fire engines," he would have said it, I thought, and that "trucks with red lights" must be some term of aviation art with which I was unfamiliar.

My ignorance read as calm, I think. A stewardess with a pageboy haircut rushed by my seat a few times, first to see if I was okay, then to note I was traveling by myself, then to double-check—if I was okay, *why* was I okay?

When we came in for our final approach, I looked out the window and saw streaking down the runway what the captain had promised wouldn't be there—fire engines and ambulances—and instead of being frightened, I was angry at having been lied to. The landing was a little bumpy, but nothing more.

We got off the plane. I had a story to tell, obviously, and as I waited for my mother, the story in my mind got larger and larger and then I worried.

The plane was empty. The crew left with their suitcases, including the stewardess with the pageboy. I had never been at a completely empty airplane gate before—it was like being backstage at a theater.

The stewardess returned. She took me behind the counter and let me use the airline phone to call home. Mom didn't answer.

I tried Peter's house. He wasn't sure where my mom was either, but I was welcome to come to his place. He asked to speak to the stewardess, and then she handed the phone back to me. "One question—is that stewardess cute?"

I said, "Yes."

"Put her back on the phone."

I did. In a moment, it was resolved. She would come with me in a cab to Peter's. As I recall, things went lightly and rapidly, with much good humor—the stewardess accepted a glass of wine from Sue. While Peter was on the phone, I tried to entertain her. She had seemed to be impressed at first with how mature I was, and she was interested in how that had happened, and yet the longer she was here the less impressed she seemed. She was having trouble understanding who exactly Peter was to me and to my mother, which I didn't think was relevant.

Peter came back with a report. My mother had been at a rock concert and forgotten my arrival time, but she was on her way over. She wanted to thank my savior, which was not going to happen—she caught a cab even though we all wanted her to stay.

When my mother came, I wasn't really angry she'd forgotten me. I liked proving I could survive without her. I was mostly mad she hadn't gotten to hear about the ambulances and fire engines. But something about the stewardess bothered me. Peter had some harsh words for her—she was cold, she was a bitch, fuck her, she's not invited back. But I kept remembering how she looked as she was trying to assess my environment, and I wanted her to understand that everyone here loved each other, we are all aristocracy at rest and at play. But I could see she had not been charmed.

When Mom asked about my trip, I didn't tell her that Dad had called her flaky, and I didn't tell him she hadn't shown up. He would have misunderstood. It wasn't evidence, it was an accident.

————

Some private schools in Pacific Heights were contained in stone Gothic Revival mansions, as if to assure parents that even though we were in San Francisco, their children would be educated as strictly as if it were the sixteenth century. Town School for Boys, however, had been designed in the 1950s and it looked like a Madison Avenue office building, which perhaps reflected the idea that school, like fear, would be a civilizing influence. But it didn't quite take. When I arrived the first day, the silence in the classroom was like that of Barbary apes interrupted in their dens by the appearance of a goat smeared in candy.

Seventh graders shouldn't go to school. They should be shipped to camp. I was being parachuted into territory that was hostile simply for hostility's sake. By the end of my first day, the next-most-junior boy, who'd only been there since second grade, was overwhelmed with relief that he was no longer the newcomer.

Nothing bad happened at first. There is a base politeness when bullies are experienced enough to be patient. *Was I new to the neighborhood? I'd been there a whole year? Where was I before? Public school, well, that must have been interesting. And before that? Southern California? The beach? Did you surf? Oh, just joking, you don't look like a surfer. You've been to Young Man's Fancy—nice sweater*. I can almost imagine them lined up on the curb as I left, waving, telling me they were looking forward to me coming back the next day.

It was difficult to explain this to my mother. She thought she'd seen me outwit some bullies when I was younger, and she was positive that a good lesson and my enormous brain would get me through this.

Peter brought her to parties and introduced her to friends who had interesting financial propositions. I wasn't invited to those parties. I don't know what most of the opportunities were. She met the guy who invented the Pet Rock. ("A schmuck," Peter said. "No grace, no dignity, just looking around like a big dope at all the women at the party," probably meaning Peter was unable to sell him anything.) A cabaret owner needed money to put on a show called *Beach Blanket Babylon,* with original songs about San Francisco. It was campy and gay, inherently ridiculous and risky and my mom passed on it. Another time, Peter invited her over late one night to meet a financial person, but when she arrived, there were already two women there, and it was obvious that she'd been invited so he could choose among them. She left and didn't talk to Peter until the next set of apologies.

One investment took a while to evaluate because it was so far-fetched. She studied brochures. She had meetings. She wrote a check and with that, my mother bought thirty-five Pong machines.

I'll never know how much she paid for them—first, she told me ten thousand dollars; I later heard fifty thousand. I used to know everything about Pong machines, the way I knew how many silver dollars were made in Denver in 1883 or who penciled *Defenders 14*. But I've forgotten who made them, or if you played to eleven or thirteen or twenty-one points. I just remember the feeling when I first saw a Pong machine: it was like the Space Shuttle strapped to the back of a 747.

My mother's machines were tabletop models, black-and-white monitors set flat in particle board with wood-grain laminate. They were a knock-off of the original design. You could play with one or two players. Each player had a single knob, like the dimmer on a light switch, that moved the blip left or right.

The machines were state-of-the-art, meaning you could play three different games: tennis, hockey (which looked just like tennis, except with more lines on the screen), and knockout, where you tried to eliminate the other player's big white Xs, eight stationary, sitting ducks.

The graphics were as simple as cave paintings. The black of the screen was a fuzzy gray, the white was bluish and veined with horizontal lines from the cathode-ray tube. The software allowed you to hit the ball straight on or at a forty-five-degree angle. No English, no rushing the net. The sounds the machine made were as primitive as a baby robot's, different inflections of "beep" or "boop" depending on what the ball hit, and a more sour "baap" when the ball went out of bounds. Then, GAME OVER, capital letters, with a mock game playing in the background to entice new players.

I don't like the inclination toward camp when people dwell on the technology of the time. No colors? No sound effects? No levels of difficulty? Just one knob? People played a game that even Samuel Beckett would have to admit had no story line. It sounds like we all must have been very stupid in the 1970s.

Pong was serious business. I was proud of my mom. This was the coolest investment she could have made. I brought the pamphlet to school. I showed it to my economics teacher. I showed it to the bullies, an attempt to dazzle them with something sparkly, and they all nodded, that was cool. Also, it changed nothing for me.

Mom had bought me a fitted T-shirt, French cut, powder blue and I made the wince-inducing decision to wear this mistake to school one day. The word went out in a whisper: Glen has tits. That went from an exclamation to a nickname to what I was expected to answer to. My name was now Tits.

I told my mother about it, and she got me a book on my changing body, a book with drawings of hairy, unself-conscious adults and curious prepubescents, probably translated from some Scandinavian language. Nothing here explained my growing breasts, which had weird, hard tissue in them. I concluded I had breast cancer and was going to die.

My father called me once a week. If my mother was home, I closed the door, listening for distant sounds and wishing I could feel things. He and Ann had gotten married, and I felt nothing about that, for instance. When I told him about school, or the things I briefly loved, no matter where I started, I ended up beginning sentences that had no exit plan, like I was guarding bad decisions. We had tried to get Leo a girlfriend, but they'd only hissed and fought. After she left, he started peeing on the carpets. Leo was sad. Pause. Pause. Pause.

"These kids are teasing me."

He'd heard that most of my life. "You shouldn't provoke them," he said. Pause. Swallow. It was like there were three-by-five cards with subjects written on them. I had run out of things to talk about. There was a new bend in my sentences, a place where I separated subject and predicate, "Did I tell you about"—and then me wondering why I was going to say this—"this cool investment mom is making?"

"Investment?"

Maybe I thought he'd see a link between cassette tapes and video games. Mom was visualizing the future. But he disagreed, he thought the Pong machines were a terrible investment. They were a fad. There was competition from jukeboxes and pinball machines. Had my mother researched any of this? What was wrong with corporate bonds? They were boring but my mother was a single parent—she shouldn't be trying something so risky. She was being a flake.

There was more like that, an avalanche of it.

When I got off the phone, I opened the door. Mom was in the living room. How was my father, she asked. I told her that Dad thought she was a flake.

Why did I say that? What did I think was going to happen? She explained that my father was threatened by the possibility that she might have good business ideas. "You don't think I'm a flake, do you?"

"Of course you're a flake," I joked and I felt like I'd slapped her.

"You and your father," my mother whispered. "You're both real put-down artists," she said.

"I mean, you know," I said. What did I say? Something like: It had come out wrong. "Flake" was a good thing, I meant that she wasn't beholden to conservative thought. No, really, it's just that you don't behave the way you used to, in Corona del Mar, when you weren't free. "Flake" means freedom, and you are free, Mom. Something like that. Whatever I tried to change, it didn't matter. She was done.

It's not like I was a normal kid who was being teased for no reason. I was a smartass. I was beginning to learn what it meant when no help was coming. One day in Latin class, when the teacher was out of the room, another kid passed me a note.

Q: What does Glen say when he looks at his chest?
A: I love my Mounds.

Catchy. A slogan for a candy bar turned against me. There were hisses of "Tits" now. Rising catcalls and jokes I was too upset to understand. I did nothing, and so it got louder. Tits! Tits! I stood up with tears in my eyes and I said, "You guys are making fun of something you don't even understand. I have cancer."

There was a pause in the hazing. It was like a question mark hung in the air, and then an exclamation point. I was claiming I had breast cancer? Holy shit, that was *fantastic*! It was like I had bought Christmas presents for each and every one of them.

Our desks were solid, heavy frames like something out of an iron-monger's shop, with a writing board fastened in place and slats below to store textbooks during exams. Hey, Tits. Hey, Tits. Hey, Tits.

I stood, picked up my desk over my head and threw it. It hit the wall.

A few minutes later, in the principal's office, I ratted no one out. There is a code of the Old West that I would not break. I was seething, and not because of the teasing so much as at how I'd behaved like a seventh grader. I wanted revenge but I wanted it to be smart, with élan. I'd let myself down. Mom had been right to not read me fairy tales.

I told Peter about this. He asked for the names of the kids who were teasing me. I told him.

"And what time does school end?"

I wasn't sure I should answer that—it seemed like an oddly specific question. "Three o'clock."

"And afterward, are there a bunch of kids milling around on the sidewalk? Okay, kid, this is what's going to happen. Not today, not tomorrow, but one day when you're not expecting it, at three-oh-five p.m., a black limousine is going to pull up in front of Town School and a pair of guys with leather jackets and sunglasses are going to spring out, grab those kids, throw them in the back of the car, and the car is going to speed away with great alacrity, and vanish. While everyone is freaking out, you'll be totally calm and waiting because you'll know what's going to happen next—five minutes later, the car will show up again and those bullies will be shoved out to the pavement dressed in ballet tutus, with lipstick, full mascara, and wigs on. That's it, bullying stops right there."

"That's not going to happen."

"As God is my witness, when that happens, I want you to make one deal with me, just one—when that happens, you're never going to ask me for anything else again. You're on your own after that, endgame."

I agreed with him. We shook on it.

He said thoughtfully, "If that doesn't work, you should just buy their souls and let them stew about it."

It turned out that until the Pong investment paid off, we would have to tighten our belts. I said all I needed was fifteen dollars a month for comic books, and when my mom was startled by that figure, I said, "I meant seven-fifty."

We couldn't paint the town with Peter anymore. We would need to move, too. We had too much overhead. It was just temporary, until our ship came in. The Pong machines needed a few months until they'd paid themselves off and soon we'd have a return on our investment.

My mother had been poor before. It built character. Besides, this wasn't actually poor—it would be good for me.

I could handle a tighter money flow. I could handle being bullied. I didn't really need anything. Once, twice, maybe more, I went up to our rooftop, where it always felt like a Sunday afternoon, and every echo of every sound seemed magnified to match the pang of long shadows. I couldn't see the Bridge, but I could see nearby hills and the mossy bricks of neighbors' houses, their kitchen counters, the strange angles of sunlight falling on their hardwood floors. I was a jewel thief or a ghost. I was hardly even a body. I could handle anything. The rooftops of San Francisco were quiet and they would be here long after my thoughts were gone. It was almost like I was calm.

Moving into our new apartment would require a change, my mother told me. I don't remember if I fought when she explained what needed to happen. I think I didn't.

It was six o'clock on a winter evening when the doorbell rang. I was watching *Star Trek*. My mother answered. A man came in. I remember him having gray hair and a combed mustache and perhaps he was a little chubby. He was from Pacifica.

I have thought so much about the twenty minutes he spent in our apartment that I no longer remember what I actually saw and what I have imagined. My mother wanted me to come meet him. I preferred to watch *Star Trek*. I might not have come out at all.

The man got on his knees on the carpet and he wriggled his fingers. He brought out treats for Leo. Leo hid under a couch until the treats and the play started to seem like fun—he was a social cat—and then he came out and smelled the man's fingertips. But he was aloof, too, not letting himself be scratched. Staying out of reach until, Oh bother, Leo collapsed on his side to let himself be rubbed accordingly.

"What's his name?" the man asked.

"Leo," my mother said. "He's a rare seal point Siamese." And Leo talked happily, his Siamese voice loud as a baby's. I could hear that even when I turned the television up.

The man had a carrier. It was easy to coax Leo in. My mother grew up on a farm during the war. She'd been sent there to escape the bombs. There were cats and they were interchangeable. Also, she knew it was different for me. Leo was my best friend and I talked to him every night when the lights were out. But we were simplifying. We were moving to another apartment that didn't take pets. He had peed on the rug, so it was time for him to go.

She knocked on my door, and she asked if I wanted to say goodbye to Leo. I said I didn't. She encouraged me. Finally, I put down my fork—I was eating something—and went downstairs.

The man was parked in front of the house. Leo was in a carrier in his hand.

I remember nothing else, except that I was missing the part of *Star Trek* when Spock put his hands on the alien Horta and performed the Vulcan mind meld, and I was mildly, distantly, vaguely annoyed at being taken from that. I would not say I felt hollow or empty. I would have told you then that I knew exactly what it meant, giving away Leo. A child's pet is being given away and that is sad. But don't insult me by assuming I'll be broken by this. When I was little, in my tests to get into that gifted school, they found I had eidetic imagery. A lot of kids have this, and it's not well understood, except that it's a little like taking a snapshot of a moment. And it fades around the age of twelve.

Here, one flash, by the lights of our building's entrance, sprays of ficus leaves over us, Leo in the carrier, the man with the mustache looking down at him with surprise and tenderness, my mother glancing from them to me with an attempt to assess me, and me looking at my feet, which were bare on the wet winter pavement. I am not even here, I am vanished, there is no longer even a boy to feel anything.

I went back inside to watch TV. I never saw Leo again.

THE NEW APARTMENT was the bottom two floors of a duplex at the Western edge of Presidio Heights. When I walked inside for the first time I knew it was haunted.

There is still something crisp to me about the layout, as if it's a blueprint I had to memorize for a jury trial. The ground floor was where Mom and I lived. Below us was a generous and awful basement. The steep staircase led down to two dim, unused bedrooms facing a failed garden overgrown with dry weeds. There was a recreation room with a floor that seemed to slant slightly, and then, if you took a turn, there was an area that was not just unfinished but to my eye a portal to dark wilderness, a workshop cluttered with dirty power tools hanging aslant off peg boards. There were cardboard boxes soft with moisture and must, and the fluorescent lights hummed and flickered without really penetrating the shadows. Beyond the workshop, there was a doorway into a storage area that I never went through. When we moved in, I closed the door and twenty minutes later it was open. I wasn't scared—I knew this was just a result of how the house had settled. But I also knew there was something in the basement that was old, patient, and much larger than I was.

The ground floor was social and happy, though, in part because my mother herself was happy—her investment was working out. It was time-consuming but worth it.

If you think about it, Pong had 100 percent of the video game market share. In a few weeks, I became the world's champion Pong player. To be sure, there were only a limited number of moves you could make, but it would normally cost about twenty dollars in quarters to perfect them. I could play for hours for free, and the machine had a one-player option. This was handy since kids from school tended to come over just once and guests at my mother's parties were too stoned to play well.

Mostly, I played single player when I was supposed to be doing my homework. I would look up and thirty minutes would have gone by, so I would make it sixty. Even when I wasn't playing, I saw the bouncing ball when I closed my eyes, and I heard the beep or boop of the electronic ball in my dreams.

The machines my mother had placed filled up with quarters every week. She went to bars and restaurants and pizza joints in San Francisco, Marin, Oakland, and the South Bay. Mom and the owners of each place split the proceeds, which she picked up in the afternoons, when business was slow.

But going from bar to bar was a hassle, both for the time it took and because she got hit on so often. Mom stopped collecting her share herself, hiring a friend of Peter's who—this was either a joke or not—used to make a living breaking people's legs.

Peter and I went collecting together once. It was my first trip to Oakland. It was one of those painfully bright days, hot and airless. We went to many taverns. Peter was fastidious and washed his hands after every stop. He reminded me that when he'd had his nightclub, it had been clean and the clientele top-notch. As we drove around Oakland, we felt sorry for Oakland not being San Francisco.

One stop was on West MacArthur Boulevard, somewhere around Telegraph. There were motels here whose signs had incomplete words made from old plastic letters.

Peter left me in the car while he went into some terrible dive. I was instantly surrounded by hookers. They tapped their fingernails against the door, which was locked.

I looked straight ahead until they lost interest in teasing me. When Peter came out, he talked to them. I could hear him bantering, and as I focused on the huge sack of quarters in his hand, I had a horrible thought: he was going to use my mother's profits to buy a hooker for me.

But no. He got into the car, alone, and we were off. He saw my expression, and he laughed. "Nah, kid, I wouldn't want to do that to you. You don't know where those snatches have been, they're disgusting. You know what syphilis is? When you're ready we'll get you laid with a pretty girl who'll be kind to you, answer all your questions, show you what to do, there are chicks who love educating young men. When I was thirteen I had to stand in line, my friend, and we'll make sure that never happens to you."

He explained how complicated sex was. There were emotional consequences to seducing a woman. "You aren't even ready to hear the Rule of The Last One In," he said, and then he told it to me anyway. The last guy to fuck a woman has control over her. She doesn't even know it. It's not something to manipulate unless you're prepared for her to also hate you. It's biology, it's something feminism can't tolerate, always be kind and don't abuse it. Endgame.

That discussion is clear to me at the expense of another one that day. We made one last stop before we left Oakland, but I couldn't tell you why. It was at a residential hotel on West Grand, across from Lakeside Park. We went in together, Peter made a phone call from the lobby to a room upstairs, then we rode in a rickety old elevator—you shut the brass, accordion-like gate yourself—to the third or fourth floor, and then we got out into a hallway that smelled like cough drops.

Peter made me wait in the hall while he went into one of the rooms. I don't know who he saw or how long he was gone for. In the hallway, I became aware of someone staring at me.

There was a chair in an alcove, next to a table with a sad vase of silk flowers. In the chair was an old man in an old suit. He wore a hat. I looked away because he had no nose.

When Peter came out, we didn't wait for the elevator. He acknowledged the man in the chair, and then took me at a jog down the staircase. When we were in the lobby, he whispered to me, "That guy? That's what syphilis does to you."

. . .

One afternoon, a truck backed up to the curb outside our apartment. It unloaded a Pong machine. It had gone on the fritz, as my mother said, and needed to be repaired. The screen did a lazy roll every few seconds. It was an easy fix. Until then, it would stay in the basement, in the recreation room. It reminded me of a soldier taken from a battlefield, awaiting triage.

In a rare moment when I went downstairs, perhaps to fetch firewood, I would see the glow of its screen, blind, rolling slowly, sending a shivering light across the ceiling. My night light.

It turned out that Pong machines were expensive to fix. Someone from Digital Games, or whoever had ripped them off, or whoever had their maintenance contract, let us know it might be cheaper to get a new tube. But it was unclear if that was true. The machine just stayed there until, a few weeks later, a truck pulled up and another Pong machine joined it.

I'm not sure how an artist came to live in our basement. Partly, it was the 1970s, and if you had a dinner party and a spare room, a guest might end up with you until the next party across town. Also, a little of my mother had never left the boardinghouse, so she was generous with allowing people to stay.

The artist's name was George, just like my grandfather. I liked George. He was confused-looking and mellow and defenseless as a teddy bear, down to how hanks of chest hair poked through the holes in his denim shirts. I have photographs of him as part of a tandem Halloween costume, where a ski mask and some netting was supposed to make him the spider to a woman whom I don't recognize as his fly. He's too adorable, hardly convincing as a predator. Women were thrilled by how gentle he was until they realized how disappointing "gentle" was up close.

He was a friend my mother made outside of Peter's gaze, and Peter was darkly amused by this. He was mean to George, casually making fun of him and then glancing at me when George didn't react. George, Peter whispered to me, was a putz. He hadn't needed to tell me that, but I also saw something unusual: George didn't care what Peter thought.

George would get stoned, line up a grid of Strathmore sheets, and slash across them with pastel crayons, filling each with abstract shapes and patterns. Then he would separate them and stare until—*ahah!*—he would outline with black pastel the scenes that the colors suggested. My mother was fond of one that turned into a man driving a car, so she framed it and put it in her office.

His process was *hilarious* to me. I couldn't believe the artwork in my old home was created like this. I tried to imagine my father telling the story about how the Fabergé chess set had been forged by a stoned teddy bear eating Necco wafers and chortling. It reminded me of how, when I was four, I used to sit in my mother's lap and hammer at the typewriter keys and ask her to circle the words I accidentally typed. By showing off his process, George had kneecapped my ability to take his art seriously.

I am no longer the Stalinist hardass my twelve-year-old self was. But even that kid saw George's method had integrity. I was reminded of a Gahan Wilson cartoon from *Playboy* with a girl regarding an artist in a quiet forest. He's painting exactly that forest, only populated with monsters, with the caption, "I paint what I see, child."

In art class I started drawing things like Ginger Rogers tap-dancing wearing a Christmas tree costume. I drew people with dead fishes on their heads, and costumed heroes coughing out paint splatters like it was a superpower. I did a detailed landscape of the Presidio, with a robot centaur who has driven a baseball bat through the forehead of a kid whose identity was only given away by the tennis shoes: they belonged to one of my bullies. It didn't make things any better, but the hours of sketching gave me a place to park my misery.

———

My father took me to New York to meet Ann's family. Now that they were married, I could, in his words, come out of the shadows and be counted. I liked Ann's parents. But since I'd never been to Manhattan I didn't understand what I was seeing.

My father did. Ann's parents lived in an apartment on Central Park West in a co-op her grandfather had built in the 1920s. The view was of the park, best seen from a solarium where there were overheated plants dried out on the radiator. They had a maid and a cook whom they loved. The first night I was there, Ann's father gestured with his highball glass toward a display cabinet filled with objects. One piece of old broken pottery was a gift from Moshe Dayan. Something else involved a memory of a wicked discussion he'd had with Golda Meir.

It was the house tour of my father's dreams. He had landed safely.

————

Here's how Peter lost my mother.

He told her if he didn't have a thousand dollars by five o'clock, he was going to be evicted from his house. My mother brought him a check. He thanked her, he showered her with kisses, he told her how great she was, and then she went home.

That wasn't his mistake. That was coming.

Peter loved entertainment and plays and movies and popcorn. Anytime he recommended something, it was because there was no finer example, he said, of whatever it was he happened to be talking about. He took me to see *P.S. Your Cat Is Dead!*, explaining that it would teach me that love is brutal. I wasn't yet a human being if I hadn't seen *Pal Joey* or *A Thousand Clowns*, and he had similar feelings about any film that he'd just thought of. There was a cinema in Jackson Square, a little rep place. "Watch this, kid," he would say, "you'll learn something about women." Or men. Or business. Or this:

Auntie Mame, awash in 1958 color saturation, is about a polite and intelligent boy named Patrick, sent to his zany aunt, who lives in a sparkling New York City where every party guest is a prince or a showgirl. She teaches him how to live! live! live! When bad times come, they're in the form of dour legal guardians or stock market crashes. Auntie Mame's financial problems, of which she has a series, end happily because of her pluck, luck, and determination. She is generous of spirit and has a heart of gold, which makes how Patrick grows up—a stiff, conservative type ashamed of her—heartbreaking.

But in the end, he sees the error of his ways, and Mame, now a published author and a wealthy widow, reunites with the adult Patrick, and teaches his own son how to live! live! live!

I mistakenly told people I'd seen this as a child. I saw it for the first time recently, but it was familiar because *I'd grown up in this movie*. My mother thought she was Auntie Mame. And when we met Peter, she thought *he* was Auntie Mame. Anyone she met with a zest for life and disdain for convention was Auntie Mame, regardless of what else they did.

The next time I flew back from Chicago, my mother wasn't there to meet me, again. The same stewardess was on that flight, and this time, there was no social visit with Peter. Instead, she rode with me right to my own front door and only let me go when she saw my mother herself.

My mother was apologetic—there had been an emergency. My room smelled sickly, like a hospital corridor. It was mostly empty. The night before, my mother had had a man over, and he had brought a friend who had kept to himself. She put him in my room. He overdosed on heroin, spraying the walls with blood and vomit and ruining my mattress. She was waiting for a new one to be delivered. I stood in my room, unable to really take in what this meant. Heroin was something far beyond my experience and no one in my mother's circle had even referred to it. It was something *doomed people* used on the way down. My mother kept shaking her head in shock. "I don't get it. He said he was the heir to the Coca-Cola fortune."

Recently, a friend asked why it was so hard for me to understand that people *are* what they *do*. It was a concept so slippery I needed to write it down and stare at it like an advanced algebraic equation.

I get it at times and then I feel like the grown-up, frumpy, disbelieving Patrick who is ashamed of his Auntie Mame. If people are what they do, then there's no room for the compelling bohemian stories of magic guiding your life. My mother didn't think people were what they *did*. Instead, they were what they *told you* they did.

And that's where Peter made his mistake. He thought my mother was stuck in that movie, and perhaps a little stupid. He didn't understand the actual boundaries of what only seemed like naïveté.

After she lent Peter the money, my mother started to stew. She hadn't heard anything from him about repaying her. In fact, he was spending more money than ever.

"Weren't you about to be evicted?" she asked.

"Oh, that. I just had a bet that I could make you bring me a thousand dollars."

My mother was horrified—she asked for the money back.

Peter shrugged. "I spent it on cocaine."

Horror. Outrage. Phone calls. Hang ups. I wasn't to talk to him again, flowers arriving, flowers thrown away. Maybe—there were so many incidents like this I'll never know all of them. I'll never know what Mom saw that I didn't. I don't know how bad it got. Did she see human slavery? What did she have to ignore? She would say she ignored nothing, but she had her eyes on a different prize. She would say, maybe, that because she was in business with him she couldn't just stop talking to him. It must have enraged her, his cold-blooded awareness that she would forgive him.

Tabletop Pong machines were not durable. Screens went black; wires scraped raw; sometimes, like on a television, the vertical hold shot. And after too few months, no one was much interested in playing anymore, so restaurants and taverns asked Mom to remove the machines even if they did work.

There was a pizzeria on Telegraph Avenue in Berkeley that drove my mother crazy. "They were complaining that no one was playing anymore, so I went in—they'd thrown a tablecloth over it, and were using it as a table!" She sighed in exasperation. "Well, no wonder no one was playing, then. But could I get them to understand that? No!"

The investment wasn't working out according to the projections she'd relied on. Every month there was less and less coming in.

Peter found her a diversion. He introduced her to his best friend, which was supposed to occupy her until the next investment opportunity. And that was where Peter fucked up. He forgot the Rule of The Last One In.

Peter said Trevor Blake had co-owned Arthur. He was a fashion designer to the stars, winning international prizes and showing on runways throughout the world. He did women's wear, accessories, jewelry especially. My sense was of a guy who woke up late, took thirty messages from his answering service, smoked and drank coffee and talked on the phone for hours, sketching brilliantly, keeping tabs on his workshop, who then went out to New York discos all night.

This turned out to be true. Trevor was genuinely talented. His work was biomorphic, cork that could have been coral, or pewter chips that looked like the ridges of vertebrae. Just as Peter claimed, his clients really did include the Duchess of Windsor and Jackie O and a cadre of other moneyed socialites.

He was a handsome man, an Armenian Jew, heavy-lidded eyes, dark skin. He could talk all night long. In photos from the time, he wears too much jewelry, but wears it like worry beads, fingers running over ridges like he's soothing himself. His eyes have a quality I don't remember in person, but I see it clearly in the old black-and-white press clippings. Just like Peter, he is arrogant, and just like Peter he is amazed he's getting away with something. Trevor, however, looks shamed, beaten down as if his success were a sign the world was easily fooled. But that blurriness might just be the cocaine.

He and Peter had drifted apart when Trevor married an heiress, but in a short time Trevor was ready to play again. I don't remember meeting him, but I want to say Peter threw a week's worth of parties, inviting everyone in town, saving my mother out for the proper rites of droit de seigneur.

Trevor wasn't remotely interested in entertaining me, but he was fine with me in the room and just as fine when I left. I was curious that he made things, even if I was suspicious of fashion being an actual art form. And if it was art, I'd just seen an artist bullshitting his way into putting his doodles onto gallery walls. I'm pretty sure I said something about that, and I'm pretty sure Trevor told me I was right. Everything in his life was bullshit, but what could he do about that now? He had a career in bullshit. He laughed about it, and the laughter was inviting and a little melancholy.

On the other hand, he brightened when making fun of Peter. "You believe anything that guy says?" he cackled. "Let me tell you about Peter Charming—he got thrown out of high school for jerking off in class. When he asked to borrow the car and his dad said no, Peter poured gasoline over it and set it on fire." Trevor said Peter was in love with his own mother. Erotically. Had Peter ever mentioned her? No? Of course he hadn't. What Peter never told anyone was that his dream was to make love to old ladies, ladies with wigs and trusses and face powder.

This was disturbing to hear, and funny, and defiant, a great, vicious puncturing. I liked knowing this. I'm not sure Peter had bargained on Trevor telling stories on him. My mother was delighted, and not just because of those stories. Trevor was one of the great talkers of the century, she said. He was funny and creative and insistent and superstitious and baffling and he knew everyone in New York. He had gone to Studio 54 before anyone else, and had decided it was bullshit before anyone else. He name-dropped, but mostly like this: "You know what, I used to think I had a problem with name-dropping until Andy Warhol told me I didn't." Followed by guttural laughter, him looking carefully around the room to see if everyone was laughing, a wince-producing drag on a cigarette, more wine.

If Peter was a chess player, I would say Trevor, who had more the soul of a poet, would have been very good at a game I admired but could never get the hang of, *go*. With a few catty remarks, he had neutered Peter as a player, ready to sweep the stones off the board. There was a much larger world than Peter Charming, it turned out.

I was at Peter's house, and Peter was pacing in his office, ranting, laughing, then ranting again, like he couldn't decide whether to be angry, amused, or impressed.

His friend Max was a big lug of a bear, a physician who lived in Sausalito. Peter kept attributing different specialties to him—neurosurgeon, cardiologist, therapist. Anyway, Max had a patient, a damaged young woman who turned out to be a Joni Mitchell fanatic. Max told her his friend Peter knew Joni well, and the woman was fascinated.

So Max put her on the phone and she asked Peter what Joni Mitchell was like. For ten, maybe fifteen minutes, Peter held forth on their friendship, showboating on how they'd met, how they were always there for each other, no doubt wondering what the woman was being treated for, if she was cute, if she might come over. She was charmed, but not charmed enough, and she said goodbye quietly, and handed the phone back to Max.

Peter said, "And then Max says, 'You know who that was, right?' and then 'click,' the fucker hangs up on me."

"Who was it?" I asked. I didn't know.

He stared at me. "It was Joni Mitchell."

That made no sense. "But I thought you knew Joni Mitchell."

"I do," he said. "Of course I do."

"Then why didn't she recognize you?"

"I know her," he explained. "Of course I know her."

"But if you know her . . ."

He didn't want to talk about it. Something about the story didn't add up for me. It seemed to go with everything else Trevor was saying about Peter.

Trevor's time should have been up. There was another party. For Peter, even if he was being an excellent host, the evening couldn't go fast enough. He was drunk, or he was stoned, or he was feeling insecure, or he misjudged the situation so that he was speaking as if it were a year before and my mother were still discovering herself.

Later, both my mother and Peter would tell me the story of what he'd said, each of them for their own reasons. Peter had taken my mother aside and whispered: She and he both knew Trevor was only a fling, right? He'd be back, they could have a seasonal thing, she could even visit him sometimes, but she understood it wasn't real. Right?

I can imagine her going glassy-eyed, nodding once, taking up the drawbridge, turning off all the outside lights, quietly putting boards over windows, turning the locks on doors. I imagine she stayed that way until the party ended.

I don't know when she and Trevor came home, because I could no longer hear the front door from my room. I was living in the basement by then. When my mother and I had moved in, the room she had put me into shared a common wall with hers, but then we saw *The Sailor Who Fell from Grace with the Sea,* about a kid my age who listens to his mother having sex and then kills her boyfriend. Shortly after that, she moved me downstairs.

This meant I was living in the basement, near the malevolent force that hovered by the woodpile. Of course I was fine. I still had insomnia, the same thing I'd fought with since I was about six years old. Mornings were tough but I got myself together and brought my tuna sandwich and diet lemon-lime soda to school. My mom drove Trevor to the airport that morning.

I don't remember what happened at school that day. Some outrage among other outrages, something about bullies that bored me to get through. During my last class, a couple of minutes before three o'clock, I was told I had a phone call.

This caused my classmates to sing a long, melismatic "Oooh" that traveled up and down its pubescent chromatic scale. There was nothing good that came of such phone calls, and the kids wanted to make sure I knew to feel ashamed.

The phone was in a side room by the lobby, down some stairs, a storage area. When I picked it up, my mom was on the other end and I wondered how she'd known to call today. I wanted to tell her the bullying situation—whatever it was—was okay.

"Hello?" she said. I could *hear* her smiling. Sometimes my mother spoke as if reporters were listening in. "Guess what? Mommy's in New York," she said.

It took me a moment to catch on. "What?"

She was excited. It had been the craziest thing—she'd taken Trevor to the airport, and she'd been saying goodbye at the gate, and it was almost like a dare, she just impulsively got on the plane with him. She was in New York. She knew it was crazy, but there was money hidden in her office in the house, I had things for dinner, she'd probably just be in New York overnight, I shouldn't worry, lots of love, it was an adventure, maybe a day or two, I could handle it, wasn't this amazing? There was something about our lives that was so brilliant and exciting, she could follow her heart that way. She had never felt so light or free.

As I listened, I can't say I was paying close attention. I remember she made me promise I wouldn't call Peter. He was trying to control her. She told me lots of love, she didn't have a number yet for where she was staying, goodbye.

The receiver was ancient, black, industrial, heavy as a hammer, the type of thing that would have glowed for hours had I been able to throw it in a fire. I was already charting my way through an evening that had no guide rails. I was going to have a house without rules, which was a dream.

And I had this pang in my throat. It wasn't fear, or sadness. The literal motions I was making were shifting my books, shuffling up the stairs, pushing open the door that led out of school and to the street. But in my mind I was shaking off wet sand and kelp, improbably trying to catch my reflection in the surf, looking for scars and bruises, feeling my muscles for tenderness. I was so excited.

I bought candy bars and the latest *Howard the Duck* and I went home. There wasn't adventure to the evening—it wasn't much different than any night my mother would be home after I fell asleep.

When she called the next morning, she said she was probably coming home the following day, but there was a possibility, a slight one, that it might be a little longer, just a little, because she was learning about a situation. Trevor needed guidance with something, so she was going to stay another day or two at the most. The money I had should hold, and she could send me more if necessary, and I was okay with this, wasn't I? Of course I was.

Two days went by. It wasn't bad. I had a routine. I went to school. Three days. Four. Afternoons, I put some orange juice in a metal cup in the freezer for two hours and while it cooled I watched *Fractured Flickers* on the television and listened to NPR at the same time. When the theme for *All Things Considered* came on, the juice was the perfect consistency, harder than slush but not like a block of ice, and I would carve into it with the head of a spoon.

I thought about doing homework before dark but I didn't. There were comedies to watch on TV, and detective shows, and comics to reread. I made frozen macaroni and cheese. There was the news, which was important to catch up on, then I started doing my homework. When I got tired, around three, I decided to sleep until six, and I set my alarm. I was late to school most days because I tried to finish my assignments while walking. But otherwise I was handling this just fine.

Mom called to explain why she wasn't home yet. Trevor's business was in trouble. It had nothing to do with him or his potential, but something else, and if I get the specifics confused, the reasons will become clear. She might have told me Trevor had a business partner who had done some shady accounting, and he was trying to get back on his feet by reorganizing. He had an avalanche of ideas and materials and a clientele thundering for his next collection, if only he could get this financial hardship sorted out. My mother was going to turn his ship around. She was sure this would only take a few more days.

She said helping Trevor was about investing in our future. I understood. Fashion designers made a lot of money.

A week after my mother left, I was in her office at night, ordering a pizza. I was going to use the same voice on the phone I did when ordering a pizza from Peter's house, the voice of someone who would tip well. While I was dialing, somewhere in the house, a door closed.

I was alone in the house. This chill came up my back, a chill so deep it froze my arms to my sides and my shoulders jumped up. The sound had come from downstairs, the basement.

I thought about calling the police. I thought that was silly. Then I thought people in horror films always said calling the cops was silly. If I called the cops the first question would be: Where was my mother? I didn't know what would happen after that.

The front door was locked. The doors downstairs were always locked from the inside. *A child left alone by his mother hears a strange noise in the house,* I thought, *proving he is in fact only twelve years old.* That made me mad. That wasn't who I was. I walked to the stairwell, and leaned down and saw the band of light from a Pong machine rolling across the ceiling. But there was something else, a rustling noise that when I listened closely became voices. Something in the basement was whispering.

I shut the door to the stairwell and went back to my mother's office. I closed the door. *I am not frightened,* I said to myself, even though I was shivering so thoroughly I would still be twitching even after whatever was in the basement had eaten the heart out of my chest. I knew there was nothing in the basement. I knew that no one had been killed by ghosts.

A child who was pathetic would be frightened. I was going to open the door, have dinner, watch TV, have a regular night. I wasn't going to fail.

A few seconds later, something was scratching against a door frame or a wall. I could hear it. Something insistent, like a fingernail.

I dialed Peter's number. When Sue answered, I started apologizing for calling, but I couldn't talk. Like they had come from somewhere outside of my body, I was overcome with sobs. A stupid, frail, shivering boy was lousy with terror. I wanted to apologize for crying, but I couldn't.

I was at Peter's house within the hour. There was pizza on the way. He was already on the phone to New York. He told my mom what a terrible mother she was, listing all the bad things that could have happened to me. She didn't want to hear it. She got on the phone with me and told me I was being manipulative. Trevor needed her. I was fine, she said, I was resourceful and should have been able to handle the house on my own. She didn't believe for a second there were noises or that I was scared—I was smarter than that. This should be an adventure for me.

Peter took the phone back. He shouted at her, and he slammed the receiver down. I was eating pizza. He and I shared a look. I knew exactly what was going on—he was going to play unfair. He was checking to see if I was on board. Without saying a word, I let him know I was. He had Sue call Town School and tell them I would be out for the rest of the week.

The next day, the three of us went shopping for comic books. I was perfectly aware, as he said to me, "This is one of those popcorn and candy days—let's be bad," that I was his hostage. He could count on me to get my mom back from Trevor.

I was out of school for a couple of days. We flew a kite. Sue and I went to galleries and looked at ceramics. We had brunch at a diner in Half Moon Bay and watched the ocean waves afterward. On the way back, "Wake Up Little Susie" came on the radio, and Peter, inspired to deliver a monologue about having been a teenager, pulled into a high school parking lot and started doing donuts. He looked over at me to see if I was thrilled or scared. But I don't think there was an expression on my face. When I see myself, it's like I have a soot-singed blanket over my shoulders and I'm sipping hot tea.

When we were back at his house and I cried again, Peter called my mother as fast as possible and held the phone up to me. She was aggravated. Was I jealous of Trevor? Was that the issue? He had done nothing to me—why did I have to try to manipulate her?

I felt terrible for being manipulative. I wasn't a thirty-six-year-old midget. I wasn't even mature for a twelve year old. That Peter and Trevor and my mother were negotiating didn't matter to me. I just felt embarrassed. I didn't want my mother, I was already grasping the sensible nature of not wanting—but on a chemical level, with as little control of myself as a wolf pup, I *needed* my mother back.

Ten days after she left for New York, my mother returned to San Francisco. She was tremendously upset with me. She made it clear she wasn't staying—she was only going to organize things so she could leave again. Trevor's business was in a critical stage and he needed her.

She interviewed live-in help. She hired Bob and Sally, a couple of hippies, to look after me. Then she gave me strict instructions to have no contact with Peter again. She returned to New York.

Bob and Sally both looked like Art Garfunkel. I don't remember them exactly acing the interview process, but they were adequate for my mom's needs. In the first days, they made a lot of brown rice, smoked dope, and fucked with their bedroom door open. I think they were striking a blow for the revolution, or whatever the revolution still looked like in 1976, by living in Pacific Heights. I was a rich kid so they made fun of me. Sally in particular was fond of listening to whatever problem I was trying to explain, then tousling my hair and laughing at me.

Within a week, Bob and Sally left, writing down a number to call if I got into trouble. I'm not sure where they went, but they did show up to call my mother and tell her everything was fine. Otherwise, I was alone.

When my father learned I was living by myself, he phoned me to ask if I wanted to come live with him and Ann. I told him no. I was fine. He didn't press the issue.

I went to school. I was teased no more and no less than before. A few afternoons on the school steps, I faintly wondered whether I could hear the squeal of brakes as a limousine finally kidnapped my bullies. It wasn't really *wondering*—it was more the discovery of a new private cynicism.

When I walked home, I made up stories about Marvel Comics' chief spy, Nick Fury, Agent of S.H.I.E.L.D., who was grizzled and had an eyepatch. I thought about him so hard the walk from school to home felt impressionist, pointillist, leaving me dimly aware of passing sidewalks and breaks in the curb. On some days, a pair of kids I'd never seen before, two guys riding bikes, took to circling me and spitting on me until they got bored. They didn't even go to my school. I'm not sure how kids I hadn't even met knew they could do that to me.

My mom came back from New York for a few more days. She gave up on Bob and Sally, telling me an old boyfriend of hers would move in instead. He was a handsome guy with thick sideburns and I had no opinion of him one way or the other. I looked forward to making fun of him, even if at this point my heart wouldn't be in it. I was nervously hoping he would be nice. His name was Glenn, and as much as I distrusted it when someone burdened my name with an extra N, I wanted us to be friends. I worried that neediness might leak out from me.

After my mom left again, Glenn was physically supported into the house by a couple of friends, as he had pneumonia. They carried him into my old bedroom, leaving him there with what they explained was a good supply of homeopathic remedies, since he was a vegetarian. He didn't wake up for the whole weekend. When I came back from school on Monday, he was gone, leaving a note thanking me. He was going for a bike ride for a few days at least. He didn't actually come back.

So the deal was that I would take care of myself. I shopped for groceries. I drank a glass of Carnation Instant Breakfast every morning, with Breakfast Squares. I packed school lunches of tuna fish sandwiches and diet lemon-lime soda, and, every night, cooked a tub of Morton's macaroni and cheese dinner, watching *Star Trek* while I ate a dessert of chocolate Zingers. One night, I bit into a Zinger and came away with a mouthful of hair. I ate it anyway.

I scared the hell out of myself with the creepier sections of *The People's Almanac,* the unexplained disappearances, the prophecies of the end of the world. I drew pictures of sharks, vampires, and a weird specialty: creatures with hands for heads. The hands were slanted, with motion lines around them, waving hello or goodbye.

School projects piled up. I was supposed to write a history of the space program, typed, with impressive diagrams and evidence I'd read at least several books. All I managed to turn in were a few pages in handwriting, with a model of a Gemini capsule that I'd half-finished because I didn't know how to assemble the rest. D−.

There were floor-to-ceiling bookshelves in the basement. I kept my comics there. In the dead of winter, during the rains, I saw silverfish. When I pulled out some issues of *Strange Tales,* I couldn't open them. The pages were crisply adhered to each other and rippled like riverbeds. Water had ruined them. There were no other leaks in the house. About half my comics were damaged. I felt like this had happened on purpose, to test me.

I would make my own comics. I stayed up at night with my door wedged shut against whatever was outside it. I had a typewriter. A new issue of Marvel's fan magazine, *FOOM,* explained upcoming plot lines, so I decided I would write them myself and see how my stories compared to theirs. *The Avengers* were going to have a story with every character Marvel had ever created in it—that sounded big enough for me. I typed pages and pages. When I needed to think, I turned the TV volume up, poured a reservoir of Elmer's Glue on my palms, rubbed them together to spread it from the heel of my hands to my fingertips, and waved my arms around until the glue dried, pacing and talking out plot ideas to myself. I would peel it off carefully, trying to make complete scurflike impressions of my hands. Some nights, the thinking went so deep I did that two or three times. Sometimes I pissed into a soda bottle to keep from leaving my room and passing the dressmaker's dummy on the way to the bathroom.

The Tonight Show ended so early, one a.m., and then *The Tomorrow Show* ended, and some channels played the national anthem but others just went to static. If I kept changing the channel upward, into thinner air, I could get at least the fuzzy outlines of Jay Brown's *All Night Movie-Go-Round,* broadcast from Santa Cruz on a station so deep into the UHF dial it might as well have been ham radio. Jay Brown would show 1930s melodramas featuring actors I'd never heard of performing without conviction on sets I thought I'd also seen in better movies. I sensed that neither the directors nor writers cared about the story lines, that there were bathtubs of gin on the set, that the players could have freely said or done anything and no one filming them would have noticed.

Every fifteen minutes, regardless of whether the scene had ended, there was another commercial for a used car lot, hosted by an apologetic Jay Brown, who seemed to like watching movies more than he did selling cars.

I had to squint through the electronic sandstorm to guess at the details of his set. Jay read letters from viewers. Mostly retirees who asked him if he took the same kidney medications they did, and who wanted reassurances he didn't like drivers who broke the speed limit. I enjoyed hearing these because it meant there were other people awake like I was.

It would start getting light, and I would feel a sense of dread, as I had once again not gone to sleep, and there was another school day ahead. I felt ashamed of myself for not having taken better care of my evening.

Outside my door, which was closed, was a roomful of Pong machines. Dozens of them.

The Pong fad had gone belly-up. Most of the machines had been removed from restaurants, though my mother left a few of them in the more distant locations. The basement was filled with Pong machines stacked in the corners three tiers high. Some worked; some didn't. They were scarred with cigarette burns, coin slots scratched up or jammed, chipped edges where brass belt buckles had caught the particle board. I plugged in all the machines I could, turned out the lights, and watched the luminescence spraying across the walls. Then I played the remaining machines to death. Repeating games until the knobs came off or the screens flickered out.

It took weeks of play, but I did it, I killed every single one of them. I was the champion and sole survivor.

When I'd gotten past the darkest part of the evening, I would go upstairs, to the living room. I would open the curtains. Gradually, I'd see a mixed-blessings kind of gift, purple light behind the skeletons of the trees.

In the future I would have friends. We would sit here on this couch, waiting for more friends who would be in the kitchen, chopping up herbs for complicated pasta dishes. People in the kitchen would have a whole set of jokes people in the living room wouldn't know until we all shared dinner and then afterward we would dance, maybe in couples, maybe more free style. We would have adventures. I was convinced that there would be an earthquake and we would all be heroes, but we wouldn't be conceited about it. We would save each other because we loved each other. I would have an Asian American girlfriend who tended to wear white painter pants and no bra. We would sleep in. I would be able to sleep.

I started leaving the house. I'm not sure how often I did this, but it happened in spring and summer, when I had to be on the streets no later than 4:30 a.m. to truly feel how empty it all was. There was fog sometimes, mist blown in a slant across the arc lighting of streetlamps. The first time, I stood on the curb outside my house, heart in my mouth, feeling like Columbus, like Reed Richards at the maw of Subspace in *Fantastic Four 51*. Ahead, darkness and streetlights making ovals in it, a man-made pattern of stars blending together as they ascended toward the horizon line of the nearest hill.

When I walked, the sound of my footfalls was muffled. I wore a down jacket, and I had to keep taking off my glasses and rubbing them against my shirt to blot the fog away.

Along Jackson Street, I looked at the lights in the windows of mansions. All the rooms I saw felt empty, but that was just the angle I could see from—the high part of a wall, the cake frosting of plaster around a chandelier. It wasn't at all frightening to walk before dawn here, as every house gave off the calm impression of sleeping money. I imagined that the night before, parents had made dinner, homework was done, teeth brushed, pajamas put on, and then lights out, heads on pillows. The bullies were asleep in their beds. They were missing out on what I was seeing.

I wouldn't see a single car in Pacific Heights, not even on Broadway, more of a thoroughfare than Jackson. Peter's house was dark. It didn't feel like anyone was sleeping inside. It felt like a cardboard backdrop this time of night, ready to be inhabited only when the camera was pointing its way. When he realized he couldn't use me as leverage, I'd stopped hearing from him.

I left Pacific Heights. I could see a glow of traffic lights ahead, green, yellow, red, green, yellow, red, waltz time, changing without cars in the streets. When I did see headlights I knew the driver was so far away he couldn't see me.

Henry Africa's, dark in the hours after last call, was where the adults played. I was curious what happened after they left, hoping that there was a sophisticated shimmer left over like a spray of rhinestones. I expected to see barkeeps watering down the sidewalk or women in cocktail dresses woozily hailing cabs with one high heel shoe in hand, but I didn't.

I hardly lingered. Polk was where the teen hustlers were, so I rehearsed what I would say or do if someone accosted me—my plans were inadequate. Yell, I think.

In the saddle of Russian Hill, I was aware I was too far from the Bay to see it, so I walked north on one of the less picturesque crosstown streets. When there were deep alleys in sight, I walked in the middle of the road. I avoided the nude bars of Lower Broadway, crossing through Chinatown instead. There was a vital, warm sort of feeling here, as if the sidewalk and the buildings were always awake and alive regardless of the time of day. It was the only place I remember seeing people, usually just one or two older men walking with purpose as if someone were clocking them.

When I hit North Beach, the sky was usually turning blue, and streets smelled of something I couldn't identify, but the air was heavy with it, a warm hickory scent that I associated for years with the opening of the day, promise, the city yawning and stretching. It turned out that I was walking by a coffee roastery. Then, bakery smells, windows damp with condensation, the metallic clanks of ovens opening and closing, AM radios turned to the news.

Sometimes I wanted to go to Coit Tower, but the park surrounding it scared me, so I would just walk around Telegraph Hill, to the Bay side, as tourists were starting to wake up. Sometimes I stopped in Washington Square and watched old people doing Tai Chi. No one ever talked to me, but maybe once, twice, there was a shout in the street as I walked by and my skin tingled and my shoulders climbed up to my ears in fear, and I kept walking.

I didn't ask myself where I was going. The point wasn't to find a place so much as it was to have walked and to have burned a new bit of the city into myself. When a vista was pleasant, perhaps the overwhelming vertical of a hillside with houses riding it like a wave, I might stop and tell myself how lucky I was. I could imagine a time when I looked back on this moment, this view, with a sense of loss. I would be nostalgic for now, and this thought soothed me—surely what was happening to me wasn't sad. It couldn't be sad if in the future I looked back with regret that this time had passed.

I knew how adults loved the city. *You should have been here when,* said every adult. Maybe that time had never existed, but pretending it had was part of our social grace. If enough of us didn't believe it, it collapsed. Believing was on my shoulders now.

My mother's shelves had interviews with artists, the long-form ones in *City* magazine or *The Paris Review,* about how they'd overcome hard times and I pretended that this, right now, was a hard time.

Maybe this was normal, and common, and maybe other kids were walking in a syncopation that prevented any of us from actually seeing the others. Maybe we all drove ourselves in the dark with a need to explain what was going on. Later, years from now, we would realize that we each had been narrating our lives to no one—ironically, if only we knew, *here we all were for each other,* each of us members of the other's invisible audience. Walking in the dark was so long ago, we would say, and how we ache for the way the roasting coffee smelled. It was like we were royalty back then, with the empty city around us. It was great. We wish you could have been there. It was so beautiful and now it's gone.

There was a little more to the walks for me. Why am I still embarrassed to admit this part? There was a block near Nob Hill that I tried to walk each way, coming and going. There was a cramped alleyway there, the kind of place I would normally avoid. It was lined with angel trumpets, yellow bell-shaped blooms that at night gave off a potent and friendly perfume. It seemed like a trap you would find in fairy tales, so I never went down it.

But I thought that if I weren't expecting it, I would startle when I heard a familiar meow. I would look down the alley and see Leo trotting toward the curb. He would throw himself down on his side, showing off his belly, convulsing in pleasure at having found me. Oh Leo.

But I knew he was gone. The world didn't work like that. Leo was fine where he was, his little sweet cat mind having forgotten me, him sleeping on the bed of his new owner without regret. Straighten up, Glen, stop it. No one comes back just because you miss them. My heart was broken, but it was better it broke without me showing it off like that.

When I was at home I spent a lot of time going through my mother's files, looking for things I wasn't supposed to know. There were papers relating to the divorce and there was a huge file on me, with everything from my birth certificate to my current, terrible report card.

I found my IQ test. There was a printed sheet showing the IQ bell curve, and how around 130 was "gifted" and 150 was "genius." 170 was at the flat end, where the oxygen ran out. There was handwriting by the Eldorado School headmistress, notes from 1969 about how she'd administered the test and how I'd gone off the charts, 170+. The "plus" meant I had surpassed their ability to quantify me.

The number, with the weirdly imprecise yet clinical-looking plus sign, burned into my retinas. It was proof. I wanted it to be higher. I wanted it to surpass all ability to measure. Then I looked at the date. I felt suspicious. How can you tell how smart a five-year-old is? Also, it wasn't a standardized test—it seemed to be a set of mimeographed questions the headmistress had made up herself. *Draw a diamond.* Which

I did by drawing a square, then passing it to her at a forty-five-degree angle.

I wasn't a genius but I was *clever,* and it felt to me like that test had mistaken the difference between the two. My parents had bought into an exciting fiction that had started the moment they'd seen that 170+ and continued until now, when my mother had left because she was convinced I could handle myself.

Then I turned the page and something in me broke. It was terrible to see. It was another IQ test, a commercial one, the type you might buy at a bookstore and administer to yourself. It wasn't mine. It was my mother's.

My mother had decided to see how she measured up to her impossible child, and she had scored exceptionally high, 135 points. She could have gone to Eldorado herself. And yet I knew she looked at that and found herself not good enough. It was evidence that I was putting her down, again. I felt this dull ache of guilt and sadness, as if I were responsible. Long after I put the files back, I could see the numbers as if they were projected right in front of me. I could imagine my mom taking the test dutifully and sighing like she'd failed the 11+ exam, which she hadn't. Our results, hers and mine, confirmed to her that she was no good and that I judged her.

I understood something further, without steps of deduction—it arrived full-blown like divination. Looking at me while I was in my mother's office was the portrait of her father, long dead, unassailably a genius. Somehow, my mother had confused me with him. She loved me and despised me like I was her father. She had fled to New York to show me she wouldn't be crushed under my impervious, mighty thumb.

So much learning in such a brief time. I had no evidence to really support it except for how it sat in my clever heart. It felt correct and awful and it made me miserable for my mother. I felt like I'd sneaked a glance inside her medicine cabinet or her dresser drawer. I wished I hadn't seen any of this.

For four or five months in 1976 and 1977, I lived like that. Adults were around sometimes, but mostly not. The longest consecutive time I was totally alone was about two weeks, I think. There were plenty of shorter stretches, too. I didn't take up drugs. I didn't get mugged or raped. As a result it took a while for me to understand it meant anything. In my twenties I had a well-oiled version of my basement story. I talked about it casually because it felt like nothing to me, and that seemed to shock people. I told it to get sympathy and also to look down on whoever was giving it to me. *Oh, that makes your heart go out to me? You're weak,* I would think.

There are gaps in my emotions, the places where other people find continuity. I feel love and then it's like I'm driving on black ice with no contact against the road. I love three days out of five. I have heard gentle suggestions that maybe I am trying to avoid being abandoned again, but that doesn't seem right. I've taken on what Peter Charming said—the one who needs the relationship less controls it, and I have been with an unfortunate exception or two the one who needs it less.

Baby, you know they love you when they're there. My mother used to say it ruefully when a Saturday night sputtered to a close without a phone call or explanation. She said it in that way of beating herself up for not having learned. Then she would fall in love again, stubbornly, forgetfully, as if knowledge like that would only knife her vital, over-flowing heart.

Trevor was the first man of many she would discover, all in trouble, all ready to be pulled back with enough love and patience and some-times cash. It would never work.

The price of understanding her with some compassion goes like this: if you know they love you when they're there, then my mother loved Trevor but didn't love me.

That should be painful. It's not. From a distance I find her behav-ior brave. Why shouldn't a woman love a man more than she loves her child? All I knew when I was twelve was that I had a challenge like sur-viving in outer space—your mother chose to leave and you're clever or a genius or something, so how do you live well, Glen David Gold?

However, it's more complicated than that. Trevor, regardless of being intriguing and soulful, was a terrible person. My mother knew it. That's the part that's painful. Neither Trevor's situation nor my mother's grasp of it was apparent to me when I was twelve. When she and I talked on the phone, she explained things elliptically, even by her standards. She was living in a hotel and Trevor was somewhere else. He visited. Things were tense. Sometimes they managed to go out together but mostly she had to wait by the phone for him. She wasn't sure what was coming next, but if they could get through this rough patch, things would work out.

They would work because she loved him. She loved him so much I could hear the ache in her voice. She would never fail a man like that, even if he disappointed her. She would have a bigger heart than his, and that would show him the way to be a better man. She would be a better person than the man to whom she was devoting herself and that made her stronger, and he would see it eventually. Her love was a beacon and the result had to be inevitable.

Things could have stood like this for a while. My mother would have stayed in New York but for one thing: Peter Charming got the shit beaten out of him.

I had obeyed her and stayed away from him. Maybe I broke down because I was lonely; maybe he manipulated me into coming; maybe there was some arrangement between him and my mother. In any case, I was alone in his house one night, waiting for him and Sue to come back from a bar, and they were gone far longer than expected. I fell asleep on their living room couch.

Around three, the front door flew open and Sue ran into the kitchen for ice; Peter limped in afterward and collapsed on the stairs. His face was bloody. His nose had been broken, and his eyes were swelling shut. And he was laughing. For a moment, I thought he'd fallen through a window again—a few months beforehand, he'd snorted too much cocaine, smashing through a Union Street storefront and going into convulsions.

He clutched at his side. "Hey, it's the midget," he said. He started stripping off his clothing. Bloody leather coat, bloody shirt. He had a story to tell me, he said with a smile. Sue returned with the ice, and a hunk of steak, which he held to his eye as he tried to stand up straight, nude in his foyer.

I remember her holding him upright. They had been walking down Polk Street, Peter said. He'd bumped into a guy, and the guy had picked a fight with him. Peter had tried to talk his way out of it, but the guy swung at him, and you can't walk away from that. So Peter started wrestling with him on the sidewalk, and Peter was winning. "Sue Blue, I was winning, right?"

"You were," Sue said. "He knew he didn't stand a chance."

"So the guy pulled a Peter Charming on me. I can't believe it. He broke away from me, and he saw we had a big crowd, and he said, 'That's right, motherfucker, I *am* a fag! I don't care what you call me, I'm proud to be a fag!'"

"You called a guy a 'fag' on Polk Street?" I asked.

Peter snapped at me. "Of course not. But all of a sudden, the crowd was on his side, and they started in on me, too. Kicking me. Sue Blue got me out of there."

He took a shower, drank brandy, smoked dope, yelled at Sue as she patched him up, and they told me the details over and over again. The guy became bigger and more cowardly, the crowd more vicious, Peter the consummate pacifist.

"I mean, fuck 'em if they can't take a joke," Peter said, more than once. I wasn't sure what that meant anymore. It was sounding like a way to seem he'd won something when he clearly hadn't.

Peter's time was up. I would like to say I saw it in Sue's eyes while she was dressing his wounds, how when he flinched and cursed at her for the bite of the rubbing alcohol, she was already picturing her suitcases, thinking of which friends whose numbers Peter didn't have might be awake and have a couch for her.

A couple of years later, Sue did leave him. My mother was in touch with her quickly to ask something she'd been wondering since all of them had met. And yes, Peter had taken Sue's money, too. Sue had a large divorce settlement—she'd been a dental hygienist married to a wealthy dentist. Peter had come in as a patient, and the moment he looked at her, her husband no longer mattered. I think she felt bad for how she'd ended up as the obviously good-hearted bait standing at the door with a glass of wine for a number of women like my mother.

But back to the night of his beating. One of those flashes of memory: Peter clean and in his robe, his eye blackened, mouth upturned with a half-million-dollar smile. Him saying, again, "The guy pulled a Peter Charming on me."

· · ·

My mom came back a day or so later. I don't think I had much to say to her—our relationship had changed. She quizzed me. Wasn't I upset? I wasn't. Peter was fine. It proved to me that people could get beaten senseless and survive. I came away from it with a weird sense of urgency. I needed to get out.

Eighth grade was ending. It was time to apply to high school. Town School fed to University High, whose aspirational name indicated exactly what it was, a prep school for the neighborhood kids heading to college. With my mother back in town for a while, she let me know her own plans: she was moving to New York permanently. I was free to stay in San Francisco if I wanted. I wasn't sure how that would work.

Living with my father and Ann was no longer an alternative. She was pregnant and they were going to have a child soon. There was no room for me in their apartment, which they didn't even have to explain to me. I didn't want to live there anyway.

High school counselors came to Town School to give presentations. Boarding schools on the East Coast, Andover, Exeter, sounded like attending school on Jupiter. But there were also boarding schools in California, and one of them was called Thacher.

Thacher's presentation was led by Mr. Livermore, after whose ancestors the city was named. Mr. Livermore had gone to Thacher himself, then Yale. He was a type I hadn't seen before—even though he was wearing a tweed jacket and a knit tie, he was also wearing cowboy boots. He looked uncomfortable indoors, but he spoke kindly, with an instant moral clarity, like a sheriff who, when things were slow, would bring out a broken-back copy of Thoreau to read trailside.

Thacher was a small boarding school in the rural town of Ojai, which I couldn't place on the map. North of Los Angeles, south of Santa Barbara, it turned out. It was in an east–west valley that was near the ocean and yet it had a desert climate. Freshmen were required to feed, groom, and exercise a horse. "As Mr. Thacher said—'There's something about the outside of a horse that's good for the inside of a boy.'"

And now girls. Thacher was going coed. The first slide Mr. Livermore put on the screen was a view from Thacher into the deep bowl of the Ojai Valley. Here was the upper soccer field, Mr. Livermore explained, with tennis courts to the left and stables to the right, and then beyond that, ranches and then, five miles away, the town of Ojai (population five thousand), and beyond that, rings of mountains.

It was like my first night in San Francisco or my first bid at a coin auction. It was obvious to me that I belonged at Thacher. I wanted to sleep every night on a campus where there were girls sleeping nearby. I predicted I would be popular and that sex would occur. I would become athletic. I would become interested in the outdoors. I have no idea why I thought those things.

It was shockingly expensive to go—almost six thousand dollars a year. And no matter what Livermore said about the atmosphere there, it was equally likely to be a prison population of despicable rich kids contained there in lieu of being forcibly set adrift on ice floes before they murdered any more relatives.

I decided it would be friendly. I ignored the horse situation. I was going to apply to Thacher and be admitted and go there. Then I was going to Yale. Then I would move back to San Francisco and start assembling the team of friends that would include artists, rivals, musicians, and a girl in white painter pants.

My father was puzzled by this—he asked me if my mother had put me up to applying. She hadn't. After balking at the price, he noted that there was financial aid, so perhaps the money wasn't an issue. This was more complicated than I understood. My father had plenty of money—rather, Ann did—and to their credit neither was that troubled by spending it on my education. They were hesitant to have any more of it go through my mother, as they suspected she would figure a way to siphon it off. So my father told me we would look into financial aid if I was accepted.

Which was going to be a huge problem. It was highly competitive to get into Thacher. I had learned a great deal in the previous year, but I hadn't exactly been doing any schoolwork. My grades were mostly Cs, except for the Ds.

The Thacher application was many pages long. I think it was assumed by the school that an adult would help me. There was an essay question. Who were my heroes? I wrote: "Bill Cosby. And whoever planned the raid on Entebbe."

But that was all I wrote. I didn't know what an essay was.

There was more like that, my chunky and terrible handwriting, my incomplete sentences, my evasions. What intramural sports had I played? Willingly, none. I was always picked last in softball, after Wade, who had one eye.

I wrote down "baseball" and "soccer" and "running" and, since I knew they played it at Thacher, "lacrosse," even though I'd never seen a lacrosse stick. I didn't play those other sports, either. I had played baseball once and been hit in the face with a baseball bat so hard it broke my nose. I put "running" down because technically, after school, when being teased I did run places. I said I'd camped even though I hadn't and I listed books on my mother's shelves as ones I'd read myself.

After I sent it in, a wave of shame swept over me, and I felt like I was drowning in my own mistakes. I knew I hadn't done well enough to get into that school, and I knew I had to do better somehow. I felt it could help if Thacher met me.

The road from Ojai to Thacher was one-lane, with waist-high stone walls marking orange groves next to corrals and ranch houses. It seemed to follow, more or less, a barranca of huge white rocks worn smooth thousands of years before by a river no longer there. My father drove.

A few months beforehand, he and Ann had left Chicago and moved back to Los Angeles. The weather there was better, making it more appealing to start their new family. They had a three-bedroom apartment in West Los Angeles, close enough to the ocean for a nice coastal breeze, and a tiny Mercedes with a backseat a thirteen-year-old could just barely fit in.

We went uphill, gently, for a few miles. I yawned from nervousness. There was a fork in the road, and my father slowed down to figure out the map. Turn left on McAndrew? I wondered if there would be a time where I thought "once, I knew so little about being here I didn't even know whether to turn left on McAndrew."

Thacher's white stone gates appeared under the shade and litter of pepper trees. The campus was, like the valley, dotted with orange groves, and the buildings were Arts and Crafts or Mission stucco. When I saw students, I could decode how they dressed—preppy, not surprisingly—but not how they walked, which was a slow lope, with some swagger and ease. They walked as if nothing terrible was about to happen.

I was introduced to Mr. Twitchell in Admissions. He was East

Coast, atrocious plaid sweater, and a sunburned pink face that came with an appraising squint. As he described Thacher, I could barely hear him. I was too consumed with the realization that if I didn't get in, I would die.

I was trying to memorize the photographs in the office, the names of the staff, and I was trying to anticipate how to dress for dinner. I hadn't brought a tie. Suddenly that was all that mattered. *I hadn't brought a tie.* It was very possible I needed to dress for dinner even though I hadn't seen a single tie since I'd gotten to campus.

Also, I was being looked at.

"Glen, this is Weston Richardson," Mr. Twitchell was saying. Weston was a freshman, and his job was to show me the school. I would sleep on the floor of his dorm room that night.

Weston didn't shake my hand. If Mr. Twitchell was evaluating me, Weston was already finished. He wasn't wearing a tie, but I wasn't relieved by that, as his demeanor was frightening. He was only a year older than I was but from the confidence that wafted off of him, he might have spent that year in an urban militia. Khakis, Top-Siders, no socks, preppy clothes worn not as if they indicated club attire, but as if he couldn't be bothered to think of wearing something else. He had, beneath his blond bowl haircut, an utterly dismissive expression.

"Glen's visiting us from San Francisco."

"That's a thrill," Weston said. "Stuart Hall?"

"Town School."

"Oooh," he said, as if he'd caught me bragging. I wanted to protest, and then from his cool look, I understood he actually didn't care. Not even slightly.

"Weston's great-grandfather was something of a Thacher legend," Mr. Twitchell said. "He was the first person ever expelled from here."

"Really?"

Weston nodded. "I think he knifed a guy. That your sleeping bag?" He threw it over his shoulder, and gestured that I should follow him out of the office.

I ran to keep up with him. He looked at me again. "Dinner's at six-fifteen. Did you bring a tie?"

I shook my head.

"Classic."

. . .

Weston gave me a tour of the campus. He talked. And talked. That it was a great school academically was something he didn't dwell on. He focused on the only important thing: the school was going coed.

We were standing in the art studio with another freshman. Craig, who didn't quite have Weston's presence, said something about how things would change when the girls were finally there.

Weston said, "What, for you? Not for you. In your dreams. Even the sloppiest gash who shows up here won't give you the time of day." Somehow, Admissions had only let in ugly girls. Not a one of them was hot.

"Joni Katz is hot," Craig said.

Weston sighed. "Son, you think anything with two legs and a twat is hot. You reek."

I listened hard to all Weston said, and his vocabulary for saying it. I wanted to be blasé about girls.

After dinner, he took me to his dorm. We sat in his room starting at seven-thirty, when study hall began. The schedule was deliberately overloaded. There were chores in the morning and inspections and required breakfasts, then classes, and then required sports in the afternoon, and you had to care for your horse, and there were formal dinners five nights a week. Study hall, and something called "check-in" every night at ten, which even Weston treated with respect. One senior, a prefect, knocked on Weston's door to see why he was talking, saw he was talking to me, and moved on. Weston continued: had I seen that guy? That was a senior, something that had been molded into a human being from the blob I currently was.

The school made one specific deal with its students: unimaginable freedom in exchange for following the honor code. The contract went something like this: "Promise us that while you're here you'll never cheat, steal, do drugs or alcohol, promise never to go into the dormitory of someone of the opposite sex, and above all never lie to us if we ask you questions about any of this, and in exchange we'll trust you to do more or less anything else you want. That way you get a safe place to grow up and take chances and we get a better society out of it. Civilization is based on the balance of responsibility between the individual and the group, and if you can abide, you'll become responsible enough to handle anything, and fast. Plus all the avocados and oranges you can eat." It was a Southern Californian version of being welcomed to Athens, circa 800 BC.

I wanted that. But there was so much to know. If you wanted to leave campus, you had to fill in the sign-out sheet (the what?) on the pergola (the what? where?), and get permission from the TOAD (not a real toad) and it was hard to keep up with what he was saying about "wandering."

"Wandering is something only seniors get. It means that after ten p.m. check-in they can do any fucking thing they want. Go anywhere. Walk the Perimeter Road, smoking cigarettes and jacking off into each other's mouths if they want to. And some of them *do* want to, pretty boy. Just kidding," he said. "The truth is, you're ugly. Here you go," he said, throwing a *Hustler* at me.

It turned out that evenings ran on porn and junk food. I could do that. At ten p.m., as promised, the prefect pounded on the door again, confirmed Weston was there, and at 10:30 the lights were out. In ten minutes, Weston was snoring and I looked at the ceiling.

I was thinking about all those rules, and how the reward for following them was to be a senior and *wander*. It wasn't lost on me that I longed to earn that ability again, the one I had when I was twelve simply because I declared I could. I needed to impress the admissions department.

There was a meeting during which I sat in a captain's chair and I very carefully said nothing to Mr. Twitchell about how I was living in San Francisco. It was important for me to not seem weird, I thought, so I concealed as much as I could.

When I'm clearly in the wrong, I tend to speak from the corner of my mouth, eyes averted, my words coming out with an aural flinch, as if I'm already agreeing with whoever disagrees with me. That's how I talked to Mr. Twitchell at the interview. My grades were mentioned. I had an explanation ready, but I didn't need it—Thacher sometimes overlooked grades when an applicant had other aspects that made him or her seem like a good fit. Did I ride a horse already? No? What sports did I say I played? Oh, so when I said that, it was more like "I could play those if necessary." Any hobbies? I didn't mention that my hobbies included rolling joints for grown-ups. And I wasn't very good at that.

What did I read?

Now I had something to talk about. Well, comic books, I said, but good ones. Now I wasn't flinching. I was describing how I'd finished writing a very good origin for Nick Fury, Agent of S.H.I.E.L.D., and had sent it to Marvel Comics. Before Mr. Twitchell could ask anything else, I was in full-on *Paris Review* interview mode. I'd been waiting for the moment where someone would ask me about my work. It was twenty-six pages, I explained, and would last twelve issues, a whole year, and it featured every character in the Marvel Universe. I'd introduced a new character named Amatnon (I explained that it was Latin) and he had alternating plates of vibranium and adamantium that meant he couldn't be harmed. In fact, he could feel nothing, he "loved not," hence the Latin name, and it was, I could admit, autobiographical. I got even more about that out in an excited rush before I realized from Mr. Twitchell's eyes that I had made a mistake. This was not impressive. This was weird.

On the way out, I thought I should have mentioned instead all the science fiction I was reading. Those books, at least, were novels.

I sat in on Weston's math class, which might as well have been theoretical biophysics. Worse, it was taught by Mr. Twitchell, whom I had already lost. He gave a pop quiz. In the awkward moments when I was looking around for a clue how to behave, Mr. Twitchell knelt down in front of me and asked with concern if I'd followed anything in the class so far.

I admitted I hadn't. Instead, I'd been thinking about *Dune*. He didn't know what *Dune* was, so I explained: it was science fiction, not a comic book, and I was wondering how to turn it into a movie. So while he was teaching, I was imagining sandworms and vast deserts through which they swam. He looked at me with what I can now identify as concern. Then he smiled, tapped on the desk a couple of times as if sorting out what to say, then went back to the front of the class and taught the rest of the lesson without having actually said it.

When my father asked how it had gone, I didn't have much of an answer. I wished it had gone well, so maybe I lied to him.

I won't prolong this. It turned out that there really was such a thing as a permanent record at Thacher. Mine began with a note from Mr. Twitchell. *He's weird,* it said. *But I like him.*

It was true—Thacher had some standards beyond reading grade point averages. One thing that trumped grades was "weird." I got in.

————

There was a school dance right before graduation from eighth grade. I had never danced before, but I felt pretty good about my future so I went to the dance, to critique it. I spent the first two hours standing by the punch bowl, telling Jon Epstein how stupid everyone was for dancing. I talked about the psychology behind it. All our unmet need for gratification marred by our flaws and shortcomings, our lack of insight into what we actually wanted. Movement didn't solve anything. Dancing was a mistake. Eventually, he left, then came back, with girls.

"Tell them about the dancing," he yelled, over the music.

I didn't know where to put my hands. I remember I was leaning over one girl, who was trying to hear me, while Jon was paraphrasing, for another girl, my argument against dancing. Then she whispered it to another girl, and then the girl I was talking to took my hand and led me to the dance floor.

I danced for forty-five minutes. When the first girl was tired I found another. I'm fairly sure I danced with several girls at once. Other people stopped dancing, and I stopped, too, but they gestured that they wanted me to keep going, so they could watch.

By the time the dance was over, I had untucked my shirt, and kicked off my shoes, and I was sweating, and I could barely speak. There was a crowd around me. They all wished the dance had continued, if only so they could keep watching. Also, my philosophy against dancing had spread around. Everyone agreed I was really smart. I understood that they weren't watching my dancing because it was good. It was more like watching a chimpanzee that had been chained inside a barrel until he was twelve years old explode through the staves, hurl the oak lid away like a champagne cork, and fling his body against the rafters until he exhausted himself. I would want to see that.

"We were all at a party last Saturday," Andrew Vaupin said. "We were trying to think of who was straight, and we listed off a bunch of names. Then someone said 'Glen Gold' and everyone laughed really hard."

Everyone laughed again when he said it. I laughed, too, like this: *Hah*

hah? hah hah hah? I was trying to figure out what he meant by "straight." I knew it usually meant "heterosexual" and yet I knew he wasn't talking about that. There wasn't much homophobia at Town School; we were in San Francisco and some of our teachers were gay and no one cared. Further, in this context, *straight* seemed to be something shameful. And regardless of how gay-friendly our junior high school might have been, it would never get to the point where anyone actually looked *down* on being straight.

I had no idea what was going on. So I kept laughing, to show everybody I knew exactly what they were talking about.

"So, are you?" a girl asked.

"Am I what?"

"Straight?"

I was about to say yes. But to be straight was to be laughed at during parties to which I hadn't been invited. I was being invited *somewhere* now, maybe. All it took was giving the right answer. "No, well, yeah, sort of, I'm sort of, pretty much, no, sort of straight, kind of, you know."

Only when the conversation had moved on did I realize they meant *straight* the way Peter said it, like stepping out of the shower to pee. That my classmates might have anything in common with that other life had confused me too much to make the connection then.

The kids around me were talking about how they figured I read Latin and spoke Greek and knew calculus. They didn't know anything about me. They couldn't have a clue that when I arrived in seventh grade, I'd already been banned for life from the Washington Square Bar & Grill. They didn't know my grades were miserable. All they knew was what they saw, a sweaty, chubby, hyper-verbal kid without any grace. Of course they assumed I had to be smart.

The girl I had danced with the longest was nicknamed Froggy. She introduced herself that way. She had a raspy voice, and she was from some former British colony that produced girls with raw accents. "You're smart and you're funny," she said. "Your mates want to see you dance again next week at Hamlin's." This was a girls school. She wrote her phone number on my hand. Then with some amazement, she swept her palm up my forehead and through my hair. She wiped her hand on my shirttail. "Nice heat," she whispered.

There's no reason to assume I slept that night. I went to bed sweaty and woke up with a sore throat from, I thought, having shouted and laughed so much. It had been the greatest social event of my life. In the halls on Monday, the other boys actually nodded at me.

Later I called Froggy. I was so nervous I'd prepared a joke "hello" that was so convoluted it was like dropping a *New York Times* acrostic in her lap. Five letters, sweaty, Freudian for "I want" with scrambled French "you," remember? Oh yes, *idiot*.

She seemed a little abrupt but still open to me coming to the dance. I believe this was the moment she artfully let me know they'd allowed her to invite three boys, meaning two other boys in addition to myself whom she had invited before me. She knew we'd each have a good time with all that company. I couldn't put my finger on why this seemed slippery. I wondered if it was possible that when girls issued invitations, you might not always get all of the story.

This, though it seemed like a plateau on the way to a better place, was actually the high point of eighth grade. I had found a tentative acceptance in that world, just as the component pieces were to scatter to different high schools. I learned about anticipation, for the coming dance was five days away, then four, then three, and I was out of my mind wondering what was going to happen. I did not kid myself that I would get to kiss Froggy, or rather I told myself that wasn't going to happen so that I could be pleasantly surprised when it did, not that it would, et cetera.

The sore throat became walking pneumonia. The evening of Froggy's prom I lay on crusty-feeling sheets, wondering what the dance was like. I also tried to talk myself into feeling like this was for the best. Writers aren't really made to dance, I thought. We're the ones who press against the window outside the ballroom, noting the beauty of skirts twirling in advance of a surrender, before we walk away alone, perhaps stopping on the damp pathway to make a brief, tubercular cough into our fists. There are more writers than babies conceived on prom night.

After I recovered, I was no longer teased at all. For the few weeks before eighth grade ended, I was the crazy guy at the dance who was moderately entertaining.

———

That summer feels jumbled and confused, an epilogue of misplaced packing tape and last-minute changes of address. My mom was finding her place in New York and she traveled back and forth. A freezer not quite defrosted, and typed notes left for the landlord. I was getting ready for Thacher, buying a sleeping bag for camping trips, reading the required novels. I was trying to start growing a mustache. I had very little to work with. I didn't really want a mustache. Also you weren't allowed to have facial hair at Thacher. The teachers would order you to shave if they thought you needed to. But that's what I aspired to, to be told I needed to shave.

It was the summer I saw *Star Wars* repeatedly at the Coronet on Geary. Maybe this was the time I went to tennis camp? Why do I remember seeing *Annie Hall* with kids from my school?

My mother's sister Susie came to town from England for a few weeks with her husband, Barry, and a scrum of cousins roughly my age. They were rightly prepared to fight with the rich, snotty, egotistical jerk they remembered from our last visit. But I had been humbled a little bit. I'm sure I was still kind of a dick, but I was also lonely. I shared my comics. I showed them how to play a somewhat-functional Pong machine for free. They taught me the words *snide, wank, anarchy, Cadbury.*

"You're being snide, Peter."

"I am not. Bollocks."

"Don't say 'bollocks.' "

"What's 'bollocks' mean?"

General laughter. I didn't know what "bollocks" meant, and even the adults weren't sure if you could say it, given how it was all over the radio now. Hadn't I heard of punk rock? No? We stayed up at night, me telling ghost stories about the basement and them terrifying me by singing Sex Pistols songs.

Rosemary, my mother, Elizabeth, Anna, Susie, Georgina, Jonathan. Susie was as pretty as the rest of the girls, maybe prettier. Peter and Paul agreed it was weird how much their mates wanted to come over after school, just to look at their mother. Though she had the same sense of humor as my other aunts, the same belief that life ran on zest, a feeling that any day could be improved with the circus in it, there was something different about Susie. She was deeply responsible, which was weird for my family. Debbie, her daughter, told me Susie looked remarkably like a photograph of an American soldier that Elsie had kept in a dresser drawer for murky reasons.

My mother had told Uncle Barry he could make a living building houses in San Francisco. They could start a new life here. But the contacts she had lined up didn't work out. It turned out there were union issues my mother hadn't known about.

This caused my mother and Susie to fight. My mother was annoyed at her family's inability to adjust to all the freedom she was showing them. Susie didn't approve of her friends, Mom said. Trevor needed her, so she got on a plane again.

Susie, Barry, my cousins, and I took a road trip for a few days. Susie kept asking me who Trevor was, how Peter really made his money, what did my father think of all this? But she also didn't press the issue. She had other sisters with more insistent problems.

When we arrived back in San Francisco, there was a message for me on the answering machine in my mother's office. I can still hear the timbre of the voice, slow and deep. "This is Jim Shooter . . . Marvel Comics. Calling for . . . Glen . . . Gold."

By the time he said that, I had already fallen over. I was faceup on the carpet. I was having so much trouble breathing I started to belch. Susie worried—what was wrong with me? It was a small office. Barry, Peter, Paul, John, Debbie, I think all of them crowded in to see what was going on. The boys dragged me upright, telling me to stop being so dramatic, and then there was an argument about who among us was being snide. It was decided: probably me.

I had to play the message back to understand it. I played it so many times I worried I would snap the tape. Jim Shooter had gotten my story about S.H.I.E.L.D., and he wanted to talk to me about it. I should give him a call when I could.

I was curious whether I should be weeping. I jumped up and down, but that didn't seem right. I kept saying, "This is so surreal." Susie didn't understand what was going on—I said that the editor of Marvel Comics, my favorite comic book company, had called me, a kid, about a story I'd written. That still didn't explain anything—it was just a plot summary that she understood already.

The rest of the pack fell away, and it was just me and Susie in the office. She was kind and her reactions to things were so deeply normal that they startled me. She asked me if I wanted to tell my mother about these Marvel Comics. Oh. Yes, I guess.

Susie had been right to suggest it—I wanted Mom to know. It offered evidence I had survived. Here was my faith in the power of words. I had written my way out of the basement.

On the other end of the phone, I could tell my mother was beaming. Also, unsurprised. I don't know what her actual words were but I could feel her pride overshadowing everything else. I was entering a world larger than myself, one she already knew, where there was magic and reward. How simple her reaction seemed as she was saying, *Of course you did it, darling. Of course.* We were both living our dreams.

Thacher started in September. In August, my mother had some business to attend to in Reno. I came along.

I had talked to Jim Shooter of Marvel Comics. Shooter had started writing comics when he was twelve, too, and he wanted to encourage me to keep writing. Learn about science so I could make up inventions that sounded like they could exist. He added a hesitant beat to that. When I was in high school, I should read all the literature I could. Updike, for instance (I wrote down the name). I thought this was to polish my comics skills, but he said that wasn't quite it. He said I might read enough that I'd forget about comics. Which was fine, he added.

I wasn't quite sure what he was getting at. I tried to rephrase what he was saying so it sounded more like "you're so talented we're going to hire you soon." There were some killing silences until we agreed I would keep sending him stories from Thacher and he would critique them. But no, I wasn't hired.

The truth was that I wasn't as exceptional as I'd hoped. And I hated having patience. But I read Updike short stories while my mother and I were staying in a Reno hotel casino.

My mother met with a high roller who had a big house at the edge of town with a swimming pool. He drank cocktails with lunch, swore a blue streak, and called my mother "lady."

We left his house at high speed. My mother was furious to the point of tears—he'd talked her down in price, giving her something like half of what they'd agreed on.

I'd like to say I had some reaction to the fact that we had abandoned at a stranger's house—a cheap bastard's house—the Fabergé chess set. But it meant nothing to me then.

I took in something as I was in that hotel room, looking at the flashing marquee sign. Downstairs was a cathedral-sized room full of people who were leaking money into the casino, quickly or slowly. They were suckers. They didn't look at a situation from an angle to see what choices they really had.

I understand fate is unjust. Fate is a bully. My mother flees across the country with baskets of valuable things. There are bumpy roads and bridge tolls, cops on the take. By the time she limps into the city, she has been picked clean, and it's just her and her empty basket and the story of all the hard luck she has faced.

I can see it as it's happening. Is it a betrayal when I'm wondering this, also—The wheel is cold, or the wheel is hot, but why is she playing?

I wish that before I'd left San Francisco I'd walked across the city again to take in what I was leaving. I wish I'd stood on one of the peaks whose names I never learned—San Francisco below Market was for me as distant and hot as the Martian landscape. It would have given me some perspective. It was 1977, which was the apex for a certain gentle kind of San Francisco life. The doomed George Moscone was mayor, the ascending Dianne Feinstein was on the Board of Supervisors with Dan White and Harvey Milk. Bars would have ferns in them for a little while longer, and the music people played still had a disco beat and a horn section. The Sex Pistols had just been booked at Winterland. There were bathhouses in the Castro now. There really was a page turning.

I made myself some promises. In high school I would find something athletic to like. I would be less sarcastic and more genuine. I would tell people my name was David.

Days before I left for Thacher, I did something terrible. During the shuffle of all our possessions, the collection of coins was in my bedroom for a few days.

From the 1969 series, there was a one dollar bill, five dollar, ten, twenty, fifty, and hundred. They were still face value in 1977, in other words worth $186. They were never likely to be worth more than that, even in uncirculated condition. I pocketed them. I put all the rest of the coins back where they should be, but I kept those bills in a secret compartment in a Chinese chest in my room. I knew it was wrong.

That weekend, there was a comic book convention at the Jack Tar Hotel. I faced the dealers' room with a sage look on my face. I ran into the dealers from Comics & Comix on Columbus and the Best of Two Worlds but I didn't buy anything from them—there were much better deals to be had if only I was prudent. As I was combing through the back-issue boxes, I was narrating the story: this is just fine to do, I will feel no guilt, I should feel no guilt, I am a kid on my own, making the best of this situation. At the same time I was explaining it to myself as a rehearsal for what would happen if my father found out I was stealing.

Who was I stealing from? Myself? My past with my father? Ha, that was the thinking someone *straight* would use. This was the best choice I could make, and not at all motivated by darkness and rage. How could I ever think this was rage at work?

Carefully and wisely, I thought, I comparison shopped. I spent $186 on old comic books.

My first investment.

NOVEMBER 1974. I was ten years old, lying on my stomach and reading comic books. The phone rang, Peter Charming calling, him telling my mother to stop packing, come to a party, and then a few hours later my mother and I were on the PSA flight from Orange County to San Francisco. We caught a cab at the airport curb and my mother gave the address, 1974 Broadway.

On the ride into town, it was dark outside, so all I could see were lights from other cars and houses on hillsides, not a clue what San Francisco was like yet. My face to the window. It's not a pretty drive from the airport at first, but then the sight of downtown is impressive and strange, a distinctive pyramid surrounded by more obvious skyscrapers, and suggestions of hills and bridges in the distance.

We were on an ugly multideck freeway that spilled abruptly into North Beach, a sleazy fiesta of neon and flashing lights. Topless clubs advertising "He-She Love Acts." Sailors. The deep bass of amplified music trying to convince the people packed onto the sidewalks that anything sticky and awful must also be sexy.

The cab idled at the stoplight. My mother looked at the address Peter had given us. He lived on Broadway. This was Broadway. She looked disturbed.

A thud of a body, the cab jumping on its shocks. There was a blur I couldn't quite resolve. A pimp and his hooker had gotten into it, and for a second there was a snarling face pressed up close enough to mine to leave a film of breath on the cab's window that remained vivid after we peeled off.

I was blank. Nothing. No reaction, not even a racing heart. My mom asked if I was all right. The cab went through the Broadway tunnel, and on the other side of it was Pacific Heights. Fussy Victorian flats, Edwardian town houses. In other words, the bulk of Russian Hill filtered out the tit bars and Broadway became respectable. We were saved.

But the moment that face hit the cab, something happened to me. At the party that night, among the biofeedback and the pinball and the adults smoking weed, I tried to say something like this: You know how, right before you speak, there's a moment where the words in your brain start lining up? Just as there's a tunnel from North Beach to Pacific Heights, I became aware of a kind of tunnel that the impulse to speak travels, from someplace primal and prelingual into the place that civilization understands. There's a distance between when I perceive something and when I form the words to describe it, and my perception only becomes real when those words finally hit me, and I am anxious. What happens when I perceive something before there are words for it? Is there something in that darkness, before words?

I realized that I was telling myself about what had happened fractions of a second after it happened. After that collision with the cab, that sense never left me.

There was a comic book hero named Captain Marvel, who, in issue 29, gains "Cosmic Awareness." It's not exactly specific what that means except that it's a superpower. I felt like that jolt in the cab woke me up to what being in tune with the universe must be—following the chain of perception back into that tunnel so there's no longer a space between what you see and how you react. I could never explain it to adults in San Francisco because they, to a person, wanted to tell me about their acid trips. This was different. I didn't know why.

A WEEK OR SO after coming to Thacher, I stood outside the pay phones that lined the side of the dining hall. I was waiting to call my father, but I was also eavesdropping. Another kid who was new was trying to explain a word to his parents. "No, 'face.'" He said. "*Face*. Like, you're—uh—*faced*. You know?" A brief pause—obviously the person on the other end of the phone didn't know what he was talking about. Just saying "face" repeatedly hadn't helped.

He tried again: "When something goes wrong, like when you think something and it turns out not to be true, only you had a lot riding on it—we'd say *face*. Only, it would be like, *faaaaaace*, because you'd be faced." Pause. "No, it does make sense. But I guess you kind of have to be here. It makes sense when you're here."

I sympathized. When I talked to my father or my mother, I couldn't explain this place. Plus, I was having trouble talking to my father anyway. I could not sleep most nights. I had stolen $186.

The problem was, even though I'd moved from San Francisco, I'd brought myself with me. I felt guilt. At night, instead of sleeping, I looked at the ceiling and I plotted the pathway from my room to the pay phones. I'd have to wait until after eight in the morning or so, to be polite. It would need to be a collect call. I would tell my father everything.

But every morning when I woke up I realized I was being ridiculous. I'd made an investment using my own money, right? Those comics were going to be more valuable than those bills ever would be, and years from now my father would applaud my foresight. Except that I had broken the covenant that held us together. Except he had broken it first. Except I was using that as an excuse to try to not feel bad.

These thoughts didn't last very long in the daytime. There was too much to do. At a school assembly one morning, Dr. Chase, who had been the headmaster in the 1950s, got up to tell a story. It was an urgent one. He needed us to know that everything he thought he'd known while he was at Thacher was wrong.

Dr. Chase had been retired for a while. He'd been brought out that day to be a charming fossil, but fossils from Thacher didn't behave the way normal fossils did.

"I was in a bar in Manhattan a couple of weeks ago," he said, which was shocking enough to hear, then he backed up. When he was headmaster, before coeducation, Thacher bused girls from Emma Willard in for dances. It had been Dr. Chase's job to stand on the dance floor with a ruler, making sure Thacher boys stood twelve inches away from Emma Willard girls. Many years later, he was in a bar in Manhattan and he ran into a former student who had been his nemesis. There was one nemesis in every good class, he explained, "like in Milton." This one was kind enough in adulthood to buy Chase a drink.

"Did you know," the former student asked, "when you were on the dance floor with your stupid ruler? Do you know where I was? In your office. On your desk. With my girlfriend."

This caused our assembly to riot, which Dr. Chase took in quietly. It looked to me like he was curious what we were learning. *How simple your laughter is,* he was silently saying. Mine had a subtext: you never knew what was actually going on. There was always a way around the system. I liked this lesson.

Dr. Chase's story made me suspect abstract thinking might be rewarded here. Every day, among all the duties and homework assignments, Thacher presented you with a pile of unfinished material, threads of daily life, and it was up to you to decide what to make of it. As a freshman, there was little chance to do much—just trying to do my homework on time was hard enough—but as you cleared hurdles, slowly, you were given more free time to use, maybe wisely.

I saw seniors smoking cigarettes and arguing on the Putting Green after dinner. They talked to girls. They knew how to arrange weekend dances. They dressed in tweed vests and frayed Brooks Brothers shirts that they'd stolen from their brothers' laundry hampers. They lived life of *sprezzatura*, elegance without effort, an art history term I learned my first semester.

I wanted to know the same ease they did. Seniors understood music in a way that made me feel queasy and small. The first time I was in Ken Everett's room—a senior—I could not take my eyes off his satin-gloss Technics amplifier or his speakers, which were tall enough to be end tables. I still had the Panasonic all-in-one I'd had since I was ten, and the receiver was built into the base of the turntable, and the speakers were as crushable as Coke cans.

The music I heard coming from seniors' rooms was incomprehensible. It was Roxy Music and Traffic, Stanley Clarke and the Grateful Dead, jazz I'd never heard of, and Frank Zappa sometimes. The only thing the songs had in common was a sense of jaded exhaustion that the seniors had managed to embrace by the age of seventeen.

I longed to be jaded, but the problem was that someone preferred me dead.

The freshmen boys lived in Middle School, a handsome Arts and Crafts shingled dorm in the center of campus. From memory, from north to south, six rooms housed the following boys: Cliff, Heitz, Flohr, Herron, Sparrow, Robbins. It turned out that Mr. Shagam, a faculty member fond of wordplay, had done the room assignments. So upstairs, again in a row, Pinkham, Brown, Brown, and Dunne. Of course, I was in that row, but more to the point, I had a roommate. I cannot imagine the cry of joy Mr. Shagam must have let loose when he realized they had incoming freshmen named Glen Gold and Francis Fish.

There weren't supposed to be roommates, but the class of '81 had overbooked, so some of us had to double up. I was the youngest in the class, Frank the oldest. I was from San Francisco; he was from antipodal Newport News, Virginia. I was perhaps the least experienced horseman, Frank had his own saddle. I was Jewish; Frank hated Jews. Rather, he was under orders from his mother to get a single room at any cost (I was actually standing next to him during this conversation, as at least one of them thought I was too stupid to understand what she was saying), and so a quick course of anti-Semitism seemed to him to be the best way to accomplish that.

One time, I was struggling to stand up while Frank was grabbing my wrists and trying to force me to my knees. He was saying, "Go on, tell me that Israelis are passive pussies. Say it. Say, 'Israelis are passive pussies.'"

I did collapse to the floor but I didn't say it. He got bored and went on to doing something else. More than anything, I was shocked by his choice of insults—the Israeli commandos had just rescued a planeful of hostages; clearly there had to be more stinging ways of making fun of being Jewish. It was clear even he didn't really believe it—it was just the first tool at hand.

If I seem more exasperated than threatened, that's about right. Frank was mediocre at being a bully—I could tell that his heart wasn't in it.

I had a terrible, stinging crush on Debbie Taylor, who was from Montana, who knew everything about horses, and who was a better student than I was. I used to write and tear up letters to her, and on rainy days I sat in the window and imagined what it would be like to listen to ELO's *New World Record* with her. One afternoon, Frank came into our room and shook the rain off his hat and told me I might want to put on some sad music instead—he recommended the *Best of Bread* or anything by David Gates—because Debbie had just started going out with an expert horseman with whom I could never compete.

I thought Frank was taking the opportunity to tease me, but it turned out he was a romantic. He shared his Doritos with me. He told me dirty jokes and then he became serious. "You and me, we're not like other guys," he said. "We respect girls—everything about them. I hate it when my heart gets broken." I was amazed but it was also nice to have him on my side.

He was also helpful a couple of weeks later. I had a crush on Kirsten, who before realizing her mistake had held hands with me on a school trip to a production of *Arsenic and Old Lace*. "No, you shouldn't write her a letter telling her how you feel," Frank said. I also had crushes on Rachel, who was an artist, and Jean, who was one of eleven children and who lived to argue about things. If you were a girl and you talked to me when I was a freshman, I was interested in being your boyfriend.

Six weeks into the first semester, I came back from dinner to find a strange person in the room. I recognized him instantly: John Spencer, a senior. He was sitting on the radiator, window open, smoking, one of those privileges reserved for seniors. Finding a senior in my room was like finding a yeti. My first thought was that I was about to be killed.

Spencer was strange, donnish like an Oxford scholar. He kept his own hours, tending to cook late meals in the student kitchen by himself. A Prince Valiant haircut, a slack body that didn't walk so much as stumble forward, floppy hands that always held a Player's Navy Cut, which had the most nicotine in any commercially processed cigarette.

Whenever rules were explained to me, Spencer was cited as someone who had found an asterisk. He didn't play lacrosse or have a horse—he took fencing lessons. All of his classes were AP or independent studies. He'd computerized the seating arrangements for formal dinners. Somehow Spencer kept getting seated, week after week, next to the prettiest girls in school.

"Gold, right?" That cigarette was certainly not allowed in a freshman's room. He was watching me and taking in how I was taking him in. Finally he took out some sheets of paper. It was dot matrix, two hundred rows of names and numbers.

"The administration asked me if I could computerize the grading system, so I did," he explained. "They don't know what a back door is. These are everyone's grades."

It was like being handed plutonium. Nothing he had done so far suggested I wasn't going to be killed.

He continued. Here was the freshman class, by rank. I had the fourth-highest GPA. "Eric Heitz has the highest grades, but he's a fac brat—he knows how the system works. The second highest is Debbie Taylor, and I think she does it by studying hard. She's the one you have a crush on, right?"

"How—"

"Don't be dull. I have a crush on Heather Findlay, and she has the third-highest GPA. I have no idea why you have the fourth highest but it might be you're a genius. Are you?"

"I am," I admitted.

Ludicrous as that was, he still nodded. "Good. Who have you read?"

"Read?"

"What books have you read? You have atrocious musical taste— ELO? Come ON. Haven't you even heard of Rick Wakeman?"

I hadn't. And if I had, knowing what I know now, I would have shown him the door. Spencer was a fan of prog rock, music that didn't count unless it told a story about the Book of Lindisfarne, and used an eighteen-minute organ solo to do so. But he was passionate. He had a lot of books to recommend, too. Roger Zelazny, Walter M. Miller, Clifford Simak.

At some point, probably about now, the door slammed open and my prefect, Ken Everett, was standing there ready to shout. Smoking? Busted! Then he saw Spencer, and he was as confused as I had been. Seniors didn't fraternize with freshmen. But—recovering—Ken still shook his head. Spencer wasn't supposed to smoke in freshmen's rooms.

"Are you sure?"

"Yeah," Ken said. After all, only one of them was a prefect—Spencer technically had no responsibilities here.

Spencer tapped ashes out the window. He had a smile that it's hard to call anything other than smarmy, the kind of thing a super-villain withheld until the moment he was assaulting the hero's girlfriend.

Ken left. Spencer said he'd be keeping an eye on me, and then he helped himself to some of my Doritos. He left, too.

I was baffled, still. I'd half-thought I was about to be offered the keys to a secret society, and that hadn't happened. I heard the word "provisional" a lot because the first year of Thacher was a winnowing process. You were in the school but you weren't quite accepted as part of the landscape until an odorless, tasteless change had occurred. The school was so small there were no groups of jocks or snobs—you had to keep recombining with the same people throughout the day, first at breakfast tables, then in classes, then riding horses, then in study hall, then in the dorm, like reshuffling a deck of cards. You might be good at track but you probably also were trying out for *The Madwoman of Chaillot*.

This increased your chances of making friends. Alex Calhoun, who lived near me in San Francisco and who had the same glasses as I did, was a decent sort. Butch Cliff, a motocross champion at home, seemed to find my jokes funny enough to not dismiss me entirely. But no one was sure if he was meant to be here or if years from now he would struggle to explain to people how, for one semester, he'd gone to a place called Thacher, and it hadn't worked out. People might point at the one blurry photo of me in the yearbook and wonder what had happened to me, and no one would know the answer.

My guilt about the $186 was crushing me and on one particular night in my bunk bed, I focused on the ceiling and tried to explain myself silently to a stone-faced invisible judge: I was a kid. How could I be trusted with that responsibility? That interrogation was endless, full of fretting and tossing and turning.

The next day, Frank told the other freshmen boys that he'd heard me jerking off all night long. Suddenly, my problems with my father weren't important. Frank had hit on an almost perfect way of getting me ostracized. There was no argument I could make to get out of it. *You're accusing me of doing the thing that everyone does, you know the surveys, 97 percent of men say they masturbate and the other 3 percent lie.* I didn't say this aloud, as it would put me in the strange position of seeming to admit to doing the thing I'd actually stopped doing because I had a roommate, in order to never be accused of doing it. I was angry there were no points awarded for having had such restraint.

For a couple of weeks, my reputation was on a seesaw. I was sitting on a lawn with Kirsten, who blushed easily, who was forthright and had managed to befriend me in spite of my crush on her. I thought it would be a good idea, maybe a great cleansing, to tell her what Frank was saying about me. I was specific. I even used my own defense. I remember finishing up, "and the other 3 percent lie," and realizing with a flush that I had just made the type of mistake someone who'd been in a boys school for two years would make. I'd been talking to girls regularly for only a few weeks. Anyone could have told me you just didn't talk to girls about stuff like this.

I stammered a bit. "So, yeah, you think, maybe, uh . . . ?" as if that wasn't digging me in deeper.

Kirsten, blushing, "Yeah, I'd say the same percentage of girls are liars." And she looked away.

I mention this because I walked around that day thinking that after Frank Fish had attempted to ostracize me, I'd accidentally learned that girls *jerked off.* What other guys in my class had stumbled over this? None of them! Things were kind of horrible but I was also having the best day of my life, if only I knew how to get out of being harassed.

Late one afternoon, maybe a week later, I was tied into the bathroom in the upstairs hallway. I had gone in to use the toilet and Frank had lassoed the door shut and tied the rope to the railing across the hall, so I couldn't get out. He taunted me for a while then had something better to do, and he left.

Somehow, eventually, I managed to open the door enough to get about halfway out.

I saw Mr. Robinson, who ran the dorm, standing quietly in the hallway. He was an English teacher and a lacrosse coach, with a demonologist's Vandyke. He had an abrupt, dark sense of humor that I looked forward to one day being a good enough person to bear the brunt of. I should note that as I was pressing myself flat to get out, I wasn't crying or red-faced, just a little bit bored about how my day was going so far.

Mr. Robinson met my eye. It was an interested look. My first thought was that he could have untied the doorknob at any time. And he hadn't. But not because he was a bully. Something else was going on.

"How you doing?" he asked, not unkindly, as I squeezed myself through the door frame.

"I'm okay," I said.

"You sure?"

"Yep."

Finally, I was all the way out, my body a mess of abrasions. I looked at the lasso, which was still intact.

"Anything you need to tell me?"

I shook my head. I started to undo the rope, but he stopped me. "Next time, bring a knife. Don't be so nice to Fish." He padded away, all khaki trousers and penny loafers. He knew whose rope it was. I realized what had happened. He was seeing if I was the kind of person who could help himself.

"Oh, and one more thing," he said. He shook his head and with a sigh, as if he'd told me this a hundred times before, moaned, "*Shave,* for God's sake, Gold."

I was delighted.

Over Christmas I visited my mother, who was living in New York. We stayed together in a hotel near the Empire State Building in advance of a Christmas that Trevor had planned for all of us. He was supposed to call and give us instructions about where we were meeting him. Mom took me shopping at Bloomingdale's, where I bought a tin of Famous

Amos chocolate chip cookies and, because it amused us both, she also bought me a Famous Amos baseball cap.

When we got back to the hotel, Trevor hadn't called. No matter—she and I went to the movies. We went out to dinner. She took me to bookstores and candy stores. We got cheesecake from Lindy's. Back to Bloomingdale's. Still no phone call.

She went to the hotel window often, looking at the street outside and I could see in her face that look she got when working through a feeling of almost sublime unfairness. She didn't deserve this, and yet it was happening to her.

I told her stories of Thacher. In late October I'd been on a weeklong camping trip, a forty-mile loop through Mineral King in the Sierras. We'd done the first thirty-eight miles, saving the last two, a climb over something awful called Sawtooth Pass, for the last day. But at four in the morning it had started to snow, and by daybreak there was over a foot of snow on the ground, making Sawtooth impassable. So we turned around and hiked the thirty-eight miles in a blizzard, without proper snow gear. Since it had been my first camping trip ever, I thought all camping trips were like that. I'd gotten frostbite in two toes. I'd only learned this when I tried to thaw my foot in front of a fireplace and my sock had caught fire, but I couldn't feel it. It sounded terrifying, and it was, but there was something fun in getting to say I'd survived it.

She tried Trevor again, to no response.

I tried to make her laugh. I told her about my English teacher, who was a dwarf, and who had nude photos of herself in her house, and who taught us grammar lessons based on her own unpublished novel. I could tell my mother wasn't actually hearing me. "One of the photos," I said, "is of her on a trampoline." I hadn't seen that photo, or the others, but there were rumors. Boarding school, it turned out, had truly heroic rumors.

But my mother was looking right through me. She found a pay phone, fed it dimes, got the answering service.

One night after Christmas, she called me into her bedroom in the suite—I brought with me the book I was reading, her gift to me that described the history of comic books. My mother was propped up on pillows in her gown, phone on the bed with her. She asked if my book had anything in it about Garth.

"Garth was a comic strip I used to read when I was a little girl," she said. "All I remember is that he was a strong man who'd been called away somewhere and who promised he was coming back home to rescue everyone. It never happened, not in my life at least. I had to learn not to believe those promises." She sighed.

I looked in my book, and yes, there it was, an entry on a British comic called Garth. She looked at it. She said that her father had been gone so long when she was little that it had shaped all her life since then. She had learned to wait for men. She didn't know why she couldn't learn anything else.

"When you were little," she said, "I never read you fairy tales. Do you remember that? I didn't want you to think anyone would rescue you."

On New Year's Eve, she wanted to go out in the crowds but she also didn't want to miss a phone call, so we sat in the room together. It was overheated in an East Coast way that was beginning to become familiar to me, and Mom wore a festive red turtleneck. I had a pile of gifts she'd bought that week, books by Kurt Vonnegut and a gigantic Hershey's Kiss that must have weighed a pound. As we waited together, I read and I hacked at the Kiss with a butter knife to break off manageable bites. Trevor never came.

I felt bad for her, because of a detail I haven't mentioned. I don't know when I learned of this fact. If I learned it before the trip, I felt sorry for my mother in a certain way, and if I was still ignorant of it then, I felt sorry for her in another, more naive way. Trevor was living with someone else. My mother explained this to me as if the woman were a gangster and she had a knife to Trevor's throat. It was terrible for him, he didn't want to be living with her but there was some circumstance that was forcing this to happen. My mother explained his agony, and then the details of what sounded like house arrest for Trevor, but the more I listened the less I heard. At some point in the near future, just a few weeks, he would be free, she said. It's a hard thing to describe. I believed her, but I was also beginning to tune to different stations. I was fading away while she talked.

At midnight, we could hear cheers and she was sitting in the window, peering through the curtains, and I could see the city lights reflecting on her face, which was beautiful. "I'm almost forty-three years old," she said softly. "How much longer do I have to put up with this?"

Maybe I knew about the other woman, in which case that question struck me as hopeless. Maybe I thought Trevor was unattached, but in that case the question was still hopeless to me. In either case, while hugging my mom, being funny for her, something had changed—part of me, an ember, frightened me with its wayward travels into the possibility of ignition. I thought there was an answer to her question, in that she didn't have to put up with it at all. But here she was, choosing it. This was the part that did not sympathize.

A couple of freshmen didn't come back after vacation (and for them, the single Thacher yearbook on a shelf, or in a garage, is the kind of mystery that defines adulthood). This meant there was a room free. When I returned to school, my new spot, a single room, was directly across the hall from a boy named Ronald.

Ronald was friends with Frank, which meant he was a problem. But he had little use for anti-Semitism. Instead, he didn't like me because I was weak. Ronald had a face pockmarked like a battlefield, and a perpetual sneer, and terrible grades that would eventually get him kicked out of school. But not yet.

I had returned from break feeling melancholy. After visiting my mother, I'd seen my father and Ann and my new half-brother, Seth. I don't remember my first impressions, but shortly after seeing Seth I decided I didn't need to tell my father about the $186. Guilt subdued.

At Thacher I wore my Famous Amos baseball hat and a silver Porsche racing jacket that was a gift from Trevor. These got a few chuckles. I was starting to make a name as a kid who was odd, but there was good odd and bad odd, and no one cared enough yet to make the distinction about me. It was a strange sort of low, in that I technically had three homes but no one in any of them cared much about me.

Ronald was bigger and more determined than I was, and there was nothing I could do to stop him if he wanted something from me. He would steal bags of Doritos, say he'd pay me back, and then that would never happen.

One evening, he opened my door and told me he'd heard I had the new issue of the *X-Men* and he wanted it. I have no idea how the following came to pass—either I put up some kind of real fight, given that this was a comic book and not just food, or Ronald made an offer outright. Thirty cents. Only he didn't have the money right then.

It was obvious what I should do. "You don't need to give me money," I said. "Trade me your soul instead."

He laughed. "Right."

"No, really. Take the comic. You won't owe me anything. Just your soul. Ha. Ha."

"What, you want me to be your slave or something?"

"No, nothing like that." I got out a yellow pad and handed him a pen. I dictated: " 'I, being of sound mind, hereby bequeath my immortal soul to Glen Gold for him to do with as he so pleases. This contract will become binding upon my death.' " And I gave him a place to sign at the bottom.

"You don't have any control over me," he said, double-checking. "I'm not cleaning out your corral for you."

"It says 'upon my death.' "

He thought about it. Then he signed. I countersigned, handed him the comic book, and pointed at my door.

"So you don't want a quarter or anything?" he asked.

"Goodbye," I said, as calmly as possible. He chortled once and left.

Our prefect came by to make sure we were in our rooms at ten p.m. Lights out was 10:30. Around eleven, I was awakened by my door opening. It was Ronald. He had the comic book in hand. He told me he hadn't read it, it was in perfect condition, and he wanted to give it back.

I said sure.

"So we'll just get rid of that contract," he said, carefully.

"No. That's done," I said. "Your soul is mine even if you give me back the comic book."

"Don't be a dick. Here, take the comic."

"The pact is made."

Ronald told me to go fuck myself, and was on his way to searching my room, but by then the prefect was already standing in the doorway. He asked what the hell Ronald was doing. No answer, just a death stare. He left.

When I came back after school the next day, my room had been turned upside down. The sheets were off the mattress. My drawers had been rifled through. A couple of guys were in the hallway, alert that something was going on. You just didn't mess up another guy's stuff.

I went to Ronald's room with a small crowd around me.

"Is this what you were looking for?" I handed him the contract. He tore it out of my hands.

He did two things at the same time: announce that he didn't care about it, that I was some kind of freak and he didn't care about me either; he tore up the contract.

Then I showed him the photocopy I'd made. Well, one of the photocopies.

Within a day, the whole school knew I'd bought Ronald's soul, that he was weak enough to want it back, and that I was tormenting him. After a few days, I let Ronald buy it back for two dollars, and afterward, maybe strangely, he had a small respect for me. I never got bullied again.

A few days later, I came back from the stables to find something strange in my room. There were four seniors in it, John Spencer and three I barely knew—Ross and Jaime and Steve. They were sitting on my bed and on my chair, feet up, reading comic books. My mother had given me a five-pound canvas bag of peanuts for Christmas, and the bag was open, and there was a pile of shells on my bed. I'm not sure that any of them looked up at first; they were having a conversation that didn't include me. So I just listened.

Finally, Spencer said, "Is it true that you bought a kid's soul for a comic book and sold it back to him for five dollars?"

It was true enough. I nodded.

Spencer wanted to know all the details. How had I worded the contract? I showed him one of the copies I'd made. He read it aloud. "Have you read *Black Easter* by James Blish? Never mind, you'll never find a copy but I have one."

Ross said, "Oh, God, here we go."

"You should read the sequel, too." In a few minutes, Spencer had specified five or six trilogies I needed to read. I should read books by Larry Niven except where Jerry Pournelle was his coauthor. He wanted to know if I had plans for my junior year yet, as there was an exchange program with Andover, where the girls were hotter, and a smart person would start planning to apply now.

Spencer had been looking to mentor someone. Ross and Jaime and Steve made fun of him for it. He'd been talking about this all the previous year. There were so many secret spots on campus to know about, places to take girls, he figured, though that was still theoretical. But then there was the occult: Had I gone to the Krotona Institute yet? It was home to Krishnamurti, the messiah of the Theosophists and it was the largest occult library outside the Vatican. And it was walking distance from downtown Ojai, he said.

At some point, there was a knock at the door and Frank Fish appeared. He looked startled. I think he was going to kick my ass for what I'd done to Ronald, but when he saw the seniors there, he did a perfect three-sixty—started to retreat, then got a better idea of how to screw me. He stayed. He tried to joke with the rest of them, to moderate effect. Then he said, casually, "Surprised you're hanging out with this guy after I caught him jerking off like that."

Dead silence. But not from anything dire. Just . . . no reaction. Ross shucked another peanut. "What the fuck would you say if you were *my* roommate? Jesus."

Frank was ignored. Seniors, it turned out, were much more Realpolitik about this kind of thing. But Spencer understood why Frank brought it up. As Frank was about to leave, embarrassed, Spencer stopped him.

"Frank? *Face*," he said.

Ross agreed. *Faaaaaace.* The rest of the seniors joined in.

So that is the story I told my father when trying to explain the meaning of the word "face." He understood. It got a laugh. My work was done. Time to move on.

NO LONGER AT THIS ADDRESS

I BEGAN THIS MEMOIR by saying I have become autonomous. It's not like I arrived, stepping off a boat and onto a bedrock land whose maps all promised a certain *distance*. Much as I like stories of immediate transformation, the bond between a child and a mother doesn't work like that. Mom and I had estrangements and reconciliations, sometimes fueled by that feeling so deep it felt mercilessly like genetic truth, that if only I jiggled the kaleidoscope one more time, I would love her.

There isn't a moment. There's an accumulation of moments.

Do you sweep them away because maybe there's another moment upcoming, the one that makes you realize you were wrong about all the prior moments? That's tempting if you have needs only a mother can provide. In other words, if you're human.

When I was thirty-one, she called me. She needed surgery to restore her hearing. There were possible complications and she worried she was going to die. So before the surgery I visited her and sat with her on her couch and she tried to understand why I distrusted her.

I shied away from saying things that might make her angry or defensive. I learned to speak from an acute angle to absorb the shock. Also, she had increasing difficulty understanding conversations. So communication was one-way, and prone to me finding the right moment to insert a word she might hear. I listened, then didn't listen, as her word avalanche swept down a hillside and I thought things like, "I am now the same age as she was when she began to get rich. Do I understand her better now?" My mind wandered. My mother was saying, "I never read you fairy tales as a child, you know. I didn't want you to think you had to rescue anyone," and then she was on to some other topic, citing the names of people I didn't know, or would know if I were better at paying attention.

I tried to get her to go back. She couldn't hear me. Her topics of conversation were now singing full speed down distant tracks. I was on my own.

I had thought it was "no one will rescue you." Had I spent my life having heard the opposite of what my mother said? Or was I the type of person who would disbelieve myself in her favor? Yes.

But I thought she might die, so I got forceful. I said a few sentences from the story I've just told: when I was twelve, I lived on my own for a while. I wanted to know why that had happened.

After I said this, it went dead quiet. She looked at me agape. She shook her head in horror. "No," she said. "No, that never happened. Never. I didn't leave you."

"But—you did. You got on a plane with Trevor and you called me from New York."

"Oh, no, no." She put her hands to her mouth. She had gone pale. "I would never do that. But I can see why you'd feel so strongly toward me if you think that happened."

This is why I can imagine her horror if she heard I thought I should save her. It's the same face. I was having one of those experiences where I was floating out of my body. For years, when I wrote scenes in which one person confronts another, I made him float, because I didn't know it was possible not to do that.

My mother didn't know what to say, but she felt sorry that my memory was so sour. She wondered why I remembered it that way. Still, the 1970s were strange times, she said, and she would have done some things differently if she knew then what she knew now. But most of all, she said, she did everything for me. She made all the choices about the men and the money to try to find me a good father figure.

For a week, I cross-examined myself. Had I made it up? Did I need to imagine that set of wild circumstances? Did I have to create a mother like that so that I could—what?—feel abandoned? Maybe I had to make up an origin story for myself.

Her ear surgery was successful, in that she lived. I'm not sure her hearing was restored. It was sort of hard to tell with her. A few weeks later, she got in touch and said she'd read over her notes, and what I'd said was true. She had left me, something she hadn't remembered until now.

I couldn't bear, again, the understanding that my mother believed deeply and exactly whatever allowed her to survive from one incident to the next. I didn't know what to say, so I said nothing.

She said, "I guess Mommy fucked up."

PLEASE FORWARD

IT'S RARE WE SEE OURSELVES in a life story that makes sense. But there are moments like, for instance, sitting in the back of a cab on Broadway in 1974, when a body falls against the chassis. I look up and am aware for the first time of a gap between when something happens and when I make words to describe it. That might be my birth as a writer. I don't have emotions so much as I describe them. That is how I was made.

My mother visited me at Thacher in the spring of my freshman year. I took her around the perimeter road. Here was the Outdoor Theater, constructed in the prior century from the white stone, *piedra blanca,* that was scattered around campus. Here was the horse they'd assigned me, Louis Houdini, who was so clever he could open the gates to the corral with his mouth. Back at the dorm, I told her about buying Ronald's soul and selling it back to him. Here was a copy of the contract. Funny, right? She agreed—mischief among boarding school students, rather what she'd expected of me.

It wasn't much of a tour, nothing to compare with what I'd grown up with, but I'd only been there a brief time and didn't have much accumulated yet. I had almost nothing—almost—to my name. She had to go soon, so that was okay, but there was one thing she had to take care of first.

We walked across the Pergola and into a room by the auditorium, where there were overstuffed couches facing a giant fireplace. I asked after Trevor, and I asked after Anton, whom my mother had started mentioning recently. Anton managed musicians. He was tall and handsome, an air force vet who spoke with eloquence about life on the road with talented, famous people.

Anton was under a lot of stress. A singer had canceled a concert and because of some technicality, Mom said, Anton was financially responsible for it. She said a very partial, almost biased judge had frozen his assets. Mom was hoping to help him get back on his feet.

It was hard to follow this story, which had more odd details than I remember, but I felt bad for Anton. It wasn't clear to me what he had become to my mother, but it did seem that life in New York was harsh, especially for people who lived by their dreams. My mother had confidence in him, and she believed that in the near future, maybe only months, he was going to organize a college tour of musicians that would get him out of this fix.

She had an errand. Concerned and responsible, sitting on a couch, opening her purse, bringing out a manila envelope. I know she made whatever she was wearing look good. She had been a model, remember, and she had a flair that made anything simple look elegant. She used to sing to me when I was a child, "Moon River," and when I had ear infections she would stay up all night, listening to me howl in a pain she felt miserable about since she could not ease it. When I was four, she led me through the tide pools and she slipped, knocking loose her front teeth, so her very smile was traumatized by being a mother to me. When she asked me for a favor I wanted to do it.

She had put me into adventure and danger without knowing the difference. She had let me sit with the adults and the freaks. Because of her, I had an education. At fourteen, I was looking at her in a way children might never get to see their parents. I was evaluating her. I was thinking, *She looks nervous. She looks awkward. She knows this is wrong to ask.*

She fanned out some documents allowing her to cash in the corporate bonds that had been earmarked for college. My mother told me that the interest rate was paltry. If this money was freed up to invest properly, the return would be phenomenal. I would get every penny back and so much more. She sounded embarrassed. She sounded like she couldn't believe it had come to this, the world so unfair and chaotic, her being forced to turn to her only child with such a beggar's dilemma.

At the same time, she was embarrassed for an entirely different reason. She didn't believe what she was saying. She was already preparing for the moment where all my money would vanish. She was already feeling shame. When she talked, she sounded upbeat in the manner of a saleswoman who has memorized a brochure offering me great advantages for my future. Both the lie and the truth were true to her. Seeing that then *crushed* me, a shove in the chest so violent I barely felt it, if that makes sense. I took the pen.

I hated my signature. My first name came out the same way it had since learning cursive, so it seemed immature. My last name I always signed with a weak collapse of the capital G, exactly as my mom did. I disliked how it looked as if my name were a part of her in a way I wished it no longer was.

But when I signed I did it boldly. I did it to prove I was my own person, and I knew the real consequences. I told myself and my invisible audience exactly why I was doing it, as I was doing it. I was setting the record straight. My mother's world was populated by abandoned princes down on their luck and pitiless landlords. But it didn't have to be that way, not with your shoulder to the wheel and a little luck on your side. So simple, done, signed, here you go.

Our business was concluded, the ballpoint on the table, the sun not yet set behind Casitas Pass, the afternoon wind picking up and loosely shaking the burgundy-colored flakes around the pepper trees. My mother had not yet gathered up her things. Her flight back to New York was still ahead of her along with all the possibilities in the world.

Adulthood, I'm convinced, is among all those other measures when you can feel nostalgia and remorse at the same time. That's what I felt right then. I felt the urge to be where I was and somewhere else, also.

It would be so beautiful if I weren't here, I thought.

My mother gathered her stuff, I walked some part of the way with her, and then I hugged her goodbye.

Watching myself from a distance of decades, I'm waving to her as she leaves. My awareness, born in the back of a taxi cab, made real now: an event has happened and instead of feeling it, I am telling myself about it. I'm able to tell you about it, and sharing that strikes some tiny flint that may be visible from very far away. I have given her all I can and I'm sad it isn't much, a few thousand dollars, all I have to my name. Here's just a bit, Mom, a life raft and one burst of wind to make your trip a little easier. There is something terrible out there, I know. You're not really going to escape.

2

THE

COUNTERFEIT

CHILD

---

for Jason Roberts

My observation of people leads me to conclude, generally speaking, that even people with some degree of intelligence are likely to go through life supposing they have ample time before them. But would a man fleeing because a fire has broken out in his neighborhood say to the fire, "Wait a moment, please?"

To save his life, a man will run away, indifferent to shame, abandoning his possessions. Is a man's life any more likely to wait for him?

Death attacks faster than fire or water, and is harder to escape. When its hour comes, can you refuse to give up your aged parents, your little children, your duty to your master, your affections for others, because they are hard to abandon?

—*Essays in Idleness,* Kenko, 1332
(translated by Donald Keene)

REMAINDER TABLE

IN SUMMER 1983, when I was nineteen, I fell in love with a woman who swore she wouldn't love me. She let me know I would have to settle for learning from her about books and the classical arts and how to go to bed with someone without fussing about my heart. She would introduce me to the rules of how to live cleanly, perhaps poor as alley cats, but with cats' autonomy. She emphasized, however, that she would never actually want me.

I am however unpersuaded by people who say they don't want me, and this is where the story gets complicated. You could say I run hardest after the people who are running away. That's something I recognized about myself that summer. Another is that for reasons I didn't question I had an impulse to rescue women. Alas.

But before I tell you about who I became, I need to tell you about the person I no longer wanted to be.

When I graduated from high school in 1981, I was only seventeen. I went to college in the East for some reason. It's very possible I decided to go to Wesleyan because Mary Goodrich was going there, and she was cute. And then I was in Connecticut, which depressed me every day for not being California.

I can't explain why I was a Japanese Studies major. It might be that the classes fit my schedule, and in the classrooms I found cute girls to talk to (Mary Goodrich, it turned out, was uninterested). I wrote out Zen teachings in flabby Kanji. The more I smudged things like "The way of the sage is work without effort" the more angry I got, which I suppose is an illustration of irony.

I enrolled in a fiction-writing class. I wrote badly. There were only six people in it, and the rest of them quickly had enough of me. We met at the professor's house, in her living room, and she seemed to eye me in every session like I was about to steal an ashtray. I didn't know how to convince her otherwise, and the more vulnerable I made my fiction the more hatefully it read. There isn't much that causes people to recoil more than sensing someone wants to be liked.

September was humid, and so was October, and in November it kept getting colder in a way I wasn't familiar with, a brutal muscle-piercing cold, as if the weather actually wanted to kill us all, but people who understood seasons told me that it still wasn't winter. I was trying to fit in, so I raced some dorm mates down the corridors one evening. I didn't see a shelf sticking out of a wall, and I hit it nose-first. I'd broken my nose once as a kid, and I thought it was broken again. The next day I went to the campus doctor, who explained to me that it wasn't broken. If it were, he said, putting his hands on my face, he could break it back into place, like *this,* and there was an awful snap.

He was silent for a moment. Now I'd broken my nose three times. I don't remember that part as vividly as him telling the nurse to bring the pharmaceutical-grade cocaine.

When I left his office, I was numbed up (he made me sign some release forms after the blow submerged my brain). I had a cast on my face reinforced by surgical tape that went over my forehead and cheek-bones. I was confused. I had homework, and I was hungry, and I was supposed to buy some antibiotics at the drugstore, but I wasn't sure what to do first. I walked through Middletown as the sky darkened and the first snow of the season started to come down and stick. I was surrounded by Connecticut winter, finally—and when people saw me shuffling toward them, they crossed the street.

The cast stayed on for weeks. The tape dirtied and warped, holding on to every stray piece of lint and fuzz. I slept at odd times. I missed classes. I felt strange, like I was in a space suit that I didn't know how to take off. Other students learned that when I came into their rooms,

I tended to ask unanswerable questions, like if they ever felt alone even when other people were around.

Mom visited me. I'd invited her up from New York to see a concert, the Moody Blues, her favorite. One of my dorm mates had promised to give her a ride back to the city afterward, because there wasn't train service. But he disappeared, and I was unable to understand where he went. My mother needed to get home, which was a problem so insurmountable I couldn't function.

It's hard to explain what I thought about her then, or what she was going through. It might have been stability. My own semester had been dire enough that seeing anyone else's situation was almost impossible. I was so lonely that I called my high school friends, hours on the phone, long-distance, to hear voices that were familiar with whom I'd been beforehand. When I talked to my mom, it's not like my defenses were down—since high school I'd suspected something was wrong with her—but I had this faint idea that a young person who was having a rough time might reach out to his mom.

So we saw a concert together and the next day I had no way to get her back to Manhattan. I sat down on my bed, then I was lying on it, fully clothed, staring at the ceiling. I was familiar with difficult problems. I knew how to think my way through them. But now, my thoughts were going in circles. And then they were frozen in place.

I could feel how my boots gripped my feet too tightly. They were double-knotted, and thinking about the effort it would take to unlace them started to break me. My mother was sitting in a chair in the corner. I didn't know how to communicate to her that I was completely lost.

Mom got up, kissed me on the forehead, above the bandages. She took her things with her and, just like that, she left. Apparently she'd figured out how to get back to New York. She was resourceful. If I were the needy sort, I could have been upset, I suppose, but I didn't want to be around me, either. I didn't mind her leaving me. It felt familiar.

Then I was alone. I didn't move for a period of time I don't know how to define. I felt like the fabric onto which the day was sewn had ripped, and I was seeing through it into a void. The sky outside my window caught my eye, and I was unable to tell if it was dawn or dusk.

It makes no difference, I thought. *That's not a new sun. It's the same sun. It's the same, always.*

With this thought, I fell into an awful, hollow place that revealed an essential daily lie, that having a good spirit is enough. But in truth there are no feelings, just chemicals that make us feel things, and when the chemicals recede there is no solace. There is nothing.

The worst part was this had no air of discovery, but of return, like I'd known all this on an atavistic level. This was confirmation of something I'd glimpsed when I was awake in the middle of the night at six and seven years old. The terrors were real, but they weren't of an approaching burglar. The terror is that no one is approaching. I had touched nothing, which leaves a permanent mark.

It's not like anything specific brought me out of this. The awareness was always there as my nose healed up and the cast came off. Months went by. I was impatient. I didn't exactly recover socially, but I applied myself, pretending to fit in until my self-consciousness died down a bit. Spring helped a little. Sun on my skin.

I wasn't sure what the point of anything was anymore. I was thinking that if I were the protagonist of my own story (and I did think that way), it wasn't about coming-of-age—I'd done that already. But when I read in my Eastern philosophy classes about how life was mostly suffering I had a faint inkling now what they were talking about.

I joined Alpha Delta Phi, Wesleyan's literary fraternity, which was coed, and whose brothers and sisters terrified me with their sophistication. They wrote sestinas. They lived in apartments off campus. They took group showers and had mushroom trips and knew how to cook tofu and perform African dances. They spoke about professors by their first names, they hosted readings by Joyce Carol Oates and Trevanian and John Irving and there was supposedly old graffiti by Jack Kerouac in their basement, which they called a grotto. After readings, some of them snapped their fingers in place of applause and the rest gave tired but patient looks to the finger-snappers.

I wanted so badly for them to like me that I had to calm myself down. The writer Jim Carroll said there are two types of cool: the chimpanzee and the panther. The difference is the chimp has to keep working at it. I wasn't cool at all, but if I'd managed to get close to one sort, I was the chimp. And the panther—a mystery, and effortlessly so—was the right choice.

Be here now, I wrote, a lot. It was shorthand, a bastardization of Taoism, the kind of wisdom that would fit on a T-shirt or on the cover of one of my notebooks. It was supposed to keep me from feeling anxious or guilty, because those were emotions from the past and the future, two places not to live.

I was in love, by the way. Heidi was a Richmond, Virginia, Lutheran minister's daughter, which, if it's the first thing you know about her, unfairly suggests she was as horny as a drunken pirate. She was intoxicated by the idea of "know thyself." In adolescence, she said, she'd read books on teen psychology to anticipate the crises and emotional cul-de-sacs she was supposed to suffer through. She decided to avoid them by skipping straight to the mature outcome, a developmental shortcut she figured would save everyone time and grief.

"And it didn't work!" she cried, genuinely irked that her mind couldn't out-think itself. This made me love her. I judged her for giving up, though. I thought, "I could probably do it," the way I often did about things that someone said were impossible.

Heidi had the soul of a kindergarten teacher. She carried Crayolas and Scotch tape in her purse, had glitter on her nightstand, sewed her own Halloween costumes. There was no reason for her to stand up for this kind of domestic work publicly at Wesleyan, where feminism was cutting-edge in a humorless denim skort kind of way. Further, arts & crafts would be humiliatingly uncool at Alpha Delta Phi, gender-based uncool, multidimensionally less cool than finger-snapping, and yet she could not be persuaded out of it. She took over the wine and cheese parties, and added crayons and butcher paper.

But just as I was flinching, the coolest poet in the house, who was a lesbian that semester, closed her eyes and remarked on how the smell of Crayolas brought her to a beautiful, innocent place, and then everyone used the crayons. Safety scissors came out of hidden drawers. Heidi was a hit.

This should have been a lesson to me in the power of being yourself. Heidi was funny and she cared about me, and this shook away questions I'd been living with for a long time. Freshman year questions, like:

"Who am I?" and "Does anyone see me?" and "What happened to me after I broke my nose?"

One weekend, I brought Heidi to my mom's apartment in New York. Mom was in the midst of moving back to California, so we had the place to ourselves. We cooked, we saw a play, we were served drinks at restaurants, we took our room keys, which the university had stamped DO NOT DUPLICATE, to a bored locksmith on 72nd Street who promptly duplicated them.

My mother was moving, I told Heidi, because a great opportunity awaited, and fortune favored the brave, and it was make-or-break time. This seemed glamorous to Heidi and that made me believe it a little more myself. In a way, we were making an agreement: she was the one who was slightly sheltered, her parents still together, good church people; I was more worldly, and my mother was a little bit exciting.

In truth, I wasn't quite sure what was happening to my mother, except it was clear that none of her investments in her boyfriends—first Trevor, then Anton—had panned out. To me, her move to California was a way to restart her life without expecting anyone else would come through for her.

On the last night in the apartment, I stood behind Heidi in the living room, wrapping my arms around her and kissing her on the neck while she stared up at the wall. Here was the 1930s oil painting of George, my grandfather. I had seen it so often I could no longer see it clearly. I wanted to apologize for the figure peering out of a mire of history, enrobed in muddy colors, that cool white stare from a face that might be louche, judgmental, or campy.

Heidi said he was sexy.

I hadn't thought of that before, and it made me look at him again. I decided she was right—George *was* sexy. A sexual gaze broadcast desire or autonomy, and his was about autonomy. That thought—*I am autonomous*—was attractive. Long after we went back to school, I thought about it, and I thought I had an answer to those old questions about myself. *That's me,* I thought, or *That should be me,* which is different.

One Sunday evening just before I turned eighteen, in deep March, the kind of March unknown to me in California, high snowbanks behind

Olin Library and wind rattling empty bleachers, I stood still on the football field under arc lights singing with the strain of winter on them. I was listening. There had been a voice inside me my whole life that said "I can be happy when . . ." When I get published. When I have a girlfriend. When my mother is happy. When it's safe.

Safe? It was the streetcar theory. I'd read the first few pages of *The Master and Margarita,* and had concluded that if I declared myself happy, a streetcar would leap its tracks and smash me flat. But right then it occurred to me that Heidi was happy. Nothing bad had happened to her in response.

I unzipped my jacket and I stood for two or three minutes, feeling warm. I had just left rehearsal for a play. I was on my way to my dormitory, where Heidi was waiting for me. But I wasn't wishing I was at rehearsal or at the dorm. There was no "when." I wanted to be right here, right now. I couldn't name this feeling and wondered if it was what being happy was.

When I walked into my room, Heidi was reading in my bed. I wanted her to know how I felt, but I didn't want to cheapen it with words (for some reason I thought that actually explaining myself equaled cheapening). I took off my jacket and sat on the bed. I wanted to be *known.* I hoped she would see whatever this feeling of peace was that radiated from me, and I took her by the back of the head, brought her to me and kissed her.

When she came up for air, she said, "Thank God you kissed me. I thought you were going to strangle me."

I explained to her, quickly, no, no, it's this good feeling I have, but the more I talked the more it was like I was covering up a crime I'd accidentally committed. The more honest I was being, the more dishonest I sounded, and as my anxiety filled up the overheated dorm room, Heidi took on the hooded-eyed expression of my fiction-writing teacher.

There was a distance between how I saw myself and how everyone else did. This wasn't going to clear up easily.

I spent the summer between freshman and sophomore years living in my father's house in Brentwood, California. I worked at a Shakey's Pizza on 26th Street, in one of the less utopian sections of Santa Monica.

Duane, the assistant manager who hired me, was unimpressed, beginning with my application, on which I'd put WESLEYAN prominently as my current address. He concluded that as an intellectual, or something, I wasn't qualified to actually use the oven. So I made the pizzas and put the metal tags on them with the order numbers and they were shuffleboarded onto the burners by Martin, a surf rat with a dirty pelt of blond hair and the Santa Monica native's accent, afternoon-length *rrr*s that almost made him sound like he was from Missouri.

When Duane's back was turned, Martin let me put a pizza in, once. Two seconds later, I recoiled with a burn from the oven's lip already rising on my wrist.

"Don't worry, dude," Martin said. He showed off his forearms. They were shiny with welts. "You get used to it."

"Wow—that looks painful."

"Nah, bud, I take a Quaalude every day before work. I don't feel a thing."

This was the first job I'd had where my co-workers understood they had maxed out their earning capacity. There was a sense of fatalism in the air, as if everyone had paddled away from a sinking ship onto the island that was Shakey's Pizza, supplies were running low, there was no search party coming for us, and making pizzas and doing bong hits was only going to last so long before we ate each other.

I don't remember talking much. The others all had nicknames—Hoss, Dutch, Tango—but I didn't get a nickname. Whenever I added something to the conversation, the others tended to fall silent, as if they were trying to interpret how I was judging them. The fact was, I just wanted to fit in, and the baldness of this, too, probably made them fall silent.

After I'd been there two weeks, Duane pulled me aside. He whispered to me, eyes ducking left and right as if looking for eavesdroppers. "Wesleyan? My cousin just told me about that place. Wow."

I brightened. "Yeah."

"I mean, that's amazing."

"Yeah, well . . ."

"How'd you end up in an all-girls school, man?" He had such respect for me at that moment, and by extension for himself, for having known to hire me in spite of everything else I was. I could see in his eyes that he just *knew* I had stories of disdainful girls in English equitation outfits and tough, kilted lacrosse players and pledges in pink sweaters lining up, nails dug into palms with anticipation, outside a sorority house in whose chapter room, by candlelight, on a mound of silk underpants, I was the altar.

"That's Wellesley," I said. "I go to Wesleyan."

"Oh."

And just like that I was demoted again. I remember him walking away and me thinking, "Why am I that kind of person?" and wishing I'd just kept my mouth shut. How hard would that have been? The world would have been mysterious, bold, and a better place for both of us.

Wesleyan was humorless. The term "politically correct" was rumored to have started there, and in 1982 it was the front burner on which all discourse carbonized. One debate in the student newspaper was whether you could be a feminist and not be a lesbian, and the answer came down like a double-headed axe: No. No, you couldn't. The Feminist House changed its name to the Womonist House, there was a woman's history class for men called "Educating the Oppressors," and men took it.

Lust was male and aggression was male, and both were clearly *wrong*. And so, just as political jokes flourished in the Soviet Union during the Khrushchev era, Wesleyan turned out to have a hidden, spectacular misogynist humor.

Q: Why do women have vaginas?
A: So men will talk to them.

That was my second-favorite joke. My favorite was courtesy of a mean-looking junior named Dan, who took the villainous roles in the theater department. One evening, as we were about to go onstage in a play, Dan pulled me aside. Dan had never actually spoken to me before and I thought he had some kind of emergency direction for me.

He whispered, "How do you make a woman come?"

"How?"

"Who cares?" He shoved me through the curtain and onto the stage, dazzled. It was an old trick to fuck with your cast mates, and I was impressed, and from then on, I had a new favorite joke.

At Shakey's Pizza, orders started with #1 and went to #100 before going back to #1 again. When a pizza came out of the oven, any of the crew could go to the microphone and call it out. It was simple enough that Duane let me do it.

Except for one number. Every time, when it came up late in the rotation, there was a shoving match among four or five guys to grab the order and the microphone, and the winner would cry, "Calling Number *Sixty-nine*! Number *Sixty-nine*, please!"

Whoever won was looked upon as heroically as Alexander Pope pinning Dorothy Parker to a chaise longue, although I was probably the only person there who thought that. I never competed. I just quietly made my pizzas and bided my time, because I knew I could do better, somehow.

It was early August when I piped up, which meant there was still a month left for me to live with the consequences of trying to tell my joke. It also meant I'd been there long enough to understand my place if I'd been paying attention. It wasn't that I was shunned, or even looked down on. My job was to be the guy who was in college.

There were five or six of us in the kitchen, and though it was early in the shift, it was busy, so the calling of Number Sixty-nine had already occurred. My co-workers were in a postcoital drowsiness because of that. There was some attempt at joke telling. There was subdued laughter. I was listening, nervous, waiting to make my move.

"So! How do you make a woman come?"

There was silence. Martin was looking toward the ceiling.

Duane was clenching his brow. Finally, he said, "You play with the clit, right?"

"No," I said. "Who cares?"

Had there been crickets in the kitchen, we would have heard crickets.

Martin said, "I care, man."

"No, no," I said. "It's a joke."

"Tell it again," Duane said.

"I can't tell it again."

"Sure you can. Tell it again."

You can't tell a joke twice. It's like trying to chew the same stick of gum again. But: "Okay. How do you make a woman come?" As if enthusiasm would make it work, I shrieked it. But Duane was holding up his hand.

"Wait," Duane said. "Tango, Dutch, come on in here, Glen's telling a joke. Glen, wait, hold on for Tango and Dutch."

I looked down at my prep table, at the cold slices of pepperoni and mushrooms and green peppers, in other words at the actual tools of my actual job. "We don't have to . . ."

But Tango and Dutch were there, arms folded, waiting for me to speak.

"What's going on?" This was Deirdre, whom I haven't mentioned. She was the only one of us cute enough to work the counter, so she was rarely in the kitchen, except now, because she'd heard something great was about to happen.

"Glen's telling a joke," Duane said. "Okay, Glen, tell it again."

There was a ring around me. I was faced with expressions of serious intent, a group of refugees around a hand crank radio during wartime. Duane was utterly sincere, hand on his chin, waiting for the joke, so he could get it this time.

"I can't," I said.

There were cries and wails. I had to tell the joke. Come on! But I couldn't. I was red and shamed and I turned toward a phantom order as if it had to be made immediately.

"Okay." Duane sighed. "I'll tell it. How do you make a woman come?"

"How?" someone asked.

"Who cares?"

A spurt of laughter. Deirdre, who'd been drinking a root beer, coughed and hacked and as she recovered, she howled. "'Who cares?' Ha! That's so funny! What a guy joke!" Duane told the joke over and over, all night, each time getting fresh laughter as I glowered from the sidelines.

There, take a picture of that: that guy, the one standing behind the counter with his little paper hat on, the one who lacked courage, the one fuzzy around the edges, the one who wasn't quite himself yet, or prepared to defend who he actually was. That was the person I no longer wanted to be.

GENEALOGY & SCRAPBOOKING

M Y JOURNALS from then are punishing to read. I was self-centered, the kind who goes out of his way to show he is *not* self-centered, and thus struggling with why he's so distracted by his profile reflected in store windows. My notebooks are abattoirs for hundreds of pages of crossed-out, rearranged, gutted sausage casings stuffed with poorly raised fiction. Every word there mistakes clever for genius. My stories have characters named Upton, Ilyssa, Austin, Lamont, Marshall, names no actual parent has ever given a child, and the dialogue is arch, aging as badly as situation comedies with laugh tracks.

On the cover of my first journal, next to the Wesleyan University crest, is a list of books I read, with dates inked in to indicate when I'd finished them. Lies. I finished maybe one in four of those books. I recorded them thinking I would fool my older self, whom I apparently thought would be unscrupulous and forgetful.

But I can't hate everything there. The words also describe an attempt to be a better human being. I was still struggling to finish a sentence, like this: *I am the kind of person who* _____ .

"Write a scene," I wrote, "where it develops backwards—dialogue not spoken backwards, but each following scene actually precedes it, chronologically," along with a disappointed note that it turned out someone named Pinter had already done this.

I worried that I wouldn't remember the things I hadn't written down. I worried that what I was writing down were the wrong things. My emotions, I wrote, were the depth of a penny's edge. Among a lot of badly done Kanji, I set out rules for behavior, one of which was "You must be arrogant. Without being pretentious." If you are wondering whether I'd meant not "arrogant" but "self-confident," this is the remainder of that entry:

> Not self-confident. At the end of the night, self-confidence feels good enough about itself to take the bus home while arrogance is fucking self-confidence's girlfriend.

I'm not sure how I meant this arrogance to fit with my simultaneous urge to radiate a Zen master's calm.

I started taking notes on things beyond myself, as my family suffered a tragedy. I wrote on March 10, 1983, that my mother's older sister, Rosemary, had died in England.

Rosemary had washed down a handful of Valium with gin, which the coroner recorded as an accidental death. The family wasn't saying "Valium with gin" aloud, much less speculating how that could have happened. My mother suspected they were being British and more discreet than she wanted them to be. She hinted that Rosemary had spoken darkly of how depressed she was. What was an accident, anyway? I had only met Rosemary a few times, so the news came with oddly syncopated echoes: I was sad, I hardly knew her, I was sad for the people who loved her, I pretended I knew her better and that her death meant more to me than it could. There is a shameful feeling in adolescence where you make fictive kinship with the victims of terrible news, a way of feeling excited without the pain of actual involvement. Jeremy Leven in *Creator* calls it "keeping the marquee lights flashing." A kinder way to say it is that I had never suffered a close loss and this was my way of trying to feel something.

I'd already taken to answering friends' questions by saying, "I was raised by wolves." But Rosemary's death reminded me that I did come from somewhere. Mom's family myth was about potential, and it was a complex one. It was as if each child were taught, along with how to tie her shoes, and not to make crumbs when she ate, that she should always keep her hopes up, and know they would never be realized. Something would reliably hunt down your dreams and kill them. But still, chin up.

I have a typed history my mother gave me, a hundred or so single-spaced pages transcribed from nineteenth- and twentieth-century notes. It's a catalogue of all the fortunes the family made by hard work then lost by disaster or betrayal or profligate offspring. (A startling number of officials, shifty bankers, and ugly merchants who did us wrong are identified as "no doubt Jewish," which makes me wonder how accurate the rest of it is.) It seemed like we were cursed, and our only inquiry was whether we could break free of it, and the answer was obvious to everyone: We would never be free. So don't struggle. Chin up.

When Rosemary died, I realized: *I am a person who is 50 percent made up of this.*

It was spring break sophomore year and I was staying at my father's house. He was doing well, working for Atlantic Richfield in their solar division, where he claimed he was in charge of a project to sell the sun to the Arabs. (My father was the kind of engineer who had an engineer's sense of humor.)

A few days after I learned about Rosemary's death, I met my mom for dinner at a restaurant nearby. An old friend of hers was going to join us and as we waited for her, my mother told me about her current situation.

I can't remember when I started referring to my mother's "situations," but the word was meant to indicate something transitional, a way station ill-suited to her but certainly not of her choosing. I'd been using it long enough that I didn't think twice to use it now.

Mom needed a neck brace. She had been doing laundry at a Fluff and Fold, and had stood up into the dryer door. She needed to see a doctor, but couldn't quite afford it. However she had been to a lawyer, who thought she had a good case for suing the laundromat, so things were looking up, she said. She tested me with a glance to see if I thought they were looking up, too.

She had a business plan, but it was on hold for now. In the meantime, she didn't want to type and file for a living. She wanted to work in sales, phone sales preferably, so she wouldn't wear out her shoe leather. Her English accent was something she'd learned that people responded to.

But she hadn't landed that kind of job yet. She was working at *a* job, an office job, but not *the* job, driving there in a terrible car she'd bought at a police auction with brake lights that were always on, one door unworkable. For now, she said, everything was a compromise, there were sacrifices to make in the short term for her greater ambitions.

"Bear says hello," she said.

My mother was dating a man named Bear. I'd met him once. He wore aviator shades, cargo pants, and a bandanna neatly folded into a headband. He lived in Long Beach, by the oil derricks. He told my mother he was a deposed Samoan prince, which she repeated to me in wonder, but even I recognized the ink on his arms as Mexican gang tattoos. When I went to the beach with my mother and Bear, who was very polite, and who didn't ask me any questions, but instead talked about the ways karate could make me a better person, I was thinking, "My mother is under stress. When she's not in this situation, she'll be calm enough to see this clearly."

Jen arrived at the restaurant. She and my mother hugged. They had met in the 1960s, when my parents had bought an apartment building as an investment and Jen and her then husband had managed it while setting up their own businesses. It had been a good arrangement—though my parents were in a better position than their friends, there was enough prosperity for everyone. Jen and my mother both got divorced, and for a while they'd been two attractive women with money and options.

I liked Jen. She was pretty and funny and cautious, a little conservative, maybe what an anchorwoman was like off-camera. She often told stories about men, one eye on me to see if I might learn how to treat women right. She was a successful banker now, and that was often a problem. I remember her saying, "You go out with a guy, he realizes you're driving a Mercedes, and that's when the competition starts, but he doesn't want to admit he's uncomfortable so soon it's all, 'Hey, Flat Stuff, what happened to your tits?'" This was addressed to my mother at first but she was also looking at me with a faint smile, and I thought, "Yes, I will never insult a woman's tits, especially if she's making more money than I am."

I can tell you what Jen was wearing that night: a couple of elegant pieces of gold jewelry, sandals, white linen slacks, a striped silk shirt unbuttoned a bit too much, as if it was still the 1970s. I remember her outfit because it was the last time I saw her.

I don't remember what my mother was wearing, but her makeup would have been immaculate. She was just as stylish as Jen as long as you didn't notice how her fingers drummed on her pocketbook like she was tapping out a message to assuage unknown forces.

Jen asked me about school. I told her about my Japanese classes, and she was quick to leap past the philosophy and language and into how smart I was to study Japanese from a business perspective. It showed foresight, she said, and she was now looking from me to my mother.

"How's the job search," Jen asked.

My mother said she was working and she had a job. It wasn't ideal, she was doing more secretarial work than she wanted, but she knew there was opportunity to take on more responsibilities if only she could get over this hump. Her boss, Ken, was too demanding. He found flaws in her when she was actually helping him more than he knew. She would do work after hours to help out and he never acknowledged it. Sometimes he yelled at her and she could smell alcohol on his breath. He was writing bad checks and asking her to sign them. He'd stopped paying her a salary. After he lost his apartment he'd started living in the office.

What was so different about this story this time? Only that I was seeing Jen hear details accumulate until they formed a kind of teetering stack.

When the check came, Jen took it. "Pay me back when you get a job," she said. I thought this was kind. Then I saw my mother's expression. It was a nonexpression, her face caught between one reaction and another.

"I have a job," she said.

"But he isn't paying you."

"He will. It's just a crunch right now."

"You want a more steady job, right? What about being an executive assistant? There are benefits you could use."

"It's important to keep your options open," my mother said.

"What sort of salary are you looking for?" Jen asked.

"Commissions," my mom said.

"Just get an office job," Jen said. "What's wrong with that?"

It was the kind of question I didn't know the answer to. I knew my mother would have an answer. But she was just staring at Jen with a half-defended expression, like she was going to run or strike her if necessary.

"I know you don't want secretarial work, I know it's boring, but it's safe. Do that while you look for other work. Okay?"

My mother had a friend who cared about her, I thought. But my mother's eyes flicked from Jen to me, and she realized she was sitting with not one enemy but two. She said nothing.

When dinner ended, my mother led me to her car. She tried to open the passenger door, having forgotten it didn't work, and then she had to open it from the inside. We both got in. She put her key in the ignition. We sat quietly and I wondered what it was like at the beach right then. It wasn't a cold night and the stars were out.

My mother exploded. She slammed the palms of her hands against the steering wheel over and over. "How can people be so ungrateful when you give them a piece of your soul?" she cried. "She doesn't know what it's like to take dictation when you're almost—almost—" She heaved and sobbed.

"Fifty?" I was only trying to be helpful, but she looked at me like I'd stabbed her.

"Jen loves to give advice," she said. "It's why she can't get a man. She's too aggressive," she declared. It was a condemnation, an underlining to Jen's flaws. "She's always asking me why people think she's a dyke," she yelled. "Well, now you know!"

We sat like that for a while, my mother sobbing, and me feeling the urge to get to the beach so strongly I could barely stand to be in the car. I was feeling this dire force, dark as angels, pulling me out of my body. I saw myself on a beach, swinging a golf club at the sky, driving a ball up the coastline. I'd never held a golf club. I wondered where you could get one late at night.

"She thinks she knows better than I do. The typing pool. She wants me to work in the typing pool," she said. She was wiping her nose, blowing it, her eyes at once hard and watering.

I was supposed to drive with my mother from here to Long Beach, forty-five minutes on the freeway, and then I was supposed to stay with her overnight. Then wake up in the morning at her apartment and spend the day. This was like imagining holding my breath while diving under a glacier.

I no longer thought that if I were smart and empathic enough, I could come up with a comment that would make adults laugh in any situation. Instead, I started to say something that I'd learned in my Eastern philosophy classes, as it struck me as helpful. I said the cessation of desire could be a key to happiness. When it came to courting enlightenment, there was a wisdom, I said, in *acceptance*—

She said, "Never borrow money from a friend. They think they own you."

Then she started the car and drove, jerkily, brake lights on. Along the way, she told me details of her debt to Jen, a crummy, lousy four hundred dollars that I didn't want to know about.

She stopped at my father's front door, which hadn't been the plan. This was awkward. I was relieved we weren't on the way to her house and I felt guilty because of that. Pausing here, or maybe stopping here— there was a difference—was to give me a choice, I understood. She said carefully it was okay if I didn't come with her.

I said I thought she might need me.

She told me not to come. She said she could be fine without me.

Was I going to lean into this permission? She needed to hear a response. In my mind I was running, and I could see palms by the cliffs of Santa Monica in my mind, and I could imagine the sweat running off me as I flung myself at oblivion. Golf club. Sand fanning out when I drove it against a ball.

"I could come," I said.

Her eyes almost clicked as they swept back and forth across mine. "Next time," she said. When I came back from school in the summer, I could come down and visit. That would be better for her, actually, now that she thought about it. Really? I asked. Yes, she said, sure, her business would be up and running more, and there would be more to do. Plus she would pay me five dollars an hour then, she could afford that. We could make a weekend out of it.

So I said, "Okay." "Okay," I thought, was a word that meant *acceptance*. I hugged her goodbye.

She left me at the curb, and as she drove off I could hear the sound of an axle scraping like a knife sharpener.

No matter how long your parents are divorced, the transition between them, even the steps across a well-trimmed lawn, past a swimming pool, feels like a trip in a bathysphere. In those seconds I was thinking about Lao Tzu. I was trying to understand the difference between feeling acceptance and feeling nothing. When I closed the door inside my father's house it was like my ears might pop.

My father already had a low opinion of my mother. I didn't want to tell him how the evening had gone. But here I was, about to start talking to him for reasons I didn't understand.

When I'm confused or I know I'm missing the key point of a story, or when I question my own perceptions, my explanations come out backward. I seize on details that mean nothing and then I try to make them spring to life with meaning. I am trying to find a perch from which I can seem like I'm not ignorant.

In the kitchen, leaning against a counter while my dad thumbed through mail, I half-explained what had happened, and then wondered how he was taking in what I said, then tried to adjust what I was saying so that he wouldn't think poorly of me or Mom, and then I wasn't talking for a while.

I tried to wrap up.

"I guess she'll muddle through," I said.

He said, immediately, "Into another muddle."

"You don't know that."

"People don't change," he said.

I wanted to challenge this. He'd changed since marrying Ann. Maybe he understood that me not bringing that up was a kind of loyalty to him. He and I would not notice, together, how he was gruff and impenetrable in a way he hadn't been when I was growing up.

My dad was, with exceptions we'll get into, good with money. He wanted me to be good with money, too, and he often said aloud he worried I would inherit my mother's sensibilities rather than his. So he tried to teach me things at moments like this.

"Your mother lacks self-awareness," he said, then nothing more. With that, he was back to the mail. Lesson over.

This means something, I thought. I tried to absorb it like modern poetry or koans, until it bypassed my brain and sank into my body. Be here now. I felt heat on my face. My father was saying my mother was in this muddle because of *her*. Not because of fate or curses or the cruelty of her bosses and boyfriends.

I wanted to argue about that. My mother had had a terrible run of luck, I thought, and blaming her seemed like tying an anvil to her when she needed sympathy. I didn't argue. I went up to my room instead.

This was a few days before my nineteenth birthday. I already knew to never have a character in fiction stand in front of a mirror, because people never look at themselves in real life in the evaluative way authors need characters to do it. However I did look in the mirror then to confirm I was no more and no less handsome than I'd been earlier.

Rosemary had taken Valium with gin because—maybe—she saw no way out of being herself. If depression is blackness, does it fall on the end of the spectrum where you lack all self-awareness or have entirely too much?

Here was an avatar: Heidi, reading psychology texts to get ahead of all that ridiculous work an uninformed mind had to do, so she could be more efficient at being human. My classes in Eastern philosophy bubbled with parables about simpletons, dough heads, who were unable to see the light. But sometimes enlightenment hits you like the crack of a stick, subitism. I had a plan. The pathway to happiness for me was to, unlike my mother, become completely self-aware. Self-awareness would lead to tranquility—no, start with tranquility, then let self-awareness settle in. I would be exactly the person I was capable of being.

I would spend the whole summer trying, if necessary, but I thought it wouldn't take that long.

THE NEXT MORNING, my father listened with mild patience to my explanation of how I was looking to change. I was going to reflect the cessation of desire, I was looking directly at the uncarved block—that went nowhere. Anything that smacked of trying to plug an existential crisis struck Dad as a luxury better indulged after I had a paying job.

Finally I realized what would make more sense to him: I was turning nineteen that week. I asked him to take me shopping for blue-and-white-striped cotton shirts.

Dress shirts don't come up much in Buddhism, but changing within is hard. Also, I was in Los Angeles, so my externally based approach made some cultural sense. I must have seen an article in one of Heidi's issues of *GQ* about how to dress appropriately. Choose natural fibers. Skinny ties and tiny lapels are in. Be neat and crisp. This is what Tenax hair gel is. Here are actors and models you wish you looked like. Glance at a unifying vision and see how you measure up. Feel the terror of looking like you care how you look.

My father bought me four blue-and-white shirts. Button-down collars on three, a tab collar on one, a compromise. He wanted me to get cotton-poly blends, for convenience; I was determined to get some all-cotton shirt with collars that came to starched points. (He did not believe I would actually iron them and I was determined to prove him wrong.)

We got the cotton ones. Calvin Klein. Perry Ellis. Some were white with faint blue pinstripes and others looked flashy, like distress flags from a sinking yacht. Also black jeans. Ray-Ban Wayfarers. Black Converse high-tops. I wanted to buy a skinny silk tie, but my father told me he would not buy me a skinny tie as long as he lived. If I were getting a tie, it had to be something I would wear in the workplace, which he wanted me to join when I came back home for the summer.

For some reason I argued strenuously for a straw fedora, which I authoritatively checked off my list as if it completed my outfit. I will not bring it up again.

My hair was of no discernible style. I'd done myself no favors when I'd grown a beard after Connecticut raised the drinking age to twenty-one. So I shaved. I went to a barbershop near the Veterans Administration and got the same haircut everyone got, short back and sides, and when I left I looked like I was on my way to see Josephine Baker in Berlin, circa 1928.

There was not much I could do about my nose. It was now a backwards S and not particularly functional. The careful haircut actually made the nose more aggressive, as if I was telling people I was proud of my flaws.

The effect when I returned to Wesleyan was that I was well-groomed and I dressed in clothes that fit. I wore my neckties with the black jeans and the Converse high-tops and even when it wasn't sunny I wore the sunglasses.

I got better at Japanese. I dreamed in it a couple of times. I thought I looked serious, perhaps even, if you caught me looking intently at something, mysterious.

Heidi didn't buy any of this. She and I had been arguing tentatively anyway, but my new clothes and haircut seemed to her like an assault on the relationship. Once she walked into my room with newly curled hair, and when I looked at it and said nothing, she burst into tears.

Later she brought me a magazine folded back to show off the advertisement for an upcoming movie called *Risky Business*. It featured a handsome actor wearing Ray-Ban Wayfarers like mine.

"You kind of look like him," she said.

"Really? You think so?"

She looked at me witheringly. "No."

A few days later, I wrote in my journal a comment about my heart ("black ice"), then Heidi's name and the phrase "until one day you no longer see what you once saw." Did I mean she didn't see me? Or that I no longer saw what I'd seen in her? She had kissed someone else when she was home for vacation; I found out; it was a good excuse for me to be outraged and to look at her with detachment. We broke up.

In May, it was time to go back to Los Angeles. I felt a little bit strong—my clothes a kind of armor, my detachment a minor superpower—but not strong enough. I was nervous about seeing my mother. If I was still the same on the inside—churning, awkward, looking for the approval of people I hadn't even met yet—I had changed on the surface. Only the surface. I was all image and no substance. In other words, I was prepared for my hometown.

MUSIC & HI-FI

OWEN PICKED ME UP from the airport. We'd gone to high school together and he was thrashing against college in Berkeley just as I was Wesleyan, with uncertainty about whether he belonged. He'd discovered punk rock, so when I climbed in his car, he got to business, playing a tape of bands he'd seen live or heard on KALX, the student radio station that ran as if it were a pirate ship parked three point two miles off the coast.

Owen was good at detailing the sociology of punk. The bands had names like the Meat Puppets, the Germs, the Circle Jerks, the Vandals, the Dead Milkmen. There was a thing called slam-dancing. I'd heard of this, but was scared to learn more.

Owen explained. "You know those cartoons where the Tasmanian Devil spins around and it's a whirlwind with thunder and stars and lightning coming out of it?"

"Yeah."

"That's what slam-dancing is like."

He liked punk because punk didn't care what people thought. Punk didn't brush its teeth and it drank beer for breakfast. It was incoherent and angry and uncompromising, excellent for a genuinely nice guy like Owen, who still lived with his mom. The lead singer of Flipper sang with his back to the audience. "Just total arrogance," Owen said. Once, Fear had a string quartet open for them, to piss the audience off. The Pop-O-Pies were famous for sometimes playing only one song, a cover of "Truckin'" by the Grateful Dead, but then doing the song for forty-five minutes or until the crowd finally pulled them offstage.

As he was talking, I decided to show off what I'd learned at Wesleyan. I put a tape I'd made into his deck. I turned it up.

After about fifteen seconds, Owen said, "What the hell is this?"

"Philip Glass."

"Who?"

"Philip Glass."

His face puckered. "This is horrible."

"I'll take it off."

"No, Glen. We're going to listen to it."

It was minimalist piano from the afterworld, frosty and intellectual, probably the kind of music Bach would play after being dead for five hundred years. I reached to pop the cassette out, but Owen stopped me with a glare. He listened to confirm that I had intended to play this. "You like this? You actually like this? Is it that a *girl* likes this?"

At the next stoplight he stared at me with such disappointment I finally took the tape out. It was obvious to Owen that Wesleyan had done a shitty job of educating me.

On Wilshire, a few blocks from my father's house, there was a billboard for a Spanish language station's eleven o'clock news team. The weather girl had breast implants. The sportscaster had dyed blond hair. The seasoned, serious anchor had an obvious toupee. All of them had teeth like searchlights and though it was hard to tell from the ground, I'd swear the photo had been retouched so their eyes were blue. The slogan read: "*Auténtica.*" I can't believe I was the only person in all of Los Angeles to note the irony of this, but now, in my new rush to keep my eyes open, it struck me as important. Was this me, in my new clothes and haircut? My Philip Glass music? Yes. I was *auténtica*.

My father lived in a house that could have seemed affluent or just middle-class, depending on how sophisticated the eye evaluating it. After people have known me long enough to have heard stories about my dad, they are shocked when they meet him. In person he seems so nice. He's curious, funny, gentle, and he loves to share what he knows. He wants to know if you know anything interesting, too, and he wants to hear your stories.

His laugh is famous in family history. Once, he saw a performance of *Beyond the Fringe* off-Broadway, and he laughed so hard Peter Cook and Dudley Moore stopped the show and did their routines directly to him. His name was Herbert, and when bookstore clerks asked if he was "that" Herbert Gold, he always said yes, because in his mind, he was that Herbert Gold.

He was the eldest and blackest sheep of a tight-knit family which he wanted to leave immediately. Grandpa Ben had met Grandma Frieda when he was sixteen and she was thirteen, and they dated for five years before they kissed for the first time on the Tunnel of Love ride at the White City amusement park. They were together for seventy-five years, solidly, and had three boys, all successful, many grandchildren, Frieda screaming at Ben every single day they were both alive.

They tried to inculcate three things in my father: family, Judaism, and baseball, and he made sure he taught me nothing about any of them. As a teen he was mentored by a surveyor who taught him about science, and it turned out he loved science. It answered questions without getting hysterical or the answer being "because we're your family."

At the University of Michigan he joined what he told me was the engineering fraternity, and his family told me was the Jewish fraternity. He was there for one reason only: to become their social chairman. My father's party planning was limited to making sure the dances were held on the weekends that a girl named Alva could attend them. This courtship went throughout college, and was a success. Like many of his successes it was brief: he married her.

As a child I sorted through the photos of my father's life before me. I was deeply curious what his first wife looked like. Slides from vacations they took together, labeled in his engineer's print, might say "Alva by the waterfall," but someone had removed the transparency from the cardboard frame. Finally I found a small photograph from their wedding day, and my father looked the happiest I have seen him, and Alva's entire form was cut out so that not a trace of her remained. He told me a jealous girlfriend did this, but the precision of the cut looked to my eye scientific.

I asked him years later when he knew Alva was a mistake. "On my honeymoon," he said. "I remember walking on that beach alone that night and looking up at the sky and asking myself what I'd done."

I'm glad I know this story. It illuminates for me what a young Herb must have looked like the first time he married a beautiful woman who turned out to be complicated.

When he met my mother, he had a job that paid well, a Porsche, his sense of humor (now darker), and that attractive, cheerful amorality. Mom was beautiful and funny and could beat him at Scrabble, and there was that English accent that made people stare, and when they stared, they saw a handsome, loving couple that radiated *success*.

A decade later, while that was falling apart, he was doing consulting work on the Board of Trade and the Commodities Exchange, contributing to computerizing their systems. It was supposed to be a brief job, a few weeks here and there, but the weeks kept getting longer and he was gone for months at a time.

He was desperate then. The first important event he missed, perhaps one of my birthdays, he sent me an envelope with a joke note inside: "Stop saying I never give you anything," and with it a crisp ten dollar "HAWAII" note from World War II, for our collection. When I remember these gifts, and there were a few as several years went by, it's as if my mother were standing nearby every time, eyebrow raised to see if I agreed that these were transparent bribes.

They were. But there was something else going on. Dad's letters to me got longer, and weirder, each one tallying how long he'd been awake before writing them. Twenty-two hours. Twenty-six hours. He was programming, his mind overrun with the thrill of Fortran and C, and I thought he was just having fun.

Sometimes he would call the house at odd times, and if I answered, he would just say "thirty hours," and tell me to tell Mom he'd said hi, and he was going to bed. Once, my mother answered instead, and they almost immediately got into a fight. He hung up. She looked at me, and said, "Your father wanted me to tell you he's been up for fifty-six hours."

I thought this was boss, and I bragged about it at school, insisting it was boss even when Gary Abraham, whose father was a sports medicine doctor, said staying up that long was impossible. Which might be true except for how much speed my father was doing.

It was 1974. My father had just had five million dollars slip away, and he lived in the remainder of that expensive, diminishing, impossible-to-maintain lifestyle. My mother tells me he became paranoid about IBM stealing his work, and there were rough phone calls where she talked him down.

Many years later, his sister-in-law told me this story: his brother, who also worked on La Salle Street, was waiting for the train. He saw my father standing, reading a newspaper, at the same stop. This was a surprise to him. My father had been living in Chicago for two years without telling his family.

My father disputes that story, but it's a much stranger story to make up than to deny. I think it happened, but not because my father didn't like his family. I see *shame* in his choice. He had gotten fired and had lost everything. The project he was working on now didn't pay as promised. There were mysterious hierarchies among traders and also he fucked up trading at least once.

His new wife's money was wealth generations deep, a family portfolio of real estate money, shopping center developments, and skyscrapers built by industrialists on a scale my father could never compete with. It was intimidating money.

After they moved back to California, he got up early every day, showered, dressed in a boxy suit, left for work at Atlantic Richfield, came home, put his briefcase down by the mail table, and listened to Ann tell him about the day she'd had. He made somewhat funny comments to her in return. They now had two little boys, Seth and Marc, who also had days my father listened to. He gave off two distinct impressions: one was that he was relieved to be working a job that ended at five p.m. The other was that he was insisting to an invisible witness that he was happy.

He and Ann had landed not in the secluded estates area of Brentwood, but its more shapeless flatland cousin, where the streets were a mix of condominiums and ranch houses with lawns. The garage had a Volvo station wagon and a 1970s midline Mercedes. It was a corner lot with a big backyard with three-story palm trees and a nice-for-the-neighborhood, but not flashy, swimming pool. Two stories in a vague Spanish style, and every wall covered with artwork.

He and Ann still collected the photorealism my father loved, but they'd expanded to the work of local artists whose careers were in the ascent. They commissioned portraits, so when guests sat in the living room, there was a life-sized watercolor of Herb and Ann sitting on a couch, him leaning forward, about to make a point he found important. It was clearly a commemoration of having arrived, and that's what I think my father was saying to himself every day when the gears of the automatic garage door opened, and he drove into the garage, then opened the door to the kitchen, with a chirp of the alarm, and came into the house to be greeted by wife and children: *I have arrived, I have arrived,* because he wasn't sure he had.

When I came back that summer, my father spent evenings in his study, reading *The Wall Street Journal,* listening to classical music on his excellent KEF 105 speakers. The music was for him what punk was for Owen, a badge of belonging. In my father's case, the resonance of Tchaikovsky wasn't its emotional engagement, but a man like himself, in a house like his, listened to classical music.

The music didn't really do its job, I think. He bought more albums and he improved his stereo, but nothing could change his nagging feeling that an amoral person who didn't want to be where he'd arrived, again, could cheerfully insulate himself from discomfort with money.

ARCHITECTURE & HOME IMPROVEMENT

IN SUMMER 1983, when I came home from Wesleyan, my father and Ann were interested in moving. There was a house in Bel Air, recently built, that was an architectural wonder, "a showpiece," as my father said. The current house wasn't a showpiece.

I told him he just wanted a place to say, "Look upon my works ye mighty and despair," and he said, "Probably."

They were negotiating with the current owners. He told me I should see the place. I wanted to go, but I had to go to my mother's in Long Beach first. She had said she had a good eight or ten hours of office work for me, which meant forty or fifty dollars to start my summer out. Since I didn't drive yet, I would take the bus there. When I came back, Dad would pick me up and show me the house he was interested in. And then, he reminded me, it was time to look for a summer job.

When she was still in New York, my mother had started a business. If you were an entrepreneur and needed someone with typing or other office skills, and if you weren't yet in the phase of your business where you had an office, you could call my mother. She was an excellent typist. She knew many professional résumé formats. She had a "can-do" attitude, and she was unafraid to work long into the night if necessary. She leased copiers, and had sign-making equipment. Sometimes she had an assistant, sometimes I worked there on school breaks. But it was on the second floor of a building in Midtown. No one knew she was there, and if they did, no one would hike up a flight of stairs to get copies made unless her prices were good, and they weren't.

When she relocated to California, she brought her business with her, but she'd had to get work like the office jobs she'd complained to Jen about. It wasn't clear to me if the office work she'd asked me to do was for her own company, for someone else, or maybe in pursuit of a new career in sales. When I took the bus from my father's to Long Beach, I was unsettled. I wanted whatever she was working on to be successful, so I could prove my father wrong.

When I got off the bus, Mom immediately took me to a bookstore to buy me a couple of books. Unlike my father, Mom wasn't that concerned with me getting a job. She worried that I'd have enough time to write a novel. When I was in high school, she'd bought me a copy of *The World According to Garp,* describing it as "about a mother and son who write," a way no one else has ever described it, but the way I've thought about it since.

At her apartment, we ordered Chinese food, she asked me again about my writing, and volunteered that when she got settled she would have so many more stories for *Money Matters.* So many people had such crazy ideas of what they could get away with when you were an individual proprietor, and a woman, not that she was calling foul on all men. And then it was like she woke up to actually seeing me for a moment: did I realize how much with my new haircut and clothes I looked like my grandfather now?

She was right. Now that I was clean-shaven and my hair looked like it had been razored by Leni Riefenstahl's stylist, my face had the angular shape that supported his intense stare.

But something else was up. Everything my mother owned seemed to be in a box or on a counter. I had the sense that if I opened the kitchen cabinets, they would be empty.

She had a typewriter set up for me. "You can write if you want," she said, because she had some paperwork to do. I didn't feel like writing, but I had the sense that it would soothe her to hear her son typing. The phone rang and she ignored it. I tried not to look at the phone. Instead, I typed, "When a phone rings, you have two choices. Answer it. Or let it ring." My mother made a different choice: she unplugged the answering machine, wrapped up the cord, and then put it into a box.

She put me in charge of packing. There were files that had to be boxed carefully. When everything was stacked and labeled, it was time to take the cartons out to the car. Mom was leaving her apartment and moving to San Diego. So it wasn't really office work, but she was going to pay me to help her move.

When the apartment was empty and the car full, the last thing to go in was the typewriter. It was an old top-of-the-line IBM Selectric whose font bobbins had fascinated me as a kid, and as my mother was typing now I thought of the film ribbon that passed before the hammering letters. If you stretched it out in front of a light, you could see all the characters making up all the office needs, résumés, and business letters that my mother had typed out. And as you unspooled them you could take yourself back into the past, where her business started, and then you could read forward into what it had become.

Now she was typing this, to her landlord, "Making the best of a poor situation, I am returning the key. As you and I both know, I would be unable to—" and then I stopped reading.

The door to her apartment was closed and we were on the outside. The note went into an envelope with the key, then went through the mail slot, and she closed the door. I had never seen someone skip rent before. We were both pretending I hadn't seen it now. I felt frosted over, and supremely careful, as if by breathing too hard I would accidentally ask a question.

Ninety minutes south, the apartment in San Diego was just off the freeway, across from the abandoned El Cortez hotel. It was six hundred square feet, and she would be running her office out of the front room for now. The carpet smelled of cigarettes and mold. I wondered if her luck would change here. I wondered if my five dollars an hour would include the hour and a half the drive had taken.

My mother said she thought the apartment was nice. She was close to downtown but not so close it would make her rent go up. She confessed that she'd chosen San Diego because someone had promised her a job, but between then and now, it had fallen through. She didn't have enough for the first month's rent, and she didn't know what was going to happen. This led to an awkward pause. Then she admitted she didn't actually have the money she'd hoped to pay me. I said that was fine.

"But I promised," she said, and she listed off ways she would be paid soon. There were men who owed her money.

"I don't need the money," I said, more quickly than I'd planned. What I meant was that I didn't want to be part of this. I didn't want money to come out of her situation and toward me. But what she heard was me bragging.

During our remaining conversations she wouldn't let me out of her sight, as if she might miss it when some sour assessment crossed my face. She seemed afraid of me except for the moments where she would announce an optimistic slogan about how things would work out. She tried to ask me questions, but got tangled up in them and instead talked about her prospects again.

No, there was one question. Within minutes of my arrival, and every couple of hours from then until I was lining up for the bus, she asked me, "When are you coming back?"

My father met the bus in L.A. He drove me into Bel Air, and then we went airborne above Sunset on one of the streets I'd never driven on, because even though it was public, I strongly felt that I wasn't rich enough to be there. It was a long way uphill. We passed the houses that were close together, then the ones that were far apart, and we kept ascending.

We didn't talk about Mom. Instead I'd had enough amusing college incidents that I could tell him stories that ended with a good punch line. He noticed that every Wesleyan story had a melancholy twinge to it.

He finally said, "Do you actually like that place?"

"Maybe?" I said.

"Maybe?" A long pause. "Maybe." And we both knew what that meant: it cost over eleven thousand dollars to go to Wesleyan. Berkeley, the state school I'd declined, was about six hundred dollars a semester. "Then why are you going back?"

It doesn't matter what I said. We would have this conversation because we would never have the real conversation beneath it. Once, a couple of years before, I had broached the subject of how Wesleyan would be paid for, and it had ended badly, and I was unable to bring it up again. My father had never wanted to pay for Wesleyan, in part because my mother had squandered my education money, which meant he had to pay for it *again,* or rather Ann was paying, which meant I represented a prior debt he was bringing to the relationship. I—not that I understood this—resented the hell out of that attitude so I was committed to going as long as he hated paying for it.

Also, I was carrying an ember of shame with me. I wondered if it was betrayal to suspect that my mother's luck wasn't actually going to change. Rather: that it wasn't luck. If I believed that, I would be aligning myself with my father, and that struck me as a grim way to live.

Here's how I thought: "My mother is going to do well, now that she's landed in the right place. And I'm going to make the most of Wesleyan. If you think that's impossible, let me show you how I do impossible things."

Our approach toward the house was from below, and it loomed over us, a sophisticated radar-station-like array of cool blue metal boxes. It looked like it was made of sunglasses. It looked angular and Dutch, contemptuous of weakness, and in its relentless brutal simplicity it was almost *evil*. We parked outside and stared at it. Bold houses can make statements. One look, and I understood it was better than I was. It knew that, too.

My father was looking at it with an expression I'd now say was of Moses sighting a distant hill and knowing to his bones that he was within reach of the promised land.

You could shoot perfume commercials there. If Catherine Deneuve stood on one of its balconies in a red dress, looking pensive, it would make sense. The house made me want to wear finer clothes, have an even better haircut, toned muscles, and maybe a diamond embedded in my lateral incisor. If I could live up to that house, I would feel better about myself.

My father clearly wanted it because he could see himself living there. The house was his blue-and-white-striped shirt, his sunglasses, but maybe just a little bit his straw fedora.

As we drove back to the old house, my father asked when I was going to look for a job. He said that it was getting late in the summer to still get a shift at Shakey's, and I told him, No, I wasn't going to work fast food again.

"I want to work at Hunter's Books," I said.

This surprised him. It surprised me, too. It pleased him. It was a step up from what he'd imagined. It was an independent bookstore, not a chain. People working at Hunter's wore ties. They were smart and eclectic, actors training for work and authors working on novels. Celebrities shopped there. But the competition for a job was probably fierce, my father said, and then something dawned on him: "I doubt they take on summer hires."

I hadn't thought that through. But he was right. If I got the job, he said, it would mean I was working there through Christmas, and I knew what that meant, too: I wouldn't be going back to Wesleyan. I would be living with my father, in his house, and maybe proving him right on many counts.

This was a problem, because when I looked at him, I thought: *I am the person who is 50 percent made up of this.* This annoyed me.

CAREERS, BUSINESS, & MARKETING

I N HIGH SCHOOL, Owen had been a soccer player and track team captain who favored white overalls and whose long hair was set off by
a ball cap to which he'd affixed a raccoon tail. We had similar senses
of humor, and his childhood—which we never talked about—was as
inexplicable as my own, which is all that men need to become friends.
He sometimes exercised by putting his bicycle on rollers in his room
and riding to all four sides of Lynyrd Skynyrd's *One More from the Road*.
In other words, like the other people I loved best he had the courage of
his eclecticism.

In the years we'd known each other, he'd introduced me to Earl
Scruggs, Johnny Cash, James Brown, The Who, Buck Owens, more
or less all people so tortured by love of music that they had substance
abuse problems. Punk was the latest in a line of such sounds that spoke
to his higher aspiration: to be courageous.

He told me he wished he had Keith Moon's reputation for tearing
hotel rooms up, but without having to do all that problematic destruction stuff. If he ever really destroyed a hotel room, he knew he'd feel so
guilty it wouldn't be worth it.

In a way, summer of 1983 began for me when Owen paid for a simul-
cast of a concert by The Who so we could watch it on television at his

house. After getting some chips and beer, we were driving down Sunset in his 7UP-green Saab turbo. It was a sporty-looking car that gave the misleading impression that whoever drove it would have a well-planned personal style.

At a red light, a GTI pulled up next to us. Inside were two very cute girls. They rolled down their window.

"Hey, what's up!" The passenger was leaning across the driver. She was smiling.

"Hey!" I waved back.

"What are you guys doing?"

"Who concert—" was all I managed before I was knocked backward into the door frame; Owen had floored it, running the red light. On the other side of the intersection, he swerved into parking spaces illegally to cut ahead of traffic, and at the next light he swung right so hard we almost fishtailed.

A minute later, I looked at him. His eyes were determined and fixed. "Owen?"

The flush from his face retreated. "Okay," he finally said. "I regret that."

"We could have had them come over and—"

"I know. I regret that."

"They were cute!"

"Yeah. Bad decision. When I tell this story in the future, it's going to have a better ending." He thought about it. "I'm going to say they asked, 'What are you guys doing?' and then I leaned over and said, 'I'm going to fuck *this* guy.' And I jerked my finger at you and you gave a big thumbs-up."

We watched the concert alone. I opened beers for the girls who hadn't come, and Owen glared at me. By the end of the evening, we'd told the story so that it ended with him promising to fuck me, then us both mooning the girls, only to accidentally trigger the automatic windows, so that our asses were sticking out into the night, us wailing in awful harmony as, somehow, the car kept driving itself around Hollywood. That still seemed like a better story than him panicking.

Owen concluded that fleeing like that hadn't been very punk rock. Would Lee Ving have fled those girls? Greg Ginn? The guys from Black Flag? They would have jumped into that car *with open containers*.

He declared that he was going to live this summer with all the courage he could. He was going to *go for it,* and I agreed. I agreed so much that I, too, would go for it. I would go to a punk concert with him. This would be the summer I had courage. I would finally apply for a job—at a *bookstore.*

Owen stared at me. "What?"

The next day, I was on Westwood Boulevard, in Tower Records, dressed in my blue-and-white-striped shirt and fancy silk tie, thumbing through albums. I was in Tower not for the music, really, but to avoid Hunter's Books.

I had no prior experience. My fast-food résumé, my part-time work, my summer work all counted against me. I kept glancing down at the tie my father had bought me and trying to lie to myself, "Sure, I wear a tie, every day."

Westwood was a dozen geometrically diffuse blocks of stores, movie theaters, and restaurants that serviced the UCLA campus. The streets came together at eccentric angles, and alleyways led to hidden courtyards as if the planners hoped people who weren't paying close attention might mistakenly believe they were in Europe.

Students were getting richer. This led to boutiques with four dresses on a rack, where drama majors poured Chablis for customers and the proprietress was someone's *cinq à sept.* People started coming to Westwood to be seen shopping. The cafés were filled with incomprehensibly fit and handsome students joined by the people they would grow up into, meaning movie stars.

Tower Records was full of gorgeous people I thought I recognized. Or they were behaving as if I should know to recognize and not acknowledge them. I'd been working on my image for a few months but I was in the company of people who'd been thinking about such things for a lifetime, so I felt like I was behind. It's a feeling that Los Angeles generates: it was disheartening to be the least handsome person in a given aisle of Tower Records.

I left Tower, and in the courtyard saw something I assumed was a good omen, a pushcart of men's ties for sale. Since it was near Tower, the ties were skinny. They were five dollars. Made of viscose, some black, but mostly Day-Glo pink or that unknowable popsicle color between green and yellow. Some of them had silkscreened piano keys or musical notes on them, which I was smart enough to know were tacky. Then my world lit up as I found, one rack down, the skinny black leather ties. They were more expensive, ten dollars. I needed one. I took off my conservative tie.

Sometimes a good leather knot around your neck gives you confidence. The tie fit me and to my eye made my outfit finally viable, from my high-tops to my Ray-Bans.

I walked the few doors up toward Hunter's, where they were obviously going to see through this facade instantly. I am a terrible liar and tend to flush deep red and stammer through things like, "No, I'm taking the year off from Wesleyan, so sure I'll be able to work this fall."

Hunter's window displays were mild, just books, nothing flashy. Attempting to attract customers was gauche. Hunter's was more discreet than that.

Inside, it was as quiet as a Beverly Hills Mercedes showroom. It was the kind of silence that comes with selling a life of superior thoughts.

Behind the counter was an ephemeral blond man, skin as white as the pages of a coffee-table book, who turned away before I could talk to him, leaving me alone until a woman with half-glasses and salt-and-pepper hair noticed me.

When I inquired, she whispered that they weren't hiring. I asked if they might be hiring later, and she whispered, "We doubt it." She said it kindly, or perhaps *politely* is more accurate. They did nothing bluntly at Hunter's.

The phone on her counter buzzed. She excused herself, but with a finger in the air, as if she hadn't yet explained all the ways I wouldn't be hired.

She was having a quiet conversation with someone looking down at me, also over half-glasses, from the mezzanine. He was bald, with fringe, and he seemed confused.

The woman behind the counter was saying, "No . . . no. No, it's not, Mike. He's really not. He's here to apply for a job." She turned away from me and whispered further into the phone.

Then she returned to me and she said with disappointment, "Mike would like to talk to you. He's the manager."

Mike twinkled his fingers at me from the mezzanine. I walked across the store, and went up the stairs. He steepled his fingers and looked managerial, I suppose, but mostly what I remember was falling into a strange, circular conversation with a sweet, self-deprecating man who at two in the afternoon was conclusively drunk.

He let me know that there were no jobs, true, but he'd seen me come in, and thought—ha!—I looked like Timothy Hutton. Wasn't that funny! Now that I was sitting here, I didn't, obviously, but hadn't anyone ever told me that? No? Was I local? I was looking for work, right? Where else had I looked? I told him the truth—nowhere. I was only interested in working in a bookstore, this bookstore. He asked why. I said because it wasn't a chain.

That was the truth, but I had no idea how much Mike would vigorously nod. There was a Crown Books a block away. Mike said that unlike the chains, Hunter's didn't sell books stupidly. "Not like Crown, not like it's toilet paper."

He asked about my favorite books. I thought of my writing class and my fraternity. What authors did people slightly better than myself tend to like? Raymond Carver, John Cheever, I. B. Singer. I mentioned my interest in Eastern philosophy, and he asked for examples of that, and I talked about the *Pillow Book* and Yukio Mishima and the weirdness of Junichiro Tanizaki. He didn't know Tanizaki, so I described how perverse his work was: decadent aristocrats, nose fetishes, submissive husbands. He was quite happy to hear about that. I seemed to him remarkably self-possessed for someone only nineteen. And it was just too bad they didn't have jobs to offer.

He meant it. Hunter's was part of a local handful of stores that wouldn't survive the new realities of commerce. They had slightly profitable branches in Pasadena and Beverly Hills, where he said "there are still ladies who shop," eyeing me to see if I knew what he meant. Hunter's provided a level of personal service, but people who didn't know better, who valued price over value, were going to that damned Crown, siphoning off Hunter's business. With Westwood on the ascendency, rents were doubling. Hunter's had a lease that would be up soon and there was no way they could afford to stay. So, he shrugged, sorry.

That makes the conversation sound more organized than it was. At some point, he seemed to be juggling the questions of whether he might find a job for me, and whether he and I might step over to the Hungry Tiger for a drink, before he corrected course. He was haphazard, not predatory. I shook hands with him and agreed that I'd probably find work in another bookstore somewhere.

He saw me down to the counter. He seemed embarrassed, either because he'd thought of hitting on me or because he couldn't offer me work. "This really doesn't faze you, does it? Looking for work, it's the worst."

"Nothing fazes me," I said, and it was true.

"The way to do is to be," he said with a smile, like it was a bumper sticker he'd just seen.

The slim, white-haired guy behind the counter was having a problem and he waved at Mike. There were two tourists, Japanese girls, who had a question for him. Only he couldn't understand them. One of them bowed her head and then tried to talk to Mike, who couldn't get any further with them.

"I'm sorry," I said. "What are you asking?"

One girl said, "The books upstairs? Are they on sale today or always? If we come back tomorrow . . ." she said.

I explained to Mike what she'd asked. He looked at his co-workers then back at me. "They're on sale always."

"Always," I told the girls, and then they laughed, took my photograph, and left the store.

"You speak Japanese," Mike said.

"I do."

A pleased look crossed Mike's face. This was helpful, he explained. Hmm. They were always getting Japanese tourists. (They weren't, really.) They needed someone to translate. (They didn't, really.) Now that he thought about it, this was fantastic. (It wasn't.) He wanted to tell the bean counters in Beverly Hills he was hiring me.

When could I start? Forty hours a week, minimum wage. "Wait—" he put his finger to the corner of his mouth. "You weren't just looking for summer work, were you?"

"No."

"What about Wesleyan?"

"I'm taking the year off." I lied so quickly I didn't even have a chance to blush.

I was still sure he was going to change his mind when he introduced me to Barbara, the woman in half-glasses, who politely conceded my existence with a silent "this will make no difference when we're dead" expression and a more friendly "welcome to a sinking ship" handshake.

Mike started to indicate where all the books were, but didn't finish. He figured I'd learn that later. As co-workers passed, he flagged them down with a kind of feisty pride, like he was getting one over on his bosses by hiring me.

He waved toward the blond boy I'd seen before. "This is Jeffrey. Jeffrey's been here a year and a half now."

"Nicolas."

"Pardon?"

"I'm Nicolas." He was already reaching into his pocket and taking out a checkbook. He unbuttoned the snaps on it and smoothed out the checks. Mike looked as if he'd parachuted into the wrong cocktail party while he took in the checkbook that Jeffrey—Nicolas—was showing off. He'd just legally changed his name to Nicolas et in Arcadia Ego, which was printed on his checks. "It means even in paradise, there is death," said Nicolas with quiet pride.

"Okay, then," said Mike.

Nicolas shimmered away. Mike looked after him and shrugged, as if admitting, ninety seconds after hiring me, that he didn't understand anything that was going on. But still: welcome to working at this independent bookstore.

I'm not sure who else I met that day. Later, Melanie told me she'd seen me but decided to hide in the back until I left. "I already had enough on my plate," she said, which was true.

More than one person asked if Mike had me meet Rick yet, and Mike laughed, and said, No, not yet, and I got the impression that everyone wanted to see Rick, whoever he was, meet the new guy.

I left soon after, full of cheer, and walking to the bus stop I rehearsed telling my dad the good news. Full-time employment at a bookstore. I thought briefly of my mom.

Mom, yeah, I'll be in L.A. all summer, but it's a forty-hour-a-week job so no I can't visit, yeah, I know, I'm sorry, too.

I replayed for myself the conversation with the Japanese tourists, who had been *kawaii*. No, cuter than that: *taihen kawaii*. I was going to work at a job that brought me into contact with very cute women.

When I got on the bus on Wilshire, the driver did a double take. "Weren't you just here on my bus?"

"No."

"You know who you look like?"

"Timothy Hutton," I said.

The bus driver laughed at me. "Who? You? No. What, does Timothy Hutton look like he rides my bus? No, you look like a guy who got off on the last stop." Laughing to a guy sitting in the handicapped seat. "He thinks he looks like Timothy Hutton."

When I got off at my stop, the bus driver waved at me, and when the doors closed I could see further laughter breaking out.

I wasn't going to tell my father that part of the story.

It wasn't until I was on the front steps of my house, key in the lock, that it occurred to me the word for "always" was *itsumo,* not *nidoto.* I had told the girls the books were on sale *never.*

CURRENT EVENTS

I WAS SOMETIMES THERE AT 9:45, when Mike came in to open up, or at the other 9:45, when we closed. The rituals weren't complicated—turning lights on or off, setting or disarming the alarm. Counting out the register drawer. At the end of the day, sometimes I was the second man in the office upstairs, standing and watching, as was protocol, while Mike or Harold or Fred counted the day's cash into piles for deposit. We were allowed to buy books at 40 percent off, and we could borrow them for a week at a time as long as we checked them out.

I loved it at Hunter's. I loved being surrounded by books. I loved it when someone asked if we had a book—if I knew where it was already, I loved uniting them with it, and if I didn't know where it was I loved looking it up on our microfiche and, if necessary, ordering it. I'd read almost nothing that people asked for. It was a store for some popular fiction, but more people came in looking for something classic or smart, and being able to hand over classic, smart books made me happy. I even loved grousing about customers who paid by check, the transactions which took the longest, especially the ones who only made the move to get their checkbook after I'd rung up the books and presented them with the receipt. Inevitably the checkbook was at the bottom of a purse that needed to be unlocked with the complexity of a Kansas missile silo.

My first day, still being coached to use the register, I saw a man waiting in line wearing a cardigan and half-glasses. People were staring. Finally, the woman behind him said, "Aren't you Bob Newhart?"

He gave a soft chuckle and said, "No, I get that all the time, though."

"You even sound like him," she said. His reply was a sad shrug that implied a burden: he got that all the time, too.

He handed me his credit card. BOB NEWHART. His eyes flicked toward mine for less than a second, and I knew I was supposed to stay quiet, so I did. He bought his books and left.

When he'd hired me, Mike, in his beautiful radio announcer's voice, suggested certain skills were involved when dealing with the famous. It wasn't something that could be taught, really, but he could see I grasped the whole Tao of the thing, he said. He kept using Eastern philosophical words even when they didn't line up with what he meant, but I nodded anyway, because I could see that it pleased him to say things like "Zen" when he meant "tact," maybe.

Mike didn't bring this up, but it was widely known among the staff that the true test would be if Timothy Hutton or, worse, Sean Penn came into the store. All of Mike's tact would go like chicken feathers out of an open blender.

Linda Evans came in. I beamed across the store at her, because my mother had been told she looked like Linda Evans. I told Mike my mom looked a lot like Linda Evans. He said, "Our bookkeeper looks like Betty White," and I said, "Yeah, I know."

It was a regal bookstore but it was also terrible. It was in no way ready for the modern world. We had some complicated reporting relationship with the Beverly Hills flagship store, revised many times over the decades, that no one quite understood. We didn't know how to organize our computer books. We had no language tapes. If we didn't have a book a customer wanted, we ordered it from Baker & Taylor or Ingram and it took weeks to show up, at full price, whereas Crown could get it faster and cheaper. There was a box of yellowing slips of paper showing which customers were in arrears (Peter Bogdanovich, for instance).

What we had on our side was eccentricity and its cousin, deep knowledge of books. There was an index card file box under the counter where employees wrote down what books they'd borrowed and when. This is where I felt shallow again—I didn't know what to read. Almost everyone else did. Everyone had read multiple books in every conceivable subject, mostly for their own interests, but also so they knew what to recommend to customers. Melanie's card was spotless: one neatly written high-end literary title after the other, check-out and return dates as regular as the movements of the sun and the moon. Rick's was that of a lunatic. In lush and yet careful cursive, the first title was *Gidget Has an Orgasm,* and they only got weirder from there.

My fellow employees were mostly grumpy, attending to customers as if disturbed from a good nap. Bernie looked like he'd slept in his dress shirt and tie. He listened to Bill Evans, only. He had seventy-three albums by Bill Evans. Rob made the same puns to customers every day, and had to shave his throat and the back and sides of his neck to get his shirt well enough buttoned to support the bow ties he favored. Barbara, who was listless and bored, usually stood behind Rob and made fun of him in ways he didn't understand.

Harold, the assistant manager, was ambitious, only doing the job until he could launch another career he was too savvy to tell us about. Chris was a writer and Anna a performance artist and Mitch was another writer. Melanie was a dancer, with straight black hair that fell down her back. I thought she was about my age. She had a tidy way of dressing in white pressed shirts and jeans, and she never seemed to make eye contact with me. Fred had once run an underground newspaper in Boston. Kim wore khakis every day and Naomi was a feminist and Dana drove a VW Squareback she named Chloe, and was nice enough to drive me home a couple times.

Mostly I was interested in whatever Melanie was doing. I was assigned sections to inventory—music and history—which were on the opposite side of the store from the children's books that she stocked. If I was assigned to the register, she seemed to be in the stockroom. If I was shelving, she was helping customers. Her lunch breaks were scheduled around her classes, and she tended not to eat anyway.

I tried to ask her something that would get a response. "What's Rick like?"

She considered this. "I think I'll let you see for yourself." She helped another customer and I understood she hated me.

· · ·

Then Rick came back.

I'm unclear where he had been. It's not like he'd worked there long enough to earn vacation time. I only remember his return metaphorically—as if I were shelving books and the hairs on my arms started to stand up.

More mundanely, at some awkward time that was definitely not when a shift began, a compact guy breezed into the store. He was wearing sunglasses and he was holding a knit tie, then hugging Melanie, and then Nicolas, and Dana, then studiously not hugging Rob. Rick Savilla.

At first glance, Rick was as vivid to me as if I'd made him up. Muscular and little, with a Caesar haircut and a complexion just bronzed enough and teeth just white enough to seem healthy but not vulgar. Preppy, in a low-key Lacoste kind of way. No straight nineteen-year-old like myself could have guessed his age. He once said he was approaching thirty, and had I been smarter, or old enough myself, I would have asked, "From what direction?"

That summer, a health book called *Life Extension* was a big seller among the ladies who shopped. One of them was asking if we had it, and Rick was listening to her carefully. "We do have that," he said. "It's in the health section right there."

She didn't look where he was pointing. "Bring it to me." I'd already noticed how some customers asked for things like they were dictators. She was genuinely looking down her nose when she said it, as if she'd never seen a dowager in a movie before.

Rick walked to the health section and brought the copy of *Life Extension* to the counter. When the woman reached for it, he took it away from her.

"Ma'am," he said, "you don't deserve to have your life extended." He put the book beneath the counter. He then ignored her and kept talking to Melanie.

Melanie was blushing on his behalf. "Rick?" Like: how could you do that?

"I feel like Atticus Finch putting down that dog. It's for her own good. It's for your own good, *madame*." He said this while making eye contact with the woman, whom I could tell had, you know, *shopped* for most of her life, but hadn't run into this before. She had something to say about that, but this was the moment Rick saw me.

"Oh my lord, is this *him*?" Rick looked at Melanie, who grabbed him by the shoulder and tried to tear him away from the front desk. He released himself, regarding me like he was trying to take in the features of a horse at a stable. He deflated. "Straight. Oh well. Melanie, you go out with him," he said, sounding almost helpful. "What?" Then looking at me, "Where did you come from?"

"The I Ching," I said.

"I bet you did. Where else?"

"San Francisco."

"Mecca! But not for you. You don't even know about the bathhouses."

"I know about the bathhouses."

"What do you know?"

I knew nothing, but I said, "Never wear a green handkerchief," which was a guess close enough to something profound that Rick nodded in agreement.

"My favorite is fisting," he said, making a fist for me. He said it required massive amounts of amyl nitrate, not to mention a fresh manicure.

So, within about thirty seconds of meeting me, he was talking about fisting. I knew why, and I wasn't going to do what he wanted: be shocked. "Do the bathhouses still have glory holes?" I asked.

"Do they ever!" he exclaimed. "And you hear all these screams around you—part of the trip is figuring out whether they're pleasure or pain. How do you know about glory holes?"

"Guys talk, you hear things."

He then announced that in the last year he'd slept with a thousand men, which made Mel laugh—she thought he was exaggerating—but Rick did a little tally and nodded. Three a day, roughly.

"Am I shocking you?" he asked me.

"No."

"Well, why not?"

"I'm a clear-running stream. Zen."

"Zen?"

"I like the interior calm it—"

"How did you learn about it?"

"Japanese Studies major."

"Where?"

"Wesleyan."

"Connecticut Wesleyan?"

"Yes."

"Bucks-a-go-go. Are you rich? Did you like Wesleyan?"

"I liked my fraternity."

"Fraternity? You were in a fraternity? I'm talking to a boy who was in a fraternity?"

"Coed."

"Oh my God, what does that mean?"

"Group showers."

"I like this fraternity." Then, cooing, "But Glen, how do I get you to join *my* fraternity?"

"I don't know, Rick, what can your fraternity do for me?"

"Oh, Jesus," Melanie said, closing her eyes.

I was just getting started. I felt energized. Straight men like myself are always flirtatious with gay men. We might not go on safaris or to bullfights, but we push on different limits to show how tremendously secure we are. Plus, the more calm I was, the more impressed Mel seemed to be.

"The initiation ritual alone is worth the price of admission, young man." Rick looked at me as if I should be afraid. "We have to have a dinner party," he said. "Melanie, will you come to my dinner party? You can bring Glen."

Mel looked startled to have the spotlight on her now, and said, "Sure?," and then there were customers or other distractions, and the banter was over for now, which disappointed me. I'd never been to a dinner party as an adult. If flirting like this got me the invitation, I wanted to know what the event itself would be like.

Earlier, there had been an exchange I didn't understand.

Shortly after Rick came in, and they'd hugged, Melanie asked, "How's Lolly?"

Rick gasped. "Lolly? Lolly is a *slut*. Oh. My. God. That girl!" He winced. "She's only fourteen years old and she's behaving like a divorcée."

Mel said, "Maybe it's just a phase."

"I keep telling myself that. Children go through a phase where they just have to piss off their parents."

"There's always Fausta."

Rick softened, and blew out a sigh. "Fausta is a dear." Lolly had already gotten into so much trouble with drugs and boys that Rick had put her into a special school in Switzerland, where she was just one demerit away from being sent home. Sometimes she sent him disquieting photographs of herself with boys, and now he dreaded getting mail from her. He had a well-behaved son who was thirteen, and Fausta, age nine, who was the gem of the bunch.

Rick mentioned something about Fausta's dance lessons, and he asked Melanie about a performance she'd seen. I don't remember what troupe she was describing, or even if she was describing something positive or negative, but the way she used her whole body in delivering her review—imitating moves she'd seen, showing off graceful, expressive motions—made her come alive. Her straight black hair was like a living, liquid fabric she could shake out for emphasis. I wanted to ask her something she would have to answer by moving like that.

When we were alone at the counter later, I couldn't think of anything to say that was as interesting as I'd thought I was when Rick was around. After some silence, Mel said, "So Rick doesn't freak you out?"

I tried to explain. I'd been brought up in San Francisco. Wesleyan was like a laboratory for ideas, and this bookstore, among people who'd thought more about how to live than I had, was the marketplace. Whatever I was saying was cribbed from lectures I hadn't paid enough attention to. I used the word "evolved" a lot, as in, "As someone who's, y'know, more *evolved* than other people—"

Mel had a fantasy about living on a solitary mesa in the desert, making dances, sometimes drinking wine with friends. When she drove around town, her mind went toward making dances. She reacted to the world by choreographing it.

She couldn't believe some people just wondered all day what they'd have for dinner. I'd been thinking the same thing—how was it possible not to ask questions about how the world worked? How could people not want to make art out of it, she wondered, too.

I said, "That's because they're dough heads."

"Dough heads?" she asked.

"People who don't think." It was a paraphrase from one of my classes in Buddhist parables. "People who don't even know they don't think."

Mel was still evaluating me. "Yeah, I think you're pretty evolved." She chuckled. "Young Buddha of Westwood," she said, and then she helped out some customers.

The rest of the day, I walked around feeling like the young Buddha of Westwood. I tried to engineer running into Melanie and alternatively avoiding her if I saw her too much. For a girl my age, she seemed like she'd managed to live a few extra years of life. Every once in a while, at the counter, in the otherwise silent atmosphere, I would hear her chuckle, "Dough heads," under her breath. I wondered if I was going to dinner at Rick's house with her. Would that be a date?

Her shift was over before mine. She left without saying goodbye.

TRUE CRIME

W ESTWOOD was designed to be walked in, but someone had discovered a market for pedicabs. They made no sense, because the village was about four blocks by three blocks in size. They were popular because the drivers were sun-swept, radiant men and women, most of them athletes from UCLA, some of them training for the Olympics. So the value provided was that rich, lazy people got to watch the backs, asses, and legs of beautiful students who would otherwise never let the passenger within a hundred feet of them, while providing a mildly demeaning service designed to cause them to sweat attractively as they advertised the wealth and status of the person being towed across the village. The pedicab drivers always smiled. It was a capitalist sociology experiment.

Because there was so much traffic, I could walk on the sidewalk at roughly the same speed as pedicab drivers. I kept seeing one of them more than the rest. She was Asian American, I didn't think Japanese, possibly Korean, with a gymnast's body, and what startled me was how serious she seemed. She had a Louise Brooks bob and high cheekbones. When she was looking for fares, it was like she was gazing into the darkness of need, and when she was working, she did so as if hauling tourists to the donut shop was going to rescue her from a dire fate I couldn't imagine.

I wanted her, of course, but that confused me. Lust was primitive and wrong, but appreciating the beautiful was the basis of aesthetics. So I decided that seeing her was like the unexpected grace of seeing a painting from a museum sail by, and that my urge to see her again was like wanting to study its composition at length. It was an energetic contortion for a nineteen-year-old, but I could manage it easily, as long as I never actually talked to her.

I went running in my neighborhood almost every morning before work. There was a woman up the block who had a lovely front garden, designed rather than planted, with a good understanding of what I might now call *wabi-sabi,* but at the time just recognized as inherently Japanese.

She worked every morning in her yard under a huge-brimmed hat. Every time I thought, "I am going to speak Japanese to her," I managed to lose my courage when I saw the glint of her sunglasses.

Finally, feeling like I was dangerously veering into *auténtica* if I didn't speak up, one day I slowed to a walk, caught my breath, and approached her. I wanted to say that her garden was very pretty. She looked up at me.

"Anata no niwa wa taihen kirei desu," I said.

She stared at me. It was a sentence almost impossible to fuck up. No misplaced honorifics, no weird "to give" verbs that I couldn't wrap my head around. Maybe she hadn't heard me.

"Anata no—"

"Your parents live in the house at the end of the block," she said, in English.

I nodded.

"How much did they pay for their house?"

"I don't know."

She went back to gardening, ignoring me.

That was the second-to-last time I spoke Japanese aloud.

There had been little movement in buying the house in Bel Air. When Owen came by, my father said the owner was going to throw in a car. A BMW. The guy ran a dealership.

"What kind?" asked Owen.

"I have a model in mind."

"733i?"

"Exactly. What color do you think?"

I said, "Black," and my father winced the way he did when I played a sour note on my flute, age eight.

"Anthracite Grey," Owen said, and my father approved.

My father approved of Owen more than he approved of me at the moment. I was adamant about going back to Wesleyan in the fall.

"I will pay you twenty-five hundred dollars to drop out of Wesleyan and go to Berkeley instead," my father finally said.

"No," I said.

Later, when I recounted this to Owen, he was impressed not so much with my intransigence as my father's offer. Owen and I were drinking beers in his swimming pool, which is what happened whenever we thought we should try to work on a screenplay together. Generally we got a couple of ideas out, and spent the remaining hours making each other laugh. He lived in Hollywood, a few doors down from Drew Barrymore, in a converted garage–pool house behind the bungalow that his mother and stepfather lived in. This was a tense place. His mom tended to fall in love with artists or actors or producers who'd had potential when they were twenty years younger.

So the bungalow was ruled by Bob, a mean gin drunk. He did the lights for Las Vegas shows. He was a writer, too, in the sense that he had worked on a novel for many years.

Bob kept getting in fights outside a gay bar he insisted on walking the dog past. Owen and I talked about it like this:

ME: Why does he keep—
OWEN: I know.
ME: Because if he didn't—
OWEN: Right.

Owen kept to himself, then, working at a bicycle shop during the day and otherwise drinking beer and watching TV in his pool house. There was a great punk rock show coming up: the Dead Kennedys. I should come, Owen said.

Punk was almost dead by 1983. There was talk about how it was becoming part of mainstream music in the form of "New Wave," a cheery breeze blowing through production studios that was "fresh" and "fearless" and "passionate." In other words, not scary and not angry. But punk without aggression was like Quasimodo without the hump. The radio played New Wave all the time, insinuating it was groundbreaking, and that it was the same thing as punk, which was infuriating. How was it different than punk? Simple: for New Wave, there was a boutique in Westwood where you could buy the clothes from the music video.

New Wave was Owen's enemy. He had patience for the B-52s, and the B-52s alone, because they were genuinely weird. But he witheringly condemned other bands' harmonies and kookie sunglasses. The Red Rockers made him actively angry when he saw their mild, synthesizer-based video "China" on that compromised venue, MTV. "I saw them at the Berkeley Square," he said, while cute Asian dancers jumped around on screen with flags in their hands. "They were frightening. They were the most frightening band I'd ever seen." He was looking at them like an old boyfriend whose girl now had implants and no self-respect. The Red Rockers lacked integrity, and integrity was one thing that didn't travel from punk to New Wave. Owen sang along, bitterly, falsetto, *Chiiiii-Na, Chiiii-Naaaah.*

The bands who hadn't sold out were fading away. Owen thought this summer could be our last chance to see the Dead Kennedys, the final hardliners, the most uncompromising. Few clubs would book their shows anymore because of all the violence. They were coming to Wilmington, an industrial town so far south of L.A. it might as well have been in Patagonia.

Punk made me anxious. I was pretty sure that if I came to a show, someone, more as matter of policy than malice, would decide it was necessary to kill me. But Owen's stories suggested there could be a howling moment of throwing off expectation and convention and fully committing myself to something. If I went to this show, I might become authentic. But fear won, and so I told him, No, not this time.

I had a dream so horrifying that trying to wake up from it was like pulling myself out of a grave. After I struggled into consciousness, my jaw was clenched so hard I thought I'd popped the hinge free from its socket.

In my dream, my father was winding the grandfather clock downstairs, only I knew it meant he was about to murder my half-brothers. And then it was clear he had already wound the clock on previous nights, and murdered them, and when he was finished this time, he would come upstairs and murder me.

It was a tense house, too. It was never completely quiet, because my father had populated each room with clocks. Some were boxy and contemporary, and they stared quietly out from shelves like Donald Judd sculptures, but most of them were old, handcrafted. They ticked every second and chimed on the quarter-hour. Every time a new purchase joined the rest, my father positioned it precisely and he catalogued it in his portfolio, as if that would be enough. Then another one would come.

I kept thinking, *This is like measuring out your life in coffee spoons*. My father was counting the hours as they passed. Hence my dream.

To drown out the clocks, I would put on headphones and listen to music. KROQ played all the synthesizer hits, which felt like jingles that ignored how awful life was. But they also managed to sneak in hard stuff, like X, kind of rockabilly-on-adrenaline, broken-glass harmonies about the decaying life in Los Angeles. The lead singers were visibly and unashamedly married. They had a song about it called "We're Desperate," and I wondered if my dad would get more out of hearing that than Tchaikovsky.

At work, I was at the register, and Rick was carefully making elaborate invitations, using the request forms we were supposed to send to distributors. He turned one over and carefully traced out a calligraphically precise letter to Melanie, asking her if she would come over and play.

Rick handed his notice to her, and she replied, delighted, "Yes, of course I'll come over and play. I love it that you ask me over like that."

"Glen, do you want to come over and play with me? And Melanie?" He gave me what I think he hoped was a saucy look. "We should have that dinner party," he said. Now I had two invitations, punk and gay, to be nervous about.

A boy came to the counter, and looked up at us. He wanted a really creepy bedtime story to scare his younger sister with. Melanie took him to the kids' books, leaving me and Rick alone at this crucial moment: Rick asking me to help out for dinner. "Bring wine," he said.

"I can't."

"Why not? I thought you were rich."

"I'm nineteen."

"WHAT?" He said this so loudly, customers across the store looked up. "You mean nineteen—as in years old?" Then his voice got quiet and wicked. "Does Melanie know you're nineteen?"

I didn't know. "Why, how old are you?"

"Approaching thirty. I love nineteen-year-olds. Your dick is always hard then." He watched Mel, who was returning to the counter. "Let's play a trick on Melanie," he whispered. "You stand here." He positioned me so I was facing her, across the store. When she was close, he leaned in and ostentatiously whispered in my ear. "Just look straight at Mel. Okay. Now look surprised. *Really* surprised!"

I did. Mel was smiling and ready to be let in on the game.

Rick said to me, "Are you embarrassed?"

I said, "No."

Mel asked, "What are you guys talking about?"

Rick said, "Nothing. Well, no, something—I just told him what you told me when you and I were shelving books."

Melanie's face went—elsewhere. Her freckles disappeared, and she went a shade of red I don't think I'd seen on a face before. She stammered out something like, "Oh," and Rick looked at her kindly. "What, was that wrong of me to say?"

And then he smiled so hard that Mel realized he was lying to her, and she started hitting him with a stack of index cards, harder and harder, until he burst into laughter. She wasn't laughing, however, just angry. I stood there, fixed smile, dumbly, unclear on what strange games they played with each other.

This was another day that no real dinner party invitation happened.

Over the next couple days, Rick took every chance to test my nonchalance. I knew he was getting desperate when he gave me a back rub while I was at the register.

"Rick," I said, flatly, ringing up a sale, "you're giving me an enormous erection."

"I give up," he said. "Why aren't I making you nervous?"

As he'd never talked to any straight man about sex before, a perpetually unfazed nineteen-year-old seemed to strike just the right note of investigation for him. "Why are you straight? Don't you like men? See that guy over there? The one in the muscle tee? Do you think he's attractive? You do? But you still don't want to kiss him? Well, why not?"

I explained that I figured people were born bisexual and society conditioned us to be straight. Among my friends at Wesleyan, bisexuality was the preferred state in which to spend your junior and senior years. Myself, I'd never been interested in guys, but the idea wasn't alien to me. It wasn't like raw lust was something you should act on, but of course, being interested in someone's essence—

"Wait," Rick said. "You don't act on raw lust?"

This seemed obvious to me, as obvious as anything I'd learned at Wesleyan about the personal being the political. Lust was authoritarian and arose from crippled egos, more or less. Lust wiped out Zen. *Dough heads* acted on lust. Melanie was standing there, and I'm sure she contributed something to this, a nod or something, enough to keep me going.

Rick said, "If people are born bi, what happened to you? Have you ever had an emotional connection with a man?"

"Sure."

"But you've never wanted to sleep with a man?"

"No, I mean, men like that, they're my friends." I turned the idea on its head. "Have you ever slept with a woman just because you're friends with her?"

He nodded emphatically. "It seems to me that if you haven't slept with men, you're repressing something. Especially if lust isn't a motivator for you."

I had no response. It seemed like a neatly framed argument. Having failed to shock me, he'd confused me, and that was enough for him. And I was confused. What was wrong with me?

I think this is when my self-confidence hit a wall. I had thought I'd buried raw lust the way society had organized to take care of diphtheria, and now a set of questions came in at a strange angle that made me think the issue was *dormant,* not dead. When I looked at that pedicab driver, what was I feeling? *Lust.* I didn't actually have any of the interior calm I was pretending. Would a dinner party at Rick's be like an evening at a bathhouse?

Rick selected a date in his day planner for a dinner party. I accepted. But he'd chosen the very evening of another kind of party that had until just then frightened me more. In the end, I chose one fear over another, and I told Rick I couldn't come because I was going slam-dancing.

ANTHROPOLOGY

OWEN AND I were supposed to go to the Dead Kennedys with our high school friend Mike Conway, but he had to pass. His current girlfriend was about to come over to his apartment, and unbeknownst to her, he'd invited over a previous girlfriend, who had done pornos. For years, Conway had been obsessed with executing a ménage à trois, a higher mission we couldn't argue with. He figured tonight was his chance, which it really wasn't. Owen and I went to the show without him.

After a forty-five-minute drive south, we were . . . somewhere. There were warehouses and giant machines that turned piles of gravel into other, siltier piles, and the air seemed dusted with chemicals. We weren't sure if we were going to find the Longshoreman's Memorial Union Hall that easily, given that punk clubs were always small and out of the way. But then we came around a corner, and Owen braked. There were roughly four thousand punks standing on the sidewalk. They fanned out around the entire block.

"Is this normal?" I asked Owen.

He shook his head. A good turnout was two hundred, maybe. This was roughly four thousand. I use this number because later, in the newspaper accounts, the cops kept using the phrase "roughly four thousand punks."

We parked the Saab a smart couple of blocks away, in case there was a riot. The line of punks extended through an otherwise deserted neighborhood of warehouses and train tracks, gravel pits and galvanizing plants. There were wrist studs and tattoos, mean boys in camouflage shirts and tartan kilts. Each costume was torn, mangled, folded, shredded, the fashion statement of the day being "I have recently been dragged behind a bus."

When I was in first grade, and studying Indians, a kid came to school wearing a hat. When someone knocked it off him, he started weeping and we discovered his mother had forcibly administered a Mohawk on him. I've since wondered if that kid invented punk hairstyles as revenge. One guy just ahead of us had a thrilling rainbow-colored Mohawk that was only a single hair wide. It stood perfectly on end, as if its owner were perpetually scared out of his wits. It was beautiful, and we admired it.

In front of us, a conversation about injuries sustained at shows. One guy turned in profile to show off how his nose had been broken. The Mohawk guy nodded, as that was pretty good, but then he raised the right sleeve of his leather jacket. The sleeve was cut off about halfway down, and a wicked stump of a forearm poked out. The broken nose guy admitted defeat before he even noticed how the stump had a swastika carved into it. *That* was punk rock.

I was treating the evening like a frontier anthropologist.

I kept asking Owen what certain things meant—why was that guy wearing a kilt? What did the black-and-white checks mean on people's jackets? Increasingly, he was irritated. "Nothing," he kept saying. Almost everything meant nothing. The styles, the attitude, even the swastika all seemed like costumes worn by Disney theme park characters. It was like we were standing in line for a soon-to-be-closed attraction in Nihilismland. No one was trying to be smarter than anyone else, and being kind of dumb was kind of okay. Could I fit in with that?

The line wasn't moving. There were rumors of evil: the show was sold out; they'd raised the price from four bucks to twenty; security guards had just sent a guy who wasn't doing nothing to the hospital; cops were waiting to ambush us. Owen brushed all this off. "You never hear good news when you're in line for a punk show."

A single patrol car came up the block, slowing down to a crawl, awestruck local cops looking at the line with bewilderment.

A guy in line yelled, "Goddamn fucking pigs!"

Looking wounded, the Mohawked guy with the swastika on his stump said, with a surprisingly high voice, "Hey, don't say that. Cops are our friends."

By the time we got in, we'd missed the opening band, the Minutemen. There was a break before the next band, D.O.A. I kept being derailed by the few women I saw. Each of them radiated a hostility that seemed to be ignited by sexual tension. One with Siouxsie Sioux mascara and facial jewelry would make furious eye contact with me and I would look not just away but away and *down*. It was like something out of a Tanizaki short story: a woman's glare could let me know my own inadequacies.

As D.O.A. was taking the stage, I assumed that the moment they started playing, all four thousand people would commence drop-kicking baby animals through plate-glass windows, something I would witness from a headlock administered by some golem in black leather breaking beer bottles rhythmically against my forehead to the polite applause of his friends.

D.O.A. played like they were all trying to catch up to a song running away from them that needed to be played faster and louder and meaner than any human being could manage, but they didn't care if they died trying. The crowd bubbled and a mosh pit appeared in front of us like a special effects tornado. Owen and I were in a group watching the pit, which swirled with jumping, slamming, pogo-ing kids who inflicted damage on each other in a way that seemed strangely friendly. If someone fell down, two or three people pulled him back up.

I screamed so loud I was instantly hoarse. "Is this normal?"

"Yeah. People are actually pretty nice," he yelled at the top of his lungs.

"If I lost a contact lens—"

"No, they would not help you. But basically nice."

Owen launched himself into the pit. He whipped around the center and across the edges, slamming and shoving and then returning without incident. I was jealous. He was happy and sweaty as a hockey player. "Come on out, man, it's fun."

Was I the type of person who participated or who lingered at the edges of things, an observer, a creeper?

A new song started. It was faster, angrier, apparently more familiar, because tremors went through the crowd so the spot I was in liquefied. The dance floor now surrounded me, so I was in the pit regardless of whether I wanted to be. Be here now? I had this sense pulsing around me that if I tossed back my head and started slamming around, I would be free of my brain, and hair would shoot down my wrists and across my face, talons grow from my fingertips, toe claws burst out of my high-tops, and my body would belong to the world as I let out a pure moon-shattering howl of lycanthropic ecstasy.

I *could* participate, I thought, and that made me feel fear, queasy, dark, awful fear. I carefully, slowly walked to the new edge of spectators. My heart rate was as low as ever. My breathing was fine—not excited at all, just observing everyone else get emotional. That narrative voice kicked in. I was paying attention to the catharsis of violence.

There was a short, grinning punk at the fringes of the pit who wasn't participating, but as bodies flew by, he reached out with a fist or the toe of a boot to kick and punch without the risk of being hurt. When he made particularly good contact, he half fell over, laughing to himself.

Onstage, the singer noticed the mood of the crowd darkening. "The next song is called 'Unity.' Not fighting. Unity." It was slower, with a little ska to it.

Owen shot out of the crowd like a wayward ball bearing, and smacked into me. There was a gash in his forehead, and blood was gey-sering out of it.

"I'm fine," he said. Some dick had smashed him across the face with wrist studs.

"Is this normal?"

"I'm fine."

I pushed ahead of him through the peristaltic crowd, toward the bathroom. It had probably been a serviceable bathroom for the many years of its sovereign existence, but in the last couple hours punks had colonized it and it had fallen. The walls now dripped with fresh graffiti and the toilet seats were smashed and each toilet was overflowing. A guy with a safety pin through his cheek and no pants on was balancing on one of the sinks, testing its shattering weight.

Owen pushed a wad of wet paper towels against his wound, which had left trails of blood across his face. He stood at the sink and tried to take care of himself. One sink away, a spike-haired guy whistled at him in admiration. He then opened his mouth, which was bleeding, to show off a chipped tooth.

Owen nodded politely. "That just happen?"

"Yeah."

"Does it hurt?"

The guy smiled. "Yeahhhhh!"

Back on the concert floor, Owen held the towels to his head. I was not really having a good time, not because my friend was hurt, but because he was hurt and I wasn't. I was feeling like a coward. The mood was surly, like the entire room had been promised something they suspected they weren't actually going to be allowed to have. I was one of them. I hadn't had an authentic moment yet.

But that was my fault. I wanted to go back to work and tell Rick and Melanie that while they were having a dinner party, I was having an experience. I was going to participate.

On stage, the Dead Kennedys were setting up. They were the only band tonight whose music I knew. The lyrics, when I could understand them, were sarcastic and political, and I assumed they were intelligent because I mostly didn't understand them. I didn't know who Pol Pot was, but when I heard "Kill the Poor" or "Chemical Warfare," it was clear Jello Biafra, the lead singer, was pissed off about something, and so I was pissed off, too.

Owen had told me there was a moment after a song launches when it casts a net over a punk audience, and a feeling of "we're all in this together" spreads. This wasn't happening now. There was a lot of talking at microphones, cautious mumbling from Jello toward unknown persons about things we couldn't understand. The amplification system made every word unintelligible.

They started a song, and maybe eight measures later, stopped. More muttering by Jello. More confusion spreading outward. A guy leapt onstage and stole the microphone, which left Jello clearly unenthusiastic.

To our right, a security guard outfitted in the then impressive Mr. T look of muscle tee, gold chains, and evil patterns shaved into his beard growth, was spinning his baton like nunchuks. He grabbed a skinhead by the back of his leather jacket, pulled him off balance, and ran him through an emergency exit. The guard kicked him in the ass hard enough that the kid became a completely concave figure. The guard slammed the double doors and the frosted glass shattered.

A second later, we could see the bewildered punk outside picking himself up from the asphalt. He was backlit by distant spinning blue lights. None of us registered what *that* meant yet.

The band was still trying to successfully play a song, in this case the ominously named "Police Truck." A mysterious crosscurrent ran through the crowd, a ripple away from the stage, the way schools of fish are driven by the approach of sharks. The rear doors, all of them, shattered, the sound drowned out by the band, who were playing what would be the last song of the evening, "Holiday in Cambodia."

I was starting to become transparent, floating over the room the way I did sometimes at my mother's house. I was barely here now. I could feel the crowd's tension ratcheting up, and there were little explosions of anger and fear everywhere, just not coming off of me.

Fog was billowing through the back doors, like someone had clapped chalk erasers into the crowd. A fire extinguisher, I thought. But people were running away from the vapor, and I thought, "Oh that's what panic looks like."

Owen said, "Tear gas."

"Pardon?"

"Run."

"Is this normal?"

"Run!"

With the rest of the crowd being driven elsewhere, we slipped alone out the side door the punk kid had been thrown through. I was on the sidewalk, looking back and regarding chaos through the frame of the door—a blur of bodies colliding blindly, trying to escape. *Oh,* I thought blandly, *we have just escaped a riot.*

"RUN!" Owen yelled.

I said, "Why?"

Later, Owen would tell the story as if I were dim-witted for considerably longer than I remember it. In any case, he ran away alone because I was busy regarding what he was running away from: a wall of police in full riot gear, body armor and face shields, skull-cracking batons extended over their heads. They were running directly at me.

As a frontier anthropologist, I felt exempt, as if the cops would run right past me. Furthermore, running would suggest I was scared. I thought, and this was critical, that not reacting was a merit badge, a sign of being calm. This was incorrect.

I am lucky Owen was my friend. He darted back, grabbed me, and forced me to run. A block later, we looked backward. The streets were choked with a few dozen police cruisers. There were police wagons lining up and detainees handcuffed beside them. Overhead, incredibly, there were two police helicopters orbiting the block, billion-watt searchlights sweeping the streets with metallic blue rude light for signs of fleeing black leather.

Owen noticed the cop cars were from different jurisdictions. Los Angeles, Wilmington, Long Beach. This was coordinated. The cops had planned this.

How far away was safe? Two blocks away, a catering truck was doing good business selling soft drinks and burritos. We stood in line behind some cops, who chuckled in our direction (the two of us, in boring clothing, had no signs of being punks, so we were harmless).

Owen took the paper towel away from his forehead. "I think it's stopped bleeding," he said, and a heartbeat's worth of blood fountained out of the gash and splattered his shirt. He put pressure back on the wound.

There was an ambulance nearby, and one laconic paramedic was leaning against it. He beckoned Owen with the curl of a finger. Bored, he held a flashlight near the gash, handed over a bandage, and told Owen he needed to go to the emergency room for stitches. The paramedic listed off the injuries he'd had to repair at punk shows: broken bones, caved-in skulls, don't even get him started on how fragile punks' noses were.

"Why do they do that to each other?" he asked. Owen and I reacted differently to that. Later, he said he was happy the paramedic hadn't included him in that "they." Which was an ironic way, I guess, to say that Owen had just concluded he no longer wanted the reputation of trashing hotel rooms, starting fights, living the rock-and-roll-into-punk life.

I felt the paramedic had tagged me as a dilettante. He was right. I had participated in nothing.

Owen and I walked outside the police lines, to the Saab. A small group of three or four kids walked tentatively toward the sounds of the riot from the opposite direction, the neighborhood. They were local kids attracted by the brilliant lights. They watched the scene—the punks, the cops—as if they were seeing it on television. One of the kids picked up a rock, and heaved it through a store window.

"What the hell?" I yelled. An alarm went off in the store. The kids ran away.

Owen sighed, "Opportunists," as he and I got into the car. Punks were starting to flee up the sidewalk, past us, and the streets were about to get jammed. I looked at the fleeing local kids, and the wrecked store-front, and thought, "Well, *they* participated."

Punks were steaming past us. Engines were starting all around like an amateur Indy 500.

There was a traffic jam. We told each other stories of what had happened. Owen came up with the concept of "story yeast." It's the ingredient that, when you add it to your story, makes the details grow. Owen decided he'd stage dived, and the crowd had parted, so he'd landed on his forehead. And I was clueless, a Paul Bowles character, a professor about to be eaten by the tribe he was studying.

There was something else going on while we inched toward the 405. Headlights from approaching cars would illuminate for one second the severe faces of punks crammed into cars, all of them sweaty and grimy in black leather, mouths snarling as they all, too, in their individual boxes, were telling stories. They were driving slowly and carefully, not just because there was a traffic jam, but because they were in Honda Accord sedans clearly not their own.

I saw one person—I can't swear it was the actual guy with the stump and Mohawk, but it looked like him—driving soberly in a car full of companions, his giant gelled hair flattening against the ceiling of his mother's station wagon so it pointed to the side like a horse's tail brushed backward. He looked terrified of getting the car scratched.

The postures and the act and the police breaking up the show were as ritualized as the Main Street Electrical Parade closing down Disney-land on a warm summer night. Here they were, one lane after another, four thousand punks going home, peeling off costumes, showing up to work the next morning promptly so they wouldn't get fired. Owen took them in with a glance and said, "This is not very punk, not really."

How complex. I was frustrated for not having slam-danced, but just because you participated didn't mean you were having a real experience. And there we were on the freeway again, one among many cars coming from all over the Basin, and among us all the stories were being told, the yeast rising. I looked out the window, and saw it at some point, maybe around Manhattan Beach: an old billboard, one panel falling down over a spread of smiling faces, news team jackets tagged with graffiti. At the bottom, I read aloud the familiar slogan: *"Auténtica."*

We made a stop at the emergency room at UCLA, where Owen got ten stitches. When we got home, I knew I was going to Rick's next dinner party.

MEMOIR

RICK DISAPPEARED from work again. He called in sick this time. Even though no one believed him, he didn't get in trouble. The store wasn't going to last much longer, and enforcing rules seemed pointless.

Mel rolled up to me quietly and said, after a careful moment, "I've heard some unusual rumors about you."

"Like?"

"I hear you're nineteen," she said.

I nodded. I watched her face fall. "Why, how old are you?" I asked her.

"I'm twenty-six."

I thought "twenty-six" must mean something else. I couldn't make sense of that.

"How old did you think I was?" she asked.

"Nineteen."

"Nope." She wasn't my age. This meant I wasn't her age, either. Wasn't she a dance major—Oh, graduate school! Then I realized that, yes, around the eyes, there was some evidence of desert living. And I understood why she was avoiding me—what twenty-six-year-old wanted a teenager hanging on her?

"When do you turn twenty?"

"Late March." So it wasn't like I was even almost-twenty. Mel was looking at a definite teenager.

An hour into my shift, Rick called. He asked to speak to me. I wasn't sure why.

He whispered, "I'm not really sick, but I just got the worst news. *Lolly* is in town."

"I thought she was still at boarding school."

"Well, so did I, but her mother called me late last night and said that not only was Lolly expelled, but she also got on a plane for the States. She's looking for me, which means she's looking for money, and I'm through with just handing her one dollar after the next. I'm staying home today because she doesn't know where I live, but she does know the bookstore's address."

He paused, as if what he was implying was obvious. I said, "Okay."

"I want you to listen very carefully. If she comes by, you don't know where I am, but she should leave a number where she can be reached."

"What does she look like?"

"I haven't seen her in a year, so she might have changed, but be on the lookout for a fourteen-year-old girl, overweight, probably wearing too much makeup. She knows how much I hate rock music, so she'll probably be wearing one of her Pink Floyd T-shirts. She makes a point of eating junk food around me, so she might have a slice of pizza in her hand. Oh, and she doesn't talk, she whines."

I spent the rest of the day awaiting this apparition. I was a little excited, and then disappointed when my shift ended and she hadn't shown up.

When Rick returned the next day, he wore his sunglasses indoors. He pulled me aside—he was just pretending to be sensitive to light, he said—had I seen Lolly? I said I hadn't. He looked relieved. He thought she'd moved on to San Francisco, where she had other friends to sponge off of.

"So what else? How was your evening of slam-dancing?" he asked. "How do Zen and slam-dancing go together anyway? Is it like being straight and bisexual?"

He was smiling, I could see, but I was still taking this very seriously, and I presented some thin theory that I thought explained both of these things. Rick listened, nodding with what seemed a lot like understanding. He'd taken on the role of my concerned older brother so firmly he'd begun to believe it himself, as if perhaps he'd traveled to the continent on the Grand Tour with my parents and agreed there to chaperone me through difficult thinking.

He told me about a trip he'd once taken to Wales. He'd brought along a copy of *Madame Bovary* and had finished it at sunset on the side of a hill near a mining town.

"There were tears in my eyes, and it was getting cold, so I stumbled, literally, into this pub, and ordered an ale. I sat down at a table, all alone for a few minutes, calming down. Then the door swept open and a pack of a dozen boys, boys your age, sauntered up to the bar and ordered beers. I was watching them and one of them saw me and there was something in the way I looked that was *wrong*, like they could smell this *otherness* on me. In an instant, some strange instinct for self-preservation came over me, and I wasn't gay anymore. I was just a man on vacation. As soon as I opened my mouth, they were charmed by my accent.

"One of them saw my copy of *Madame Bovary,* and assumed it was pornography, so he grabbed it. And so there they all were, peeking over each other's shoulders to look at the girlie book, and maybe I was only projecting, but I thought one of them was pushing and shoving extra hard to convince his friends, and himself, that he actually wanted to be there, to see it. Can you imagine what it would be like to be different— I don't even mean gay, I just mean sensitive or creative—and to be trapped into acting along with the pack? I hope that never happens to you."

It sounded sincere. It sounded true. I've described Rick's trip to Wales to friends over the years, and some of them wrinkle their brows and half-start in recognition, not at Rick's feelings, but at the scene itself. It's familiar, but no one can quite place it. I'm pretty sure he made it up as he went along. Or it was from a book I have yet to read.

When I walked around Westwood I thought of Rick's Welsh pub night. That summer, men tended to wear distressed leather jackets, without the benefit of having ridden a motorcycle—just the pre-disastered shell, as if they'd once been dangerous and they were still carrying that on their shoulders.

Experience was a fashion statement. I realized that if you followed this line of thinking, eventually you would see men with eye patches they didn't really need. Peg legs. There were definitely jeans with holes in them on both men and women, but they were cunningly placed. No one here had slid off a motorcycle during a barrel race circuit. *You did nothing to earn that damage,* I thought, *but it does become you.* How similar it was to the subtext of the punk look, really, where sixteen-eye combat boots and safety pins inserted through flesh were also meant to convey that you'd actually done something with your life? *I am ready for action and ready for pain.*

Speaking of that, I agreed, finally, to go to Rick's.

"Are you excited, young man?" he asked, and I was aware he was teasing me.

"Why do you want me there?" I asked him this, but mostly as if he were a proxy for Melanie.

"For *balance,*" he said after a while.

"To balance out the guests—"

"No, silly, to throw you off yours."

Mel would give me a ride.

She said, "You'll have fun."

"When am I coming back?"

"Whenever you want."

Was she saying this as a friend? Did twenty-six-year-olds *have* friends? I began to add up the differences between what nineteen meant and twenty-six and I was embarrassed.

I visited every used bookstore under the somewhat gentle Santa Monica sun. I bought a few strange periodicals, literary journals, that were so intelligent I couldn't even understand their names. *Antaeus. Ploughshares.* They were like speakeasies, and the code to get in was knowing why naming your magazine after a Greek wrestler made associative sense.

I understood some of the writing in them! This felt like a triumph, as it was the first time I'd read literary fiction without a classroom to explain it to me. I had been calling myself a writer since I was five years old, but you couldn't just have the attitude of being a writer, carrying around a highly visible copy of *Ploughshares* like it was a beaten leather jacket. Or you ended up like Owen's stepfather. Here was a formula: attitude minus work plus time equals bitterness.

I started writing a short story. It wasn't good, but it was weird, at least, with dream logic that could have tricked people into believing I knew what I was doing, so I continued with it. Instead of telling myself I was a writer, I said, "I write, but I'd like to get paid for it," which felt honest.

At work, I saw we had *Water Music* by T. C. Boyle, and when Mel saw me holding it, I said, casually, "I just read a short story of his in *Antaeus*," and it felt perfectly natural.

She walked to the middle of the fiction section and returned with a small paperback pressed to her chest with palms crossed against it. "This is white magic. Anti-dough-head literature." It was a novel called *Easy Travel to Other Planets* and it was based on the work of John C. Lilly, dolphin expert. It was Ted Mooney's first novel and she said it was so cryptic and beautiful and funny it reminded her of how I probably wrote.

When I read it in my room at home, I thought, "I could write like this," which actually meant, "I wish I'd written my short story this well," and I understood why this book was so much better than my work. The author looked outside of himself. He knew things like emotions and how other people acted in ways I didn't yet. I read it in an afternoon with jealousy, awe, and appreciation suspended over the thought that recurred like a quick heartbeat: Melanie thinks she knows how I write, which means she thinks about me.

THE CHILDREN'S SECTION

THE NEXT MORNING I was awakened by the sound of something sliding under my door. It was an article from *The Wall Street Journal* explaining how many first-time novelists never sold a second novel. My stepmother had clipped it for me.

I should explain this. The house I was in wasn't my home, of course, but during high school and college I'd camped there during the vacations when I wasn't visiting my mother in New York.

One morning when I was maybe fourteen or fifteen and on break from boarding school, I heard my stepmother on the phone to her parents. I wasn't trying to creep around; the house was large and her voice carried across a few rooms. "Herb's ex-wife is looking for money," she was saying. "She's scrounging like an alley cat, trying to sell us her old jewelry. We're pretending we don't have any money, and that we need to borrow it from you." A pause. "Yeah, right, like when we put in the swimming pool."

She was talking to her mother. I walked up behind her. I tapped her on the shoulder. Ann's face didn't change expression as quickly as mine did—it didn't change now, but she was silent and glancing away from me as she added up what I'd heard.

"Tell me when I can come back inside the house," I said. I went out the front door and sat on the stoop. It was a sunny morning in West Los Angeles. Mostly it was just pops, clicks, whistles, and shards of glass going through my mind. "Who says 'scrounge,' anyway," I thought. Also: I liked cats. So fuck Ann. Also, waiting out there, I had to admit I understood why she and my father were lying to my mom. I didn't know what else you could do with her.

Ann appeared on the porch. She said she was off the phone. So I went back in. I don't recall any discussion of what I'd heard, which would mean both that I didn't confront her and that she didn't apologize. It's likely she did and I didn't want to remember it.

So that's how it stood between us. I understood that to her, I was, among whatever else I might be, the residue of that poisonous person who had to be kept at a distance. Further, she thought at the time that she and my father were both on the same side. But she was young and my father was an unusual case.

When she slipped the newspaper clipping under my door, she was being helpful. She knew my mom wanted to be a writer, and I think Ann thought she was giving me data that might send me in a more promising direction.

She lacked malice, but she had an awkward, brilliant efficiency that skipped over social graces. Whenever Owen rang the doorbell, Ann would acknowledge him, then come find me and tell me he was outside so I could open the door myself. Owen, whose upbringing had been as weird as mine, didn't notice things like that, but I'd specifically noticed that at other people's houses, they tended to let you in when you came over.

My room was upstairs. It had a fold-out couch for a bed, and it had a demoralizingly thin mattress that pressed against a cruel set of metal support bars, so I slept on the floor. I had a couple of shelves of books and comic books, and an electric typewriter on the desk. There was a deck outside my window that overlooked the palm trees and the swimming pool in the backyard. I rarely used the latter because looking at it, I still thought, "Oh, you lied to my mom about that, too."

Just because they might be right didn't mean they could get me to stop being loyal to her.

That oversimplifies things. It's not like I accepted my mom's worldview anymore. A couple years after my moment with Ann, Mom asked me to do something for her. I was living with her in New York and working at her office. She wanted me to call my father to tell him I needed him to come up with the money for college. The original bonds supposed to pay for it had probably gone up Trevor's nose. Or maybe they'd gone to help float Anton—my mother's explanations had so many hairpin turns I couldn't follow them. I had a net of loans, grants, and a work-study job, but there was still money owed before I could start at Wesleyan. She told me Dad had been playing games with her, being cryptic about whether he and Ann actually had money or had to borrow it from her mother. She felt I would have a better chance at getting him to commit to paying for school.

She sat me down at her desk in her office, the one on the second floor in Midtown Manhattan. I had her close the door for privacy, and I made the phone call to my father's office in Los Angeles as directed. I'd never told my mother about the conversation I'd overheard of Ann's. Nor had I told my father.

I was more nervous talking to him than I normally was, but only in part because of what I was supposed to be asking. I started as she had asked ("Mom wants to know if you . . .") and he cut me off. He said I would be taken care of. He said nothing further.

At the time, my father was in management at Atlantic Richfield. He was in the brown suit phase of his career, where his sense of humor had been submerged, and our talks on the phone were always awkward, like I was the loose beatnik progeny he wasn't sure of.

He continued: I shouldn't worry. I would never be out on the street, but I shouldn't get into details with him, because there were things I didn't really need to know about, regardless of what my mother was insisting.

I said that this phone call was hard for me because I didn't trust him. I said I also didn't trust Mom. I said that they were playing games about money and I didn't understand it, and that I just wanted everyone to be honest. He pointed out that I'd once had a college education fund.

"But Mom made up for that," I explained. "Remember, she got me a scholarship at Thacher to balance that out."

"No she didn't."

Finally, something I was sure of. My father's anger at my mom had clouded his memory. "She did. I filled out the paperwork. I saw the scholarship grant. I was on scholarship at Thacher," I said.

There was a long pause. "What are you talking about?" I explained it again, and my father said, "I wrote a check to your mother every semester for the full tuition at Thacher." Then he said, "I suppose that went to her boyfriend, too."

There was more in this vein. My father started telling me things I hadn't known about how Peter Charming had negotiated the part of the settlement that set aside property to be used for my education. What he was saying wasn't exactly accurate, but it was a fuller accounting than I'd had. My mother had left out many details. My father was adding them, not carefully, but coldly and with a bit of knife-twisting, the way you do when something has been on your mind every day for a decade.

I was only seventeen, but something had been on my mind, too. I said, "Do you know this? A couple of years ago, I walked in on Ann telling her mother that you and she were going to lie to my mother about having money. She said my mom was scrounging around like an alley cat. She knows I heard it."

Silence.

"Dad?"

Silence again. I knew he understood exactly what I meant. He hadn't expected this story, and he couldn't contradict it. I was the kid he'd had with a woman he had to protect himself from, and I'd managed to find a new way to remind him of that.

"Dad?"

My father at his desk at Atlantic Richfield, in ARCO Towers, in downtown Los Angeles, many floors above the ground, views for miles, holding the phone away from his mouth. "Oh, Glen David," he whispered. Then he hung up.

I didn't know what happened. I waited on the phone, thinking there was no way he'd hung up. Finally, that strange, urgent sound of the long-distance company telling me to replace the receiver and try again.

I called back. My father has a steady phone voice. He had answered the phone exactly the same way every time I had called him, since I was perhaps three or four years old, when my mother, even then, had put me on the phone: "Herb Gold." I had always felt, in just the two syllables of his name, his affirmation that he belonged at that desk and could answer any question thoughtfully.

The receiver picked up. I waited for "Herb Gold." Nothing.

"Dad?"

He hung up again.

I held the phone. I put it down. I stared at the office door.

Eventually, there was a knock. My mother came in. "Did you get the money?" she asked.

Two summers later, when I was nineteen, whenever returning to Wesleyan came up, my father and I were both not thinking about that phone call, the way you don't think of any chronic condition, and neither of us talked about it. So there was that tension. There were others, too.

My half-brothers: Seth was six and Marc, whose life was a living hell, was three. Seth had come out of the womb at a dead run, talking, crying, asking questions, breaking shit, talking more, figuring out he was the smartest person in any given room, and making demands on his mother's loyalties like he was an Eastern Bloc dictator. His nickname among my father's side of the family was "the Prince," and for a kid to have earned that distinction over me was a significant achievement.

Marc, on the other hand, was an orchid of a kid. He was quiet for long periods of time, and unlike Seth, who loved to dance to whatever punk songs I put on the stereo, Marc liked to sit on the couch perfectly still, listening to Mozart and gazing into the middle distance like an infant Henry James. He was just as smart as Seth, which only made his life worse, because he could anticipate exactly whatever awful thing Seth was planning on doing to him next, but because he was only three years old he was unable to prevent it.

Once, I was in the kitchen with Marc, when Seth came in because he had a question to ask me. "Glen," he said, punching Marc in the face, "is Owen ever coming back to visit?"

Marc at that moment was glowing with his first, and thus purest, expression of disbelief that the world could possibly be that unfair. He threw his head back and wailed. Seth looked at him not with disdain but real confusion. Punching Marc in the face was so normal for him he didn't realize he'd done it.

But there was no punishment for that, nor anything else he did. Seth could do anything he wanted. If his feet had been able to reach the pedals, he would have driven the family Volvo to the market to pick up smokes. For about twenty-two hours a day, he bossed Ann around.

But then my father would come home. It wasn't that Seth trod lightly then—he behaved exactly as he would otherwise—he just knew he had a tougher opponent.

My father was unscalable and monument-like. In part that was because he had to be the voice of Moses when he was at home. There was always a list of promises and treaties Seth had negotiated with Ann that my father was learning of the moment he arrived. Once, before he'd even put his briefcase down, my father was greeted by Seth twisting his arm.

"Seth, if you do that, I'll do it back to you."

"I don't care."

"You're going to lose," my father said.

"No I'm not."

There had at one point been countdowns, but there weren't countdowns anymore. Nor were there second warnings. My father took Seth's arm and began to twist. Seth laughed. But it became a strangled laugh. And my father didn't stop. Seth let go of my dad, and tried to push him away, but of course, he was six and my father was fifty-two and probably weighed two hundred twenty pounds. As I recall it, my dad just kept sorting through the mail with one hand, using the other to bend Seth's wrist back until he was yelling.

"You giving up yet?" my dad asked.

"No!"

"What, does it hurt? You do this sort of stuff to your mother and your brother all day long and now someone stands up to you and you're about to cry?"

"I'm not going to cry," Seth said.

Part of me was horrified Dad was being so cruel and the other part, the stepbrother part, was perfectly fine with the little brat getting the snot whipped out of him.

"I'm going to kill you, Daddy!" Seth screamed. "Let go!" My father released his arm.

"There was a boy in Montana who killed his father," Dad said. "It was in the newspaper."

"How did he kill his father?"

"With a shotgun."

"I'm going to get a shotgun and kill you, Daddy."

"You'll go to jail."

"Good." Seth's eyes flashed. He went over to the newspaper and started rummaging through it.

"What are you looking for?" Dad asked.

"I want to know about the boy who killed his father."

"What about him?"

"I want to write him a fan letter."

It continued like this until Seth was crying again, which set Marc off into that desolate land of childhood where you're crying but don't really know why, and those two wails were the only noise as, otherwise, Ann continued to prepare dinner.

My father said to Ann, "Let's get out of this shit."

She continued attending to the chicken she was cooking. "But where would we go?"

It wasn't a solicitation; it was rhetorical. It was, "We have nowhere to go." She wasn't happy either, she seemed to be saying. I wasn't sure what she would have changed, though.

I knew what my dad was thinking. *I should be going to that new house, the cool house, where this wouldn't be happening.* Even if, of course, it would be happening exactly like this because the rest of them would ruin it by moving there with him.

After dinner, I went upstairs and closed the door, but the weird tension outside seemed to seep in. I imagined bringing Melanie over, passing by one weeping brother being punched by one cheerful brother, my amoral father, me showing her the swimming pool that symbolized the lies my mother engendered, and taking her up here for the big finish, a room that didn't even have a bed in it but a fold-up couch that I now noticed had been duct-taped where I'd let a reading light singe the fabric. Not an iota of this fit my self-image.

When I tried to go to sleep that night, I keep feeling earthquakes. But that was just me, shaking.

HISTORY

I WAS IN MY ROOM when Ann walked by. "Melanie's here," she said, and I immediately knew what that meant to Ann: she'd left Melanie standing on the porch.

I let her in. From the patient yet confused look on Mel's face, I could see her factoring in all the ways I was nineteen years old. My father came to the foyer to say hello. I could see him making a silent but sympathetic judgment of some sort. He wasn't creepy or inappropriate with women—but curious? Always.

They talked for maybe a minute: yes, she was at UCLA, yes, dance—modern dance—from Arizona, originally. Lived in New York once, lived on falafel and yogurt, dancing eight hours a day. He smiled as she described this, and I realized how much I missed the part of him that was at ease. He enjoyed hearing from intelligent strangers. Also: I *wanted* to be a writer, but Melanie actually *was* a dancer.

She was describing trends toward androgyny in dance, which he knew about, he'd read something in the *L.A. Times* about it, and then with an appraising nod, he wished us a good night.

I got into the passenger's seat of Mel's old VW Bug. While she drove, I asked questions, a lot of them. She liked to answer questions. Mel was intrigued by my summer of transformation because she felt her own coming on. She was self-sufficient, defensively so, the type of woman who paid her way for every meal, who had no credit card debt, and though that meant she was thin and went without any luxuries, there was something about her spartan lifestyle as she described it that was incredibly attractive to me. I could picture her room clearly though I hadn't seen it: the frameless futon right on the floor, bordered by all those novels borrowed from the bookstore, the Dr. Bronner's peppermint soap that doubled as detergent and tripled as dish soap. It was the life of right angles and wire-rimmed glasses, an unscented candle on a dustless milk crate, two pairs of faded jeans, three white starched shirts, and a single, tight body that fit in them without effort.

She was beautiful but I didn't know how to tell her that, so I talked about art in a cowardly, precocious way. Sharaku, who was all about Kabuki artifice, and Yoshitoshi, whose woodcuts were so steeped in blood that they'd been banned. I only mentioned them so I could ask if she knew Hashiguchi Goyo's *Woman Combing Her Hair,* a 1920s woodcut. She didn't, so I talked about how finely drawn it was, how you could tell the artist loved not just details but the woman herself. To me, that image was the peak of sensitive aesthetics, creating a kind of longing that you had to be evolved to appreciate. I said he drew it so you wanted to touch her long, straight, thick hair.

She loved art. Independent women like Georgia O'Keeffe. She liked how O'Keeffe and Stieglitz were only together six months a year, and how she was his muse but she had her own art. Or Diego and Frida, how they lived in houses that connected but they got to invite each other over. It seemed so ideal. I had only the faintest clue about maybe one of those names, but at least I owned up to wanting to read about them. That excited her, recommending books, she liked to be helpful.

Rick had given her Alice Miller's *The Drama of the Gifted Child* and she'd recognized herself. She told me I had to read it. I would probably recognize myself in it, too. It was about responsibility takers. Only now was she realizing she hadn't had much of a childhood. She'd had to take care of her mom when her father disappeared into the desert. He'd had dementia, and had vanished after clearing out the bank accounts. Mel had supported herself since she was sixteen. It was why she had clear boundaries.

I enjoy long interviews. This was like hearing a novelist in *Writers at Work* describe the life of an artist. Mel seemed as deep as any poet describing travels across sand-blasted lands, and I wondered about kissing her.

She asked: What music did I listen to, besides punk? I might have stalled, but ended up telling her, sheepishly, owning up to it, "Philip Glass."

She exclaimed aloud, thrilled. "You like him? Have you heard *The Photographer,* his album about Muybridge?" She had to explain Muybridge, as he was an inspiration to how she wanted to make dances. The calibration of motions made in everyday life, the infinitesimal study of time, turning what seemed like thoughtless motion into art, that's what got her brain into making dances.

She was about to turn twenty-seven. Did I know what a Saturn Return was, she asked. Saturn took about twenty-seven years to orbit the sun, she said, and so when you were twenty-seven you tended to transform into a new person. She hoped it was happening to her. It sounded corny, but it was true, she said, listing off friends of hers who had gotten married or divorced or had massively changed circumstance at twenty-seven. So everything was up in the air, in a way. Except this: First Person Singular. It was a kind of Rosary she brought out every so often. It was like "be here now."

Did I say it aloud at some point? Maybe I only thought it: twenty-seven was Janis Joplin, Jim Morrison, Jimi Hendrix. Maybe I would have said it as an observation in the spirit of "Right, twenty-seven is a milestone," but not meaning anything more, just because Melanie worrying about death would never occur to me. It was another way I at nineteen was different from her. I didn't know how worried she was about twenty-seven.

If I haven't captured exactly what made Melanie so attractive, it was that she had set up her boundaries precisely so she could make art. If I could have articulated it, I would have said I wanted her to be First Person Singular, with me there, too.

Maybe I was already in love by the time we got to Rick's. I just know that a combination of circumstances was putting me on track to know more about Mel than she intended. When we pulled up at Rick's apartment, it was 8:15. We wouldn't leave till 4:15, and we wouldn't sleep at all.

· · ·

Rick's apartment, in the Greene & Greene style, was so nice that in summer 1983 it cost $1,100 a month. How he managed this on $3.85 an hour from the bookstore was suspicious to Melanie. Sugar daddy? Kiting checks? It wasn't secret family money. His family didn't speak to him.

"Right," I said, "and there are all those expenses for Lolly."

I'm not sure how she looked at me when I said that, because the door was thrown open with force, as if the party within was too big to be contained. Rick pulled us in, apologizing for his "breath out to *here*." It was a nice place, beamed ceilings and original tile and hardwood and Moorish touches.

Rick pointed out a tall, curly-haired man who was slouching shyly against the stove in the kitchen. He wore, badly, a Greek fisherman's cap. "That's Philippe," Rick hissed to me. "He used to be Catherine Deneuve's lover. He was in *Valley of the Dolls*. He's only been gay for a few months so forgive the hat. He doesn't know anything yet, but he's really really really gay, like a thirteen-year-old boy is really really really Jewish after being bar mitzvahed."

Melanie went into the kitchen to get something to drink while Rick showed me the rest of the place. There was a stack of Moleskine journals in the hallway, by the phone alcove. They came up to my thighs. Rick said, "Those are my thoughts. I'm transcribing them now for a book."

"What's it about?"

He thought about it, as if this was the first time someone had asked. "About being a man. In this culture."

There was more to the house tour, but I was watching Mel, still in the kitchen. She was in deep conversation with a woman whose posture was described by her hips pointing toward Mel in aggressive slouching.

Rick had a roommate. His roommate was depressed because he'd just learned he had HIV and he was worried it might become AIDS. "He slept with this flight attendant who gave it to, like, everyone."

Recently, a young gay friend who hadn't even been born in 1983 reacted with awe when I started telling him this story. He wanted me to explain every detail of what it was like to be at a dinner party in Hollywood then with gay men discussing AIDS. But I would be a disappointing witness. It's hard to account for how Rick was talking. He wasn't really worried. It seemed to me that night that the men in the room, who were smart and funny and who had learned how to ask the right questions, would be genuinely shocked that they were supposed to be more concerned. Also I wasn't paying close attention. I was a straight nineteen-year-old with a little bit of empathy, but with a deeper curiosity about what Melanie was doing in the kitchen.

I decided I should go there to get a beer or something, leaving the men behind, and Mel showed visible joy when she saw me. The woman she was talking to had fixed her with an unbreakable Rasputin-like gaze, as if she was waiting to be found overwhelming. That's a look that couldn't go well, I thought. That might have been what I looked like when I was looking at Heidi in my dorm room. I swore I would never look that way at anyone again.

When we were alone, Mel said she was in frequent trouble because she was the only straight woman in the dance department. Her best friend was disappointed that Mel didn't even want to experiment. " 'You aren't even a little bi?' "

I asked, "Have you always known?"

She nodded. "You?"

I was reminded of being in eighth grade, being asked if I did drugs, and knowing that "No" was boring and it gave off the tiniest whiff of being narrow-minded. "Yes" was the truth here. Was I . . . boring?

A few hours later, most of the crowd had gone home. It was down to maybe a half-dozen of us sitting on the floor in front of the fireplace. Of course we hadn't had a fire that summer night, but the effect was like listening to crackling embers, the evening on its way to history.

Someone asked about Lolly and Rick said Lolly was a slut. He'd just learned she'd given a flight attendant a handjob so she could ride on the Concorde for free. Fausta however was excelling at her riding lessons, and he was hoping she would be going *en point* soon, though not too soon.

Somehow, I jumped to this: "Is Lolly short for 'Lolita'?"

"Yes."

I said, "You have a kid named Lolita Savilla?"

"I do. And one named Clayton and one named Fausta."

This was getting confusing. Melanie's last name was Clayton. "Have you ever been married?"

"Not that I know of—have you?" Rick had this crafty smile that let me know he was enjoying being cross-examined.

"Who's Lolly's mother?"

"Her mother, and Clay's mother for that matter, is a wonderful, very special woman. A fine, educated, *clean* woman. Their mother is Miss Bette Midler."

"Rick!"

"I'm serious. You don't believe me?" People were laughing, and his face lit up like he was challenging gossip. "What kind of world is this anyway? It's unfair. If I want to have Bette Midler's children, I should be allowed to have Bette Midler's children."

And then he explained that for years he had told his friends he wanted to adopt a little girl. He would give her a classical education. She would learn to play the cello and write poetry and ride English equitation. She would learn about the finest literature, not that Dick and Jane garbage.

His friends laughed, because no one would ever let him adopt *anything*. Not a box turtle. And if he did somehow get his hands on a little girl, when she hit the age of eleven or so she would rebel and become all the things he hated. There was no Lolly. None of the children were real.

"Clayton, well, I realized I shouldn't push my son so hard, and that's why Clay still loves me and he's still at Exeter."

I said, "What's he doing at Exeter, still? It's summer break."

"I mean, generally," Rick said as if explaining the obvious. "He's vacationing in Montauk now. With the Kennedys." He didn't dwell on it. A few minutes later, he was telling me he'd been dating Sal Mineo when he was murdered, which I was impressed by only for the amount of time it took me to realize there was no reason I should believe that, either.

I said, "When did you know you were gay?"

"I'd say getting a blowjob when I was twelve was an eye-opener. Oh, this is good, I've never been able to ask this: When did you know you were straight?"

"That's a good question. Maybe I'm repressing something."

"Oh, stop that. You aren't that interesting. Guys just don't make your dick hard. It's not a mystery. But," he said, lowering his voice, "why are you a writer?"

I liked the question. It wasn't, "Why do you want to be a writer?" I had a good story I already knew to tell, about my mother writing her memoirs from my point of view. I told it now, and it went over well, and as the laughter died down, Rick continued.

"So you're a writer because your mother wanted to be one?"

"She's still writing."

"Sure," he said carefully. "But are you doing it because she wanted to?"

There was probably something funny to say in response, but I couldn't think of it. I didn't have an answer. It threw me.

It was hours later. Not quite dawn. Mel and I were sitting at the curb in front of my house. The car's engine was off. We were saying things that made little sense. It was so late my head was beginning to hurt.

"Do you mind if I kiss you good night?" I asked.

"Okay."

We kissed, but it didn't explain anything. A dry, tight little kiss. It might well have been politeness on her part, except for the small part of me that suspected I just *had* to be irresistible. I wished I had the ability to let things take a natural pace, but there was thunder in my ears. I said, "You're good-looking."

We kissed a few more excruciatingly vague kisses, lip on lip and no more. She didn't pull back but she didn't encourage me. I had no idea what was going on. When I opened my eyes, she was smiling at me.

"Get out of my car," she said.

I let out the word "Jeez!"

She put her face against my neck. Her hand cupped my lap, a maddening gesture somewhere between careless and intimate, and then she drew a deep sigh, her breath crossing my throat. "Now get out," she said, not unkindly.

I'd thought I was familiar with the signals given in the adult world, but I had no idea what the hell was going on. I got out, holding on to her hand, which clutched at me until we finally parted.

ANATOMY

THE NEXT NIGHT, Mel met me after work. She'd come from dance class. It turns out you can read the bruising on dancers' legs. Ballet dancers have a different map than contemporary, Mel explained. She unzipped her bag to throw her glasses in, and a smell came out like a mushroom farm under a summer subway platform.

We went to the Hungry Tiger, the lounge across the street, for beers. While we were walking in, she was discussing a performance she'd seen, and she illustrated it while moving, which made me want to kiss her again, but I didn't know if I was allowed. Also: I was walking into the place illegally, of course, which she seemed to have forgotten. I didn't want to bring it up.

She introduced me to the bartender, who was a Hunter's customer. There was a kind of arrangement between the employees at the establishments, it was said with a wink.

The bartender was friendly, and shuffled through the things necessary for getting a beer. "You look familiar," he said to me.

"I look like a lot of people."

"Where'd you go to high school?"

"Thacher."

"That boarding school? Fancy. When'd you graduate?"

"Nineteen," I swallowed, "seventy-nine."

"Damn," Mel said under her breath.

His smile didn't even change. Neither did his eyes—they were still on me while he disengaged the beer from his hand and passed it to me. "Pretty good math classes at Thacher," he said, and left us alone.

Mel was poor. She drank at the Tiger because of the discount they gave us. She'd pawned her jewelry to stay in graduate school, and not even for the classes. I didn't know enough to ask her what else graduate school provided, but I now know the answer was health insurance.

There were no nicknames for Glen, I said at one point. You can't shorten it. There's no extension for it really. Melanie got one on the first try: Glendale. It was the town for evolved people, like us.

This was not a date, because only dough heads dated. We kept talking.

We went for sushi. I was ready to speak Japanese in front of her, and when we sat down at the counter, I said the ceremonial greeting/grunt that a customer gives, and I started ordering.

The chef was holding an enormous cutting knife about ten inches long. He interrupted me. He shushed everyone around us. "HE—SPEAKS—JAPANESE!" he cried, and punched the butt end of his knife into his chest, and under his thick glasses rolled his eyes back, wincing as if I'd murdered him. "OH—MY—GOD! Hey, everyone, this guy speaks Japanese!"

This was the last time I spoke Japanese publicly.

There is something about getting caught showing off that goes to revealing your character. I said something to Mel about learning to cede control sometimes.

Mel said she hated people who knew how to control conversations. "Like who?"

She shrugged. She wasn't going to tell me yet. The word "control" reminded me of something Clint Eastwood had said in an interview, and me quoting him made her laugh before I even said it: his only interest in power was how it related to his own autonomy. She stopped laughing. That struck her as wise. She liked the idea of being fully autonomous. "Melville," I said, "Population 1."

We went to Santa Monica to see *Koyaanisqatsi*. Afterward we said it should be required viewing. It made her want to make dances. It made me want to write things, even if I was wondering a little how much of that was me, how much my mom. I pointed out how people didn't really want to have experiences, just buy the jacket or the faded jeans to suggest they were deeper than they were. She said that she'd stopped wearing leg warmers outside of class. *Flashdance* meant women who'd never even bloodied a toe in dance class were wearing them in line at the Häagen-Dazs store.

It was after midnight and we were in my house. My dad and Ann were asleep. Mel and I were downstairs. While she was talking to me about something, I was envisioning taking her upstairs. What would we find in my room? A fold-out couch.

"Do you want to see the pool?"

I took her outside. It was a huge backyard, the house on a double lot. The pool was behind a gate, the pool sweep skimming along.

"We should go swimming sometime," she said. "Are there jets? A friend has a Jacuzzi with jets," and I swore to myself that when I finished my beer I would kiss her. I am a slow drinker, however, and quite a bit of conversation would have to pass before then.

I put my beer down. I grabbed the belt loops on her jeans and pulled her toward me hard enough that she bent backward, almost spilling her drink. I grabbed it.

"May I see some ID?"

"I left it at home," she said.

"I suppose you're going to claim you're twenty-six or something."

"Something."

I kissed her, and she kissed back, and I wondered how do you make a perfect kiss? How do you be fully aware and maybe disappear into it? Is it just turn off the mind and keep breathing? I was thinking, *There is no past and no future but this one moment, under the moon, feeling how my fingertips press against the points of your hip bones.* A little overpacked for haiku, but a similar vibe.

I said, "Until five seconds ago I wasn't sure if I annoyed you."

"Oh, the evening at Rick's? Disaster. Ten feet from your house, I thought, 'Why did I say, "Get out of my car"?' That was so stupid. But I've never done this before. Given in to lust."

Lust? It was like confessing to loving bacon, or the patriarchy. Because in the back of my head, I was thinking, "You mean that's okay?" And then: "Does she mean lust for, wait, me?"

"Goddamn Rick," she was saying. "He is such a queen sometimes. Do you remember that game he'd played where he'd pretended to tell you my secret? What I told him was that I wanted to suck you off. It meant so much to me to say that aloud, because until now I've always been someone else's fantasy." She continued, rapidly: to have her own desire first, to be reborn at age twenty-six as a woman enacting her desire rather than just being acted upon. To say it aloud had been liberating, and then he'd been the worst kind of asshole to embarrass her for admitting that.

I nodded. In a reversal of the world as I understood it, Melanie was looking to me to tell her it was all right to say she wanted to suck me off. But it took a moment to get there, because I was having trouble snapping all the pieces of that sentence together. No one had ever said anything like this about me before, so I was mentally double-checking that I hadn't misheard it.

I said, "Aren't you hot in that sweater?"

"Yes." Off it came.

She promised not to love me. That was part of the deal. I was fine with that, and I didn't ask questions. Watch me be fine with that.

We had to wait a couple of nights until her roommate was gone. In her house there were candles everywhere, no lights. Melanie made me dinner, organic chicken and vegetables. She put on Tom Waits and then Joan Armatrading. Joan was a tease, her lyrics were usually gender non-specific, but everyone knew she had to love ladies.

A beer each. No need for dessert. I didn't recognize a single cleaning product in her house. The soap looked like someone had made it in his garage. The toothpaste, which I was sure would have to be something I'd heard of, turned out to be Tom's of Maine, which I'm not sure anyone else in Los Angeles had in 1983.

Dinner was over. I was standing in her bedroom. She'd gone into the bathroom for a moment. When she came out, she was nude. Seeing my expression, something like a doll's button eyes, she asked if she'd done something wrong.

"No, it's just that I usually spend most of the night trying to talk girls into taking their clothes off."

"I can put them back on if that makes you feel better."

The answer was no. I caught up.

Two people together on cotton sheets on a futon in a room in a bungalow in the flats of Hollywood. Those small, squared piles of books with a single lip balm or hairpin or ballpoint pen atop them. Mel had hair down to her waist and each strand had a point like the bristle on a brush. Dim lights in the other room, candles trembling in the breeze by the window, and outside of us there was another house and another and another, and in places all across the city there were other people going to bed together for the first time.

I knew Melanie had a boyfriend. He lived in Arizona. His name was Jeremy. He'd seen other women sometimes, and she'd made herself okay with that. I, she explained, was an experiment. I was part of her Saturn Return.

I was so okay with Jeremy, so quick to assure her that of course this is just bodies, not hearts, of course, you'll be going back to him, I know, I know, look, if you think about it, I'm a stream you can walk through, and I'll be in your footprints for a while, and that will fade. This sounded so mature it was a relief to her, which was a relief to both of us. She traced the weird curves on my nose, asking about their origins, looking at my face with pleasure.

About Melville, Pop. 1: because she was a dancer, I could see muscle groups under her skin, and she knew all their names. In the morning, she pulled back the sheets. There was an anatomy lesson: these are traps, these are lats, here are the quads. She was especially proud of her abductors, which lived in wonderful display on the outside of her thighs, and she told me how you kept them separate, in your mind, from another group, adductors: abductors are the muscles that you flex when you want to pull away.

MYTHOLOGY

A T THE COUNTER, Rick was doing a dramatic reading from Christie Brinkley's *Outdoor Beauty and Fitness Book*. It was an in-joke between him and Mel, in that the women who bought the book were either already gorgeous or, as he said, "beyond all measures of help." He approved of putting lemon in your hair and cucumbers over your eyes, and maybe we would all go to the beach to let the sun work its magic, as Brinkley suggested. On the other side of being human salads we would be glamorous. It was a weird kind of campy appreciation—despite the author being, you know, Christie Brinkley, there was valuable information inside. Rick, Mel, Glen, Nicolas et in Arcadia Ego, Dana, if she has enough sunscreen, we'll all go to the beach. We knew this wouldn't happen. Mel had asked that I say nothing to him about sleeping together, which made sense to me.

A couple of days later, he was gone. Apparently one of Mel's guesses was right—he'd been kiting checks against the register drawer, and when they bounced, Mary, the bookkeeper who looked like Betty White, told Mike.

This isn't exactly the end of Rick's story, but I would never see him again. Though I was disappointed—he was entertaining—I didn't think much about him at the time. I was busy not being in love.

Jeremy, I learned from Mel, was handsome and tall and his body was so hard it didn't seem to be made of skin and bone but lightly buffed, polished wood. He was funny and charming and he wasn't in Los Angeles. And he knew about me now. Mel had told him she would be seeing other people, and Jeremy was as evolved as we were, so he wasn't bothered by it.

The second time I came over to Mel's house, it was midafternoon. We went into her bedroom and shut the door. A few seconds later, her roommate, Nancy, knocked gently. In response, Mel said something that didn't make much sense, so through the door, Nancy asked, "Are you . . . taking a nap?"

". . . yes," Mel said.

The phone rang. You couldn't tell who was on the other end of a ringing phone, but I looked at Mel, who knew as well as I did that it was Jeremy calling.

She smiled. "Let it ring," she whispered. "I always manage to turn the answering machine on unless I'm fucking someone."

I liked this—it suggested a general reliability, something I found sexy—trumped by a passion that I'd ignited.

We continued kissing as if I'd won a midway prize, and Jeremy left a message with Mel's roommate that turned out to be that he was moving to Los Angeles *immediately*.

Mel's house was on a side street off of Santa Monica Boulevard in the middle of Hollywood. I volunteered to take the bus back, and she was grateful for that. Driving across L.A. was a drag. So I stood in the dusk among a half-dozen men who were mostly my age, and I waited for the bus—obliviously—while thinking about Jeremy.

It's hard to say exactly why Jeremy was coming. I'd like to say I irritated him and he was coming to reclaim Melanie, as this appeals to the part of me that likes making men who are said to be hard as wood feel insecure. But the reason he gave was that he'd gotten a job writing a television show, and this was the first real pang that defied my ability to make everything okay. Jeremy was being paid to be a writer.

Mel didn't see any reason she and I should stop seeing each other. I agreed. This would be easy, I said. I asked the questions adults would ask until I could ask: What was the show?

She was proud of him, as it was a big deal. He would be writing scripts for the most anticipated show of the season, the follow-up to the most successful comedy of all time, *M*A*S*H*. The working title was *AfterMASH*. I hoped it would be canceled before it even got on the air, but I agreed with Mel aloud: wow, great, that's great.

I say I'm not competitive, but that's because I tend to immediately lose any contest of strength, speed, or agility. However I still automatically rank men standing near me by how I'm better than they are. Even while waiting for the bus on Santa Monica Boulevard. The other guys were all what you might call *tuff*, not actually tough but dressed in fatigues or cowboy denim that only made their open, vulnerable faces that much softer. They were like New Wave models who were all about to cry. I didn't talk to them, but scowled the way they did, hoping no one would talk to me. They might be looking sullen because they felt blue, or because it looked good, but I looked sullen because I was jealous a guy had gotten a job on a TV show.

There was only one bus that stopped there. If you didn't get on it, it meant you were waiting for something else. When the bus arrived, I got on. I was the only one. I turned around while putting in my quarters. The other guys ignored the bus entirely. As we pulled away, I looked back at them posing and looking at each other like they wanted to be rescued from how good they looked being sad. It dawned on me that they were all whores.

At work the next day, I asked: did Mel know there were male prostitutes about fifty feet from her front door? Yes, she did. There was about a mile of Santa Monica Boulevard where you could find them. She said it so casually I realized this was another thing I should just absorb as part of the adulthood quiz.

Later there was a phone call for Mel. Jeremy. I was ringing up a customer while, perhaps three feet over my shoulder, I heard Mel laugh for the first time at something the man she actually loved was saying. It was a full-body laugh.

I went to shelve some books. It had been a week since we'd first kissed. I had no rights, I said a few times to myself.

She suggested she and I have lunch. We went to the Falafel King that dancers tended to eat at, if they ate at all. Jeremy would be moving into her house until he found his own place. I hadn't thought about that. I didn't know if this meant we were no longer sleeping together, but asking that seemed like confessing I didn't know the rules of a game I might have been winning.

I asked other questions. They'd had years of experience together while both of them were poor and struggling with art. Mel slowly told me that it was hard sometimes because Jeremy couldn't be faithful. I immediately said I couldn't stand that. Monogamy was more important to me than anything. Two-timing was selfish and—she sort of nodded, staring into her cappuccino—I realized I was being a fucking moron, because of course Mel had trashed her own monogamy with a certain idiot teenager.

She said Jeremy wasn't just coming soon—he'd called because he was on his way out now. He would be here the next day.

"Does he know about me?"

"Oh yes. He made me tell him everything."

"Everything—"

"Everything. All the things you and I did, he wanted to know all of it. He asked which of you had a bigger dick."

"And you told him?"

She nodded.

There was an obvious question to ask. I felt that not asking it was wise. She started talking about her past like she was reporting a crime she'd witnessed. Her voice sounded dreamy. Jeremy had a control over her that she couldn't explain. He'd started hanging around the restaurant she waitressed at, then at a party he'd taken her drink away, ripped off her clothes, and fucked her right there. She was engaged to another guy, but not after that happened. Once Jeremy had touched her, she felt only as fondly toward her fiancé as a stuffed animal that had fallen behind a shelf. She didn't sound happy about this, but amazed, as if she were under a hex.

"He wants to fight you," she added.

"What?"

"I told him not to."

"I'd fight him."

She smiled sadly. "I wouldn't want you to lose your beautiful face."

I felt a deep, uncomfortable tug, a feeling of unfairness that went beyond not wanting to get punched. Why was someone as strong as Mel so helpless when it came to this asshole? This—substituting different names over a course of years—was a defining question in my life.

That night, my father asked me how my day went. He was sitting on the living room couch under the portrait of himself and Ann sitting on the same couch. I told him about my conversation with Mel. As he asked questions, I explained the dinner party, then Rick, Lolly, and Clayton, then Jeremy wanting to kill me. I concluded with something about how this was all fine, I was just fine with it.

He nodded. "You're cannon fodder," he said, and went back to *The Wall Street Journal.*

THE DAY AFTER JEREMY CAME TO TOWN, I showed up at Hunter's to open the store. Mel was coming in at noon, and I was happy that she'd be spending the day here, at the store, instead of at home, with him. But she called in sick. This was the first time she'd called in sick.

I should call to see if she's okay, I told myself. I didn't call for the entire first hour I was there. Finally, I dialed her number, and I rehearsed what I would say if the answering machine picked up.

With every ring of the phone, a little piece of my calm peeled away, revealing something at once hot and sick inside. I felt like the bookstore floors had warped under me. The answering machine *had* to be on. I didn't like what it would mean if it weren't. If ten rings wasn't enough—

It picked up. It was her roommate.

"Hey, Nancy, it's Glen—is Mel there?"

"She's," a micro-catch in her voice, "taking a nap."

"Right." I thanked her. I had a customer. Christie Brinkley was at the counter.

"Do you have the Christie Brinkley beauty book?" she asked.

We did—I directed her to it, and she came back to the counter with a copy.

I didn't recognize her. I was distracted, but also she was blond and pretty, and without a photo shoot going on, she looked almost inter-changeably like one of the many gorgeous women who didn't need the book. So I gave her a dry chuckle.

She heard it. Handing over some cash, she said, "Yeah, I know, it's embarrassing to be buying this."

I said, to reassure her, "Oh don't worry, I hear that in spite of the author, it's got good tips in it."

This made her laugh especially hard. When I handed over her change, she said, "Christie Brinkley is my favorite model."

"There's no accounting for taste, I guess."

I think that came out so quickly because I was feeling bitter at the moment, and wished Rick were around to say something awful. She laughed again, and took her book and left.

When I turned around, my co-workers were staring at me, and I said, "What?" and then it dawned on me what I'd just done. Insult a super-model to her face and have it amuse her, because neither of us had the slightest clue what the other was actually saying. This felt like insight. The world was stupid and I was cannon fodder.

I had some kind of miserable burrito for lunch. When I came back to the store, I went to the counter to help out two guys who'd been wait-ing there a while. One was Timothy Hutton. The other was Sean Penn.

Hutton looked at me for a second, during which *I* at least was notic-ing the intensity of someone else's eye color, then he asked if we had a book he said no one else had heard of, *Sideshow* by—

"William Shawcross," I said, way too quickly.

The intercom at my counter was already buzzing. I looked up to the mezzanine, where Mike was jammed between his desk and the railing. He was waving at me. He had his phone in his hand, and he pointed at the receiver. I ignored him.

I led the customers to the history section. Penn asked if we had any-thing by Bukowski. I pointed toward fiction. They both thanked me. I left them there.

When I got back to the counter, Barbara handed me the phone. Mike was on the other end. It came out like this, "WhatdidTimothy-HuttonandSeanPennwant?"

"They were looking for *Sideshow* by—"

"WE HAVE THAT. Did you show it to them? Do you think they're going to buy anything?"

A moment later, they were back at the register with *Sideshow* and Bukowski's *Post Office,* one I'd actually read. I thought about saying something to that effect, but that felt like the desperation of fictive kinship, so I just rang it up. Penn still didn't make eye contact, but Hutton gave me another brief glance that I told myself meant that, yes, he'd noticed he and I had the same color eyes.

Then they were gone, and Mike was bouncing up and down beside the counter, asking me to recount what had happened, which was more or less that they'd asked for some books, we had them, and then they bought them, using money. In other words, we had provided the service that the bookstore was designed for. His excitement about this was boundless.

I felt embarrassed for trying to, by the compelling force of my will, force my having roughly the same color eyes as Timothy Hutton into meaning that he and I were, by inference, basically the same person.

I had an ego on me and I was looking to take up space somehow. I wanted to have an aura of accomplishment and wonder. The problem was that I hadn't done anything yet.

That night, as I was walking to the bus through the crowds, I saw Penn and Hutton sitting on the curb, at least one of them smoking. A girl was walking past, and Hutton said, "Hey, Betty! Betty!" and he was ignored, so he tried again. "Norma! Norma!"

The pedicab driver I liked eased up to the intersection. Penn waved at her. "Betty! Hey, Betty! Norma! NORMA?" She ignored him, and when the light changed, she pedaled away.

He looked after her, sighing. "Whatever."

No one else was looking but me, as they'd made themselves invisible by behaving like dicks. Strange games the young gods played on a Saturday in Westwood. I was curious what it meant when gravity warped around you so much that it was fun to think of new ways for girls to shoot you down.

Pretending to be losers was a weird cutting-edge art form. It was almost punk, almost Taoist, in its stripping away of their egos. They seemed so comfortable in being themselves that they could be entirely different people.

Neither of those guys would sweat Jeremy. I decided I didn't care about him either. Watch me not care. Watch me *shine* while not caring.

HEALTH & EXERCISE

A FEW DAYS LATER, Melanie invited me to the beach. We had brunch at the Yellow House, a café walking distance from the part of Santa Monica Bay she liked best, north of the lifeguard tower, where the crowds thinned out. It was relaxing up there, she said, which was good. I wasn't calm. I kept imagining Mel relaxing into domesticity with her actual boyfriend.

But once Jeremy had unpacked, he told Mel that he was in love with another woman. I was still young enough that this amazed me. The woman he loved was married, and Mel said this was typical of Jeremy, chasing the thing he couldn't have. He slept in the same bed as Mel, then went to Karen's to fuck her.

I wanted to ask something, but didn't know how to without sounding weak. Mel volunteered it: she wasn't fucking Jeremy. He was involved with someone else, so she wouldn't touch him.

"Why is he sleeping there if—"

"He said to tell you that you're intruding on him so he's intruding on you."

"Me?" I said.

"Yep."

"But it's your—"

"Yep." She added that ever since I said I would fight Jeremy, Jeremy had been talking about it.

"Wait, you told him that I said—"

"He's fantasizing that he'd come into the store, you'd provoke him, and he'd kill you."

"He's fantasizing that?"

"He keeps telling me about it," Mel said, shaking her head. The biggest problem for her was how this was challenging her own autonomy. He was finding ways to siphon off whatever power she had over her own life. I commiserated with her about that, even if I maybe should have been more worried that a guy who was stronger and meaner than I was wanted to kill me.

She said she was thinking about a boxer she'd seen interviewed before a fight, and the announcer had asked, "How will you win?" The boxer said, "I *will*," glaring at the world as if that was an answer. How do you deal with your boyfriend loving another woman? "I *will*," she said.

She thought she should step back, she said. Just step back from everything. She was going to retreat a bit, and she hoped I could be patient about that.

"I'll be flexible," I said. "Or malleable."

She laughed, but maybe she shouldn't have. I was looking at her, hard, for clues. Was she manipulating me? I wondered if her taking a rain check to spend time *alone* would really be that. Maybe she was sleeping with Jeremy, maybe she was pushing me back just to feel the power of it? What if her autonomy was based on kneecapping *my* autonomy? I said some of this aloud, swallowing the rest, in that involuted way I do when I'm not confident.

There were not many moments where it was obvious that one of us was a whole third of a life younger than the other, but this was one of them. Mel considered me before continuing. She said, with kindness, "You'll feel stronger when you resolve your mom in your head."

I had no idea what she meant. I certainly didn't realize that with that comment, Mel knew me in a certain way, meaning young, meaning not ready, meaning there was a limit to me. I didn't quite hear that. I heard an invitation to be strong.

I tried to emulate that stance. I said, "If I don't see you, that'll be a drag. But that's lust. Tomorrow it won't matter."

She narrowed her eyes. "Says the cannon fodder."

"Yeah, well, at least I'm not poor."

The part of my brain that knows how to hurt the people I love moves faster than the part that knows whether I should. Ask anyone who loves me, especially those who don't anymore.

Mel kept her eyes on her coffee, but her face was reddish, and the smile she had went fixed. She stirred her spoon around and the table was silent because I didn't know how to both apologize and sound strong.

"We should go to the beach," she said.

It could have incinerated us. Does a relationship get annealed in the weeks after the first waves of heat? Every moment is a choice about whether to stick together or to leave someone at the curb. Mel was walking with me out of the restaurant, onto the sidewalk, not looking my way, and we walked together toward the Pacific Coast Highway, into the shock of wind coming from the broad slope of the beach.

We stopped at the corner. A line of scooters was turning up the highway, one, two, three, ten, twenty mods on Vespas and Lambrettas, riders bundled up in parkas, ridiculous and fashionable in August. When it was safe to go, Mel hesitated, and I took her hand, which seemed like too much, so I went to her belt loop instead.

I'd belittled her and I wasn't apologizing. Accidentally, I was being like Jeremy. Which would be a horror to me, but for this: after a second, Melanie took my belt loop also, as if realizing it solved a problem. As if I were Jeremy, then, we walked, fingers-in-belt-loops, to the beach.

It was one of those wind-blasted days where it's more fun to have gone to the beach than to be there, but neither of us wanted to leave quickly. A little girl asked me for help with her kite, and as I unwound the string and the kite blew into the sky, she introduced herself ("My name is Jessie Frances Olvine. Pleased to meet you.") and told me a complicated story about having gone to see *E.T.* and not crying, because she was actually very brave. "Then E.T. died and I cried and we had to leave. The end."

I don't remember Mel interacting with the girl. In my mind, she was standing to the side, in her sunglasses, gazing through her. When a woman I liked fussed over a child, I always felt disappointed, as if it meant she was living an unexamined life. Mel was so much an artist—she had to be too evolved to want to be a mother, right? I had never thought about motherhood, except having a mild suspicion that it was never any woman's actual choice. Of course, any suggestion that I hadn't exactly thought this through would have startled me.

And as my talk with Jessie Frances continued, and my fumbling with the kite made it take not one minute but maybe three, Mel was looking instead at the ocean, where shifting light on the waves made the whole day start to feel like a benevolent hallucination. She seemed so strong to me, as if her appearing to be unaffected meant she really was unaffected.

"Goodbye," I told Jessie.

"No."

"We'll be back."

"When?"

Mel and I started to walk away with stiff gusts against our backs. She said, "You're good with kids."

Her Volkswagen was parked on a residential street, against a curb that jutted out of a hillside so I had to struggle into the passenger seat. Mel had been oddly quiet the last few minutes, and I was thinking about how I wanted to reassure her. I wanted to say the thing that would make her feel good, and that would also perhaps lead to getting to keep her. But something had started to shut down in her, throwing up asymmetrical corners around which I didn't know how to see. I was obviously in love with her and I knew in this moment that the most loving thing I could do was to say otherwise. I am so in love I will not be in love.

She was behind the wheel of the car now. She hadn't started it.

"You know," I said, "I don't love you, but—"

"I can't love you. I don't have time."

I didn't know what she was talking about. She had something to add.

She said, "I don't have time," again, but that's not what she meant. It seemed important that I stay quiet. "God-fucking-damn-it," she said. "Glen, I have cancer."

She looked resolutely away from me. It was like she'd failed to make a clean getaway. With that one word she'd had to reveal that everything else I knew hadn't been the whole story. She had cervical cancer, rare for a twenty-six-year-old woman. The prognosis was mixed, but mostly not good. There wasn't a great treatment, but there were some new hopes. The student health insurance was excellent. The thing was, the cancer had to do with sex, but they weren't sure why. Recently doctors had put it together that nuns and lesbians didn't get much cervical cancer. So she was thinking of how when she'd been sixteen, seventeen, maybe she'd slept around too much? She didn't think so, but it was like nature was telling her otherwise. She was going to have experimental surgery in a week or two. It involved freezing the cells around her cervix. But even if it succeeded, it might leave her unable to have children. "I have cancer. I have four dollars to my name and I have cancer." She announced this calmly, and then she cried for no more than fifteen seconds. Then the crying stopped.

She put the car into gear, and then drove me to my house.

I invited her in. There wasn't talk of the surgery, as she'd said all she wanted to. It was going to happen soon. She wasn't interested in telling me when.

She came upstairs with me. I'm not sure she'd been in my room before. The carpet we lay down on was all synthetic nylon and the pillows I grabbed for us were polyester blends that smelled of the Tide that Ann used to wash them. The hollow-core door of the room was closed and outside my brothers were yelling at each other and beating plastic toys with little brightly colored hammers. My life wasn't curated and it wasn't really under my control. And yet Mel needed something badly enough to be here, now. She was enjoying, as hard as she could, how I really was nineteen years old.

She rolled on top of me. She whispered, "I've decided you shouldn't go out with someone whose life is so complicated. You need a girl your age who you can call and she'll say, 'Sure, Glen, come on over.'" She made it sound more like the sum of difficult circumstances than her own desires. But she said it in the local, embarrassing air, in the surroundings that spoke of my temporary storage here as a stepson.

She was saying words, but it was hard to think about them, because I was ready to burst. She was kind. I remember shamefully little else, except that even then I understood this was her way of apologizing to me one last time for not loving me.

When she drove off I knew it was over between us. I kept walking down the sidewalk. It was warm against my feet. I wasn't wearing shoes. This was dangerous and stupid, I suppose, but I wasn't interested in putting on shoes and thus feeling less under my feet.

I felt calm. This was confusing because I had lost Mel. Worse, she had cancer. It didn't sound like it would be fatal, but there could be permanent damage. And the word "cancer" led to thinking of how none of us can avoid our unknowable end. *All of us might die,* I thought. *No, all of us will die.* Instead of this being depressing, the anticipation of death siphoned out, soggy air wheezing from a hapless balloon. *We aren't dead now.* Worry was about the future, and if you skated a little further, worry was about death. If you were really experiencing a moment, there was no future to consume you.

I said aloud, "But I want—"

Then, "No, not really. I don't want more."

I wanted Mel to be okay, but that was more of a prayer. I didn't want more for myself. Jeremy flashed through my mind and so did a solution: If he hated me, I would be his best friend. If he wanted to fight, I would hand him a bouquet of flowers, and if I had more time to prepare, I'd get him a little tiara and sash that said "Winner" on it.

It was a good walk in the last moments of the lingering sun. Some days are like that in Los Angeles, when there's only the mildest breeze, and the warmth is friendly, the occasional people walking past me nodding in silent agreement: *We, too, have noticed the city is pretty benign right now.*

I finished the walk around the block. I was happy. I'd been happy for a full fifteen minutes, the longest time in my life. I wasn't sure if this was a perversion of all my studies, but I suspected I'd landed on exactly their point, that considering the nature of suffering could lead to a contented emptiness. It turned out I could carry this with me if I wanted. I didn't have to pep talk myself—this is what being here now felt like, without effort, the wayless way that can be traveled, everything made sense.

The concept of semesters struck me now as small. There were larger stories in the world that I wanted to follow out. When I came back to the house, I told my dad I accepted his offer. I wouldn't go back to Wesleyan—I would stay here and work at Hunter's through the fall. Berkeley in January.

TRAVEL GUIDES

MELANIE WAS SCHEDULED for surgery at UCLA on a Friday. Her friend Mary would drive her back home when she was released from the hospital. Mel said Mary was only coming because they forced her to sign something that said a friend would pick her up, but she was sure she could drive herself afterward. Thanks for asking.

"I'll come by anyway."

"Why?"

"Hold your hand."

"Only if you want to."

I asked if she was scared. She said no. The next day she told me she put on a Pep Boys T-shirt I'd bought for her and she'd burst into tears, and she couldn't figure out why.

I didn't want to crowd her. The last thing to do is chip away at a woman's autonomy. But Mary told me Melanie was terrified, and didn't want to seem needy. Asking for something was more terrifying than the surgery itself. Mary said I should come to the hospital.

I asked Mel when she would be going in, and true to form, she told me a time in the afternoon, hoping she'd be on her way home when I arrived. I found her just as she was leaving the recovery room.

For her, it was one struggle after another, beginning with getting her perfectly faded jeans on over the layers and layers of surgical bandages. The doctors wanted her to ride in a wheelchair, which she got out of when the orderly turned his back. Then there was a trip to the pharmacy for some kind of vaginal cream, the necessity of which made her roll her eyes, and then Mary drove her home, me in the back, as Mel realized there was no possible way she could make her body work well enough to do it herself.

When she was back at her apartment, I placed a glass of ice water next to her futon. I remember her lying there in a T-shirt and a thick diaper, her fighting sleep, her asking me to check the back porch.

I did. There was a copy of a book there. Stephen King's *Cujo*. Mel had borrowed it from the store, but had put it out there because it was too scary. She held my hand again as I asked if I should return it, but she said she would do it. She said she'd probably go into work the next day, or she tried to say it, her hand finally relaxing and falling away from mine.

She was asleep. I had never seen her pushed all the way past her limits into exhaustion. It was strange to feel like she trusted me like this. This was what it was like having a friend who was a woman.

My eyes kept going to the steel-toed engineers' boots at the edge of her bed. They were beaten from use and they were enormous, perhaps size thirteen. Jeremy had not come to the hospital with her, as he had to work on the *AfterMASH* set. But he managed to be a presence, even when absent. Here he was, not attending to Mel's needs. So I sat, feeling altruistic love and anger, an amazingly heady cocktail.

Mel didn't come back to work for a while. She'd been lying to herself about how long recovery would take. I was thinking about her reading *Cujo*. The last book she'd read was something ethereal by Marguerite Duras, whose new book was getting a lot of attention. But Mel read her earlier work, and that became a mark of respect for me—loving the writer everyone would only discover ten years later. But Stephen King?

Just because something was popular didn't mean it was diminished. Now that I'd worked at Hunter's past summer break, and it was turning into autumn, I understood what a forty-hour workweek meant. You could buy the new James Michener without knowing what it was specifically, because you already knew what it was generally. That was a comfort. I started reading Stephen King, and Robert B. Parker, and John D. MacDonald. They each had a worldview with predictable elements, but that was part of their charms, like picking up a conversation with a friend every year or two.

One day Mike came to the counter humming with excitement. He had a stack of Len Deighton's new novel. He put it in the center of a display close to the entrance, and behind the book he placed a large backstop with red letters: PRICE WAR! He straightened the sign a few times, put his hands on his hips, and asked me what I thought. He'd gotten permission to discount the price on this book. This would stick it to Crown.

That all of Crown's books were discounted, and that we had one discounted book struck me as an incomplete business plan, but I wasn't sure. Mike had been selling books longer than I had. He placed a "Price War" card in the window, with a crafty pride in our resources, like Churchill enacting air defenses over London. He started hiring new people in anticipation of actually needing them.

We had a signing by Andy Summers, who'd done a book of photographs of his band The Police. Their album *Synchronicity* had come out that summer. He showed up with a tall blonde who radiated that otherworldly kind of beauty that made her seem like a different, better species than the rest of us.

I flagged down Summers's driver and asked who she was. Apparently Summers had told him to stop at a corner, and he'd rolled the window down. She was standing at the curb. "Hi, I'm Andy Summers. Get in."

I was impressed. That level of arrogance was incredibly attractive. There were three guys in The Police, and Summers was the oldest and probably the least handsome, and yet he didn't let that stop him. We sold a few hundred copies of his book, and no copies of the new Len Deighton.

A few days later I went back to the dentist because my jaw hurt. The exam was brief. He said I needed to be fit with a mouth guard. I was grinding my teeth because of stress.

This didn't sound right to me. He asked some questions about how

I felt when I slept and when I woke up. My answers didn't match what he wanted to hear. I kept telling him I was empty and content. "Look," he said, "you're grinding your teeth. Otherwise, you're telling me you're walking around with your jaw clenched all the time, voluntarily, and that's not—"

"That's it. I'll stop doing that."

"No, I'm telling you that if you're not doing it at night, you'd be deliberately clenching your jaw during the day."

"Right. I'll stop."

He looked confused. "Why are you clenching your jaw?"

I didn't want to say. The videos of *Synchronicity* were in high rotation on MTV. One of them highlighted Sting's cheekbones. When I clenched my jaw, I thought I looked more like Sting. That turned out to be a losing battle. So I stopped.

One of the things I was writing that fall was a novel I'd started in high school. It was about boarding school the way *The Tale of Genji* was about the Heian court, minutiae important to no one unless exquisitely described. I'd been trying to exquisitely describe it ever since 1977, when I was thirteen. If punching a blow-up clown in the nose so that it keeps uprighting itself is exquisite, then I have described my attempts pretty accurately. By 1983, I had about four thousand manuscript pages, and was in no danger of knowing what the story was.

I was now on the scene where a boy needs to track down his missing mother after a punk rock riot to tell her someone has died. I didn't know how to finish it. I kept changing the details, all of the nouns of the story, and yet it was still unresolvable. I was writing a first draft that I didn't know the ending of, because I had to know what my character would do when he saw his mother. This was hard to figure out.

With Melanie gone, I felt the weight of the silence in the bookstore. At the counter one day, it was just me and Fred, the assistant manager. We were both staring straight ahead. Neither of us had spoken in over five minutes.

"Yeah," Fred finally said. "The last time I took mushrooms, I fell into an ice cream freezer."

He said it as if we'd just been talking about times we'd taken mushrooms, or the times we'd fallen into ice cream freezers. And this was a goad to me—I could turn into Fred eventually. I didn't want to feel like I was drifting. It was October now, and I was living in the extra months of adulthood I said I'd wanted, and yet I wasn't doing much with it. I looked for allies.

Mike Conway, whose threesome hadn't worked out, was busy "scamming" on girls, as he called it. It was unclear to me what he was actually studying at school, because scamming had become his full new branch of inquiry, a practice between art and philosophy.

He and his friend Neal were so good at it they started handicapping themselves. They would only hit on girls at the worst times—on the bus at night, for instance. Or driving Mike's ancient, smoking, rusted, monstrous Plymouth, which he called Iron-Maiden-Man-Thing.

I went to visit Mike one night, but he wasn't there. Neal was. Though we didn't really know each other well, Neal offered me some beers. He was compact and blond and quick-witted in a narrow, specific way of being mean-spirited. In other words, he was studying to be a corporate lawyer. Neal was fascinated with my situation with Melanie and Jeremy—he definitely believed I should be fucking Melanie every minute Jeremy wasn't around. He also suggested I should shit in Jeremy's boots. But better than that, why wasn't I helping myself to the other women in Westwood? There were women out there just begging to be used.

"Let's go do it now. Let's see a movie then find girls."

We drank beer, and went to see *Zelig*, which hit me hard. Woody Allen had a critique in there for people who shape-shifted in order to fit in with other people. Wasn't I doing that right now, hanging out with a crafty asshole, and laughing with him, telling him he had some good ideas even though on a certain level I was sure he was the Antichrist of misogyny?

We had a brown paper bag from 7-Eleven with Mickey's Wide Mouths, beer that tasted like self-hatred. We took ourselves to the cemetery. I was leaning against a tombstone while Neal instructed me how the world worked. Fuck everyone before they fuck you. Give up nothing. If anyone gets ahead of you it's because you let him do it. When you meet a girl, don't be nice—be as mean as possible to her.

Uh-huh, I said. Uh-huh. I was agreeing to get him to talk more, like I was eleven years old and the kids who lived in the Egyptian consulate were telling me how the Jews had vandalized their house.

Here was someone who lived well in utter contempt for how I had lived politely. A handsome, funny, awful man vetted by women all over Westwood. He was what I should want, if I were attracted to men. But men didn't make my dick hard. Why did I even need to double-check that? How was it possible I didn't know anything about myself without confirming and reconfirming it?

While he talked, I wanted to yell, "Neal, I don't even want to kiss you!" but that's not the kind of thing you could tell another guy apropos of nothing, so I kept it to myself. I wanted to tell Rick but I didn't know where he was.

FILM

IT WAS NOVEMBER. Mel called. Did I want to go to a movie, maybe? As friends. That sounds evolved, I said.

She suggested *Risky Business*. I'd heard that even though it sounded like something Cinemax would eventually show, it subverted the teen sex comedy and its subtext apparently made you *think*. Also I wanted to know if I really looked like the lead.

There were more phone calls, and her invitation became complicated. I said, "Yes" with every iteration, as this was the first milestone of our post-lust friendship. I would have to get to the theater myself, she said. She had to leave fairly soon afterward, but not that soon, there was time for coffee. We'd be seeing it with her old friends from Arizona, Scottie and Dan, a couple whose support had kept her going in the past.

When I met them I could see how solid and decent Scottie and Dan were. We all loved Mel but other than that there seemed to be nothing to talk about. They were older, their late thirties. Every once in a while, Scottie or Dan would ask me a simple question about books or school, and I tried to be charming when I answered, but what came across was the trying rather than the charm.

The film was funny and strange and there was a sex-on-a-train scene that was erotic without showing much skin. I wondered how the director had figured that out. I wished I'd made that film. It made me ache a bit, wishing I were a better storyteller.

Back on the sidewalk, much agreement: great film. The three of them thought Tom Cruise was very hot. No matter how long the pause afterward, no one suggested I looked like him.

We got in the car. Things were confusing. Apparently they were supposed to drive to the airport now. It turned out Scottie and Dan were here because they were having dinner with Mel—and Jeremy, who was returning from a quick trip to Arizona. It's possible the confusion arose from not knowing what to do with me.

Scottie, driving, looked in the rearview mirror, directly at me. "Oh!" he said, a lightbulb moment. "That guy in the movie."

"Yeah."

"Of course—I missed it. You have the same sunglasses he did." There were murmurs of agreement, Dan saying I must have gotten them because the posters were so ubiquitous. I could have fought that, in the feeble way that never works, proving my purchase had been prescient. But all I could manage sounded like a sad attempt: my glasses fit my weird crooked nose; they were glasses I'd earned because of actual experience.

Mel, in the front seat, turned to Scottie, who was driving, to tell him something about my study of Japanese aesthetics. And that prompted Dan to say, with the interest you'd show at a piano recital, "Oh, you've studied Japan?" and I knew he was keeping the conversation going until he could drop me off and their actual lives could return.

Scottie and Dan loved Mel. But they loved Jeremy, too, and they loved Mel and Jeremy together, and whatever Mel and Jeremy did was all right with them. I was a sign of Mel's life in counter-theme, I was teenage candy, sweet and ambitious, the kid who tried to look like Tom Cruise. I was a story they would tell for a while.

It was after dusk, and my time was almost up. I said they should just drop me off right here. They were sweet—they could take me anywhere. But I could feel the car already slowing down, the curb meeting us gently. Goodbye. Nice meeting you. Good luck. Joke about Japan. Joke about movie. See you again. Click.

I watched the car pull into traffic.

It was Saturday night. I was on Santa Monica Boulevard and oh, by the way, it was raining. I wasn't that far from Mel's house, and there was a bus directly to my place, so I didn't mind waiting in the rain a little.

"Just missed the bus," a voice said.

It was a guy leaning against a concrete wall by the bus stop. I wondered: hooker or another guy waiting for the bus? He had a military haircut, combat boots, olive cargo pants, and a sweatshirt. In other words, he and I were dressed exactly alike. This didn't make me trust him.

"Yep," he said, "Saturday night rain. Chases all the whores away and the only chicken hawks tonight are total freaks or cops. What are you?"

"Mostly sad I missed the bus."

"Okay, then, me, too." He was smoking a cigarette somehow. It was Los Angeles rain, some of it coming in like cloud bursts, but mostly just an oily drizzle that smelled like weed killer. There was a bench, and sometimes one or the other of us sat on it, but it was wet, so we got up and paced. "The problem is, waiting like this makes us suspects. Everyone thinks we're whores," he said. "Like these guys."

What guys? His eye was much better than mine. A dark car cut across two lanes of traffic and before the window finished rolling down, rain disappearing inside, he had sprung off the bench, and crouched down to yell into the passenger seat, "We're waiting for the bus, so fuck off, cops."

The window rolled back up, and as the car went back into traffic, throwing veins of rain water into the gloom, he tossed his cigarette at its trunk.

"Cops. I hate 'em even more than I hate whores," he said.

It was really coming down. I'd been there twenty minutes and there was no bus. Traffic was thinning out. People who wanted to be inside had stayed inside.

Another car slowed down at the curb. Somehow I felt in the rain that I'd earned camaraderie with this guy, so I wandered toward it to tell the driver to fuck off. But the window rolled down, and there was a twenty dollar bill floating in the air. The other guy sprang off the bench. Without a word, he threw open the door, got in, and closed it behind him.

A second later, the car peeled away.

It took a second to process what I'd just seen, and I had to tell myself the story: once, this girl dropped me at a bus stop so she could pick up the man she really loved at an airport, and I was waiting for the bus in the rain with a guy who hated male prostitutes who turned out to be a male prostitute. Yep. That sounded like pretty much what had just happened.

Because there didn't seem to be another bus coming, I had time to hone this story. I imagined telling Owen what had happened, how he would ask questions that would make it funnier.

I realized the story wasn't as important as the possibility there wasn't going to be a bus. Some riot or revolution had happened up line and so I was going to stay here forever. I thought, *Be here now,* then I thought, "I don't want to be here now. It's horrible here right now."

A car idled at the bus stop. I hadn't seen it show up. Wipers going. The windows were fogged up. One window was slightly open.

I stayed away. The car didn't move. The exhaust jetted into the rain. Through the slit of the open window I could hear music. KROQ. New Wave. The Go-Go's. "We Got the Beat." Seriously?

It was a GTI Rabbit convertible, I told myself, and I looked toward the license plate, in case that would be important to the people who found my body. And then I saw something that made a blend of feelings touch my heart, fear and excitement. I was looking at a Tri-Delt sticker.

Tri-Delts were the most beautiful sorority on the UCLA campus. Tri-Delt girls were wild. How wild? It was a Saturday night, and they were wild enough to pick up a male prostitute.

I walked toward the car.

I had nothing on to cover my head. I approached the car, drenched. The window rolled down. The driver and the passenger were nineteen-year-old girls with perfect makeup and long, straight, ironed hair. They looked terrified. There was no one in the backseat. The driver leaned over to get a look at me, as if this was something she would eventually need to describe to a sketch artist.

"Hi," she said.

"Hello."

The girls exchanged looks and laughed. They talked over each other. "Would you—" "No, don't tell him that." But it wasn't the joy of playing a joke on me. It was nervousness.

"Do you want to come to a party?" the passenger finally said.

My hand was on the roof of the car. I was leaning inward so closely I could smell their perfume.

"Actually I'm waiting for the bus," I said. "Sorry."

I tapped the roof twice as a goodbye and went back to the bench.

The car didn't move. The window stayed open, as if the girls inside were consulting a textbook they had about how to get a male prostitute to come to a party. Then the window rolled up and, after signaling first, the GTI returned into traffic.

My bus finally arrived a few seconds later. I got in, paid my way, and shook my head. I was soaking wet. What a day. I started telling myself about the moments that most affected me, because I was feeling that I'd had the worst day of my life, so I was adding them up in order of the most offensive, meaning Mel's rejection, the dismissal by Scottie and Dan, Jeremy's concurrent return to her life, the girls in the car—hold on.

I told myself again the story of waiting at the bus stop and this time I got confused about the moment where I turned them down. I imagined telling Owen this and how he would say, "Wait—you didn't get into the car?" and I would say, "Of course not, because—" and it started to fall apart.

I didn't want to get into the car because I thought they would murder me? I knew they weren't going to murder me. They were going to take me to a hotel room, smoke weed, do blow, and fuck the living daylights out of me. And then they were going to *give me money*. I'd turned them down because I was scared. I could not define "of what" except fear of disappointing women who wanted me. It was that, the ignorance about myself, that made me catch a downward drifting breeze.

I'd said, "No" in the same spirit I'd refused to tell the joke at Shakey's Pizza a year before. I hadn't changed a bit—I was exactly the same person. I was *auténtica*. This was horrible. It sat with me like the onset of the flu.

When I got home, I only wrote, of all things: *I want to save you from making a bad decision. I want to save you.*

I meant saving Melanie from Jeremy. That was the most important part of the day to me, apparently. What an old feeling. Those two sentences together are as disappointing as anything I've written.

TEST PREP

ANOTHER BUS RIDE, another day, this time on the way to work. The bus driver startled when he saw me. "Don't take this the wrong way," he said as I paid, "but you have an identical twin. Just got off the bus, seriously, man."

I was a little abrupt with him, but that was because he was confirming something I was starting to feel, that whatever arrogance I'd managed to build up about myself was unfounded. There were copies of me everywhere.

The band X was signing copies of their new album *More Fun in the New World* at Tower Records. The clerks at our store had an arrangement with Tower—their people would get things signed for us so we didn't have to stand in line.

The line to meet X wound around the block. I realized the woman from Tower taking my details was both pretty and talking too much to me. I let her talk, which she did without really making eye contact. She said it was great having X here now, instead of trying to meet them in a couple of years, when they'd probably be playing stadiums. She said her name was Cindy, and when she let me into the head of the line, I meant to thank her, but got distracted, and then wondered if not thanking her was actually a good strategy.

I had two copies of the album, and I asked John Doe to draw the Flipper fish—a punk rock parody of the Christian loaves-and-fishes symbol—on Owen's copy, which Doe savaged nicely with a Sharpie.

Cindy rang me up. She had the suntanned skin and dark, curly hair of a Tuscan olive-harvesting farm girl. If she didn't work in a record store I could imagine her with a handkerchief in her hair, threshing a feudal lord's wheat fields with a flail. I noticed she gave me her employee discount. Could I be mean, as mean as possible? I told Cindy she was coming to the movies with me Saturday night. She said okay.

Saturday was uncomfortable. Early on, I started talking about the Tao, and how I wanted to be fully self-aware. I sneered at the dough heads who didn't ask questions but just wondered what was for dinner. Had Cindy seen *Koyaanisqatsi*? I started to explain it, and she stared at me as if through a thickening fog. And when I was done, she laughed. She paused and then laughed again.

She wanted to be an interior decorator. She said her sister had made her wear the jeans she had on because they made her ass look better than it actually was. She said her sister didn't like her glasses, and I agreed— her glasses were terrible. So I took them off. Bare-faced, she looked both lovely and a little confused. She was the prettiest girl I'd taken on a date and yet it was a technical kind of beauty, as if a stadium would vote her "most beautiful" but no one would fall in love with her. Thinking this made me hate myself, but here I was.

On the way to the theater, we passed a guy in a leather coat leaning against a wall, sneering at passersby. When he saw me, he nodded.

"Hey, Timothy," I said. He jutted his chin out, and I thought I saw a positive appraisal of Cindy in that motion.

Cindy whispered, "How do you know Timothy Hutton?" but I refused to answer, because I had already turned into that kind of person with her.

She took me to her apartment. It was one of those aggressively ugly 1960s buildings seemingly thrown up as an act of contempt for the future tenants. Cindy's bookshelves were rows of romance novels. She saw me seeing them and quickly said, "I hate gothic novels. Life isn't like that. They make you believe some handsome, arrogant guy will come up and shit on you, and he'll still fall in love with you."

Her problem wasn't that you were supposed to fall in love with an asshole—that part she understood—but that he would ever respond. As she talked, I wanted to ask, "Don't you understand you have a choice in this?" but she was already telling me about her last boyfriend, a screenwriter, who had taken her virginity and who hadn't called her back, even when she left him a ton of messages. The whole time, he was pining after another girl, but if he called Cindy again, I should understand she would have to see where things were between them.

She showed me her sketches of rooms she had designed. Wallpaper, furniture, carpets, chandeliers, and tiny people with cocktail glasses on couches she'd drawn with crayon. I read her handwritten notes indicating what rare fabrics she'd never seen in person that she wanted for the drapes. Were they good? I wasn't really sure what to say. My silence made her nervous. Maybe she was thinking I would say something terrible. But I wouldn't do that. I wanted Cindy to have an artistic process. I asked her questions about what her work meant. This was a mistake, as it made her feel vulnerable, and worse than that, me asking about subtext made me seem not only like a man, but for the first time *cruel*.

I started to say how making art separated us from the dough heads of life, and she asked what a dough head was again. I was explaining again, but I wasn't feeling strong about it, because as I talked I was looking at her drying rack. She had a Ziggy mug. *Oh,* I thought. No, there were *two* Ziggy mugs, so the first one wasn't an accident. *Cindy is a dough head. I'm talking to a dough head. Oh.*

I took her into her bedroom. There was a line of stuffed animals on her bed. I took Cindy's clothing off of her, and placed her on her bed and I stared at her. She was the most stunning woman I'd ever seen naked. I made her turn over—her sister had not been generous, as her ass, bare, was flawless. So was the rest of her. Her body was a puzzle, in that every anatomical detail was perfect, and yet she didn't have a spark of sexuality.

She was twenty. She was years away from the possibility of transforming from being an object to knowing her own desires. It might not even happen. She might never ask questions. I was thinking, *You are a blank slate and you are letting me do this because I'm being an asshole and because it's all that you know. You don't even know what your own pleasures are yet.*

I thought that if I made her feel something, it might mean I was slightly less terrible as a human being. My fingers teased her skin in all the places that seemed like they might wake her up. None of this had an effect.

"Show me how you do it," I said. She didn't want to, but I placed her hand between her legs, and because I'd asked her to, she started to masturbate, looking at the wall. After I took her hand away, I imitated what she'd done. I tried to clear my mind and to imagine her breathing changing, her skin bracing with goose bumps, her hips beginning to rock. But none of that happened. Her eyes were closed, less in abandon than simply being clenched. It was like picking up a phone receiver and hearing no dial tone.

I thought: Maybe this is what life is. Maybe Melanie was an aberration, or maybe she and I had never connected the way I thought we had. Instead, I was part of this world, and in uncomfortable, depressing apartments from here to Moscow, men who weren't as talented as they thought were fumbling with women they didn't even like. And women were putting up with them in hopes that they would fall in love. Maybe this was where I was supposed to be. There was a downward curve in my life, and it had not started here, but I was now aware of it.

Melanie invited me to a dance performance. I'd never seen her dance. It was a brief piece in a longer program. Set to minimalist strings that played every note for what felt like twelve measures, each chord change seemed as dramatic as a fire curtain dropping. I recall the dance consisting of a woman standing in turn-of-the-century undergarments, caught in the middle of fastening a restrictive corset. Melanie, dressed more like an apparition in white robes, approached slowly from across the floor and over the course of five minutes extended her hand toward the other woman's soft jawline. They reacted to seeing each other, and as the tips of Melanie's fingers reached the other woman's face, the lights went down and the music stopped. We applauded.

Afterward, I congratulated Mel. There was no way I understood what I'd seen, but I said something about the Sistine Chapel, the reach between God and Adam. Something about Muybridge. I was talking too much because Cindy was standing next to me, and Mel's eyes, still bright from performing, flicked Cindy's way. Cindy began to talk, and

Mel nodded a lot. Then Cindy had to go use the bathroom, and Mel looked at me.

"She's pretty," Mel said. "I bet she's fun."

"She's an interior decorator."

"Oh."

"She sketches rooms, it's an art form."

"Sure."

My time in town was winding down. I reminded my father he owed me twenty-five hundred dollars. I needed housing in Berkeley. I needed a used car, so I started reading *Consumer Reports*. Somehow, things weren't as colorful as they'd been before. But I was still trying to pay attention.

One afternoon, Seth had a girl from his class over to play. I was leaving my room and I saw Ann standing in the hallway outside Seth's door, which was drawn shut. She had a hamper of clothes against her arm, and one hand was on the doorknob.

There was an intercom in the hallway, and it was broadcasting the conversation between Seth and his friend. Obviously, they didn't know that. It had just gotten to the part where the girl was saying, "Is that your penis?"

Ann was hesitating. She looked at me. "Do I just go in and ruin their lives?"

I shrugged.

She thought about it a moment longer, then turned around and left, which I thought was a good idea.

Around this time it was clear that the Bel Air house, the showpiece, wasn't going to work out. I think no matter how well my dad could envision living there, Ann could not. So he was stuck here in this place. Ann was definitely not stuck, and this intrigued me. This house suited her, and the life within did, too. She had found a calling.

Ann was a good mom. When Marc said, "Mommy?" and Ann said, "Yessee?" she did it distractedly, thumbing through coupons or washing dishes, but she was unreservedly *interested*. "You are a *nutcase*," she would say to Seth, fondly.

My father had a nickname for him, too, taken from the *Asterix* comic strip. He claimed it had once featured a boxer named Ropus Dopus, and he tended to call his kids "Dopus," which only made each of them pause to wonder what exactly he was saying. When Ann told me one day that Marc's long periods of quiet had inspired her to call him "Harpo Marc," I realized she was better at nicknames because she was flat-out delighted by him, in her own hard-to-read way. She caved to her children too often, they had learned to maneuver around her like bankers and the SEC, but being a mother lit Ann up on a cellular level. I could tell there was nothing she loved better than that.

She had hidden angles that way. That summer was the first one I spent with a mother who loved her kids in the way that is complex, imperfect, frustrating, and also what I'd guess "normal" means. This hit me like fresh melancholy. It was a strange thing, on my way out the door, to finally think of my brothers, *Oh, you have a different mother than I do.*

Tick tock. It was a couple of days before Thanksgiving. I would be done at Hunter's at Christmas. Mel invited me to Chinese food for lunch. She told me she wanted get her own apartment with Jeremy. She used the words "and be with him forever."

I nodded. Hadn't she said she wanted autonomy? Hadn't she railed against Jeremy before? I didn't say those things, but instead I just listened.

She said *AfterMASH* hadn't panned out that well. As she described his purpose on the set, I realized that he hadn't actually been hired as a writer, but as a writer's assistant, with the aspiration that they would eventually take one of his scripts. So Jeremy wasn't as successful as I'd thought. But Mel had described him that way, because she shared his hopes.

I handed Mel the fortune cookie I'd gotten, and said I thought it was hers. It read, "New best friends and old acquaintances will affect you this week."

Her reaction was strange—she laughed for a second, but not after that. With care she put it into her wallet and sized me up in some kind of final way, wistfully, perhaps.

·   ·   ·

I was with Owen sometime after midnight. We were at Ships, an all-night diner a few blocks from Hunter's. They had toasters at every table. There were mods everywhere for some reason, and the parking lot was full of scooters. We weren't talking about our screenplay much, except to agree we should keep working on it. That wasn't going to happen.

As Owen and I left the restaurant, a woman looked up in mid-conversation with a friend. "Guy!" she said.

She was talking to me. Then she goggled in surprise.

She said, "Oh, I'm sorry, I thought you were someone else."

"That's been happening."

"I thought you were my boyfriend."

This made me laugh. If it was a line, it was a funny one. But it wasn't a line. "No, really." She pulled out her wallet and opened it. She held out the plastic sleeve of photographs. The first was, obviously, me. It looked just like me, except shirtless and playing backgammon. Guy had the same haircut, the same divots in his cheeks, the same chin, and even the same weird backwards S of a nose.

He was from France, and she thought he was back in France, so seeing me had shocked her, and she and her friends speculated about what it would mean to see Guy out of nowhere—was he more likely to be surprising her or cheating on her?

I asked if Guy rode the bus. If someone on the bus looked like me, she said, that wasn't him. Guy drove. There had to be another lookalike out there, part of a secret army.

The conversation wrapped quickly. What more could either of us say, really?

Though I'd already lost my eidetic imagery, if I ever had it, it turns out I took a photograph of that photograph as effectively as if I'd triggered the shutter and heard its rasp. It'll be there as long as I have a memory; I'm looking at it now. I would say I was mostly distressed that Guy had a better torso than I did. Then I tried to see all the ways I was better than he was, which wasn't quite possible, since we looked so clearly alike.

I wanted to look at that photograph and tell Guy I was more self-aware than he was, but even now, the snapshot in my memory gazes back with surprising self-assurance: he is clueless and self-obsessed, and *that* rather than the broken nose is why his girlfriend mistook me for him.

. . .

I was leaving Mel's orbit. Writing a love letter was the wrong way to go, but a letter from one adult, evolved, non–dough head to another struck me as the right tone to take.

It was heartfelt and thorough and sincere in a way I can no longer imagine, except for one thing: I was nineteen and I wanted to, among other things, thank Mel for having been so good at sex. I know there were other parts of the letter, and that the mention of how well she fucked was one sentence at most. In fact, the way I didn't lean on the sex, but just put in as an aside, as if sex were just one passing thing in a relationship rich with other charms, felt like the highest indication of my evolution. So not a humiliating letter, perhaps, at least not for me. I'd sent it to her house not knowing that on that particular day, she'd be away at work, and Jeremy would be there, opening her mail, as was his habit.

When she came home, the pages of my letter were scattered on the living room floor and Jeremy was in the bedroom, in the dark, smoking. There is more to that story—accusations, a fight, something like that—but my best Christmas present of 1983 was getting to imagine the sculpture Jeremy made, coiled up in bed, unmoving, angry, and to my mind utterly outfought by my scrawls of handwriting on a curated greeting card, the Goyo print of a woman combing her hair.

In my last days at Hunter's, Christmastime, I learned how to give book recommendations the moment a customer asked for one. I sized people up. *If on a Winter's Night a Traveler* was for people who liked books so much they also liked books about books. *Waiting for the Barbarians* was for people who had a social conscience and whose checks had Santa Monica addresses. *The Color Purple* was almost always a gift from one woman to another, in hopes that the latter would become more sensitive. *Ironweed* was for people who'd read all the John Irving they wanted to and were looking to pretend they were familiar with another guy's career by reading his current book. *Suder* was for people who wanted first novels before anyone else had heard of them.

I'd been there long enough to know the locals, and so leaving wasn't a bad idea. I kept seeing one homeless woman in Westwood, maybe fifty years old and quiet. I saw her at bus stops with her belongings in bags, sometimes wearing a stocking cap, always in sunglasses. On a day near Christmas, when the lines were long and they'd set up wrapping tables in the back, I saw her in our bookstore, standing at the counter. She waved at me.

No one else seemed to notice—there was this surreal feeling, briefly, like maybe only I could see her. I thought I should see what she wanted. But I had no clear idea what I was going to say.

It was my mother. Her face lit up. She had a little rolling suitcase with her.

She hugged me. Without thought, I helped her roll the suitcase out to the street. My brain plowed over whatever she said at first, as I kept thinking, "I just mistook my mother for that homeless woman." I felt terrible.

I can't remember if I knew she was coming. There are so many nuanced words for absence, because absence, like silence, can still have many telling qualities. Since I'd last seen her, I'd changed. I didn't know how to talk about that, so I told her about the things I'd seen in Westwood. We walked past the movie theaters where I had taken Cindy on dates, and the sushi place where I'd gotten yelled at for speaking Japanese, the Hungry Tiger, where I'd been served. Pedicab drivers were passing us. I recognized famous faces coming down the sidewalk, sunglasses and stubble, or scarves and tousled hair that was supposed to convey casual seriousness. *I cannot even be bothered to fully groom myself, for I am so famous I am relaxed.*

Here was the falafel place, and over there in the distance the graveyard. My mother saw her own landmarks. We passed the dentist's office I'd gone to when I was a child so small she had to carry me in. I think she came here to have her teeth replaced after she'd fallen in the tide pools. "Do you remember," my mother is saying in my memory, "how we used to . . ."

She wanted to see the bookstore. I told her there wasn't much to see. I wasn't yet perceptive enough to say what I meant: I had intended to spend the summer becoming self-aware, and had instead spent it trying to rescue a woman. And she didn't want to be rescued. And she didn't want me. I was a mess. I had no idea why I'd done any of that, or where all my failures lay. What a mystery it is when we try to live in the present, when all we have to guide us is the past.

San Diego was a great opportunity, Mom said. She invited me down to visit before I left for Berkeley. Things were looking up. I should see her business. She had friends. They were elegant and stylish and I should meet them. I would fit right in with them. She had told everyone about her son, the writer.

I protested as I always had and she smiled, and I knew she would only praise me further. She didn't know something had changed. When I was younger and she said, "This is my son, the writer," I felt like she was appropriating my ambitions. She had wanted to be a writer, and then I did, and I told her to leave me alone, like a fierce duckling. But now, I stopped talking.

My next clear memory is of when I returned to Hunter's, the disappointment crossing the faces of a couple of co-workers. "Your mom was here?" "Why didn't you introduce her?" Meeting my mom would have been great. Why didn't I show her the store, introduce her around?

"She was just here for a second," I said.

I didn't tell the truth, which is hard to write even now. I didn't show her off because she didn't look like Linda Evans. That was all. There wasn't even a deeper meaning to that—I was convinced that someone would tell her I had bragged she looked like Linda Evans, and my co-workers would see her and realize it wasn't true. She would be hurt because it would be apparent in a ghastly kind of silence, the kind that is pregnant and awful, that there had been a lie told.

I stopped working there soon after. Hunter's limped along with its overabundance of employees and terrible inventory control. Toward the end, distributors asked them to pay up front when they ordered things, and so they stopped ordering things. They lost Baker & Taylor, and they lost Ingram. No new books came in. They stopped having a second man in the room when the register was counted out. Evening drinks at the Hungry Tiger became more intense.

One morning, a couple of employees were sitting on the sidewalk, doors locked and lights out an hour after Hunter's was supposed to open. An old convertible pulled up, Mike driving, sunglasses, a beautiful young man in the passenger seat. I'm told he didn't even come to a full stop—instead, he slowed down and his tossing of keys toward the store made a parabola, and then he gunned the engine and merged into traffic. Was he actually humming whatever tune Norsemen sang at funerals?

In any case, I wasn't surprised. It was hard to remember the pride I'd felt upon being hired. I was going to be a better person back then, and that hadn't worked. Hunter's hadn't panned out as a business, either, and it had fallen apart at roughly the same point I had. It was a place that had only survived because it had deluded itself into continuing.

LETTERS

FROM

COUNTERFEIT

CHILDREN

BIOGRAPHY

I FOUND A ROOM in a house in north Berkeley, on Mariposa, a one-block street where the trees had been planted a hundred years before. There was moss between the bricks, and ivy on the stone pillars at each end of the block. It was the kind of place where the newest neighbor had been there fifty years. The landlady wore a housedress when she showed me the room, which had a view of the bay, and San Francisco in the distance. Her husband was housebound, so she said she liked quiet tenants. She was happy that I had a Walkman, because those had headphones.

I arrived in January 1984, a week before instruction began. I read and I wrote and I tried to cook things that were too complicated for me. The local hills had trails and stairways made for running, so I took myself on five- or six-mile loops through Tilden Park, ending by running across the campus. It was almost empty there for break, except for the street people. On some days the rain was so hard it drove everyone inside except Polka Dot Man, who stood still on Sproul Plaza, facing the storm front like a bow sprite, wearing a poncho, also with polka dots.

When it wasn't raining it was still dense with moisture all day. Running meant moving through these occluded fields of space where I had a bubble that traveled around me. When I did my wash at the laundromat, I sat on the sorting tables and read books I'd bought from Black Oak, next door. I told the folks there I'd worked at a bookstore, and the disdain of their response was enough to shut me up. I learned where to eat alone.

My father called me the day after I moved. He said, "I just realized something—you don't live at home anymore."

He sounded wistful. I didn't know what to say in response, because I was surprised. In my mind, I hadn't really had a home since I was twelve. When I was with him and Ann, I'd just been visiting a place I wasn't entirely welcome. That he had a wave of paternal feelings now, arising only after I was gone, was almost funny to me.

Before I left Los Angeles, I'd finished a short story called "A Handful of Stones Scattering," and I concluded after much thought there should *not* be a comma before the last word. It wasn't a good story but it was convoluted enough that friends I showed it to suspected it probably meant something. There were three interlocking narratives that—it doesn't matter. I sent it to *Antaeus*.

When I was fourteen, I'd sent a story to *Playboy* (it wasn't a sexy story—I'd heard that *Playboy* paid the most) but this was the first writing I'd submitted anywhere since. I'd had a concrete thought most of my extended summer—I would have so many experiences at Hunter's that on the other side of them I'd be a writer. This was the first step in making that happen. *Antaeus*'s reporting time, according to *Writer's Digest*, was about three months.

When three months went by, I sent them a query with a self-addressed stamped envelope asking if they were still considering the story. About two weeks later I got the SASE back, with a one-line note begging for my patience. They were still considering it.

This was almost as thrilling as if they'd accepted it. If they were pondering it, that meant "maybe," which meant I wasn't entirely insane to think I was on the verge of launching myself.

I did a daily circuit of bookstores, starting with the used places on Telegraph and winding up where the bookstores had cafés in them. I bought used mysteries and read them in an afternoon. I read a book every couple of days, like *Rosie*, which I recommended to everyone I knew, and *The Magus*, which I didn't understand but still recommended.

When I went to Upstart Crow Books around closing, I lingered so I could fall into conversation with the cute girl who worked there, but she was always interested in counting out the register as quickly as possible. I couldn't blame her, as I'd lost my spark.

And that was my ebb, I told myself, narrating as I walked down the street. I was telling myself the story of how I became a writer, finally. *But then* Antaeus *accepted my story,* I kept thinking, every time I came back to my house, only to find an empty mail table.

I kept writing drafts of a story that didn't seem to begin or end anywhere. I couldn't tell you if I was rewriting previous scenes or advancing them. It was still about a rich kid looking for his mother, who has disappeared in Los Angeles.

I also wrote out a recurrent fantasy: to have a house on an island with many rooms for many friends. I made lists of them: people I knew, like Owen; people I wished I knew. I assigned bedrooms to people whom I was sure existed: musicians and actors and poets who needn't be successful, just passionate. I wanted to live on the island full-time with a woman, and I knew nothing about her yet. This could have made me feel optimistic but instead it made me anxious. How strange not to know a single quality I was looking for in an imaginary relationship.

My anxieties blinded me in some ways that make me cringe. I remember lying awake in my room. It was seven a.m. California time, and ten in New York. I had the telephone from the hallway resting on my sternum. I had *Antaeus*'s phone number on a slip of paper. The number wasn't in the magazine. I'd had to look it up at Bancroft Library.

I called *Antaeus* to ask if they were still considering my story. The woman who answered took a few moments to comprehend that I was, in fact, an author who had submitted a story who was now actually calling their phone number to honestly ask them if they'd read it yet. I sensed that this didn't happen too often.

She took my name and she confirmed that yes, they had it, and no, they hadn't read it yet. Politely, I thanked her, and with equal politeness, she said goodbye.

I know my story didn't really show back up at Berkeley that day, but it felt like it. It felt like *Antaeus* had invested in express delivery to make sure I had my story back. There wasn't even a rejection letter, just all twenty-something pages of manuscript, paper clip unmoved, edges square. It wasn't that they'd been pondering it—they hadn't gotten to it yet, and had returned it unread. I recognized I'd done something deeply wrong by calling, and there was probably a list, and my name was now on it, and that shame drifted into the rest of the general shame I was feeling.

I talked my way into a Japanese portraiture class. This was another unfortunate idea. It was a graduate seminar, and I was an undergraduate junior with a total of one art history class behind me. The only reason the professor let me in was my confidence level. I assured her I could handle anything.

This is the problem with letting Los Angeles rhetoric apply to a Berkeley situation. Academia is somewhat about bluster, but not *that* much. The professor had us turn in drafts in progress so she could hand back comments that often ran half as long as the papers themselves. She was a good teacher, in love with her subject so much that it ate up the rest of her life. As I saw my classmates getting five- and ten-page critiques to prepare for their final submissions, I became worried.

My paper came back unmarked. Except for three words printed on the front page: "See attached cassette."

It was a C-90, and she had crossed out what had been recorded on it before (Vivaldi). She had recorded seventy minutes of comments on it. There was genuinely nothing I had said in my twenty pages that was correct. None of my citations were done in the proper style, a minor issue compared to how none of my identifications were correct, nor were any of my interpretations supported by the evidence. It was as catastrophic a collapse of an academic project as she'd ever seen.

And yet I still knew she was being kind. After the initial sting of knowing how much I'd fucked this up, I could hear the patience she was drawing on as she walked me through what might be a better approach. She tried, line by line, to reargue my paper for me. Sometimes she stopped the recording so she could catch her thoughts, and her abilities with the current technology would show themselves, as I would hear a second or two of Concerto for Two Lutes in D Minor, one of my favorite pieces, before her nasal, patient voice would continue to untangle for me the possible depictions of the Kamakura high court.

It was, by the way, a Certron tape. I hadn't known the company continued after they'd fired my father, but apparently the tapes were cheap and suited for the academic market. It took me days to listen to the whole thing on my Walkman, taking notes and trying to make the changes she'd suggested. I saw a lot of the spinning reels, the red label, and wondered when this tape, like the one Herb Alpert was listening to around 1972, might have the grace to jam up, sparing me this torture and sending me into oblivion.

I listened to most of it sitting with headphones on in Bancroft Library, at a long oak table in a room that seemed to extend to infinity. All around me were serious-looking, troubled-looking students who, like me, grasped at what to believe in, even if only until they'd finished their next term paper. By the time the tape was done, I didn't know what I was anymore.

I walked downstairs and was gravitationally pulled into a phone booth. I called my mother, collect. It's now hard to believe just how much I still needed her. I felt like my professor had kicked me in the stomach, and my response was as primal as looking for an embrace.

When the operator connected us, my mother declined the charges. The operator apologized to me, then hung up. Later, my mother would explain to me that she wasn't sure it was actually *me* calling. I didn't understand who would be masquerading as me but I also understood that there were vague elements in her life that wished her harm.

I called my father. He accepted the charges, puzzled at why I was calling. I explained I'd botched something in my major of choice, not just any class, but the foothold I had on Japanese Studies. And it wasn't a minor issue, but a conceptual disaster. It was a strange call for me, in that I knew I wasn't going to get the comfort I needed. My father had never comforted me in my life. He was the one who always believed the underlying message of his own experience—that you are on your own, the world is cold, there is no God—was learned best if learned fast. So he wasn't going to be much help. In fact, as I spoke, I had to figure out what I'd wanted in the first place. I made a pit stop at the detail that it had been a Certron tape, as I knew it would make him laugh. It did.

"Listen," he finally said. "You wouldn't believe some of the things I've fucked up in my life. I've written programs that brought systems to their knees."

"Really?"

"'Really?' Oh, really." He explained that I was lucky the teacher wanted to help instead of bounce me out of the program. He said I should take all her suggestions, go slowly, do the best I could, and then regroup. Maybe this was an opportunity. Maybe I'd get better at Japanese or maybe I'd find something I liked more. He didn't say anything about having been fired for his mistakes. But he did say that how you reacted to success wasn't as important for determining who you are as how you reacted to failure. I was now, along with the term paper, getting the results in my experiment in self-awareness.

I took a run in Wildcat Canyon, realizing I wasn't a Japanese Studies major. I wasn't obsessed enough. I wasn't sharp enough to understand the culture, and I wasn't clever enough to even bullshit my way through. I didn't know what was left to me, as I obviously wasn't much of a writer, either.

CALENDARS

I VISITED MY MOTHER in San Diego. She introduced me to her friends, a half-dozen or so men and women who seemed to travel in a pack that had accepted her already. All of us went to a restaurant on the water where I was immediately turned away for being underage. No matter, we went to the next place down, which was just as nice, and which welcomed all of us. But I had to be given a jacket and tie, which made me feel like I'd shopped in a thrift store before coming. And yet I fit in. The adults looked dressed like me, patchwork outfits, tops from the 1970s, trousers from the 1980s.

My mom introduced one man as having an exciting business of designer dog collars. He took this comment with a sideways and weirdly snooty glance, like he *also* knew his line of work was compelling, but he didn't want to talk to me. There was something seedy about the gathering, as if my mother was pretending it was a high point of 1975, MacArthur Park, brass rails and ferns, friends all about to visit Paris.

"And this is my son, the writer," Mom said, more than once. Sometimes she was serious, and other times it came out like she was pitching an album title, and she was pretending to be a Jewish mother. I wanted to say, "I'm not sure I'm a writer," but more so, "I'm not a writer the way you people are *anything*."

There was a dusky man sitting next to me who laughed with an approximation of the élan my mother had courted when she was younger. I felt like I was betraying the evening—was I being judgmental or was I just noticing things? His hair was just a little too thin, his collar too yellow, for his life to actually be this easy.

When my mother took her utensils to the lobster, he said, "No, no, you must use your hands. It is like . . . making love," as if he were naughty.

"When I make love, I always use a knife and fork," I said, in that way I have always said things to men whose innuendo is supposed to be sophisticated.

"He's being a sullen teen," my mother said, and everyone laughed, and I felt like I'd never left the dinner table at Peter Charming's house. Then she reminded me I was turning twenty soon. Which horrified me from exactly the opposite direction. I had wasted a year.

My mother had set up her company here, too. Her slogan was still "When You Wish One Call Would Do It All." Once again, she'd leased a copier, some computers, printers, and this time opened a storefront several long blocks from where any other offices were.

We stood in her window, looking outward. She was one of the few storefront businesses in the El Cortez hotel, a massive, old, boarded-up former resort that had been in a difficult escrow for many months. The corporation that owned it had gone bankrupt. The city now owned it for tax purposes, but didn't actually know there were any tenants still there, so it was a blessing to my mother that no one had cashed her rent checks for several months.

There was a crack in her window, because a local vandal stood on rooftops and used a baseball bat to drive golf balls into abandoned buildings. She had no insurance, as premiums were ridiculous, and she had once had to hide under her desk when she saw a man urinating in the bushes outside her office door. She explained that the location wasn't as bad as it seemed, as it was at the freeway exit. Thousands of cars a day passed her office. Sometimes, since she had many quiet hours to pass, she counted how many cars were going by. If only every tenth person needed a résumé and if only one in ten of those people actually came in, she'd have a thriving business in no time. The only drawback was that after dark there were bums and she had to lock the doors quickly and run to her apartment with the points of her keys poking between her fingers in case she met a robber.

She had learned her neighbor made silk flowers, and so she'd put a sign she'd made using her machines in her window: *Enter Our Contest to Win a Silk Flower by Lee.*

My mother was looking at me, anticipating a reaction. If I thought the sign was good, I would be agreeing with her that her life was going rather well. If I thought it was bad, I would be condemning her. I swallowed my response. I was reacting exactly as I had almost a year ago, spring break, the awful dinner with Jen. I had learned nothing. But I had lost one thing: my reaction now was different from tranquility or acceptance. There was nothing Zen or Tao or Buddhist in me. That philosophy, such as it was, had been stomped flat sometime before.

———

I was in bed with the most beautiful woman from my drama class. This sounds better than it was. I could tell she was stone-cold awake. Her name was Jess. She was tall and Nordic, with unblinking green eyes and intimidatingly ripe red lips. She'd been a model until something had snapped. It was impossible to look at her and think anything had ever snapped; her expression was exquisitely deadpan. This was part of what we talked about. People were unsettled when they looked at her. She said I had something similar in my gaze, and the difference between us was that this was new for me. People had once seen tranquility in my eyes.

"Are you awake?" she asked. She continued, "What do you think that redheaded girl in class is like?"

Jess was unhappy and wanted to change. She wasn't sure of further details. She strongly suspected she wanted to kiss a woman. Also she was thinking of moving to Japan, where she could teach English or even model again. Her asking about the redheaded girl made me irritated, because it wasn't the first time she'd mentioned her. I said the girl wasn't going to solve any of Jess's problems, and what were her problems, anyway? She wouldn't tell me anything.

The darkness was a net of little colorful flashes, same as I'd seen in the middle of the night ever since I was a kid. "I thought nothing bothered you," she finally said.

"I'm not bothered."

"Don't you always make things okay?"

"Yeah, I'm okay now," I said, very loudly. "You?"

Jess told me a story. It began with how many different guys she was dating, which I already knew, as I'd hidden in her bedroom once when a larger guy had shown up unexpectedly. She'd never explained that and I, so cool, had never asked.

I wanted to tell her she needn't explain anything now, only I was aware as her story began to sound like a confession that this was an exit for her. She'd made a decision. Her relief was obvious. I was being shown the door. In the way of a Victorian thriller, she was explaining all mysteries to me.

She hated herself. When she was hungry, she imagined the woman who hired lingerie models at Nordstrom's watching her, and that kept her from eating. Did I ever wonder what happened to those perfect, complex desserts she kept buying and showing to me? She ate them in the middle of the night and vomited them back up. She'd been doing this so long the enamel on her teeth was dying. She was damaged. Sometimes she sat on her bed and screamed.

She was fanning before me a catalogue of her inadequacies. I was supposed to hear it as a list of reasons I was lucky to be getting out. I heard it as ticking off the things I was not good enough to fix.

She'd gone slam-dancing recently and that was the first time she'd been able to let her anger out. She loved slam-dancing. Maybe she wanted more punk rock in her life.

It was quiet. We'd dated for a month. We were already a couple that suffered uncomfortable silences. She was someone who had actually slam-danced. She had done it the way you should, as a tunnel into bottomless hostility. She'd touched something in herself I hadn't touched in either one of us.

When it was obvious I should talk again, I said, "I'm bad at getting angry. I always pick the wrong time to do it."

"It's okay be angry with me," she said.

"I don't know how to be angry. I wish someone would do something so I could have justifiable anger. I don't know what that's like."

"Don't you?"

"What?"

"What about the person who gave birth to you?"

Jess was smarter about me than I was about her.

I was getting dressed. Even though the time of night was ridiculous, I was going home. As she said goodbye at the door, Jess added, "At least you'll get a story out of this."

"I don't know about that. I'm not sure I'm a writer anymore."

"The education of Glen Gold," she said. I looked at her beautiful, impassive, chalk-white, unreadable face. Another dead silence. She extended her hand, to shake. "Thanks for coming. And thanks for leaving."

"Yeah."

"Good night."

"I hope you get . . ." I had no idea how to finish that.

"Me too." She closed the door.

ASTROLOGY

I VISITED LOS ANGELES one weekend, staying at my dad and Ann's house the first night. The atmosphere had changed, even though I hadn't been gone that long. They'd met with the architect who'd designed the Bel Air house, in hopes of having him build them a house of their own. But it had fallen through, too, so they were going to stay here.

I was at the dinner table with them when my father said, "There's been a development."

Ann said she was pregnant.

I hadn't been expecting that. "Were you guys planning this?" I asked.

"I was lied to," my father said, growling but not with actual anger. I unfairly remember him saying it while burying his face in a turkey leg.

Ann shrugged, with a faint upturn to her mouth. I could tell having another kid was going to be an adventure for her. It occurred to me I didn't know anyone else who was so emotionally compensated by having a child. My attitude about that had been condescending, as if wanting to be a mom meant you had to be a little bit blind. But here was contentment and worry and struggle that would be difficult and have joys to it. This was what the word "maternal" looked like. Now, I'd add that I was jealous. It was a relationship I would not be able to participate in.

I looked at my dad and I saw that his reaction was almost the same as Ann's: a kind of lusty delight in the whole making-a-family thing. "Here I am," he was saying, "redoubling, recommitting, and with humor and ease."

It wouldn't be that simple.

He had already started buying clocks and watches, and it was going to become more of an obsession. By the time my brother Andrew was born, my father would have one of the finest collections of British horological literature in the world, and a safety deposit box full of American pocket watches, many of them the finest known examples. When I visited him over the next couple of years, he told me amazing and hilarious stories about the jewelers, the designers, the auction houses, the means of acquisition. He knew some forgers and con men and thugs who loved watches. But collecting, of course, is a sign of sadness. My father knew this as well as he knew the serial numbers of the watches in their velvet casings. If the pile is high enough, though, you can't see how the rest of your world is going. Which is partially the point.

How this played out for him was at least poetic. They decided to stay in this house, but to make it a showpiece, remodeling it brilliantly and extensively. My father was pleased with that compromise, but alas he never spent a night in the new rebuild. Any contractor could tell you a marriage is most vulnerable during renovations, and this one—the marriage—had more structural problems than most.

When the place was finished, my father walked me through and pointed out all the architectural gestures and technological upgrades with melancholy. "Don't you wish you lived here? Me too." He made that joke (he delivered the words as if they were a joke) several times to me. He was living in a rental in Santa Monica not far from Shakey's Pizza. No showpiece for him. He had to sell his best clock to pay for his divorce lawyer.

There is likely a Buddhist or Taoist message there about the insubstantial ways that we buttress our lives against fear and impermanence. But that outcome was still a few years away as we sat in the as-yet-untransformed kitchen.

When my father was looking back across the table, news of an imminent kid still fresh to me, I sensed assessment in his eyes. Here was a son who was not yet crushed by this stuff. I was crushed by something else, but not that. I'd agreed to switch schools, which should have felt like a win for him, and yet I seemed to have separated myself from his world-view. He asked if I was staying the next night. I could tell he hoped the answer was "Yes." I told him, "Probably not."

That day Melanie and I went to the Yellow House for brunch. We didn't go to the beach; it might have been warm, but it was February and people just didn't do that in Los Angeles. She was more tense than I'd seen her. I was thinking about cats, and how they were wild. You couldn't influence them. That made me light up when I was a kid, because the moment Leo collapsed near me, it meant I was accepted. That wasn't happening now. I didn't even brush elbows with Mel. She was in her own miserable place.

Thanksgiving had caved in on her. "We had dinner with all our friends and it was full of laughter and it was warm and I had a premonition—I knew after everyone left, Jeremy was going to ask me to move in with him. So when it was late, he sat down with me and he looked me right in the eye and he said, 'Mel, I've got the clap.'"

It was over between them, over in a way it couldn't be undone. She'd learned her lesson, she said.

We ended up at her lovely homestead, a nestlike retreat in a canyon that she was house sitting in. I thought that if I was good enough, I might stay over. This wasn't an insane possibility. Mel knew why I was there. We sat down on a couch together, I took her hand, and she rested her head on my chest, and touched my biceps with a confusing pressure. I remembered how she had once touched me in her car, at the end of a very good night a long time ago, a combination of "please stay" and "please go," and how we had ended up kissing. I was trying to figure out what was different now.

Abruptly, she recalled she wanted to give me *Lilly on Dolphins,* and she went to the bookshelf so quickly I could still feel the touch of her fingers on me.

Right to the end, Mel tried to teach me things. We had wine. After a glass she mentioned how Jeremy had once told her I would only like her until she started repeating her stories. I knew he was a villain for not wanting to hear her stories, and she told me, again, how her father had driven into the desert and disappeared. He had some kind of dementia, but since he was a physician, his colleagues had covered it up. When it became apparent he wasn't coming back, Mel's family realized he'd emptied the bank accounts and there was nothing to support them.

There are those Ancient Mariner–type stories you tell because something in their residue both forms and confuses you. Mel's were like that. But she was also compelled to tell them because she wanted me to hear something: she'd left home at sixteen and become a waitress because sometimes you have to just declare that you're enough, your family isn't a part of you anymore. She had choices. *I* had choices, she explained.

I needed to do some accounting, she suggested, of how my family life wasn't just a set of stories, but how I'd been affected.

"I haven't," I said. Other people let themselves be affected. I was a roving eye, untethered and, I thought, because I saw no connection, *I can be whatever you want me to be.*

Mel was patient. She said her surgery had been a success. It was possible she could have children, just maybe. She talked about this for an unexpected length of time, until it dawned on me that having children was important to her. To me it had been like hearing that maybe in the future she could go to the moon or learn to play the guitar. I had no idea that someone I knew would actually want children. Ann had had a child, and then she realized she liked it, and she wanted more. But to embrace that destiny? Why would you want that? Why would that be important to someone like Melanie, who had so clearly stated her desire for autonomy?

I have told my story of that year, but if the spotlight went her way, you might say that when 1983 began, Mel hadn't known what her future would be, and all the decisions she'd made until then were questionable. We live our lives in themes and counter-themes and in the latter she'd been exploring lust, in the same way a body during wartime might dance with nihilism or drink absinthe. And now, the war was over, Saturn had returned, cancer and Jeremy were gone, and her body was hers again, only this time with the suggestion that it was okay to feel safe, a little bit safe, finally, to explore what she actually wanted beyond lust, beyond me, beyond Jeremy: attachment to someone who deserved it. She was becoming comfortable with her desires.

After the second glass of wine, she told me about the work of Mike

Kelley, a conceptual artist she knew. I wrote the name down, ready to get a monograph or to look for a gallery opening. Her tone brightened by the moment. She knew him well. He was a genius. He was handsome, but he was also a genius. Once, the two of them were drinking wine together on the floor of his studio, and he genuinely leapt across the room, on top of her, and she said to me, laughing, "I mean, what was that? Was that foreplay?"

She laughed. I laughed. I was trying to make the story, which was about Melanie telling me she was sleeping with someone she liked, into Mel being open to all kinds of sex including with me, here, now. In fact she was telling me to go home.

Anyone would know that. I begged to stay. Mel let me. We slept nude in the same bed. I was awake, touching her back and telling myself how it was making her excited. But it wasn't.

I want to tell you more about Melville, Pop. 1: she ended up doing well. She married, and became pregnant, and spent nine months nervous. She had a girl, healthy and a bit of a miracle. She then tempted fate by trying to have a second kid. But fate never pays you back in the ways you expect: two weeks before she was about to deliver, her husband left her for the drummer of an all-girl rock band. Melanie told me she was having trouble driving, that she kept eyeing the guardrails and imagining flooring it, taking the Volvo and her pregnant body in it at full speed over the embankment.

But she didn't. She didn't romance the idea of her own doom. She had her second child, a boy, and then, a couple of years after that, as a single woman with two young kids, found a good man. They married, happily. What are the odds? And then, at the impossible age of forty-three, she had a *third* child.

Life, it turns out, is most often a series of mundane, unlikely events. Melanie is now the nonexotic age of sixty-one. She doesn't seek out drama. She's a librarian. She sews. When she shares photographs online, I see the huge distance she has traveled from one futon, one candle—there are dogs and cats, and mess, and a kid in college, a kid in the Marines, and her husband looks like a terrific catch. She goes to church and drinks red wine and rages about living in Arizona as someone who is not a dough head. When she texts me photos, she hopes I'll ignore the woman to the side of the kids, the woman she says has a double chin. I don't see a double chin.

But I find it ironic that her anatomy lesson has changed over the years. Though she never points it out, I'd say the adductors, those muscles which bring her limbs inward and toward this life, are flexing themselves. I laughed when I realized her email address was "Melvillepop5."

And that's decades of future she's lived. She ended up having a future to inhabit. But some endings were more complicated.

That last night I spent with Mel, I woke up irritated with myself for how I'd behaved. In a word, I felt *puny*.

As I was about to get in my car, Mel remembered something: out of nowhere, *Rick* had written her a letter. He was living in his parents' house in Nevada. It must have been rough. Reading between the lines, she thought they didn't accept him as their son. She didn't know how he was doing, as his letter—charming and funny as it was—omitted all personal details.

He did ask her a question she found curious: Was Glen still not bothered by anything?

Sometimes you get sense memories beyond words, and in this case I remember standing in the gravel driveway leading to Mel's house-sit, the greenery of trees around us, her kitchen windows steamed up from making coffee, as she said this casually. He hadn't asked about anyone else from the store, or anything else about me. Of all the things . . .

I asked for his address.

FICTION

WHEN I GOT BACK TO BERKELEY I wrote Rick a chatty letter, and asked him where he was, what he was doing. I'm sure I flirted with him.

There was no response. I was lonely and bored, and as I went running one afternoon, I imagined another letter. It would strike an avuncular tone, as if I were a fifty-year-old jaded novelist with connections to the high life. When I came back home, I wrote it out. I commiserated with Rick for Clayton having been thrown out of Andover. I said I believed the young man's alibi—that he was out with Brooke Shields when the accident took place. Further, I believed him when he said he didn't know how his textbooks and a bottle of bourbon were found in the headmaster's totaled Mercedes.

I also wrote, with enough hints for Rick to fill in the gaps, that at least it was nice his sister had been there that day to comfort him. I finished with a hasty-looking PS, telling him not to even bother thanking me for the new BMW I'd gotten Clay, that it had been swag for a Rose's Lime Juice advertisement I'd done.

A few days passed. But not many.

My landlady always put my mail on a dresser in the hall. One afternoon there were two letters for me. The first letter, on stationery with a

pair of smart, nautical blue stripes running down the left margin, was an
envelope with the return address of Master Clayton Savilla. The handwriting was phenomenal.

Clayton
Exeter—Prep
Room 128

Uncle Glen
1008 Mariposa Ave.
Berkeley, California

Dear Uncle Glen,

I guess mom probably told you I got expelled from Andover.
Honestly, Uncle Glen, I still don't know what happened. I
suppose one of the Shriver boys was jealous of my relationship
with Brooke, and pulled a rather vulgar prank involving the
Headmaster's car. Well, I like Exeter a lot, and I'm going to try
real hard to make the best of it here. I do miss my friends back at
the other school though.

Mom is being presented to the Queen of England after her
performance with Baryshnikov at the Sydney Opera House this
Spring. I'm going to spend a week with Stephanie in Monaco,
then we'll fly out for the performance opening night. John
Kennedy Jr. is my big brother in the fraternity here, and we go
horse-back riding every weekend at the country club. He's a swell
guy, Uncle Glen, and I've been giving him some pointers on his
backgammon game.

I'm writing, specifically, to ask a favor of you. Andrew is
hosting a weekend gala at Philip's manor in Wales for my
birthday. Diana and Charles will be chaperoning because we're
all under age, and there will be girls staying the week-end. Parents
are invited, but mom will be touring with Giselle, and dad hits
on all my friends, so I was wondering if you'd come along as my
family member. I realize you're busy creating the literary tome
to beat *Ullyses* [sic], but a break might do you good. Please don't
tell my dad, because he gets so hurt, being so "thensitive" as he is.

I'd greatly appreciate it if you would give it serious consideration. By the way, thanks for the car! Please write soon.

> Love,
> Your nephew,
> Clay

I laughed at much of this, and also tried to pay attention to how he was playing his game. Apparently Bette Midler was no longer their mother, but Melanie had been promoted.

The second letter had neither stationery nor a formal return address. Instead, it was written on the back of an ad with Paul Newman and Joanne Woodward asking for Save the Children donations. There were alterations: Paul Newman's sweater now had a hand-drawn heart with an arrow through it, and the name "Lolly" over his breast.

Dear Uncle Glen,

Here I am with the Newmans; I met them through my ass-hole brother Clayton and his hoidy-toidy friends from Andover. He didn't know I was coming, and I just crashed in on him one night at his dorm. I really got back at him and those fag ass friends of his that think they're so fuckin grand. Guess what I did? I waited 'til he left with that Shields bitch and then I stole his car and drove it right into the Headmaster's Mercedes! I poured a quart of rot-gut bourbon on the seat and floor of his car, and left his school books on the floor so he'll get his butt beat. (My mom thinks I'm still at that boarding school in France, but me and Patty hitch hiked to Amsterdam 'cause we had to unload some bad ass hash, then split for the States.) Clayton is such a candy ass. I'm glad he got what he had coming. DON'T TELL MY MOM!! Got to get to Wiesbaden in 2 weeks for a smoke-out with some heads, and I'm low on dough. Mom's stingy and dad thinks I'm still living on that piss poor allowance that doesn't keep me in cigarettes, much less coke. Fuck. Life's a bitch. You gotta send me some cash Uncle Glen. I know you'll understand because you go to Berkeley, where niggers and jews are equal to women. I only need about 10K to get by this

semester, and don't want to "put out" like last term just because
I couldn't make ends meet.

The next page of the letter was written on the back of a photocopy of
a half-dozen wanton-looking women clutching at their cell—an advertisement for *Women Behind Bars,* a drag queen play then running in
West Hollywood. Each girl had been labeled carefully: Patty, Monéque,
Babs, Sheryl, LaVicki, Lolly, and The Baroness.

This is a program photo of the high school play me and
some of my friends put on for the Christmas pageant at
"L'ecole Français." We got expelled, but then re-instated when
I reminded the Baroness that 7 girls gone means roughly $105,000
just in rip-off tuition alone, and that she'd have to cancel those
silk panties from Pucci's she's gotten ever so fond of. Uncle Glen,
you gotta help me!
I can't talk to mom 'cause she always takes everyone else's
side against mine. She's just like Clayton with their heads up
some ballerina's ass, listening to Clare Boothe Luce stories
about Dorothy Parker and Benchley's boring crowd. I want to
feel something goddamn it, not just live vicariously through
mom's fartin' around on stage like some 9 year old, and my dad's
inability to "cope" with anything but a thick prick up his ass and
a dinner party in L.A. I promise to stop my bulimic purges in
public if you just help out. Come on buddy, be a guy.

Love,
Your neice [*sic*]
Lolly

I was thrilled and a little horrified. It was easy to draw on my family's
toehold on culture when writing back to Rick. But the more I studied
what he'd said so I could riff on it, the more darkness I saw gathering at
the edges of what he was saying. I already had a vague idea of what was
really going on with him. I thought I should keep going.
In my letter, I said I'd decided not to give Lolly ten thousand dollars
but instead I got her a job as a roadie with the Plasmatics, the most vile

punk rock band I knew about. I accepted Clayton's invitation to the
party, and spun out the story a little further, with intrigues: the possibility of fraternity hazing, money-hungry girls, political aspirations.
I seeded it with ways Lolly could screw it up, and then I sent it off.

The next letter was from Rick. It was written around a photocopy of a
hideous snapshot of a transvestite with makeup that looked like a burn
victim's.

Glen,
    Why won't my son tell me about the weekend with Prince
Charles and Princess Diana this spring break? I've always
considered myself a rather conservative gent. Don't you think?
[Here, an arrow toward the photograph of the transvestite.]
Sure, I gave a party for the Plasmatics when they came through
town, but how was I to know the press was there snapping
photos just when I sprayed the mace in the lead singer's face?
I was coked-out; doesn't that mean anything anymore?
    I have no idea where Melanie is. She's trying to ditch me. Are
you having an affair with her? Lolly told me you were sleeping
with Melanie. Is this true? Doesn't she even have enough respect
for my reputation, let alone the fact we have 2 children in school,
and one on the road? I don't blame you, because you're a man,
but she, she should act her age and stop tramping around like
Fausta and Lolly. She has it easy. She only deals with Clayton
(when she has the time), almost never with Fausta and Lolly,
high-foots it around the world (with no forwarding address)
and sleeps indiscriminately with any foul-dicked pig she wants
(present company excepted). I'm not sleeping with other
women; doesn't the sanctity of marriage mean what it used to
before Billie Jean King and that Barnett girl aired their dirty
laundry on prime-time T.V.?
    Where is she? Huh?
    As for Lolly. Not a dime. Do you hear me? Not a dime. I got
her a job selling chocolate mint cookies outside the Bank of
America for Jerry Lewis. She's got to learn respect and love for

the less fortunate. The money may not be terrific, but she'll learn the real value lies in the hearts (and soles [*sic*]) of those crippled children.

And Clayton. Glen, we have to have a fag to man talk about my son. The car is being returned. It's not that I don't appreciate your generosity, but he's too young to start boasting the likes of such an ostentatious consumer fetish. He's beginning to turn away from me, as though I were "Stella Dallas" in cheap costume jewelry, waving a big pearl dinner ring in flamboyant gesticulations with my expressive wrist movements. I know Clayton loves me, and is probably even ashamed that he feels his friends make mock-soup of my theatrical antics, but I can't bear the pain of losing my boy. He defends me ferociously, but I understand peer pressure can be rather taxing. I remember when he was only 11. I gave a birthday party for him to rival Christmas in "Mommie Dearest." I decorated everything myself, made the cake, and bought him his first pair of top-siders, and then I heard one of his friends say, "How come your dad acts like a girl?" It broke my heart. Not for my sake, but for Clay's. That's when I decided it might be best for him to go away to school. Now I feel I'm losing him and the pain is too much to bear. So you see, I guess I'm jealous. I want my baby back. He'll always be my baby, something you may not understand. Perhaps I haven't lost him yet. I can only hope.

Rick.

I read this in my room in the early evening, in winter, with the radiator banging. The sun had set long before. It felt like whatever game we'd been playing had gone over the edges of the board and into something more darkly eternal. It was humor but it wasn't something I knew how to continue, as it came from pain much deeper than my own. I knew something was terribly wrong.

I wrote him a letter that night, long and full of detail. It didn't joke. I'm not sure what I told him about Melanie. I hope I made it a good story. I hope there was romance. Mostly, I hope I didn't get into my problems with Japanese, or the girlfriends whom I didn't understand. I hope I told him I continued to be worry-free, that I was a pure running stream, untroubled. That would have been kind.

A week went by. He didn't write back. I wrote again. Then I wrote one last time, this time feebly continuing the game we'd started, asking again about his wayward girl and loyal boy. I pointed out that all we can do is choose our family, right? I posted the letter and I waited.

I never heard another word.

When I was working at Hunter's I read for the first time that Joan Didion claim that we tell ourselves stories in order to live. It was a flashy quotation, but I hadn't felt the desperation that made it more substantial. We need to tell ourselves stories because the alternative is unbearable. Rick had written me a suicide note. Along the way he had created a family that would not fail him. Even the children who hated him.

Something happens when you see your future and your future is only oblivion. This was a familiar thought to me, because I think my aunt Rosemary had seen the same thing. Our family myth is of great opportunity taken away by great cruelty, and in that, Rick could be an honorary one of us, I thought. I could easily paint his portrait, in that he would be just as louche as my grandfather George, reclining with a joint, gazing with the same sage intensity into the viewer's eye.

Hello, old friend, he might say. *I tried to escape, too. Didn't work.*

Early one evening in late March, my mother called and when she heard my voice on the phone, she sounded very strange. She thought she'd seen me outside the El Cortez hotel. "How odd," she said. "You must have a doppelgänger."

When she hung up, I was mildly depressed. It was unclear even to my mother who or where I was. Be here now, cool running stream, the way to do is to be, those seemed like slogans written on collapsed banners with frayed ends and cobwebs discovered in the headquarters of a losing socialist campaign. I was not a panther, nor a chimp.

I looked for reasons to cheer up. I had just gotten a letter from Mel, which she signed "love (she says it now, the bitch)." There was a girl I'd known in high school, Marci, who was a flirt, who had said she might visit me, and she kept calling it off but I was fairly sure she was on her way soon. Cindy had written me to say she'd almost been raped, adding a frowny face, but that she wished I would come back and see her. There was a girl from Hiroshima named Yoshiko who was interested in visiting me in Berkeley. Heidi was thinking of flying out. There was another girl in my film class, Noelle, who had flirted with me. I made a printed list of names and stared at it and felt no better because it felt like something was missing.

One night, I was lying on my bed, sprawled among three friends, Kirsten, Rachel, and Sophie. We'd gone to high school together. We were supposed to go out and join a larger group to go dancing. But I wouldn't budge. It was raining. One or another of them would occasionally poke me in the side to motivate me, but I just kept saying things to postpone moving. We made a sculptural tangle of limbs, a Siamese Gordian knot. I wished I had a camera. I tried to memorize it: my legs were on top of Sophie's legs, Sophie was up on one elbow, saying sarcastic things, I had one hand on Rachel's knee, and Rachel was at the end of the bed, making dry responses to Sophie that somehow managed to simultaneously make fun of me. Kirsten was against the headboard, and I was faceup in Kirsten's lap. At some point, to jokingly shut me up, she pulled her sweater over my face, so I was just staring upward at the underside of her bra.

There was nothing sexual in this. The three were on my list of people I wanted on my island. It should have been soothing to be enmeshed among these bodies. I was breathing through Kirsten's sweater, my head pressed against her stomach. It wasn't like I was happy. I was thinking, "Isn't this what I want?"

I wanted more women. I wanted women to pick me up and carry me from the bed, down the stairs, and to the car, and I wanted women to laugh at my jokes and make fun of me, and to come to me with their problems, and then for them to all go away and think about me from afar. Even if all the women I knew desired me, it wouldn't quite be enough, and the melancholy it would generate—being universally beloved felt melancholy to me—would finally mean something. I would say, "Even though I have the love of all the women, I am still alone." There was something like fighting words in that.

If I could have frozen that moment, I would have, dissatisfaction and all. Because beginning now, it peeled back.

"Where are those letters from that guy you worked with?" Kirsten asked.

Making a show of how much I didn't want to dislodge myself, I got up and pulled them out of a notebook. I distributed them.

Kirsten, Rachel, and Sophie looked at them. There was a lot of laughter, and exclamation. Some reading aloud of individual, crazy bits of language. How strange these were!

"Why did you write him in the first place?"

"I don't know."

"How did you know to ask about his kids?"

"I don't know."

Someone asked, "But where is he?"

"What?"

"Where is he now?"

I didn't know what to say. "You don't know?"

It wasn't obvious to any of them.

I asked it a few times, until it was annoying. "Really? You don't know?" I looked at them with surprise, wondering what I'd experienced that made me never ask that question. I'd known, even before I wrote my first letter to him, what was going to happen to Rick.

I felt that continuing strange tug, a fishing lure embedded in my gut. When I was four or five, looking at my first anatomy chart with Mom, I saw the duodenum and the pancreas and the mysterious appendix (my father was missing his), the kidneys (my mother was missing one of those), and I ran my finger along the names. I asked my mother, "But where's my soul?" I remember her finger, then her whole palm sweeping the chart. Your soul is everywhere, she said. It's in everything. You can't see it.

We had a television when I was too young to understand what numbers were. It was a black-and-white television. When I turned off a cartoon, the image galloped away, like a gust of wind had taken it down to just a dot. The dot got smaller, and smaller, a dead dim gray image I could put my finger on but not really touch. Dimmer and dimmer, over a period of time unimaginably long to me, and yet I was always patient, needing to watch until it had finally, softly, left the set. That was the cartoon's soul, and that was how it went away. That's where Rick had gone.

I thought of the stacks of journals Rick kept, and how they vanished. His dreams of publishing the story of his life as a man had come to nothing. The three letters he wrote were the time that writing saved him, briefly. Is it ridiculous to say that when I was lying on my bed on a rainy evening in Berkeley, trying to explain to my friends that Rick was dead, that I realized the power and the limits of fiction?

I had until then written as if I had an invisible audience. Rick was writing from the depth of a man who understands that there is no reception from the world, none whatsoever. And yet, the power of fiction was stronger with him than anyone else I knew. Mike, my boss, had told himself he was running a real business. My father told himself stories about having landed where he belonged, and that lasted until his next divorce. I felt new compassion for my mother, as she was telling herself stories that were just about to fail her, again.

Fiction is a pathology. Even though it's not enough, even though nothing else, like love, or knowing yourself, is enough either, fiction was pretty much all that I had right then. Like my father, my mother, Melanie, Rick, all of us, everyone, I did almost everything because I was afraid of death and because I wanted love. I faced Kirsten, Sophie, and Rachel with a declining feeling, an elevator going down.

I needed to tell you about the person I was before I told you about the person I became. And here I was, finally. It was so familiar, how as I stood up, I felt dim, and welcomed back by an old feeling. I recognized myself: stooped slightly, my ability to make sentences slowed down, ideas bowing at the halfway point from a sense that finishing them didn't matter.

A voice whispered to me. The voice loved me. It was horrible, too. I am *yours,* it said. No one could take it from me. It was mystery, it was heavy and it was an old friend. I recognized it in the throb of my forehead, where my cast had been at Wesleyan. It was the feeling I'd had lying on my dorm room bed in Connecticut, unable to move as my mother left the room to go back home. I was already beginning to find new ways to think of the word "gray." Depression wasn't just one mood, but a whole spectrum that I needed to describe to myself.

I could not be swayed. I would keep writing and it would keep not mattering. I was helpless. This was a relief, in a way.

I got ready to go out. Nineteen was almost over. Twenty was on its way. I didn't feel better. I was a mess, but I was also myself for the first time, in a way that was going to be helpful to me. My own life no longer made sense. I no longer feared that.

We danced that night, as badly as any straight white Berkeley students ever did, at a gay nightclub that was emptier than it had been a year before.

3

THE BOOK

OF

REVELATION

---

for Owen Bly

My mother called me to ask if she could borrow
two dollars. I told her no.

CHRISTMAS

F I'M A WRITER, you'd think I might know what it means that my mother is an unreliable narrator. But I really don't. I believe every story she tells me, every version of it.

My mother once told me she met Daniel just before dawn on the morning she was to be evicted from her apartment across from the El Cortez in downtown San Diego. She was loading her van with her belongings, hurrying to be on the road before the seven a.m. visit from the sheriff. Trying to be discreet, she worked in the dark, and since her apartment was up a flight of stairs, she had trouble handling the heavy furniture by herself. Something awkward, a bookcase or an easy chair, slipped from her hands and crashed down to the street just as Daniel and a friend of his, a sailor, happened to be walking by.

Daniel would never pass up a person who needed help, especially a pretty woman like my mother. He and his friend decided to give her a hand. They quietly loaded the rest of her furniture, save one mattress, into the van, and in exchange for their help, my mother, who of course had no money to give them, concluded with a sinking feeling that she had run out of options. Everything in her life had been reduced to this primal transaction. There were the two men. There was the mattress. She did, as she would tell me later, what she had to.

Afterward, Daniel and the sailor argued. The sailor wanted to leave; Daniel wanted him to give a hand carrying the mattress to the van. The sailor relented, and the two of them took it away while my mother sat on the toilet and cried.

When she came out of her apartment for the last time, she taped a little note on the door for the landlord, put the key back through the mail slot, and found her way down the stairs. Daniel was waiting for her by the van, alone.

I can't imagine what they said to each other. She told me she was embarrassed to be so desperate, and she was grateful that her circumstances didn't faze him. The sun was rising by now, and Daniel asked her where she was going. That they both had nowhere to go at dawn seemed romantic to her. She felt like they were gypsies.

They drove the van just a block to a Denny's, where my mother ordered tea. Daniel however told the waitress they'd both have full breakfasts, sausages and hash browns, the works. My mother worried, but Daniel just laughed and for the first time told her, *Baby, with me, every day is Christmas*. He pulled out a twenty. It was his last twenty, but Daniel explained that in his life, he'd been down to his last twenty a number of times, and every time, God had provided for him.

Was it then that they got their first lingering looks at each other? Daniel, my mother would later say, could walk with kings or paupers with equal ease. He looked to her very much like the actor Richard Gere, only a bit plumper and with blackened teeth. My mother, blond, fair, blue-eyed, with a lovely and faint British accent worn down by thirty years in California, still said she looked like Linda Evans. Maybe my mother and Daniel talked about what famous people they looked like. At that point, she was sure he was just a character she would later wonder what had happened to.

After breakfast, however, they went to the van in the parking lot and climbed in, together.

It was 1986. My mother was fifty-one. Daniel was twenty-seven. Daniel said he'd heard there were jobs in Las Vegas. My mother was shocked. Could people just leave one city for another like that? Daniel laughed. How else, he asked, do you expect to have an adventure?

On their way out of town, they made one stop by an old building near the Gaslamp Quarter. My mother sat in the driver's seat, double-parked and idling, while Daniel, somewhere inside, bought a bag of crystal meth. He said it would help him stay awake while they were driving. My mother said it was okay with her, as long as he was careful. And so they drove out of the city together, my mother feeling safe and free and Daniel whistling happy songs, and I imagine both of them knew, even though they'd only been together for hours, that they would never be apart.

––––––––

It took me twenty minutes to write the paragraphs above. It was winter 1995, nine years or so after those events had happened. I was in graduate school for creative writing. I was in my girlfriend's apartment and in the time it took her to shower, I wrote it, and then I printed it, read it, and threw the pages into her wastebasket. I didn't save the computer file. I closed the laptop and it was like the writing had never happened.

A few minutes later, my girlfriend spotted the pages in the garbage. She asked if she could read them. When she was finished, she asked if the story was true. I said it was. She asked how I knew, and I said my mother had told it to me, among other, more pleasant versions. She asked why I'd thrown it away. I tried to explain that the writing had come with no feeling whatsoever. Normally when I write, I feel triumphant or cocky or embarrassed or twisting in the wind and anxious to try and rewrite it. With the story of my mother, it was like looking through water. And this suggested in a way I didn't question that there was no reason to save it.

My girlfriend, still in her robe, towel turbaned around her damp hair, was looking my way with a forensic surgeon's eye. Some women can track down, analyze, and react to color and smell more intensely than men can. So it was with Alice and emotion.

"Your mother had sex with two strange men on a mattress," she said, looking at me. "How does that make you feel?"

I wanted to please her with my insight. I also wanted to be honest. "Nothing."

I had a vision of myself having donned the cape of a superhero with the word NOTHING emblazoned on it, bullets bouncing off, and in the tiny space my mask would leave for my eyes, you could see them a little panicked, wide and blinking at Alice.

She looked at me sympathetically. She told me the piece was good. I should write more. The paper was a little wet from her fingers, and the ink had run indigo, and I wondered if I were to put a coffee cup down on it whether it would make interesting ring designs, old words evolving into patterns or chaos, depending on how you looked at it.

She asked, "Are *you* going to be in this memoir?"

"Sure." A lie even as I said it. Normal people wrote about themselves, but I knew I had a higher calling: *floating eye*. State the facts and let the readers feel the emotions rather than put my thumb on the scale. To say, "My mother had terrible things happen, and I felt sad," seemed insipid to me.

My mother told me more than once how she met Daniel. When she was feeling angry, she stalled upon approaching the most awful parts ("I had no money to pay, so . . ." and gazing down to the floor for me to fill in the rest). Other times, there was no eviction, no sailor friend, an entirely different daytime hello. When she loved Daniel the most, there were only good parts, the rescue, the buoyancy, the soul mate, and I, hearing this, wondered if that mattress was a figment of my imagination.

Or hers. Maybe it was something she had created in order to feel the worst possible shame.

When she first told me, I did not write it down. I whispered it to my girlfriend in the dark, holding her, and hoping that exposing the words would lead to them making sense, or dissolve them into nonsense, like when you believe a story and only realize you're gullible when you repeat it. Neither of those things happened. It wasn't just that I was horrified but I think my mother *wanted* to be horrified in telling it, and this is why I never wrote it down: by recording it I felt I would catch a familiar contagion that settles in on children like myself.

When I was seventeen, long before any of that, I was visiting relatives on my father's side of the family, self-contained and prosperous people for whom family is a tribe—problematic, loud, annoying as hell, but also magnetic north. They lived in suburbs and their children were of the generation who made their parents happy by becoming doctors or attorneys. They didn't know my mother that well, but she was a converted shiksa from London, which made her exotic and interesting. Given that my father had married her, she was considered de facto one of them, despite the exoticness, and the divorce.

At dinner, my aunt asked me about my mother's then-current situation, which involved a bad boyfriend and some stolen money, but I didn't get far in explaining it. My aunt interjected the following: my mother's only problem was that I didn't love her enough. I was thoughtless, she said. I had to try harder, and if I showed her enough love, the rest would work itself out.

The invocation of guilt was second nature to her. I'm sure it was supposed to be like applying a Band-Aid and a kiss on an injured knee. I folded my napkin and said, "Please take me to the train station."

She thought I was joking. I followed through. For reasons my aunt couldn't comprehend, I demanded to leave. I'm not sure she'd ever met a kid who would do such a thing.

On the way to the station, my aunt was trying to understand, sort of, in the sense that she asked me to explain, then batted away everything I said as nonsensical. This was not entirely her fault—I was terrible at explaining. I said, "If you told your son the sky was green, how long would he believe you for?"

"The sky isn't green."

"But what if you said it was? What if you knew it was green, and you had a good explanation for why everyone else said it was blue? You know they're wrong and you need him to know it, too?"

"He'd look up and see the sky wasn't green."

"But what if you thought he was betraying you unless he said the sky was green, too?"

"That's ridiculous. I would never do that."

"Do you think he'd see the sky was green sometimes but not other times?"

"Glen, the sky is blue."

I was frustrated and I shut up. I *did* love my mother. It made no difference in how she behaved. I had learned already that people who believed in the healing powers of love were idiots. I couldn't explain that everyone is just one relative away from the world unloading its lessons, in the process making what they thought they knew about the words "always" and "love" and "mother" seem trivial and naive.

I have more sympathy for my aunt now. There is alienation in having a mother like mine, in that people who can say the word "maternal" without needing to add "in a positive sense" cannot grasp what it means that I no longer love my mother. They think I'm kidding myself, or angry, or petulant, or selfish—mostly that I'm lost. For years these opinions made me angry because they felt condescending.

But it's closer to the truth to say that, as with any situation where science and psychology have failed to provide comfort, people fall back on faith. You love your mother. It's an axiom, you just do it. Until you start to ask questions about why.

While Mom was with Daniel, I still loved her because I had grown up with that faith, not even knowing it was faith, but mistaking it for biology. My love was a knot of safety mechanisms, reflexive withdrawal and emptiness. For ten years, I waited for the middle-of-the-night phone call from a sheriff's department in San Diego or Placer County or Nevada or Oregon telling me that Daniel had finally beaten her to death.

I used to imagine that phone call, imagining my relief because then I would know how I felt about her. I daydreamed about looking into that clear-running stream I'd told myself I'd become to see it cloud up with anger, hopelessness, grief. I looked forward to writing a eulogy because, in part, it would be her funeral and there would be no more shocks or surprises. I could begin a sentence with "my mother" without bracing for whatever was coming next. I wanted to call my aunt in the middle of the night and say, "You were right, I didn't love her enough and so her boyfriend finally beat her to death," because I wanted her to know how hopelessly naive she was.

But it didn't work out like that. Mom's time with Daniel ended in 1995, and I wrote about it for my memoir class a few months later. I kept myself out of it. I was as hidden as the weather, a fixed eye suspended in the blank sky over a cold industrial town. *Feel free to feel bad,* I thought. *I'm not even here.* Just as my mother had tried to tell her life story once by writing it from my point of view, I had made a complement to that by writing a memoir from which I was absent.

If you're restless, however, your brain never stops trying to pick certain locks. It turns out that what I was feeling was too horrific to take in, a loneliness I'd never heard described before. I want to explain how

I stopped loving my mother, a condition no sadder than loving her in the first place.

When I was twenty and enrolled at Berkeley, I felt a Byronic distance from the weakness of falling in love. I can hear myself saying things about my heart over coffee at Café Roma or Sufficient Grounds or standing on the stone steps outside the English Department. Berkeley was to me a series of conversations, separated by some classroom activity. Mostly I was trying to build a case for myself. "I didn't have a broken home," I tended to explain, "it was more of a scorched-earth policy."

This was me, then: 1960s narrow lapel sport coats from thrift stores, skinny batik ties, jeans with holes in them, high-tops, complicated book bags, and, I must apologize but it's true: earrings that were of the dangly sort, sometimes skeletons. I had a lot of gel in my hair. I was pretty, but mishandled that by leaning forward at the table to make sure everyone noticed the whole "pretty" thing.

I had stopped feeling happy or relaxed, and instead had adapted to the consistent background filter of depression by trying to turn it into seeming mysterious. I can see the women I talked to—I tended to say things about my heart to women—falling into those claims like I was opening up a storybook with castles and treasure. And then, bang, massive distance on my part, just when I had seemed so nice.

But then something unexpected happened. When my mother was meeting her soul mate—the very week in fact—I was meeting mine. Regardless of the pride I took in the empty place in my chest, I still had a contrary faith I believed in so deeply that I'd mistaken it for an axiom. *If I love you hard enough I can fix you.*

It doesn't work like that. This is what I want to say so it's as familiar as the stars and sunrise: your love is not enough.

MAPS AND LEGENDS

IN 1984, when I was twenty, I worked in Berkeley's worst bookstore. Our selection was thin, and we were two minutes' walk from the world-class bookstores of Telegraph Avenue. Cody's had ten times our inventory, and Moe's sold what we did, only cheaper. Though we were on campus, we didn't sell textbooks, which baffled almost everyone who tried to shop with us. The customers who came into our store had hoped to shop somewhere else.

This bookstore was far worse than Hunter's, which had a tattered, bumbling elegance. If Hunter's was like a stuffy French restaurant that had lost its Michelin star, General Books (that was as much of a name as it had) wasn't even Shakey's Pizza. It was more of a cafeteria.

A pea-soup fog of despondency enveloped the place. I remember Kevin, gangly and shy, always on the verge of coming out, and always, instead, choking back tears as he wheeled books in from the loading dock. Ryan, age seventy, a drunk, sat behind a typewriter, pecking out inventory cards so botched that after the end of his day, when he patted his chest and said, "Well, I'm going to go get loaded," they had to be retyped by Paola, whose husband had died.

It's not like *I* was fun to hang out with. I was in a slump, going through a phase peculiar to certain sensitive men, proving that I could not just date but live with a woman I didn't actually like. Noelle was French, which was very cool, and for some reason I thought that meant there was no way we would ever argue. And yet she and I argued a *lot* in an involuted style that meant an hour into it we were arguing about what the argument was about. Neither one of us knew what the other was thinking, but our apartment had beamed ceilings, a Batchelder tile fireplace, and hardwood floors, so neither of us was going to be the first to move out.

In the mornings, I would see Noelle's sleeping face on the pillow next to mine, and the apartment would be quiet, with shafts of light hitting the onyx wood framing of the exquisite floors, and I would think, "I should break up with her." It was bad enough that I looked forward to work.

Once, the bookstore had been a fun place, or so I kept hearing. The cool kids had worked there. On weekends, someone used to play guitar at the checkout counter. People would make out in the break room. There was a suggestions book from back then, a season's worth of hand-drawn cartoons, mock diatribes, and gossip, abruptly ending in June, when everyone who was good graduated. I was hired in July. Now the suggestions book was filled with suggestions.

The haunted atmosphere at the store was like Troy fifty years after the war ended. What must those Trojans have told visitors? "It's not much to look at now, but once there was this Achilles fellow who was really swift-footed, and there was this horse, but it was a trick. You should have been here."

Laura was one of the few holdovers. She was witty, but you could tell she had better things to do than talk to me. I would say something I was fairly sure was funny, and she would nod, directing her gaze somewhere just past me. I felt certain that when she left work she was swept into a limousine and taken to underground nightclubs where men snorted cocaine off her chest until it was time for her to come back to work the next morning.

There was a photo over a desk in the back office. Two former co-workers sitting on a bench. One of them was a slim man in mod clothes, paisley shirt, sunglasses, handsome but really not the focus of the photo. He and the camera are both more involved with the woman, whom I couldn't quite get a fix on. She was both mocking him and daring him to come closer. She had a vintage look, but I couldn't place the era. 1930s? 1960s? I couldn't even tell if she was pretty.

They were part of the legendary group that had left. "That's Vincent and that's Lindsay," Laura told me one day. "Lindsay was trouble. She was the resident femme fatale."

I considered the photograph. "I could have handled her."

Laura threw some books on her cart. "You would have fallen like all the rest."

That made me laugh. These people thought highly of themselves. Which reminded me of me.

I was fairly sure I was filled with untapped potential. I did not walk up the avenue when I approached campus—I loped, a determined, shoulders-forward movement that looked like I was fighting unseen enemies to get wherever I was going a little faster than humanly possible. I looked like Monsieur Hulot on his way to a tennis match.

The walk was part of my impatience. Every day, I wanted to crack open the things I didn't understand so I could write about them. I looked at every object like I was measuring how I could take it apart and describe it to people in case I had to. I treated conversations with strangers like seductions, and it was important to me who came out on top. I wished someone would describe me as *un homme fatal*.

I was writing drafts of my now-seven-thousand-page boarding school novel that was every bit as tiresome as it sounds. Occasionally however I would write short stories that were different and better, one of which was a finalist in the annual *Cosmopolitan* fiction contest. This meant it was one of twenty manuscripts that Helen Gurley Brown herself read, but when I talked about this, I shaved it to ten or to five. If I met new people, I mentioned it exactly once. When you walked past me at a party, the conversation you'd overhear would go like this:

"A writer."

"Oh, have you published anything?"

"Not yet. But *Cosmopolitan* just—"

You would keep walking.

The *Cosmopolitan* contest happened and then I accumulated only rejection slips. The early ones had handwritten encouragements, but as

I tried to be a better writer, the slips came back clean. I felt cursed. I wanted company.

In autumn, a few straggling people from that extended group of friends returned to Berkeley, landing in an 1870s brown shingle house at 1811 Rose Street. It was a dark five-bedroom over-timbered place built atop an ancient underground stream that made the basement cold and the bedrooms feel haunted.

I lived miles away, with Noelle, on the Oakland border, but I kept track of the Rose Street crew. Housemates were returning from their travels to New York and England and Africa. Bands were re-forming. People were getting day jobs waiting tables so they could write their novels at night. I thought this was incredible luck, but they were just following the normal boomerang path of liberal arts graduates who find out what the world is like. Berkeley was playing the same role as it had for generations, a comfortable town for college graduates who needed a place to be kind to them.

The femme fatale didn't come back.

The first Rose Street person I knew was Hannah. She tended to speak in complete sentences that had dependent clauses you had to listen to for some kind of excellent Homeric simile that usually was self-deprecating. She had a boyfriend named Vincent and her best friend was the absent Lindsay—the two people in the photograph I'd seen. Hannah often stopped at my bookstore on her lunch hour, where she would say hello to me and keep me updated on the old group reassembling. In exchange she seemed to be auditioning me for a place with them.

Hannah invited me and Noelle to their parties, which seemed to happen every month or so, polite yet crowded affairs where people I recognized from around town smoked in the street outside, while deep James Brown cuts played in the living room. The kitchen jammed with young assistant professors agreeing with each other about Ibo reaction to colonialism, and arrogant clerks that I recognized from Tower Records were made momentarily shy by being here. The conversations were bashful, because we each wanted to know what the other person had done to be invited. "I have the 'Love Will Tear Us Apart' 12-inch." Or, "I'm loaning Vincent *In the Castle of My Skin*."

At one point Hannah couldn't explain to me how two people dancing in the living room knew each other, and so, with appropriate music— the Bangles? the Smiths? something paisley?—playing so loudly we had to huddle together to talk, she showed me the chart.

It was a thing of beauty, a handwritten astrological map in a way, with names in place of the stars. I think there was pencil and pen and colored crayon involved. The legend: dotted lines connecting two names meant those people had lived together. A solid line meant they'd dated. There were symbols that meant they'd worked together, stars meaning they'd been in the same band, or worked at General Books, or at the *Pelican* magazine, or they'd been, ironically or otherwise, in the same sorority. Here was one band, the Mr T Experience, that some friends were in, and Dallas, who worked at General Books, had started another one called Sweet Baby Jesus that they would have to add soon.

I remember it having three dimensions and yarn, as if it were a high school science fair DNA molecule, but it was just a flat thing contained in the back pages of someone's journal, modified as new people came into their web.

Lindsay's name was at the heart of it. She'd lived with everyone, worked with everyone, dated almost everyone, and kissed all the rest.

The Rose Street crew had decided everyone who lived there should have a TV show. In Lindsay's television show, Hannah said, the opening credits would show her boyfriend putting her on a train, and as it pulled out of the station, she would run back through the cars, waving at him on the platform, but also, when he couldn't see her, accepting kisses and flowers and chocolates from all the men on the train. When one kissed her particularly well, she would hand him the flowers another suitor had given her, then turn to the window to wave to her boyfriend outside.

When she got to the caboose, she would blow them all kisses, and jump off alone, admiring her new gifts and trinkets. A redcap looking at his railway watch would shake his head like he'd seen it all before.

Oh, but the show had been canceled. Lindsay was an *ex*–femme fatale. Engaged to a wonderful man, Paul, she lived in England while he was finishing up his degree at Cambridge. He had tamed her. On the chart, the line from Lindsay to her fiancé, Paul, was maybe the thickest line on the whole page because it seemed so unlikely and such a turning point in the group's dynamic. Or I remember it as thickest.

One album after another playing in the parlor, respectable in retrospect, or just catchy: *Controversy, Deep Sea Skiving, Secrets of the I Ching, Rum Sodomy & the Lash,* and was that really Neil Diamond, only now, in this context, newly discovered *cool*? There was so much music I'd never heard before, or I'd heard it once and not known what it was, or I'd heard it when I was eight years old. On their first date, Hannah had sealed the deal with Vincent by knowing all the lyrics to "Itchycoo Park."

I didn't want to leave the party. I wanted the night to end with me having a room in this house. I wanted to be good enough to have my own TV show.

I haven't mentioned what Noelle thought. When she and I got home, she said one party was enough. She wasn't going back. What kind of assholes mythologized themselves like that?

"Right," I said.

"You aren't actually agreeing with me," she said.

I was thinking about her hair. It had never been its natural auburn since I'd met her. Noelle changed her hair color from purple to blue to violet every few weeks. I was trying to assess whether she might try blond next, and that now seemed more important, in the sense that it fully filled my brain, than having an argument.

I was bad at this part of relationships. I proposed arguments with her in my head, had them, and then resolved them, without even opening my mouth. I thought that was efficient.

Whatever she said next, whatever the words were, what she meant was, "I can tell you don't actually love me." And whatever I said in response came with the bluster of a cat inflating his tail, "How can you say that?" et cetera, but she was right, and trying to convince her otherwise led to another Möbius strip of an argument. She was loud at arguments, louder still if someone was in the next room. I kept getting distracted by wondering if she was performing her anger. I still didn't know how to be angry.

What I said was filtered through the numb brain-wipe that happened when someone was yelling at me, what *Watership Down* called *tharn*.

This is the mental state of a rabbit in headlights. Instead of anything useful happening, like a response, all I could think of was how pleasant it would be to not be arguing. I heard music in my head and sometimes it was Top 40, and sometimes it was a melody I'd made up but couldn't quite hold on to. Now it was "Itchycoo Park," a song that had once united a couple of very nice people. I wished I could get Noelle to agree that the fight wasn't as important as this lovely music.

Vincent was the group's oracle. He was handsome, skinny in a severe and tidy way, his gestures precise and measured, talking quietly, as if taking up more space than necessary was inelegant. He studied literature, and was focused on how narrative became propaganda. He and I went running in the Berkeley Hills a few times while he adumbrated his thesis in cool, measured, reasonable tones and he didn't lose his breath no matter how steeply the street bent upward.

Vincent wrote a letter to Noam Chomsky, who wrote him back. I recall Vincent was coy and didn't want to bring the letter out at first. Then he and I and some equally impressed folks all leaned over it to hear him read it aloud, with proper respect. Chomsky both agreed that Vincent was right—all information is propaganda—but also suggested somehow he was not right enough and also his foundational question wasn't rooted correctly, but good for him for thinking on this, and the rest I didn't understand. It was Vincent's equivalent of the *Cosmopolitan* contest, a message from the larger world that he had some merit, and I felt proud of him. He started applying to grad schools.

There's a kind of friendship among men that starts when two people compare the things they've figured out. Vincent interrogated me about everything I'd done so far, an evaluation of how bourgeois my experiences had been.

He asked to see my high school yearbooks. He did that to everyone he liked, which I found endearing. His dream was to find a random high school yearbook and to make up stories about the students who went there. He flipped through my Thacher *El Archivero*. Oh, the fashions! Who had a crush on whom? Oh, the sports! My God, the team mascot was the Toad? Wait—you bought someone's soul once? Did you keep it? What did you listen to then?

Music was crucial. What we listened to had to mean something, perhaps because we were English majors. Liking something without subtext struck him as witless. Vincent had been the lead actor in a video, "Jet Fighter," for The Three O'Clock. He made mock-provocative statements about my record collection. Did I have any R.E.M., he asked?

Sure—their second album, I said carefully. I had the same fear as when I was a child heading to school, afraid of having purchased the wrong lunchbox.

No, Vincent explained, it was just that Lindsay loved them. When she got their first album, she played it incessantly. Then their second album, incessantly. When the terrible third album came out, the house expected a break, but no.

"R.E.M.: Repeat Every Minute," he said. Lindsay was stubborn, and she kept discovering insupportable things to do with her hair that got dye or bleach or perm solution everywhere. She dressed up in weird costumes then changed them almost hourly. She never dressed the same way twice. She wore 1950s lingerie and gave the undergarments names like The Diplomat.

And, by the way, news: Lindsay was coming back from England. She'd been deported. She'd lost her passport, of course, because Lindsay lost everything. Lindsay was the type of girl who got deported.

For Vincent's birthday I found a late 1970s high school yearbook for Alameda High School. He was genuinely touched to the point of being silent, turning the pages in awe at having been understood. The next party at Rose Street had a theme. The yearbook was in the foyer, and there were name tags already filled out with the identities of that school's graduating senior class. There was a banner that said GO HORNETS! We were having a high school reunion of the people we had never been. As a critical theorist, it was a fever dream of a party for Vincent, and I was happy I'd helped spark it.

Everyone at the party had a blue and white name tag from the yearbook. There was one exception. Lindsay was there and she wore a name tag that read "Wet Doghouse."

I'd seen her a couple of times already. Once she was riding her bicycle from a chocolatier that had just fired her for piercing her nose. I didn't linger or ask many questions, because Noelle was with me then, performing the couple's semaphore of pulsing her grip on my hand, *leave leave leave.*

I asked Lindsay why "Wet Doghouse." She'd done something wrong, she said. Was it the pierced nose? Was that why she was in the doghouse? She looked at me kindly. She found it cute I thought that could be her worst transgression. She wasn't what I'd call pretty, but she had blue eyes that were hard to look directly at, and a face that was unnaturally calm. She seemed to move more slowly than anyone else at the party, too languid to follow the same beat as the rest of us.

We made party conversation of the sort in which the words weren't important. My mouth moved, and I kept thinking, "I don't think she's actually dangerous."

She said something that made me think we'd read the same newspaper article, only we hadn't, so I had to explain that China's TV stations were for the first time showing American cartoons. But there was a proclamation against putting animals on the same level as humans, and animals weren't supposed to talk. The Chinese government was getting around it by claiming all the talking dogs and horses and lions were actually people.

Lindsay nodded. "Huh. Did they say what the characters would be called over there?"

I said, "Manwinkle."

I could see this information parachuting into her mind. For someone so deadpan she had a remarkably readable face when she was surprised. She collapsed forward, folding at the waist, laughing. She straightened after a second, looked at me with happiness, and then burst out laughing again. I hadn't thought it was *that* funny. And it wasn't, but she had her reasons.

I said "Huckleberry Man," which got the same reaction. She looked at me impatiently like she was waiting for the roulette wheel to slow down enough to see what she'd won this time. And I riffed a little, with diminishing returns. Daffy Man. Mickey Man. Not so funny anymore. I was losing her. It took me until then to register that she actually was sort of pretty.

She stayed near me, and then when I felt secure in that, she ignored me for an hour, and I felt insecure, and I asked myself why I cared whether a girl I'd met at a party thought I was funny. I could see the blue of her veins through the skin on her neck, and her snaggletooth was interesting, and she and I were on a certain conveyor belt but only one of us knew it.

Vincent pulled me aside that night, and gravely said, "We've decided you're costarring on a TV show now." He told me the plot: *Crowned Heads,* about broke California boys abroad in England, trying to extend their visas by marrying into royalty. I was the one writing everything down. You'd see me at a typewriter, wearing a Beefeater's uniform due to some adventure, pushing my glasses back up on my nose and nodding to myself at how good my work was.

"Are you on the show?" I asked.

He said, solemnly, "When you finish your novel, my review, which will massacre it, establishes my career."

Around this time, the lease on my apartment with Noelle was up. I had asked the landlady if she would renew, and she shook her head emphatically, "No," and walked to her unit before I could ask if she heard me and Noelle when we fought.

Soon after, there was a room opening at Rose Street. Hannah was leaving for New York. I could move in.

SECOND GLANCE

From the sidewalk, the cracked front stairs of 1811 Rose Street led to a dilapidated front porch sheltered under an overhang. There was a dark living room to the left and a parlor to the right, with ceilings that were at once closed in and looming. The kitchen was bright and spacious, and there was a 1910 O'Keefe and Merritt stove that Lindsay always had a kettle or a pot or a frying pan on. Her day job was book-keeper at a French-American school, but her passion was cooking. If she could, she spent a couple hours a day shopping for dinner.

Her room was right off the kitchen, by the back porch, where the freezer was. It was one of the smaller rooms in the house. *Fables of the Reconstruction* by R.E.M. was on the turntable at all times, even though no one really liked it.

The first few songs on that album sounded like four guys trapped in a sewer drain in a foreign country during a storm. I thought the album could have been called *We Don't Want to Listen to This Either,* but Lindsay played it anyway. When Hannah left, Lindsay took a room upstairs, and I took Lindsay's room. For the first week, I kept finding hairpins and rubber bands she'd left behind.

I was a housemate in name only for the first few months, as Noelle didn't want to let me out of her sight. I stayed with her most nights in her new apartment. She was offended by the idea of Rose Street to the extent that neither one of us wanted to admit I lived there. She didn't like the narcissistic bullshit. Their stupid fucking TV shows! Where was *her* TV show?

I tried to hide how much I liked it. As Hannah said, Rose Street was the place where you could have any conversation you wanted just by going into the living room. There was always new music playing on someone's stereo, and someone was always tangling with relationship issues weird enough they deserved attention. One night, there was a tsunami warning on the coast and I sat at the dining room table while one housemate, a physics student, went through his address book, looking for a date to watch the wave with from high ground. (We circulated the insult, "He couldn't even get a date for a tsunami," for a few weeks.)

I was broke. I was transcribing lecture notes every day, but I never managed to actually make the rates the company had promised. I worked as long as I could, standing in my room as I typed, as it was too small to have both a chair and a bed in it.

The boarding school novel was starting to seem antique to me. I was reading books I'd bought at Hunter's—Cheever, DeLillo, Zora Neale Hurston, Ross Thomas, Duras, Borges—and I noticed how they each came from a deep personal confidence that I tried to emulate. My current phase was a lot of beginnings and isolated metaphors aspiring to an authority I hadn't yet earned. Write something that matters. Escape my cultural conditioning. For instance learn the difference between Laos and Cambodia (Vincent had harrumphed over that mistake in one of my less clever stories).

I tried to get into Ishmael Reed's writing class, but was rejected. The same with Alice Adams's class. Noelle got into both. She wrote a story about a nameless man whom she described as looking exactly like me, down to the S-shaped nose, who ties up a girl who looks exactly like her with a leather belt and screws her as a way to end an argument. A copy of the story found its way out of class and into general circulation. I think she distributed it herself. People gave me looks that I didn't mind, but this was not panther cool.

As close to verbatim as I could, I wrote out stories people told me, no matter how ordinary they were, as I was learning what listening meant. I wrote a story about an old co-worker who was determined not to swear, and I sent it to *Grand Street*. It came back rejected, but with a nice note from a reader named Susan Minot, whom I looked up in the library. I found a couple of short stories she'd written and decided she was a writer who'd learned to listen to people years before I had.

I also made my first imaginary enemy. *Esquire* had printed an article by a writer my age, David Leavitt, declaring him the first voice of a new, as-yet-unnamed generation, which meant I had no choice but to hate him.

It turned out there were writers my age who'd published already. Part of my routine was to stand in the new release section of Cody's and look at the jacket photographs of authors and make dark judgments about their abilities without actually buying the book. That people were establishing careers seemed unfair to me. At Rose Street I was surrounded by creative, smart, worthwhile people, and none of *them* were publishing anything yet. In reaction to this (it made sense to me at the time), I wrote a letter to the *San Francisco Chronicle* book review announcing, without explaining who we were, that the residents of 1811 Rose Street were no longer giving interviews. That was a prank, but no one else in the house understood it, so I didn't bring it up again.

I was in a film class that followed the auteur theory closely, and so we had a couple of weeks of noir: *Double Indemnity, Ossessione* (with a few chaste minutes of the 1946 American version), *Gilda,* all of which had something in common with the earlier films Professor Nestrick had shown, *Der Blaue Engel, Morocco, The Scarlet Empress, La Bête Humaine*—every female lead was a femme fatale.

This made me anxious. The idea of being manipulated was a particular hell for me. After one class, I asked Nestrick what the films he'd chosen were saying about women. He said, coyly, "Well, what does being a woman say about being a woman?"

A classmate, less than happy with Nestrick, told me there was a feminist critique about femme fatales: *they didn't fucking exist.* The term was a projection of men's anxieties about women having any sort of sexual parity. I liked this theory. It was a relief. It turned out to be a little simple.

. . .

For someone not conventionally pretty, Lindsay was arrogant. She said, "If we were walking down the street, and you walked past me, you wouldn't look twice. But if I were doing something, even sitting and reading a book, you'd look again."

True. She knew she was a type. Hers was the fatal beauty of the second glance. If a man looked at a woman like her once, he wouldn't see her. But a second time? He would see the A-line skirt, how the blouse which looked so academic was in fact slightly translucent, slightly tight. He would think: "Does she know that or have I discovered an island country known only to me?" And then answer it himself: "Only I am poet enough to have discovered this girl's unexpected, swanlike neck."

But men are dopes. Lindsay didn't just know that country's geography, but every baccarat game in the casinos of the land of the Second Glance was gimmicked in her favor. If you happen to be a person who sees relationships as expressions of power, you could say knowing Lindsay made me want not to be a sucker. I figured the best thing was never to *actually* hit on her.

Once I asked if she needed anything from the market, and she asked if she could join me. We walked together. Then it was more than one trip, and then it became a habit.

Her fiancé was coming back in a couple of months. She'd always had a boyfriend, and they always overlapped. I used to know the list by heart, with the dates of the relationships, like tombstones. Lindsay had always known how to attract men. It might have been the only thing she knew for certain at twenty-three, that with a precise flick of her wrist, she could tailor specific interest from a specific man. For instance, here was a would-be writer looking hard at the subtext of everything. Here was Lindsay revealing the underpinnings of how attraction was made. Here we were being insiders together.

I asked friendly questions, the type you'd ask to know the secrets beneath someone's emotional landscape. She said she floated over things, and I asked her if she knew the word *tharn*. When I explained it, she was happy to know both the word and that she'd met someone who also went *tharn* sometimes. She was the one who ended relationships. Some boys had begged her to stay, which was disappointing. She didn't really feel things like remorse, and to desire someone so much was a kind of supplication that made no sense to her.

She asked if Noelle was the end of the line for me. Did I see her being enough for the rest of my life?

This was in the spring, when Berkeley had come awake from a gloomy winter. When I walked across campus, it was through those Hey Nonny Nonny days when girls passing me on the paths glanced backward over their shoulders, and when I sat in class I was hypnotized by the view one row below me of a girl's skin interrupted by the tension of a bra strap. But I was with Noelle and I felt like a dog tied to a parked car.

Lindsay had read my stories, somehow (I'd never given her one), and she said she saw beauty in the world when she thought about them. I liked the compliment.

"You look like somebody," she said.

"Timothy Hutton."

"Huh. No."

"You look like—" I started.

"I don't look like anyone. I look like those portraits of French ladies in the seventeenth century." She was fluent in French. She read *La Princesse de Clèves* when she was bored. She felt like she was born in the wrong time.

Her favorite book growing up was *A Little Princess* by Frances Hodgson Burnett. It was about a girl whose parents die and she has to suck it up. The other girls in the orphanage act bratty and emotional and the heroine of the book just holds on to her doll and does not cry. Lindsay, too, never cried. It seemed needy to her.

These things were all true and said carefully. But it got less careful, because I did something she hadn't thought through—I kept asking questions.

She'd started cooking for her family when she was six or seven. That's also when she started ironing her father's shirts. He was an impenetrable one. He drank hard, he cheated on every relationship, and even his smile was fused with a darkness that led somewhere people didn't want to look.

"Where's it lead?"

No one had asked that. When she spoke, it came from a different place than when she was trying to be charming for me.

"Death, maybe?" she finally said.

Death was something her father was attracted to. So was she. Death always won. Certain men had death in their eyes. I didn't, though, she said. I had an intense stare, and she didn't know where it came from, but it wasn't death.

She seemed uncomfortable as she said this. Then we were back on track. "Is that story Noelle wrote true?"

"I've never used a belt. Have you ever been tied up?"

"I don't think they did it right. Guys always overestimate their Cary Grant index." Men thought they were suave. The one-handed bra flick, which never worked with a three-hook bra like she had to wear. Had I ever kissed a guy, she asked? Had I ever been with two girls? She'd have to try kissing a girl sometime. "I like giving blowjobs while a guy is driving. It makes him think he owns you."

"Happy Paul."

"He doesn't like that." There was a list of things Paul didn't like. When he came back from England she would have to swap out her good lingerie for the boring things he wanted her to wear. What a waste. Someone should see it. Hah. I know.

We locked eyes and I could swear she wanted to say, *You're the person who really sees me.*

Lindsay wasn't exactly telling the truth about Paul. It was a relationship with dents in it, not a prison. She knew how to phrase things. She sounded like she was saying she was in a terrible place and didn't want to be rescued. Only a man who saw her twice would wonder whether he should rescue her anyway.

Here was where that feminist theory fell down, in that Lindsay was a real femme fatale. But the mistake was to think of that as nefarious. She wasn't so much manipulative as she was twisting under the hard mercy of questions that begin when you're twenty-two, twenty-three: *Who am I? What made me? Why am I here? Where does this ache come from?*

Getting answers always involved pain. Some people, like my dad, collected things to keep that away. That's what Lindsay did. She collected men, and why not? Men were interesting, and they were interested in her. If you asked her who she was, she would say she was a woman who ate men like air. For now she had decided to become a person I would be attracted to.

This was flattering. Also it was a little sad. But you had to notice that, and I didn't. I was too busy trying to become a person she would be attracted to.

FACE VALUE

Around then, my mother called. I hadn't heard from her in a while. She said she had moved from her apartment in San Diego, and in the process had met the most remarkable man. He looked like Richard Gere. He was twenty-nine, she said. He'd grown up in terrible circumstances on the streets of San Diego—quite literally on the streets, some nights. She explained how they met. She'd been having a yard sale and was about to throw away some beads and trinkets when he asked if he could have them. He disappeared and an hour later came back with forty dollars, which *he gave her*. His name was Daniel, and he told her that every day with him was Christmas.

She still had things in storage from when we'd lived in San Francisco in the 1970s. Daniel was coming up with a friend and a truck, and could I help them? I could separate out my own childhood things. My coin collection, for instance.

I hadn't thought about my coins in years. I was no longer attached to them. If I sold them I might be able to pay rent.

In passing, my mother looped back to the story of how Daniel had started living on the streets. His mother had thrown him out of the house when he was nine years old because he was a compulsive thief. She wasn't sure he'd ever curbed that impulse, but he had a good heart, so I should trust him, she said. I knew immediately to do otherwise.

In person, Daniel didn't look like any twenty-nine-year-old I'd seen. Among other things she'd lied to me about, she'd aged him. He was twenty-seven, to my twenty-three. He'd clearly spent many of those years outside, meaning both that he seemed older and that there was something indestructible about his body, which seemed thick, like the flesh had been cured by processes that should have destroyed him. He wore Ben Davis–style industrial clothing. He seemed like he anticipated sleeping outside again.

I didn't know yet that he was dangerous. He did nothing that was alarming, unless I count him looking at me. His irises seemed matte black, neither emitting nor taking in light. When we talked in the Rose Street dining room, he seemed to be looking around me, and toward the dishware, the furniture, my housemates' backpacks, and calculating how much everything might sell for versus how hard it would be to carry.

But he didn't take anything. He smiled often and talked quickly. As we drove from Berkeley to the storage unit, he told me how much my mother loved me. He repeated stories of my youth. He told me my IQ. I'd had a Siamese cat, he said, he'd seen pictures. He and my mother had been talking to each other in the way of new lovers.

He had in common with her previous boyfriends a desire to explain how the world worked, but unlike Anton or Trevor or Peter, he had never succeeded in anything. He had observed rich people for his entire life, long enough that he looked down on them. I tried to say one or two things, but it wasn't necessary. Daniel had already learned what he was going to learn, and nothing like me was going to affect him.

Much of what he recounted on our drive over the Bay Bridge was an inventory of the house I'd grown up in, how it had been filled with endless art and treasure. This was his own house tour, fueled by imagination. I thought he was leading up to rubbing his hands together with anticipation, but instead he was telling me how none of that stuff mattered, how nothing lasted, you only really owned what you could carry on your back, right?

He explained my mother's life story to me. She had been unhappy when she was married. She'd been a fancy lady trapped with a Rolls and a Mercedes and I'd been a rich boy who'd grown up with comic books and a coin collection. My mom had told him I was broke, and trying to be a writer, and who knew where I would be in ten years? Did I know where to get any speed?

He was driving when he asked, and his eyes flicked toward mine, and he didn't pause for an answer. More talking.

There were no incidents on that trip. A few hours later, I had boxes of my childhood things in the basement of Rose Street, and Daniel and his friend were in the driveway by the truck now filled with my mother's furniture. Daniel knew where he could sell it. He told me about some great deals he'd made recently, looking for me to nod as he recited them. I remember quick, repeated handshakes, then him asking again if I knew where to get any speed, then him getting on the road. I didn't think much more about him.

I had boxes of comics that I didn't look at. I threw away some 1960s artifacts from my high-design room, like a 7UP bottle with a twisted, looped neck that was now broken. Statues of the Marx Brothers wrapped in the electric paisley poly-blend sheets off my old bed. Lindsay watched me. She was charmed by seeing my childhood suddenly appear, an array of op art and Danish modern side tables hilariously out of date.

She found some *Playboy* centerfolds I'd stuck between the pages of a book about the Marx Brothers. She asked which one I'd liked the best, and then answered before I could: the cowgirl wearing only sheepskin chaps, right? Right.

She pulled out items to make fun of (my black light, my stuffed lion cubs). When I was five years old, my cousin Christina and I had made a pretend art gallery in my closet, with posters that would light up in the dark. We towed my mother in, and made her close her eyes. We shut the door to the closet, and we turned on a strobe light so we could dance in front of it and cast what we thought were very *boss* shadows.

Mom didn't make it—the moment she opened her eyes to see the first flashes of light, she panicked and threw open the door and ran out. I hadn't remembered that until just now. I tried to tell Lindsay about it in whatever way made me seem most dispassionate and careless. "Mom didn't like closets, I guess."

She had a way of saying almost nothing, just the word "huh," so it weighed a great deal.

"Do you ever wonder," I said, "if the stuff that happened to you as a kid isn't just a story, but maybe it affects you?"

A bowling bag and a heavy canvas sack contained, for some reason, my coin collection. My father had been fond of do-it-yourself displays that relied on his engineering skills. He had chosen nonarchival materials for the sleeves which housed some once exquisite silver dollars, now tarnished where their edges touched the folders. Some of the smaller gold pieces had dropped out and were stuck in the crevices of the bowling bag, where they had absorbed the grease from crumbs of food for a decade, and were now pockmarked and stained.

I had a fresh pang of conscience about the $186 I'd spent on comics. It had been ten years but I never admitted to Dad what I'd done. The damage to the coins felt like payback.

I called my dad to ask him for advice. He asked me to ship him the coins so a dealer friend of his could appraise them.

A few days later, I received a thin envelope from my father. There was a check for the coins, less than a thousand dollars, nothing compared to what they would have been worth if properly stored. He also sent a complete set of 1969 banknotes.

There was a letter. Dad explained that when he and I had been collecting, he'd assembled two sets of 1969 currency and given me one. He'd kept the other, which he'd never told me about. Here it was. I should use it to help pay my rent.

"What's up?" Lindsay was home from the French-American school for lunch. The mail had just arrived. She read over my shoulder, because that's the level of involved she had gotten.

For half my life I'd felt a dull shame for having stripped the bills of their collecting value by using them for their face value—a term meant to distinguish the obvious from its *deeper* value. Now my father sanctioned exactly that behavior. I had permission. I felt I could move my shoulders, that they'd locked into place a decade before.

So Lindsay was saying to me, "What's up?" as I was thinking *I'm not that guilty person anymore,* and it occurred to me I was going to spend that money, and I was going to sleep with Lindsay.

THE SOLE AND SINGULAR JOY

I HAD JUST KISSED LINDSAY. It was late morning in spring, and we were on the porch. There was music coming from the distance. A neighbor played an instrument none of us could identify, at odd times of day, and though we'd tried to locate the house it came from, it was a Bermuda Triangle level mystery to us. It was percussive and yet it seemed to play melodies, too, non-Western, and the breeze brought it closer or farther away, an audio mirage.

That day had the kind of transcendent spring weather that happened rarely in North Berkeley, the air heavy with honeysuckle and the sweet peas in neighbors' yards trembling with breezes, and it was hard to think in a straight line for more than a few minutes at a time.

It was a slow, friendly kiss, throughout which I thought *I am kissing Lindsay*. She didn't kiss like anyone else. There was something eternal and quiet in its intensity, like all the time in the world had melted, and we were going slow and fast.

She said, "We can do this, but only once. We can get it out of our systems before Paul comes back. Just once."

Here was a tightrope of rational thought. Let's not be idiots, let's try to think this through, let's look at all the evidence. There is a monstrous cloud of animal lust drifting in, and being horny never made anyone smarter. Neither of us would get needy—we might not have even said that aloud, as need was an unforgivable crime.

This was the first time one of us said to the other that we didn't want to look back at this and wish we'd behaved better. Each of us hated that idea: "Oh, we were so young, so naive, how could we have been that stupid."

I've noticed that adulterers are visited by perverse angels who clear the way for them. Trains that are never off schedule run early or late that day, bringing them into contact and leaving mates unaware. Noelle vanished for a few days and I learned she was at an old boyfriend's house at roughly the same moment Lindsay whispered to me she was ready. Strange how the trail can suddenly glow like that.

At midnight, Lindsay opened my door without knocking. She knew she would be welcome. She and I stood on my futon, staring at each other. She wore a white cotton union suit that was cut above her knee. It had tears in it and big buttons up the front. She knew she didn't have to try to package herself.

I took off her clothes without touching her. Touch is a way of reassuring. *What if I don't reassure you,* I was thinking. As each bit of clothing came off, Lindsay seemed to move more slowly. She relaxed. When she was fully nude, she stood still, not posing, but tranquil. She settled down on a pillow, with her snaggletooth giving her a crooked little smile. Her chilly blue eyes stared at me. *Here's what you've won.*

When I touched her skin, I could feel what she felt. I wasn't just sensing her muscles beginning to clench, it was like I was eavesdropping on her whole nervous system, and I could feel what she felt as if she were an extension of me. How odd, and how addictive.

I could feel something else happening. Her body was starting to tell me stories. All the boys wanted to make her come. No one would even think of making it difficult for her, she was spoiled, and always had been. I wondered if I was just making that up. Men think we have inside information; we think we don't just know what we're doing, but that we are empathic and attentive and no doubt better than the last guy. I decided that whatever else I did for the next few hours, it wouldn't involve letting her come.

Eventually she grabbed my hair and pulled my face up to hers. She whispered, "Do you know what you're doing to me?"

I said, "Yes," because it was true, I did know. It was also a lie, because I hadn't *quite* known. "You want," I said. I'd meant to finish the sentence, but just saying "You want" was enough for her.

She studied me. She nodded. "I want."

When I turned off the verbal part of my brain that tries to direct traffic, I could sense something heavy and simple going on. It doesn't sound like a revolution to say "Lindsay wanted," but I wasn't sure a man had ever heard what she wanted.

Later, it was getting light outside. There were birds. An attractive pile of clothes on my floor. We were sweaty and confused. Neither of us could move. It felt like there was steam rising off of us. We stared at each other as if we'd bobbed to the surface, *Oh, we're still alive.* This had been the best sex of my life. I knew saying that was a trap. I had never felt so intensely close to someone, also a trap.

"That was five and a half hours," she said, and then, maybe realizing how that sounded, she added, in a mock heroic voice, "You certainly planted your flag, mister."

Every second she stayed was stolen time. I was thinking about how the *Pillow Book,* an eleventh-century Japanese treatise on court manners, said it was important for your lover to linger even if she didn't want to. Lindsay wasn't moving and yet I envisioned her halfway up to her room. Lindsay, courtly and appropriate.

I said, "A little piece of you already left."

"I'm a girl who leaves first," she said.

What do you do after something like that? Shake hands? We said goodbye, she went on her way, back upstairs, one perfect heist later, and we were done, never to touch, forever, until the next day, when it started up all over again.

When Paul came back, she, laconic and sleepy-eyed, pissed him off so much he threw her engagement ring down Rose Street. Then she and I continued, and it felt like a miracle to me every day for the next four years, and then it didn't.

FABLES OF THE IMPERVIOUS LOVER

I WAS SITTING ON NOELLE'S BED while she was crying. I'd broken up with her, but she was the type of person who thought if she protested enough we wouldn't be broken up anymore. "I refuse to accept this," she said.

I was looking at the covers of *Mademoiselle* and *Vogue* she had on her floor, and I was reading to myself the makeup tips, the promises of new collections for summer.

It occurred to me she was never going to let me go, so I stood. She burst into fresh tears. I took a step toward the door. It was peculiar to just walk out on her, but it was what I seemed to be doing. When I made it to her living room, she threw herself in front of the door and blocked it with her body. This was not very French. Or it was very *very* French. It was so dramatic I had trouble believing it was real. It felt like how she only argued at the top of her lungs if we had company around.

"Move," I said, quietly.

"I can't."

I looked at her. I was barely there.

"How can you be so cold?"

I moved her out of the way, opened the door, and shut it behind me. Then I started to run, because it was possible she would try to follow.

I should say this was the fourth or fifth time I'd told her it was over, and there would be more times where I hung up or shut a door on her. But this time was unusual. When I got to the end of her block, I saw a group of eight people holding hands as they walked in pairs. I'd seen them before. They had a handler. They had lopsided heads, misshapen trunks, and they all smiled in the same complete and delighted way. I thought they looked like they didn't know what was going on except that they were being taken care of. They made me uncomfortable because of the way they trusted. It was like a low pressure system of vulnerability drifting across Berkeley.

It seems unrealistic to think I would see someone further on the same day I broke up with Noelle, but this was Berkeley, part cabaret, part sideshow. There was an elderly, spidery, and thin homeless woman who had all her belongings on a bicycle. She pushed it to collect glass and cans from recycling bins. I'd seen her often enough to feel like I was looking at a familiar ghost when I spotted her from a great distance. Today, she was at the edge of campus, where Bancroft hit Telegraph. Her bike had been flattened by a car.

The woman shuffled in circles around her bicycle, holding the loose fender in her hand over her head, and she was mourning at the top of her lungs. I kept walking.

I'd seen someone's children. I'd seen someone's mother. *One day,* I thought, *I'll know how I feel about that.*

Rose Street started to fall apart. One of Lindsay's friends started dating Paul. Hannah kept calling from New York to talk to Vincent about when he was coming. But he was frequently out rock climbing with a pretty girl, and he didn't always call Hannah back. Some of the old crowd moved out; the folks who replaced them were friends but something was different and a little diminished now. Maybe I just wasn't paying close attention to anyone except Lindsay.

She didn't really care about Rose Street, it turned out. Nothing mattered enough to affect her. She said, "People tell me I'm cold because I'm afraid of being abandoned, but that's not right. I just don't feel the things other people do."

I now felt quiet contempt for the type of person who was affected by things. I kept coming into my room and finding records on the turntable, with directions about what I should play. "Temptation" by New Order. "Thick as Thieves" by The Jam. "I'm a Man You Don't Meet Everyday" by the Pogues. "Happy Song" by the Nips. "Backwards and Forwards" by Aztec Camera. "Your Silent Face" by New Order, again. Every song was supposed to be a clue to explain who she was, without her having to say another word herself.

She left me a card with her translation of a Baudelaire phrase: "The sole and singular joy of falling in love is the certainty of doing evil."

She wanted to know my astrological chart. I'd wanted a girlfriend with whom I had a psychic connection, as that seemed, for some reason, like an argument for compatibility. I did Tarot readings for her, which I'd learned to do by candlelight at Thacher, and I had her do mine, and we marveled at how the results were so unambiguously *powerful*.

I had lunch with Owen. But I hadn't talked to him in a while, and it was as if I'd taken a trip to a foreign country and was trying to explain life in a commune whose rules had evolved from observations of shadows and the green-capped fairies possibly seen among them.

"We did our Tarot last night," I said, because Owen and I had messed around with Tarot cards. He knew what they meant.

"And?"

"Do you know what the final outcome card was?" I asked. It had been the Lovers, a card I had never seen in an outcome before.

"Was it . . . the Ball Player?" Owen asked. "The Cad? Tell me it was the Cad. The Rock Star?" He cracked himself up.

Clearly, Owen didn't understand how powerful this was.

"Jesus," Lindsay said. "Is this really your mother?" She'd been reading a letter I'd dropped on my bed. "The voice is so *Pollyanna*."

It was an IBM Selectric font with handwritten amendments on a slick sheen of onionskin. Lindsay saw the dead-eyed way I read it, recognizing when a normal person would have a reaction.

I asked, "Doesn't she sound like a mom?"

"No."

I liked hearing straight talk. We talked to each other honestly. It felt like we were shining daylight on our more hidden impulses: picking up with anyone so quickly after her engagement wasn't smart; her heart wasn't her own again yet; she wanted to be ambushed, tied up, and used for sex; getting involved would be confusing. My friend Bill, a confessor of mine, had told me to beware—leaving a relationship was like swinging out on a trapeze, and was made easier by having someone to catch you.

We knew. We wouldn't mistake the person who caught us for our soul mate. We could handle this. I was seeing past a horizon line that had previously limited me. So was she. She said she'd once been a woman engaged, but now she was outside of that, looking at herself, and not making the mistakes she had before. Here's what you thought your life was, she said, now let the camera pull back and see a fuller frame. There was a way of refocusing so that the more obscure truths were visible.

I told her about my dad and myself on the porch with our telescope. Look at the dimmest stars by looking away. Later, I walked into my room and found an R.E.M. album on my bed with a note, one word, in her handwriting. *Kohoutek*.

Of course R.E.M. had a song called "Kohoutek." Michael Stipe sang about the comet, and *maybe* a girl who vanished like the comet. It was hard to tell what else. I listened as hard as I could to know what subtext Lindsay understood that I didn't yet.

R.E.M. songs reminded me of abstract paintings. The mind wanted to find a narrative, but maybe Michael Stipe was singing phrases that were meaningless. It was kind of maddening. Then there was the way the music felt, which was also hard to nail down. What did "Pretty Persuasion" feel like? Sort of joyous? With moments of caution?

This meant that, feeling joyous and cautious, I sang along to words I couldn't quite hear, which describes most R.E.M. fans in 1986. "Oil . . . has been dried?" I sang, which might or might not have been a lyric, and then, I sang, with authority, "Goddamn your confusion," because that one was at least clear. I felt that persistent inarticulate yearning that came through all the music Lindsay loved. What got reflected with every memory she told me about, every song she wanted me to hear, was her sense of loneliness. *I have felt this way,* I thought, *even if I don't exactly know what this way is.*

· · ·

Lindsay was dressing in her room. I admired her in the mirror and she let herself be admired, making fake model poses.

"How'd you get the bruise?"

She looked at the back of her leg. "I don't know."

We went out for Thai food. We were both relaxed in that postcoital way where you're soft as butter and neither traffic nor crying babies can change how you feel.

Plearn was not far from campus, and it was too warm inside, the tables sticky, and the food excellent. Lindsay was always cold, so she held her teacup with both hands. She was looking at me with tranquility. Being with her was beginning to feel like the laws of physics were different. There was a blur separating us from the rest of the world.

"I have a passion for you," I said, which was a clever way of not saying anything about love.

The smell of the opal basil, the *nam pla,* the curries, and the two of us not saying we were in love. Instead we told each other stories of how we had mauled each other. *I did this to you you did this to me I've never done that before I liked the handcuffs it felt great.*

She was looking off, over her tea. She asked if I had someone in my past, an old girlfriend, who—every time we saw each other—I just had to fuck?

The right answer, to keep up, would have been "Yes."

She continued: was there someone who, even if I was dating someone else, even if I was in love with someone else, the attraction was just too hard to resist? Because she did. His name was Charles Blank. They'd dated in high school, and back then they'd spent the summer alone together in a house on the beach. "We banged away like armed policemen. We banged like a screen door in a cyclone."

By then I'd somewhat invented an old girlfriend who this might be true about. I kept it vague, which was fine, because Lindsay didn't have questions for me.

"It's weird about Charles Blank," she said. "Whenever I see him, there's no question. It's this animal attraction that's unstoppable. No question."

I felt a tiny weakness, in a way I hadn't before. I didn't like the feeling. "What's so powerful about him?"

"He's six foot five and has a beautiful body. He has a massive cock.

When I sit on it, it fills me up to here," she said calmly, with her palm against her navel. "But that's not what actually matters."

"What does matter?"

"Death. He has no fear of anything, no regard for anything. I do things with him that I'd never do with anyone else."

"Such as?"

She didn't say. She just looked at me in her impassive way, as if me asking more would be inelegant and needy.

I was thinking, *There's no question*. I was beginning to feel queasy. "Where is he now?"

"San Diego."

Something was happening to my body. I couldn't tell if it was getting hot or cold. I was trying to relax my shoulders, and to remember to breathe. Lindsay had been in San Diego the week before. She'd called me from there.

"You're vibrating," she said.

I was. It was like a fist had picked me up, shaken me, and thrown me down again to see what would land faceup. "Did you see him?"

"I only saw him for two hours," she said.

This was a terrible answer. She was holding her tea, a little concerned, like she was taking a child's temperature. The bruise on her leg.

"Am I still vibrating?"

"Yes."

I apologized.

"It's okay. I like physical reactions like that."

I said, "I'm making it okay. This is what the process of making it okay looks like."

She understood. She explained she hadn't fucked him—she was fertile that day—so they'd done other things. I didn't want to know more, but didn't want to let her see me thinking about that.

"Has there been anyone else?"

"Since when?"

"Since we first kissed."

"No. Well . . ." She wasn't sure. She'd kissed Dallas, but couldn't remember if that was before or after me. And another guy, Nick, from Tower Records. She was gazing at a far wall, and nodding. Okay, yeah, wait, there was this other guy at a party. And—was this a problem? She hoped it wasn't a problem.

"No," I said. We were silent while I was thinking about my breathing. "I need to—"

"Oh, wait," she said. "Five guys." She said some more things I couldn't quite take in, and I responded with a statement about how cold my heart was, so this was no problem, and she responded, "Thank God. I'm passionate but not loyal."

I nodded. I thought, *This is her right. She owes me nothing. I'm free. She has freed me.*

"Wait. Six," she said.

I have always remembered taking this in without understanding it. This isn't quite right. I understood. "Oh, right, femme fatale."

Later, back at the house, I said to her, "I want to tell you a story about Charles Blank. There's a castle. And there's a princess in it. And outside the castle walls are all these confident, handsome firstborn sons, and not one of them realizes he's about to join the pile of dead knights."

She laughed.

I stopped her. "I'm not one of them."

She narrowed her eyes, fairly sure she was following me, but not completely sure.

"I won't rescue you," I said.

It was kind of a leap. She hadn't said she wanted to be rescued. Especially from something that sounded as attractive as getting fucked by the personification of death. But I thought she'd told me about him for a reason. Finally she nodded. She was surprised, she said. Every boyfriend had wanted to win. She wasn't quite sure what to do with me now.

BANK THE QUARRY RIVER SWIM

WE ARE COMING TOWARD A LESSON. It doesn't seem like much: What's under your skin is yours alone. People are separate. Your skin is a boundary, as is the rest of you.

The kinder lesson is that sometimes, the world gives you a connection, and it's like a miracle. Love does go some distance running on miracles. But not that far.

I got a job that summer writing film reviews for Dow Jones. My contact was a colleague from Hunter's Books who had to explain the gig to me. It wasn't going to be in print, but in a technical place called "online," which would be accessible to people with computers who paid for a service whereby they could access a central database. My job consisted of sitting in the library, going through the 1930 and 1948 bound copies of *Variety* and *Billboard,* and writing out cast lists and plot summaries of every film known to have been produced. It paid well.

Lindsay auditioned for and won a job at the Rockridge Cafe as their baker. She got up at five a.m. to heave sacks of flour and make pies. She still worked at the French-American school as a bookkeeper. She got me a part-time job there, a couple hours a day, as a day care worker.

My French accent was terrible enough that the kids were deliberately bad so they could hear me speak. Some of them laughed so hard they pretended to fall over, which made me wonder if ridicule was genetic or learned.

Rachel, whom I'd gone to high school with, moved into the Rose Street sunroom. She and her boyfriend had recently done Ecstasy, a drug that had simultaneously appeared on the market and been made illegal. I'd done mushrooms a few times. But after reading what I'd written so impatiently during trips, I was annoyed to realize that I'd been fervently, carefully, obsessively describing only the effects of the trip itself. A psychedelic trip was a narcissistic friend.

Rachel said Ecstasy wasn't hallucinatory, not really. The insights tended to linger. Plus the sex was indescribable.

That was all I needed to hear.

Lindsay and I got a piece of paper folded into an origami triangle by some obsessive chemist. In it was a beige powder we dissolved in apple juice. Drugs are about ritual, and Ecstasy's ritual included fasting for the day (to increase its effects), finding a comfortable place to be, settling in with plenty of water, and then waiting. If we were already close, what would happen now?

The new R.E.M. album, *Lifes Rich Pageant*, had just come out. I'd already listened to the first side, once. Mostly, the songs sounded like anthems. I noticed Stipe singing "gather up" kinds of lyrics, wanting to get people organized, mostly singing "we" instead of "I." Mobilize the masses, what a rock star might do if he wanted to direct his audience's energy toward some purpose beyond trying to figure out what his lyrics were.

The first chord of "Cuyahoga" made me stare at the record revolving on the turntable with a sense of déjà vu. I didn't move for the rest of the song. It reminded me of seeing an old photograph of a place, and staring at it to figure out whether I was in the landscape or not. I couldn't tell if I liked it. I put the album away, and figured I'd listen more carefully later.

After drinking the juice, Lindsay and I looked at each other the way everyone does while waiting for drugs to start, wondering if a given flicker of perception was from approaching headlights, far in the distance.

A few minutes later, the phone rang, and I—starting to feel something changing—answered it. It was the guy who'd sold us the Ecstasy.

I said, "How odd to hear from you."

Why? he asked.

Well, I said, I'd just taken it.

A long pause. Okay, then.

What?

Nothing. Just, he'd been calling to tell us it was a strange batch, people had had weird trips on it.

Weird bad?

No, weird weird. Really, everything was fine, enjoy it, he was being overly cautious. Just know that whatever happened, it wasn't quite Ecstasy, chemically speaking, but something else.

Wait, what?

Yeah, there had been some kind of issue in the lab, but enjoy. Really, man, enjoy.

I was off the phone, staring at the receiver, and yet feeling strangely untroubled. Not just untroubled, but actually *good*. It was like I'd gotten the best news possible. I wasn't worried, which puzzled me, as I am built to worry. It was becoming very hard to focus on anything dire.

I saw Lindsay and I started touching the fabric of her undershirt. I felt as if I were now strapped to the front of a locomotive, but *pleasantly*. Fingers on skin felt so intense it was like they left vapor trails behind them. I could *hear* how my fingers slid across Lindsay's shoulders.

Our conversation made intuitive sense and then every once in a while, a fresh push of energetic pleasure would race through her or me, and a jaw would clench, pupils dilate, and a feeling would overtake her or me, *I want to share a revelation*.

In a moment of calm, I could see her eyes were flashing. She wanted to talk. "I know secrets," she said.

"Like what?"

"I'm the softest girl you've ever touched."

"How do you know that?"

She smiled. "Heidi is the second-softest."

"I don't know how you know that either."

"I know things. It drives boys crazy."

"You like that."

"Boys are easy. I was a man once in a previous life. I died in a duel. When I got shot, it didn't kill me immediately, because I got shot in the stomach. I lay there, bleeding out, and as I died I was composing a poem no one ever got to hear. I don't remember it except for one line, where I was comparing how my mistress teased my cock with the slow, cold hands of death finally coming for me."

"So is that real or is it a metaphor?" I asked, because reincarnation wasn't real.

She looked at me patiently. "Regardless," she said, "I know what men's orgasms feel like. For some of you guys, it's like death."

"Like Charles Blank?"

"It's like lightning striking the ground for him," she said. "It's meaningless. It dissipates. He knows the same things about death that I do."

I am not threatened by him, I thought.

"You don't have to be threatened," she said. "You won me. Trust your intuition. I'm not going anywhere. But you enjoyed the feeling."

"What feeling?"

"When I told you about Charles Blank. The writer in you wanted to feel the worst it could get."

She was right. I asked how they'd met and she said that when they were teenagers they'd both worked at the same fast-food place.

"What place?"

She said, carefully, "Doodle Burger."

She told me that she no longer wanted to kiss anyone else. I said it was okay if she did. She said of course it would be okay. She just didn't want to. She liked me enough. She hadn't said that to a boy before. She had never felt this way.

"Because we're on Ecstasy."

"I felt it already. I'm *telling* you because we're on Ecstasy."

On one of those intoxicated, standing-tall, I-have-indeed-won walks down the hallway to the bathroom, I looked in the mirror and noted that this was the face of a man having fun. I yelled down the hall, "Wait, no, don't put that on yet. Don't put 'Cuyahoga' on until I come back in."

I came back into the room. Unlike earlier, my brain was crystalline clear now. Lindsay was crouched in her white cotton undershirt and boxer shorts, hennaed hair falling forward over her face, the new R.E.M. album in her hands. She was looking at me with fear and pleasure.

"How did you know?"

"What?"

"How did you know I was about to put on 'Cuyahoga'?"

"I could see you."

"But you were in the other room."

Then, the clarity was gone and I was swept up in talking. She kept finishing my sentences for me. When I talked about visiting a quarry at Wesleyan, she filled in details about what it looked like, how people sat in the sands around it. When she talked about San Diego, I could see her memories unfolding as if I were riding alongside her. Gymnastics classes. Boys she'd ruined.

She said, "You're starting to see me for real."

"One day in eighth grade," I said, "I went to school and at five minutes to three, I got a phone call. I had to go to the principal's office. It was my mom calling from New York. She'd gotten on a plane with her boyfriend. I was alone a few weeks, I think."

"I wish I'd been there with you," she said. "I would have held your hand."

"I would have hated you," I said.

She looked wounded, and then she understood. "It made you independent," she said. "You stand outside things, like how I do. You know no one is coming for you." Then, she choked up. "But sometimes someone is, and it's okay. Sometimes people just come for you because they love you."

She put on "Cuyahoga." The music was a dirge, the bass line distorted and glum. The lyrics were about tourists visiting the Cuyahoga River, where native tribes used to live. It's hard to be a citizen of a place when your very presence is destructive. You might be smart enough when starting your own country up to see how your ancestors hurt people when they started theirs, but you're doomed to do it all again.

This isn't about Indians, one of us said. It's about opening yourself up to a new relationship, because you have to take a chance even if it's going to ruin you. It's a love song from the old country to the new one that destroyed it. We'd watched our parents ruin everything. What happens when it's time to start your own country up?

It was obvious that she and I were starting our own country up. A sweet drug, a lovely way to feel, I thought.

"How am I ever going to explain this?" I asked.

"Do you need to explain it?"

The next day I felt what everyone who took Ecstasy felt. My jaw was clenching, my cheekbones popping out. I was hearing wisps of conversations from the night before, and they were vivid and consuming, but also fading as my brain was on the ferry from vacation back to reality.

We are entering here the part of a summer where I no longer traveled down rational lines. There are easy ways to make fun of it. But to imply with a smirk it was only wishful thinking, the folie à deux of two hopeful kids, is to betray that memory a bit. I'll say that we wanted all of what is coming next to be true.

I went to my job at the library, but there was something that prevented me from sitting where I always sat—construction, I think—so I took my archives into another room and sat down to work, which was difficult. Some image would flash in my mind, a gym class, a man shot in the stomach, and I couldn't tell if it was something I'd heard from Lindsay or if I was seeing her memories. I heard "Cuyahoga" as if it were playing in the library. I wrote down the time, 10:30.

Twenty minutes later, I looked up. Lindsay was standing in front of me. She handed me roses, gave me a kiss, and left without saying a word. I didn't have time to ask how she found me.

That evening, she told me she'd put "Cuyahoga" on the turntable, and when she had, she'd known where I was. She looked at the clock to see if she could bring me roses before she had to go to work, and saw it was 10:30.

There was still a lot of the drug in our systems, so we took this as a gift of chemistry.

It was a few days later. My brain was back to normal.

I put on "Cuyahoga." I was trying to understand if I liked it.

The way that both Lindsay and I had reacted to it in ways clearly beyond what any rock band could have meant was a little embarrassing. I wanted to tell people about it but I also wanted to say it with caveats. *I know this is insane, but . . .*

Three minutes and a few seconds into the song, the phone rang. It was Lindsay. I started laughing. "That took a while."

"I know," she said. "I got a wrong number first."

. . .

It kept happening. If Lindsay was out of the house and I wanted her to call me, I put the album on. But we understood it wasn't something we should use as a party trick. We wouldn't lean on it or try to make it mean more than it did. Which was hard because we weren't sure what it meant, except that we felt like four arms, four legs, one brain. Which is how the summer started to lose its edges. Everything applied. Horoscopes and fortune cookies and comic strips and quotations from books seemed to tell us how we were meant to be together. I was new to the feeling of when you literally can't fuck someone enough, your body wearing out before your need to continue does. Each orgasm wasn't exhaustive—it didn't even touch the surface.

Empirically, it was important to express doubt. But doubt is of course how magic is stamped out. There is more to the world than you can explain. Could I just enjoy it and not have to understand?

When I was eight, I bodysurfed. A six-foot wave, the largest I'd ridden, broke perfectly on my board so that I was propelled forward with a force faster than the wave itself, as if two fingers had pinched down on a watermelon seed. It was my first experience of being shot toward the shore by a gravitational bully with its own color and smell and texture, an unquestioning, uncaring force that took me past my limits. It didn't destroy me. I saw that wave every day now.

I took photos of myself to show how happy I looked. I bleached my hair, then hennaed it, then wrapped my hair in a silk scarf with the ends askew, posing shirtless and tuff as an intellectual Rambo. If there was one message the photos shared, it was "I am so self-contained I want you to notice me."

I rarely got more than a few of myself on a given roll because Lindsay kept borrowing my camera to take photos of herself in the mirror. She liked how the flash made the results hard to see, like her looks had to be handicapped to be appreciated. We hoped there was more to us than we'd known before. We hoped that made us look good. We were getting caught up in a language that by definition no one else could understand.

She came downstairs wearing a full-length blue dress.

"When have I seen you wearing that?"

"You haven't."

"No, I have," I said, carelessly, because I wasn't paying attention.
"When?"

I said, "I don't know." She kept looking at me. It seemed important to her that I think about this. I could see her wearing it in a fancy courtyard, with well-trimmed hedges. "I see—fountains?"

She nodded. "And gardens, but we rarely walked there." She paused. "Because I was married," she said.

"To an older, wealthy man," I said. It came from an unknown place, perhaps adjacent to the unknown place from which I can sometimes retrieve fiction. It felt the same as when it comes the most freely, like I'm taking dictation. But this time we were doing it together, exquisite corpse-style.

She said she was poor before marriage, peasant poor, but happy. She loved to run, and she fell down a lot, and liked being among her brothers. An old man came to the house to say a rich man would marry her. Her mother gave her a box as a gift when she left home. Lindsay said the first time she saw me I was in the audience for a string quartet.

Someone eavesdropping would smile. Yes, this was like writing a story, and now it was like having ESP and calling out to a loved one to see if, in spite of the void we live in, we can be overheard. If you look at psychology or rational thought, it's the kind of thing that should die on the vine. It's not real. "You were late," I said.

"I was. The first movement was playing and I had to wait outside until they finished."

"It was Vivaldi's Concerto for Two Lutes in D Minor," I said. I'd been obsessed with that music for most of my life, but only the second movement. The first time I heard it, in high school, I was convinced I'd heard it before.

We agreed: she made me leave because she didn't think it was fair she was married and couldn't be with me. I never saw her again. She later had a girl by her husband. When I left I lived by the sea. I often sat by the ocean and thought of suicide but knew that was the wrong gesture. I tried to compose music but wasn't skilled with it.

It wasn't like a conversation. It came and left rapidly in the sense that neither of us brought up specifics again, but when we looked at each other there was now a different dimension of our relationship. It had survived time.

I had a friend from Thacher, Jean, who worked with the Berkeley Psychic Institute. When I ran into Jean at a party, I said maybe it was unrealistic to think that people actually reincarnated, and that two of them managed to find each other two hundred years later.

"Oh, no," Jean laughed. "It's real. You had a contract."

She explained that when people couldn't be together in life, they sometimes made a deal with each other to return after death. I asked if that meant Lindsay and I were destined for each other.

"If that helps you out, sure."

I didn't know what this meant. I asked if Jean ever felt like there was a large wave out there, something much larger than herself, and it wasn't really up to her—she could resist or submit and it didn't matter—the wave didn't care?

"Oh yes," she said. "When Bob Weir stops acting like a rock star, when Rhythm Devils is over and done, and Jerry is deep into a solo, there are times the whole stadium is pushed by a giant wave." She added, not for the first time, that if I played guitar, I would probably sound a lot like Jerry.

I mention this because Jean had convinced me both that Lindsay and I were part of a phenomenon that existed, and that it mostly existed for people on drugs.

One night there was a thunderstorm and I couldn't enjoy it because I'd finally gotten into Ishmael Reed's fiction writing class. I'd learned that when a thunderstorm comes, writing classes will be filled with stories set in bed, listening to thunderstorms, because every boy writing in Berkeley thinks it came only for him and his girlfriend. It's their thunderstorm.

Reed taught a deliberately unfair assignment: write a story first person from the opposite sex's point of view. It was efficient in its lesson, which was that it's hard for a twenty-year-old to capture how someone from a different gender thinks.

Because I hate losing, I cheated. I read my mother's letters and typed them up until I got a sense of her voice. I created a story based around events she'd told me about. A woman offers copying services from a location no one wants to visit, but she's convinced things are just about to turn around. A condescending old businessman gives her advice, annoyingly good advice, that she can't take in, because he's also hitting on her at the same time, and she reaffirms how everyone is against her at this critical juncture. It felt unlike anything I'd done before, not good, not bad, just a strange feeling of mimicry.

The workshop was, to use a word I don't reach for lightly, bizarre. After someone else went first (a couple's relationship was on the rocks, but renewed by a thunderstorm), Ishmael presented "Six Cents a Copy" to the group. There is usually in a beginners workshop a silence when a story hits the table. It's the intake of breath before the room tone kicks in. This time, it broke when a woman said the story was offensive.

Clearly, she said, I had a problem with women. The room relaxed. Other students were relieved, because they agreed. No woman actually thought like this. She was a caricature, her thoughts a man's parody of a woman's thoughts. My narrator was incompetent in a way that no businesswoman would ever be, and she made fibs about what she was doing, as if I believed women lied to themselves all the time.

I have an ego on me that tells me I'm right even when it shouldn't. So I was okay with them being wrong until Ishmael agreed with them. This character was phony. He said it was interesting I'd tried to write an older person, but that was it.

I think I have never in my life said, "But it really happened." Writing fiction means you're trying to get readers to believe things that haven't happened. If you can't get them to believe what *has* happened, you've failed doubly.

Ishmael was a force of nature when it came to social issues like race, and he used satire so effectively that I wanted never to be a white guy deserving his scorn. I wanted to learn the lessons he taught. That I'd failed so miserably, with such conviction in my talents, made me feel awful.

One of the women in class concluded, as comments were winding down, that the work was in fact antifeminist, which was like a final baseball bat to the back of my knees.

Reed stopped her. "Antifeminist? How so?"

She explained. Clearly, by doing such a deep read on a woman who was incapable, someone who so failed even the most commonsense tasks she set out to perform, and still claiming that she wasn't mentally ill but just, well, a woman, I was insulting the cause of feminism.

"Hold on," Reed said. He looked at my story again. This wasn't a brief thing. Over a minute of silence. "This is an antifeminist story," he said again. He looked at me. "Okay, I didn't get that at first. That's interesting."

A few people knew what was up, but I didn't. Reed distrusted feminism. It was a secondary crusade for him, of almost equal importance to race issues. Feminists were the enemy behind many shadowy academic conspiracies, he thought. He explained this briefly, and the class thought he was kidding.

When I got my story back, his initial comments were crossed out, as was the original grade. Instead, there was just one line. "Excellent indictment of feminism. A−."

This was so confusing I kept taking the story out and looking at the grade and wondering why I felt flustered by it. Apparently my mother only made sense if her life was satire.

WHEN TOMORROW COMES

ONE LAST ECSTASY TRIP. It was obvious that the visions came at the cost of borrowing against vitality. Every recovery period was a challenge. My jaw ached for days. Lindsay and I took one and a half tabs each for a finale.

It was too much. The wave was too intense. The trip lasted for six hours, and it was at times like involuntarily bobsledding down a glacier.

She had to tell me something. "In a few years, after we get married, we're going to have a kid," she said. She waited for me to catch up with that. She continued: She's going to have long, wavy, brownish blond hair. She'll be a quiet one. She'll observe everything, and she's going to be smart and funny. Kids are supposed to look more like their fathers, but this one would look more like her mother.

What she was saying sounded exactly true, as if it had already happened, and she was reminding me. We said things to each other in wonder like, You're going to be a father. You're going to be a mother. Ha! There is still a drug in our systems, this is the drug talking. The drug is whispering these things.

After a long silence, she teared up. "Her name is Suzannah."

That name had lain dormant in me, genetic code waiting to be fired, and now I could see Suzannah as if she were a friend who had left the room but was about to come back. She whistled to herself, she favored sweatshirts, she was kind to animals. She was clumsy.

"No middle name," I said. Lindsay nodded.

Everything was happening at once. We were talking into and out of conversations, hands moving, picking up throughlines an hour later, doubling back to fallen topics.

It was deep into the evening. I was standing. Lindsay was on her knees. The space heater was glowing behind her. One of those wavelike rushes broke against me.

"What?" Her pupils were like moons.

"When you were little, did somebody touch you?"

It was a ridiculous question. It should have been mood-shattering. She considered it, though, and she started to say no, but didn't get much further before her eyes lit up. Her eyes were such pale blue. They started to water. I felt the way I did when looking at a page from one of her antique French novels. I could recognize some hints about what was going on, and make sense of a little of it, but also I understood that the meaning was years away from me.

She didn't have an answer yet. She said she didn't quite understand it, but this had to do with how she felt death's cold breath on her shoulder. It was why I was so important. She was weeping: "You're so positive, it's so positive between us."

We kept looking at each other as the drug faded out, and we kept saying, aloud or otherwise, how for the first times in our lives we felt completely *known*.

I had to work day care the next afternoon at Ecole Bilingue, hungover. Two hours of playing with children was weirdly peaceful, about what my mind could handle. *Suzannah,* I kept thinking. *Suzannah Suzannah Suzannah Suzannah*.

I was in the art classroom. Tall white ceilings, rafters painted white, kids' egg tempera paintings tacked to the wall. Lindsay rushed in. There was a phone call for me. I could take it on an extension.

It was my aunt Susie. She'd called Rose Street and someone had given her the school's number. She said my mother was about to be killed.

I immediately thought: the walls of this classroom are Swiss Coffee, and the loops of the telephone cord are dotted with paint flecks from years of service, and there are white buttons on the top of the phone's body, one for each line you could access, one red button to hang up. One white button is depressed, and that is the line Susie is saying something to me on, and I don't remember exactly what she said. Daniel owed money to some bad men. He couldn't pay them back. He'd had multiple chances. So men were on their way to murder my mother.

Something something something, Susie was going to something something, the police were something, we'd know more in a few hours, she would call me back later. No, there was nothing I could do. Goodbye. The phone went back on the hook and I thought it was strange how multiple times in my life I have been faced with impossible news of my mother delivered through the industrial, flammable plastic of telephones on school grounds.

Something was in my hand. Lindsay had handed me a note.

I'll be there when tomorrow comes.

Lindsay wrote notes rarely, and when she did they weren't extensive. This was a lyric from a Eurythmics song, and I wanted to argue with her about how lyrics weren't the best way to express yourself, not bothering to put the sentiment into her own words was cheating, like buying a pre-printed condolence card, and from a literary standpoint it was like donning the skin of a lion. That was the stupid, smart, snide, terrified side of me that couldn't comprehend the rest of what she meant. She wasn't going to leave me as long as there was a tomorrow to stick around for.

There was a taboo word between us, the word "forever." What Lindsay was saying, even by quoting something else that only tingled with meaning when sung over a beat, was dangerously close to "forever."

Later, still waiting for a follow-up phone call, I told her the note was sweet. "But you didn't have to say that."

"I meant it."

"But you don't know it. You don't know how you'll feel tomorrow. You can leave me, that's all right."

"I'm not going to leave you."

I thought about this. "Okay, that's right now. Right now, you're thinking 'forever,' but it's just 'forever' for this moment. And that's okay. I know that in this moment, you want to be with me forever."

She shook her head. "No, I know how I'm going to feel tomorrow, too."

I didn't want to be unclear about this. It had been a terrible thing to hear about my mother, I said, and emotions were running high. At a time like that, people said things they might not mean.

"No," she said, patiently, "I mean it."

"Okay. So—" Because I was warming up, I said, "You might *say* things and also *feel* like you mean them because you think I might need to hear them, which was kind of you, but I don't need anything." I added that she shouldn't mistake the way a normal person might react to news of his mother's impending murder for me needing to hear "forever" because, as I'd said, I didn't need anything and I was making this okay now. "We could end this now, and we'd both be okay," I finished.

"But if we kept going together, we'd be amazing."

I couldn't think of any more ways to turn what she'd said into language that I understood. She denied all attempts to contain it. She meant it. She didn't overemphasize it, and she stopped trying to reassure me. Eventually I just nodded, taking it in with my brain but nowhere else. Because it was obvious that anyone I loved would leave me. Who even questions that?

You'd think there would be some resolution to my mother's situation, but there wasn't. One day she called, and I asked if she was okay, and she said she was. She referred to a story of how things worked out without actually telling the story. She said she was safe. She didn't say it with relief. She was still with Daniel. That word, "resolution," didn't really apply to her life.

A few weeks later, Lindsay and I went to Los Angeles. We saw *Caravaggio,* a low-budget, mannerist movie based on the artist's life that got increasingly surreal. Halfway through a familiar, very old pressure was descending on me. I used to get ear infections as a kid. This was unmistakably a gathering of sickness in my left, scarred eardrum. I had to leave the theater. The pain was starting to rise the way it always had, a balloonlike airplane cabin pressure that tricks you into feeling it can be yawned away. It can't.

It was late at night, so we drove to the nearest emergency room, at

UCLA, where Owen and I had come the evening of the Dead Kennedys concert. The pain in my head was so exquisite I couldn't block it out. It was a weekend, so the room was crowded. I was thinking, *I am a pure clear-running stream, I am a pure clear-running stream,* which didn't work. It didn't matter who I'd been, because now all I was was a vehicle for pain that flowed through me and wiped out everything that mattered before. I tried screaming but it came out in a voiceless croak, because, to accompany the ear infection, I now had laryngitis.

Every time I heard the nurses walk by, I manufactured lies like that they were getting me medicine.

A doctor was standing in my room with a chart. He looked at me. "Mr. Webber?" he asked.

I shook my head.

"Oops." He left.

I started crying. This made me convulse, and each time I inhaled, new pain shook through me.

I thought of Lindsay in the waiting room. She loved me now and she would love me tomorrow. This did nothing for the pain, but it made me stop crying. Instead, I was angry. Something had shifted so I felt *safe* to feel angry at the world now. I washed my face and I dried it, looking at the completely angry person in the mirror whom I recognized. He'd been gone a long time. It makes no difference whether you fight pain or whether you let it flow through you. My face was dead to the world.

By the time a doctor came in, I owed no one anything. He looked in my ear and my throat. He actually gasped. He said he'd never seen a worse ear infection. "Anywhere," he added. "Ever." He wanted to show my ear canal to the other doctors. As he was about to put drops in my ear, a nurse called him and he leaned in her direction, but I grabbed his arm, not gently, and physically kept him from leaving until he treated me. Two drops into each ear, pharmaceutical-grade cocaine. I got to take the bottle with me.

I was sick for months. They had me on ampicillin, amoxicillin, Zovirax, codeine, and erythromycin at different times. I tested positive for, or had antibodies to, cytomegalovirus, Epstein-Barr, herpes, and mononucleosis. But I knew what was actually going on. My body was doing all it could to protect me from actually falling in love.

POOR LITTLE RICH GIRL

L INDSAY WAS GOING TO SAN DIEGO to visit her mother. I drove her to the airport and parked and walked her to the gate. It was 1986, so you could still take your girlfriend right to the breezeway next to the airplane, hugging goodbye with the awareness that in minutes you'd feel the emotional thud when you saw the door closing shut. You could see the plane taxi away.

That immediacy and that possibility is gone now but then it was a ritual, the departure at the gate. And this trip with Lindsay was in a way an elegy for all the other things that were about to vanish, because while we kissed, I said, "I love you," and she said it back, because we'd been saying it and neither of us had regrets.

"I wish I could come with you."

"Me too."

Impulse. We were in love and so far anything had been possible. I bought a ticket at the counter. I recognized the precedent.

I got on the plane with her. She was delighted. This was crazy. But we were able to do crazy things if we wanted to. What about parking? It would be expensive, but the hourly and daily lots weren't that different in price.

We were in the plane, and then flying for the first time together, remarking on that, holding hands and kissing. Every once in a while, her eyes refocused on my face, and she squeezed my hand. She was trying to figure something out.

She had told me about her mother, Louise, who was tough, smart, vain, and inflexible. She was a social climber. She liked important people, and by important, she meant they'd gone to Harvard or had titles before their name like Doctor or Colonel. She wanted to visit Egypt because she thought she was a reincarnated princess. She didn't tend to admit when she was wrong.

Louise would hate me the moment I came off the plane. "She doesn't like a change in plans," Lindsay explained.

I joked about that. She didn't joke back.

We had different relationships with our mothers, but that wasn't something I'd thought much about. I couldn't read how seriously she was taking this. She had spent most of her life evicting her emotions from their former home on her face.

"If things don't work with your mom," I said, "I can go visit mine." Maybe we talked about how ironic it was that both our moms lived in San Diego.

When we landed, Louise had the presence of a senator in the crowd, and when she realized I was walking off the plane with Lindsay, her smile went beautifully suspended. There was no outward evidence of anything having changed for her. And then when Lindsay explained who I was, Louise greeted me warmly and with a smile so genuine I understood she loathed me mildly, backhandedly, in a way that was never going to change, no matter what I did, for the rest of my life. I'd made a real enemy.

There was conversation in the car. I was trying to establish myself as smart, caring, successful, artistic, not a flake, curious, eager to know more about her and her undoubtedly fantastic life, but also not too grasping or too unseemly, too faux ingratiating. I had rarely been so aware of being Jewish.

Louise was a litigator. She was good at asking questions when she wanted to be. Facts came out in the car. I was a writer. No, of course, by that definition, true, I *wanted* to be a writer. And it was a lovely coincidence that my mother lived in San Diego, too. My mother was cosmopolitan, I said. She was from England. She led a gypsy's life.

Ah, then did my mother know I was coming to stay here?

Well, her job, managing business services, was a busy one, so I hadn't called her before I came. Yes, I was from one of those families where you can show up without calling.

Louise said it was so tricky of my mother to get ahead of the curve and find a place on 8th and Ash, so far beyond where the gentrification ended. In fact, we passed the exit that made my heart trip whenever I saw it, but I didn't point it out. I could see my mother's building in context of the skyline, where it now seemed like a dead tooth among many on a septic jawbone.

Louise lived in a community that was not just gated, but on the other side of the gate had an archway bridge that was designed to look as much as possible like the one that takes you into Heaven. We hadn't worked out where I was staying. Louise took me and Lindsay in through the attached garage, and she introduced me to her husband, who was a good and defeated man. Here was Lindsay's room. Here was mine. Oh.

The next morning, I woke up. Lindsay was in a nightgown that was as thick as burlap. She gave me coffee. I remember her as if she'd brought a bundling board to place between us.

"I think you need to stay with your mom this weekend." It was nothing personal, though Lindsay allowed maybe it *was*, but mainly Louise had plans and I wasn't part of them. No matter how charming I was I wouldn't win.

"But—"

"It's not worth it."

She had a dazed expression, and she looked younger, her hair weirdly regressed to high school style, her slouch that of a teenager.

"Not worth it," I said. This was a phrase we used all the time, along with "I'll make it okay."

She kissed me. "I know the day I'll stand up to her. The day I marry you."

As I got dressed, I was thinking that Lindsay and I would marry, which excited me. We had it planned out. We would get married after I sold a piece of fiction somewhere. That would be a sign I could be established as a writer.

My lifelong enemy excited me, too. I wanted to put a novel I'd written on her bookshelf. "This is my son-in-law's book. It's a *New York Times* bestseller," she would have to say to every guest at every dinner, with a grimace, because as much as it would pain her to bring me up, it would hurt worse for her to skip the chance to brag.

After I dressed, I got in the back of the car. Lindsay and Louise were going shopping at the Horton Plaza mall. They were dropping me at my mother's place.

I had churning thoughts then, most of them revenge-shaped. I didn't like how small Lindsay was. Charles Blank made sense to me in a way he hadn't before. If I had a mother like Louise, I would want someone to obliterate me sometimes. We drove over the arch and onto the mainland. I had them drop me a half-block away because I didn't want Louise to see exactly where my mother lived.

I stood on the porch outside my mother's apartment. I still thought anything was possible. I had come to San Diego on those particular wings. There was no reason for me to have called ahead. Until I was this age, twenty-three, I thought I could go home. I'd thought all the way until I was twenty-three years old that I could walk up to a house in which a parent lived and surprise them.

When I knocked, there was no answer at first. I knocked again and my mother appeared.

She had an expression on her face that I didn't recognize. Later, I would realize it was the exhaustion of having been frightened for a very long time. She was holding a kitchen knife in one hand and a white paper towel around her fingers, which she had just accidentally cut. Her eyes were searching my face. She didn't recognize me.

Abruptly she hugged me in a burst of relief. She pulled away. She looked ashamed.

The front room was mostly carpet, with wide empty spaces where there used to be chairs and tables. She didn't want me there. The room was filled with sailors. My mother didn't refer to them. It was as if they were furniture. A couple of cots and air mattresses were pushed to the walls, which were bare. In the kitchen there was a huge pot of water boiling on the stove next to economy-sized bags of buns. I had walked in just as my mother had cut herself making hot dogs for sailors.

I don't know how long I was in the apartment; it was probably only a few seconds. I recall a young black man in sailor bell-bottoms, with ginger hair and blotches of pink skin eating away his natural coloring. He was standing by a window, smoking a cigarette. He watched me.

My mother guided me out the back door. I tried to explain why I was there—Lindsay, her mother—but she couldn't absorb it. Her hearing problem grew acute under stress. It was a good thing, she said, that I'd come. She took me to the garage and tried to unlock it, fumbling with keys and pressing on paper towels to keep her fingers from bleeding. She said over and over she was glad I was here, she had things to give me.

I wanted to tell her Louise was a snob. My mother hated snobs. When she had money, she hated people who condescended to those less fortunate. Now she was shuffling through the garage. She pulled out boxes, filled-up shopping bags with old letters. Photographs. My baby clothes. I talked to her, but she was also talking to herself and she could only hear one of us.

When I was still working at Hunter's, I'd sent her a book, a rare first edition of Barbara Hutton's biography, which had been withdrawn from circulation, something I'd found by accident. The book was called *Poor Little Rich Girl,* but my mother couldn't remember the title correctly. She thought it was called *Little Gloria . . . Happy at Last.*

"No, Mom, it's called *Poor Little Rich Girl,*" I said, which was ridiculous and unimportant. I didn't need the book back. I didn't care about it. "It's called *Poor Little—* Mom? Mom—it's called *Poor Little—*" which I didn't need to say. She continued to sort through the boxes, looking for the book, unable to find it, whispering, *"Happy at Last, Happy at Last, Happy at Last."*

She ferried me to the sidewalk, looking behind her, toward the house, and hugged me goodbye quickly. She was clearly still terrified of something. "You have somewhere to go? Did you say you were with your girlfriend? You're meeting her, right?"

She left me at the corner. She trotted back inside her apartment, holding her intact hand around the paper towel protecting the wound. I heard the door open, I saw her go inside, I heard the door close softly.

It was hotter than I'd thought. Horton Plaza was just a few blocks away. At a bus bench I looked at what I had with me, five full shopping bags. She had given me every photograph she had of me, every photo of her own life, all the letters and cards she'd kept from her family. I knew my mother was in such danger she had to make sure someone else had the things she treasured.

Horton Plaza was huge, something like four stories of outdoor mall, with passageways linked at odd angles. It was mirthful or witty in design, childish colors, clashing, to make people feel that spending money was fun. I stood in the middle of a department store, maybe Macy's, with mannequins dressed in Trevor Blake–like fashions, with all of my shopping bags half-bursting with bent, crumpled, knotted, hand-annotated, historic, mysterious, magical belongings that were packed by someone who would never walk through this comfortable space as if she belonged here. My mother had once shopped in stores better than this. I bet that if I looked through the bag I could find notes on Crane stationery and photos with edges marked by having been removed from silver frames later sold at garage sales.

I looked through the crowd, sorting it for someone to recognize. This was one of dozens of stores in the mall. How would I ever find Lindsay?

It didn't take three minutes before I saw Lindsay and her mother. They were both surprised, both in the same way, in this order: *What's he doing here? Is he okay? Is his mother okay? He has all these bags.* I now imagine both of them showing the same level of recoil, which is unfair.

There was some kind of conversation. I was smart enough that in the time between when my mother put me on the street corner and when I met Louise's eye, I had a pretty good story. My mom had given me a hundred bucks to get back to the airport and catch a flight.

Louise took me to the airport. The five bags were in the trunk. Lindsay held my hand. Louise asked me some sympathetic questions about my mom. She seemed genuinely sorry for me. Later, Lindsay said, "Of course she did—she'd won. You were leaving."

I paid for the flight in cash at the gate, and got onto the plane, holding all five bags, which the attendant helpfully put up in the bin compartment overhead. I see her face now as if she were the same stewardess who rode with me from the airport to my home in San Francisco when I was eleven and my mother forgot to pick me up. She wasn't.

When I was back in Berkeley, I started looking through my mother's things. I felt like someone who'd been in front of the stack of speakers at a concert for too long. Mom had given me hundreds of photographs, some of them as old as World War I. Here was Admiral Gercke in his U-boat commander's uniform, weeks before he died under the sea. Here she was, a child in a series of photographs in which an increasing number of siblings were scattered around her. A few chaste modeling shots when she was seventeen or eighteen.

Then photos of my mother at the entrance to the emergency room, then in labor, then me, GOLD BABY BOY, a fresh raisin in the crib. The drafts of the telegram my father sent out calling me a slayer of dragons and successor to 007. I found a clear plastic tub and inside it several impossibly small sweaters someone had knitted in 1964. Here was a bone teething ring with a silver rabbit to hold on to.

There are many tricks that photographs can do, most of them melancholy, such as when I saw how hopeful and in love my parents were. My mother loved me then totally and completely. She still did. That was the most devastating thing to know, that these things were the love she had to give.

I didn't have a home with my mother anymore. I felt stupid for having thought I could just show up where she lived. That kind of trip was over, forever.

It might not be obvious, but this was the end of something, too, that feeling that Lindsay and myself loving each other would be enough. The magic we shared didn't seem to cross the threshold of my mother's house. Nor hers.

3930 ROBLEY TERRACE
OAKLAND, CALIFORNIA
94611

1811 ROSE STREET had a landlady who'd automatically renewed the lease for a few years, but she was going to move back in, and so the group of us dispersed, with a whimper. Lindsay and I decided to live together. She had a specific vision of a large one bedroom on a tree-lined street in Oakland, far from campus, a first nod to adulthood. It would need to be an older building, with high ceilings and morning sun. If it had a loft bed, even better.

She found the apartment for us immediately, first phone call to the classified ads, and why shouldn't she have? It was on a secluded, heavily wooded side street near a nice shopping district. The building had an odd history—it was constructed in England in 1911, then taken to pieces and reassembled for the Pan-Pacific Exposition of 1915, where it was billed as the first prefabricated apartment building. Arts and Crafts style, heavily timbered, with narrow slats that made it seem even taller than it was. Only five units, each of them simple, with high ceilings and large windows that looked over the steep hillside, which was mostly trees and shrubs. The owners, a pair of artists, lived upstairs in the largest flat. Our place was a very large one bedroom—the living room was so large in fact that it was sectioned into two rooms by pillars, and there was a loft bed in the far half that made Lindsay say, "We'll take it."

She treated the loft like a pillow fort, setting it up for reading and lounging and drinking tea. She decorated it with vintage photographs found at the Ashby flea market, and draped mosquito netting around it. The actual bedroom we set up with a mattress for guests. I started calling it Fifi's room, where the spoiled, clumsy French maid lived, whom Lindsay had to punish every morning.

Lindsay understood olive oils and how to make pizza dough with cornmeal. She could pick out a ripe pineapple. Sometimes she still woke up in the middle of the night, fretting about something, and the next morning I would find Linzer Tortes or crème brûlée on the butcher block.

She worked accounting and at the Rockridge Cafe as their pastry chef, which meant some mornings she was up at five. I would sleep in, but get occasional flashes of her alone in a commercial kitchen, crimping pie dough. The cooks came in at six or seven, and they were polite and shy with her even as she ate a solo breakfast at the counter before coming home.

I put a work desk in Fifi's room. On one wall I had a poster of Molly Bloom's soliloquy and on another a picture of David Leavitt, whom the photographer had tricked into posing with his fist grasping a pencil on top of his head. Leavitt had published his first book of short stories, well-received, so my fictive, one-sided feud with him continued. Onto my wall he went, to watch over me while I scrambled up the rocks, knife between my teeth, eyeing the castle ahead, cunningly, I hoped.

I worked the day care job, and I took tickets at rock concerts, but I was still in school for one last semester. I was trying to be craftier about my writing. The most exclusive fiction class at UC Berkeley was limited to something like twelve students, and about forty people applied every year. I was rejected the first time I applied, but not the second. Leonard Michaels, the teacher, wasn't just hangdog, New York style—he looked like he'd eaten a bowl of cigarettes for breakfast. He had a voice that probably sounded natural in its natural setting, a shared bathroom at the Chelsea Hotel, but in Berkeley he seemed like one of those migratory birds that was blown three thousand miles off course and ended up where the weather was nice at least, but he seemed miserably out of place.

His method was to have the students read work aloud in class, the whole story, beginning to end, which as a teacher I now recognize as a beautifully cynical way to get through an hour twenty with less effort. Once, during a read-through, his head began to drop, until he actually had his forehead on the desk. "Stop," he said. "Stop. This is a bad story. This is deeply, deeply bad."

It was my story. I'd written it and I was reading it aloud. As a teacher I now recognize something else. There are two types of fiction-writing students—the type that need to know there's room for them at the table, who need to be encouraged and inculcated with self-confidence. Then there are the other kind of students, ones who need to have the self-confidence beaten out of them. Michaels was making an accurate judgment call about me.

He didn't count on the class's response, however. They wanted me to keep reading. The story was about a bunch of friends whose vacation is ruined when dead clowns start washing up on the beach. There wasn't any sort of reason for the clown infestation—I just liked the image of a beach dotted with dead clowns, a grunion run gone wrong. I read aloud to the finish, which didn't change Michaels's mind about its awfulness.

At the end of the last class of the semester, Michaels went around the room to ask what writing people still remembered. He went last. "Dead clowns washing up on the beach. I still hate that goddamn story, but for some goddamn reason . . ."

So I decided to turn it into a novel. Part of it was that writing about friends on an island was fun, and part was understanding that any reaction, even repulsion, requires an emotional engagement that my other stories hadn't quite earned.

Orwell wrote that he had to write four bad novels before he published his first. I told myself I was fine if *The Clown Joke* would go unpublished. The better my friends knew me, the more they disbelieved that I would be fine if my manuscript was a learning experience. I think many people prepared to console me when I finished in three to five years. But I had courage based on how stranger things had already happened to me.

Lindsay and I had been together a year. I was now twenty-three years old and I was deeply in love in a way that wasn't cautious, but all-consuming and burning brightly.

Once, my mother showed up with Daniel. She gave us little notice, as if I might tell her no, they couldn't stay with us. I think they were driving a great distance to bring housewares from seller to buyer, and Oakland was a good resting point.

There was no explanation of what I'd seen in San Diego. I pretended it hadn't happened. My mother seemed happy, but Daniel talked incessantly, sweated, and she kept stroking his arms and rubbing his neck to soothe him. There was clearly something wrong with him. She said it was the flu, but his symptoms didn't match up with that.

After they left, Lindsay discovered someone had eaten the entire box of chocolate Cadbury Eggs I'd gotten her for Valentine's day. Cadbury Eggs were dense, confection-filled bombs of corn syrup and milk chocolate. Lindsay, who loved chocolate, could eat one egg every couple of days. During the evening, Daniel had secretly eaten about a dozen. When I discovered this, I got angry—who eats an entire box of chocolates out of someone else's heart-shaped presentation box? I felt petty about this, because also, who *cares* that someone eats a bunch of candy? It's the rebellion of a child, and getting angry about it is also childish. I almost felt like he'd done it deliberately, knowing I wouldn't stoop to actually be angry for long.

But Lindsay stared at the foil wrappers in a more appraising way.

"Your mom is dating a junkie," she said.

"What?"

"I think so," she said. Junkies worked through sugar in a way no one sober could. This made sense. It explained the sweating and the rambling, disjointed things he said. My mother rubbing his back. I thought it was a little badass that Lindsay knew about junkies but also this gave me a better basis to be angry instead of saying, "Well, Daniel ate some of my girlfriend's candy."

I said, "Wow, I had no idea."

"Didn't you say he asked you for speed the first time you met?"

"Well, yeah."

And then we just looked at each other. So it wasn't that she was so insightful. It's just that we had both been trained to ignore the obvious, especially when it was family.

Lindsay had discovered vintage ceramics, like Bauerware. She went to garage sales in her VW Bug, and knew how to vintage clothes shop, and her understanding of makeup was deep and complex. We went to concerts and had other couples over for dinner, which was always magnificently cooked. If I am capturing her activities rather than her character, that is approximately right, as Lindsay was heading toward that time as a woman in her twenties when she was undergoing a shift.

It was similar to what had caused Melanie to question everything she knew. In Lindsay's case, the questions had to do with desire. There is a transition from being the object of someone else's desire—a kid who obeys her parents, or a girlfriend who is hot to men—to understanding what her own desires were.

Lindsay didn't know what she wanted to do. She wrestled with depression. Once I asked why, and she said, "I feel like a chintz flower." I didn't know what that meant. "Useless. Pretty and not useful." She said she needed therapy to figure it out. I said that made sense. She should probably work through what had happened when she was a kid. She agreed.

I was about to graduate, I'd taken a semester off between Wesleyan and Berkeley, and another semester off at Berkeley, and I was taking the minimum requirements to be a full-time student. I'd spent a fairly lazy six years in college. There was a feeling of diminuendo about it. I didn't want to go to the ceremony. The secretary at the English Department told me to reconsider. They were changing the valedictorian's role.

"The smartest people don't give the best speeches," she said. So they were having a contest to write a speech—anyone graduating, like myself, could enter. I pondered this halfheartedly while waiting in line at a taquería. I jotted down some ideas on the receipt, and I typed them up when I got home. The speech struck me as funny, at least, and as I continued it, I tried to say something about the ways English majors disappoint themselves. While the business majors all are getting their résumés offset so they can field offers, people like me would be running the copy machines and trying to explain to their parents that their ability to articulate their shame in careful prose made it worth all the money college had cost.

My speech won. Berkeley graduating classes are so massive they go by department, over the course of a few days. About twenty-five hundred people were at the 1987 English Department graduation.

A couple of sentences into my speech, the microphone went out. I vamped. I told jokes. I tried to get the crowd to do a wave. I leaned into the microphone to test it, and it was now on, pumping out feedback, as I pointed at my bow tie and said, "I tied this myself," which got a standing ovation, weirdly.

I'd invited my father to graduation but hadn't told him I'd be speaking. There were two reasons for that. One was that I wanted to surprise him. He wasn't just surprised—he wept. "You had them in the palm of your hand!" he said afterward. "When the mike went out, some kid next to me said, 'Wow, he's going to panic,' and another kid said, 'Not Glen Gold, he doesn't panic.' How do they even know that about you?" My father called my stepmother, and my grandmother, and his brothers, and I think if he could, he would call everyone he'd ever met to tell them how good I'd been.

"Why didn't you tell me you were going to do this?"

"I wanted to surprise you," I said. I didn't say the rest of it.

"There's only one thing that could have made it better," he said. "If your mother had been here." And then, immediately, he stumbled, Not really, right? Not my mother as she was. If only she was the same person he'd married, the woman who had raised me, until the divorce. If that woman was still around, he would love to have shared that with her.

This was the other reason I hadn't mentioned it to him. I hadn't told my mother about graduation. As soon as I knew I was going to perform, I had to ask Lindsay what I should do. My mother would bring Daniel. I couldn't let that happen.

It's not like Lindsay had an answer. She knew that in one way I wouldn't feel like a good son, but the other way, it could be an uncontainable disaster. Who knew what Daniel would say or do in a crowd?

At the ceremony, I took what pleasure I could. In the back of my mind was an uncomfortable restraint, a nervousness that this wouldn't be contained, that my mother would find out I'd excluded her. I wanted to say to everyone, "Thank you. Please be quiet about this."

HOPE AND GLORY

WAS WRITING *The Clown Joke*. Lindsay and I were both summarizing depositions to pay the rent. If you were determined, you made good money, but if you were lazy, you could just skate by. Lindsay made more than I did because she was focused and had a good work ethic. A year went by after graduation like this.

Mom called every couple of weeks. Once, she said she and Daniel were moving into a converted school bus. She said I wouldn't be able to contact her, because she had no phone. Also, no kitchen, no bathroom, and no shower. "There's a good chance you won't hear from us for a while, but maybe we'll just drive up there and surprise you," she said heartily, and I didn't know what to say about that.

But I forced myself. Haltingly, I said that Daniel worried me. She didn't know what I meant, so I continued, he didn't seem—well, I didn't know whether he was on drugs or not, but he seemed like he was on drugs.

"Oh, no, no, no, no," she said. "Not anymore. No, he's cleaned up."

I was firm, though. "I'm not comfortable with him around. I don't feel safe having him here with Lindsay."

"I don't know why you'd say that." Her back was up.

"He ate something like a dozen Cadbury eggs," I said. "First, he stole them, but only a junkie could even do that."

"You're being unfair to him. He really does mean well." When we hung up, nothing was resolved.

A few weeks later, she called again, sunny and cheerful. They'd found a house. They had a kitten named Misty now. "She's just like a baby," Mom said. At 4:30 in the morning, Misty woke them up by hopping on the bed and playing. She brought them trophies—her hunting instinct—only there were no mice in the bus, so she bought them broccoli spears instead. I should come visit, she said, and she paused.

I didn't know what to say. There was no way I was visiting, so I was noncommittal.

Also, the house was infested with crickets, Mom said. She only said this to explain how cute it was that Misty now brought them crickets. She ate pizza and toast with jam, like she was a person. Daniel loved Misty and Misty loved Daniel, she said. I should come visit.

I understood what was going on. Misty was the evidence Daniel wasn't a monster. He had a kitten. Surely I'd like to see that.

My aunt Susie called. The specifics are hazy to me now, but my mother was in trouble again. I think she was in Las Vegas, which I am seeing now through coils of smoke, marquee lights flashing to make a strobe effect illuminating something threatening her safety. A scheme had gone wrong. Daniel's drug use had spun out of control. Mom might not have had a phone to tell me herself. I remember it as if my mom were trapped under falling debris, there were flames approaching, some terrible force had catapulted Daniel away across several states, and Mom was shrieking instructions: wire her $107 for train fare.

Eventually my mother did call me herself, numbed and supine, like the fires were out but she was hoarse from yelling. I told her I'd paid for her train fare to Oakland, anticipating her feeling a sense of rescue. I heard in her reply a shift into formality as she added me to her list of creditors.

There's an alphabet known to people with parents whose needs flatten their own. We recite it to ourselves in times of stress, which means we know it by heart. There's an emotional progression from confusion to guilt to commitment to strength to anger, a rhythm that after a while feels sing-songy, as ritualized as our ABCs.

She's only my mom, I wrote while this was happening. The "only" weighed exactly what the entire world weighs. I was trying on a new perspective. There is allegedly an unpayable debt of having been born, but I was wondering how that worked. What were my real responsibilities to someone who was my mother?

If my mother were free of Daniel, she could live with me and Lindsay for a month. I would drive her to job interviews. We were minutes from Berkeley, the one city in the country so socialist that it actually thought about the needs of women returning to the workplace. There were support groups and job boards. I wasn't naive about the search. It would not be easy. I also wasn't naive about my mom. She might not want this to work.

There was another reason I invited her. I wanted her to see how I'd changed. For years, she had been what I'd call *broadcasting* rather than having conversations. She didn't understand how being with Lindsay had changed my landscape into one of stability. My vision was simple, her in our guest room, slowing down, nothing nipping at her heels, her unwinding until she could see the life we'd made. The feeling of wonder might rub off on her.

I also was trying not to be an idiot. I called my dad to tell him what I'd planned and he said, "Your mother is a black widow. She'll drain you. To her, it's her survival or yours."

I was thinking: *Here is a warning from a man who divorced this woman. And every time she returns to my life, my father has to divorce her again.*

I promised myself I would set limits. This was the last time I would help her out.

As I drove to the train station I was blasting a cassette of X, music that bypassed my conscious mind and made me feel older, taller, surfing an angry sea with other members of my tribe. My thoughts, circular, were like this: There is no way to fail, no way to sneer at this even if in the future this attempt looks naive, because right now, loving Lindsay is getting me to the train station without fear.

I was a few minutes late because I suspected that if my mother was on the train, it wouldn't be on time. I had this image set in my mind of a small British blond woman standing among boxes, and I was thinking about how when she was a child she was sent away from London to a farm during the war, and here she would be, a refugee, again.

There were no passengers on the platform and there was no train.

The Amtrak crew were trying to figure out what had happened. The train was missing. After I waited for a few minutes, they told me the train was going to be delayed. Not by a few minutes, but ten hours. They didn't know why. Did this happen all the time? No, they said, this was a first.

I drove back home, chastened a bit. Lindsay was summarizing depositions halfheartedly, about as anxious as I was. It's hard to say for certain what she thought of my mother living with us. She knew what I hoped would happen and she was in love with me, so she would give it a chance. I sat on the couch and looked at her. I said we should get married soon.

"How soon?"

I thought about it. "Before the end of the year."

"Huh."

"Or maybe ..." I expected our marriage to be preceded by signs, fortune cookies broken open on the sidewalk with *Yes!* as their only message, three-masted ships spotted floating over Oakland, panthers running on the beach. But what if that was wrong and there were no obvious miracles? Would that mean we should get married immediately and make our own magic? Or maybe I wasn't getting published because we weren't supposed to be married.

Lindsay said, "What if you never get published?"

I didn't know what to say about that.

It was late at night when I returned to the station at Sixteenth and Wood, which I should mention was a dead neighborhood in West Oakland that was much more troubling after dark. I had to drive past blocks of corrugated tin structures that were blackened by soot, as if they'd been set on fire by bored children. The train station was just a platform in the street. There were SRO hotels surrounding it that looked frightening. If you stepped into their lobbies you would become diseased.

My mother's train had already arrived, and she was struggling under the floodlights alongside a porter to get her luggage out from below the carriage. Alongside her suitcases and bags she had an enormous, well-taped cardboard box that I couldn't quite fit into the trunk of the car.

She explained as I was rearranging the bags that the delay was because of a train derailment, that they'd spent hours stuck on the rails without anything to eat, but people were nice about it. It was a story of refugees' kindness and deprivation, and I was nodding as the trunk of the car accidentally swung down and smacked the back of my skull.

I dropped to my knees, hands on my head, which was ringing as my vision went stippled. I'd never been hit so hard in my life, my sinuses overloaded with an oceanlike smell. I thought, when I could think again, *Catch the Wave.* How ironic.

My mother had stopped talking. She wore an expression so strange it shimmered into my permanent memory. It wasn't the look of a parent rushing to rescue her child. Instead, it was a look of recognition. *You're part of my world again,* it said.

Later, with all the bags and the giant box unloaded in the study, Mom dug through her purse until she found a bottle of a Chinese analgesic she wanted to tell me about. There were many things to describe— her train trip, the things in her boxes, people she had left behind, how exhausted and happy she was to be here, the future, she was bubbling over with it. But first, here, the medicine. "I am your mother, after all," she said, with a mock emphasis on "mother" like I might have forgotten that. She put some on the bump on my head and it did spread that menthol feeling of numbness. "It keeps mosquitoes away," my mother said. "Also, it's good for foreplay, but be careful where your fingers end up."

Later, with my mother in the study, that door closed, I asked Lindsay if that last part had been a weird comment. She had to think about it. She wasn't sure. Maybe? When she was a teenager, she'd bought something called Kama Sutra powder, something you were supposed to lick off your boyfriend. It had gone missing. Her mother had used it all. So Lindsay shrugged. Who knew what mothers were supposed to be like.

Then she asked part of a question, "How long do you think . . ."

"A month," I said. We whispered even though we didn't need to. My mother was mostly deaf. We'd agreed to a month, and if Lindsay was questioning my resolve, I was happy to answer: a month, still.

We were holding each other in the loft bed. Mosquito netting around us. Lindsay whispered, "What if, in a month, she hasn't . . ."

"Yeah, I don't know."

. . .

My mother was on a clock, and she knew this. She was smart. The first afternoon she and I walked through the shops on Piedmont Avenue. It was Lindsay's birthday and my mother wanted to buy her something. At the flower stand, she shopped prices, and then bought the prettiest combination she could for three dollars.

"What does Lindsay like? Does she like toys?" We went into a toy store and my mother stared at everything until her eyes fell on a wind-up plastic mouse holding a wedge of cheese. When you let it go, it did a backflip. It was a dollar. We had it wrapped up.

When we got back to the house she worked on her résumé, and wrote a cover letter on my computer. She asked me to print it out. It was still on my screen, amber letters, gray background, and I felt my stomach drop, and then forcefully be made okay, as I noticed there were typographical errors. Should I point them out? My mother had typed résumés for a living.

She was already planning her next step, answering an ad in the paper for phone sales, when I handed her the cover letter. I'd fixed the mistakes quietly, as I thought telling her about them would make her feel judged. There were still phrases I couldn't understand, and non sequiturs. "I'm in the Bay Area currently to visit my son," it began, and there was a whole paragraph about her salary requirements, something I knew you didn't put in cover letters.

I'd found an organization in Berkeley that helped women returning to the workforce find jobs. She met with them willingly, but she was discouraged. They had asked about her typing speed and if she was up on the latest word processing software, which she wasn't. She'd been living in a bus, she'd explained, but they didn't seem to understand what that meant about being current with technology. They were grooming her for secretarial work, which wasn't what she wanted. She felt talked down to, which was a terrible thing, and women in positions like that were often so condescending. They weren't helpful about sales jobs.

That night, my mother gave Lindsay her gifts. Lindsay reacted the way I had when my grandmother, who was sweet and strange and crafty, gave me chocolate when I was four years old as a bribe to sit on her lap while she patted my shoulders and talked to me about the fairies. Sometimes gifts are barter. Lindsay's tranquil eyes communicated with the slightest narrowing. She understood my mother had done the best she could with the mouse and the flowers. She understood something further because of the story my mother then told.

It was a story about when my mother knew her first marriage was doomed. She'd married an American GI named Bob, who took her to California. This was in the 1950s. Her in-laws owned a furniture store, and they took her through it to furnish the apartment she and Bob would move into.

"It was *hideous* furniture," my mother said, "the most awful stuff that people would call 'classy,' because they didn't know any better. But I appreciated the gesture, and so I dutifully picked out some things. And on our wedding day, they presented me with a bill for all of it." She paused here for me and Lindsay to be horrified, which we were. But there was more. "I was working as a secretary, supporting Bob in school, and I arranged for ten dollars a week to come out of my salary. Week in, week out, and then on Hanukkah, his parents presented me with a scroll, with ornate calligraphy, celebrating everything I'd paid, and canceling the rest of the debt." She paused again. "Not returning any of the money I'd paid so far, just to be clear—they were telling me I was welcome to the family by canceling the remaining debt they'd forced me to incur."

It was a complicated moment, the terrible story and my mother choosing to tell it now, not so much to me as to Lindsay. My mother would say she was telling the story because she wanted to, without ulterior motive. But she was in her sweet way suggesting that it was a cold world out there, so many people were just counting their ledgers, weren't they, Lindsay? Here's a mouse and some flowers, as I am being gracious and I know you'll be gracious in return, Lindsay. Stinginess can destroy marriages that haven't quite yet gotten aloft on their own. Good night, see you in the morning.

My mother sat in our living room the first week to make phone calls. She had a script to follow, and a list of contacts. She was selling space at a medical supplies convention. She would get three hundred dollars for every booth she sold. If she made only one sale every two days, she could have enough saved up for her own apartment.

I'm not sure you'd call this a job. It was a task. It wasn't a task she'd found recently. She'd had the phone contacts in a Rolodex she'd brought with her from her last situation. She'd tried to make it work before she was evicted, but she was sure she could do better here, without a sword hanging over her head.

I worked on depositions in the guest room and Lindsay worked at her desk just on the other side of the living room, so we heard my mother between us, talking on the phone stiffly. When she addressed potential sales, she had jarring moments of excess élan, when her accent became more grand, as if she were the top of a sales pyramid and she had many minions under her. There were pauses when she was listening, or trying to, and I would anticipate from the next room the awful moments when she had to react to whatever the potential exhibitor was saying, when my mother sounded terrified and unsure of herself. *Thank you so much for your time and if you reconsider, my callback number is . . .* with careful enunciation of each syllable, as if she were translating for foreigners.

In between calls, the phone rang once, and she picked up. Her voice melted. She was glad to get this call. I could tell it was Daniel calling.

After she got off the phone, she came into the study, where I was working, and looked a bit wistful. She saw an opportunity to tell me something about Daniel. "He really is trying, you know."

I asked why he was calling, and my mother told me he'd been trying to fill out job applications, but he was overwhelmed. He had sold a pint of blood to make the phone call. He was asking if Mom could help him with his résumé. She explained something I hadn't known. Daniel didn't know how to read or write. "But he really wants to learn," she said. "Really. Look at this."

She shuffled through her pile of bags. She pulled out a laminated sheet of yellow paper.

"He asked me to teach him to write something, so I asked him what he wanted to write. He wrote this. I showed him how do to it." She read it to me. It was a marriage proposal. She had laminated it with one of her office machines. The words looked scratchy, hewn from bark, and they floated off the page for me. I remember the phrase, "Love is the Answer." I felt embarrassed, like my mother had lifted up a sheet to show me how gentle a monster looked while sleeping in the nude. She was so proud of him.

I had too many reactions trying to force themselves out at once, and so I was instead churning with nameless, dark feelings about this. My mother wanted to be a writer and I got this part of my identity, *writer,* directly from her. I once thought she would write a wonderful book. And now she was showing me how Daniel could actually, finally sign his name. I nodded, because, yes, him loving her so much that he learned to write was impressive. But I felt a stab of jealousy along the lines of "I've written so much more than that, Mom" that was so deeply buried I wouldn't have admitted it. Also, a thought was taking up much of the available room in my brain. My mother was never going to be a writer. That dream was gone.

Finally, a horror. I didn't know if she'd married him.

She put the laminated paper away. I still couldn't ask. Her reading and writing lessons hadn't really held long enough for Daniel to begin reading—he didn't see the use of books except the Bible, and he didn't need to read that because he knew in his heart what it said. Love is the Answer. No, she hadn't married him, but she thought he was so sweet for asking.

In one day the first week, my mother made two sales for her medical convention. I hadn't expected that. She wanted to take me and Lindsay to dinner, but it turned out she wouldn't get paid until the exhibitors in question sent in their contracts and their checks had cleared. That might take a week, she thought. But we had dinner and it was a little celebration.

I was quietly adding up how many more sales she would need to make to get an apartment, but a small hitch occurred. Her boss had asked her to send out 500 flyers but had only sent 250 of them, and stamps for 100. It was a major decision, she explained, whether to send out postal packages that cost 45 or 65 cents. She was unclear whether she was supposed to buy her own stamps for the rest, and she couldn't get answers for a couple of days. How ironic, she said, for this to happen now when she was on the verge of success.

Nonetheless Mom kept calling to follow up with leads, even though she couldn't send out brochures and didn't seem to be making any more sales. Finally, one of the exhibitors told my mother that he might be interested in the show, but it was the same weekend as a much larger, more established medical convention that everyone he knew was attending.

It turned out that most of her call list had already signed up for this other show. When her boss phoned back, Mom learned her two sales had canceled. The net effect was that none of her leads panned out. She was out of money, and was in fact in worse shape than when she started when you added in the cost of stamps.

Lindsay decided to go to San Diego for a few days, which I thought was a good idea. We needed my mother to find some new place to go, but until then, why not stay out of her way?

Lindsay was gone. My mother was saying, "You spoke at graduation?"

We were in our living room. "It wasn't anything big," I said. I have no idea how it had come out. Maybe I thought that someone would tell her eventually. Maybe I was still angry about Daniel's laminated note.

"It sounds like a big deal."

"It wasn't."

"Oh. Did you invite your father?"

Touché. "He sort of demanded that he come up. I didn't really have a choice . . ."

She looked willing to be convinced, but she also asked to see the speech, which she read quietly on her single bed. She noted the place where I called out to my dad from the audience.

"Well, I knew he was going to be there," I said.

"I see."

She must have congratulated me. She must have weighed whatever else she wanted to say against what she should say. I didn't blame it on Daniel, because at that moment, it wasn't just about Daniel anymore, but the two of them together. I was beginning to understand that them as a unit meant something different than what I'd thought before.

Finally my mother broke the silence, which had been terrible. "You really were class valedictorian," she said. She looked at me like she was letting me know she'd been clever enough to write my life for me.

. . .

With Lindsay gone, dinners with my mother led to details about her life that she was too ashamed to tell in front of my girlfriend. They were almost stories, but they didn't quite have beginnings or endings. Instead there was that word avalanche which picked up velocity as she connected memories of terrible things that had happened around her. She told me, again, how she and Daniel had met, but she used the word "mattress" for the first time. And said how she hadn't left for so long because she was afraid of him killing me. This linked somehow to my father having been so cold to her, to her own father dressing her down in French, when he knew perfectly well she didn't speak French. Really, it had started right when she was born. Her parents hadn't been married, and she felt such shame at being a bastard, and it was far worse in British society than I could ever know. She didn't even know when her real birthday was—her birth certificate had been destroyed, and her own mother couldn't remember. Had she ever told me she had a twin? Other relatives had confirmed it, and she wondered what had happened. It was probably a stillbirth. But when she found her parents' letters, she saw her mother repeatedly trying to blackmail her father into marrying her. "Our little one needs a last name," Elsie wrote, and when my mother read that she felt devastated and guilty at having been the bait that forced this great man into a marriage he clearly didn't want. Maybe Elsie had kept her and given the other twin away so as not to entirely frighten George. Maybe there was another woman walking the earth now who had entirely different circumstances.

She looked at me, face deep with hidden meanings I was supposed to understand. When I listened, it made sense to me intuitively, the way a lullaby did. If I actually unpacked the lyrics, it turned out I was supplying an internal logic that meant only that I was her son.

She said, "I know you must hate me." I said I didn't. But I asked her why she made such "odd choices." I called them "odd" because "odd" was a neutral word.

She answered slowly, precisely, as if she'd been waiting until I was old enough to understand. And though I wrote it down, I can't explain what she said. It's long and serpentine, with reference to her low self-esteem, to her father again, to shame again, to needing to find disreputable men ever since because she felt they were the only ones she deserved. She had cheated on my father at the end of their marriage and had gotten herpes. But he had cheated on her, and had gotten herpes himself. And after the marriage ended, when we were in San Francisco, she had gone on a date that had ended violently. The man had forced himself on her in something she had only recently started calling date rape. She had lain there quietly because I was in the house. Before I could react to that, she described her family's lack of support; never really having had a chance to be rich; events conspiring against her; how she'd be able to set up her own business if only she had one more chance. She made it all sound like she was in a small boat in the middle of the ocean, smacked around, no compass, broken mast, torn sails, spun by currents and winds she couldn't control.

Then she said that when she'd packed to finally leave Daniel, he'd picked Misty up in his hands and told my mother he would strangle her if she did.

My mother didn't deliver the next line of this story. She just looked at the floor.

"I made mistakes," she finally said. I thought I knew what she meant, but it turned out she'd moved on from that last topic. "When I was with your father, I wasn't ready for the responsibilities of money, but now I can visualize it and I'm ready for great wealth to find me."

When Lindsay came back, we lay in the loft, holding each other, and I told her that my mother had cheated on my father, my mother had gotten herpes because of it, she had been raped, I'd been there when she was raped, she'd met Daniel when she'd had sex with him and a friend on a filthy mattress. Daniel had threatened to kill me. He'd strangled their kitten, maybe. My mother had no opportunities on the horizon. She was out of money and options and I wasn't sure what to do next.

I can't say that any one part of this made me feel more awful than another. I was doing what Lindsay and I had always done, a kind of triangulation to see if it was strange to hear any of this. She said that yes, it was strange. She didn't say more. There's a battlefield triage level of compassion that runs thin after a while.

. . .

After three weeks, my mother had numerous inquiries into sales jobs for multilevel marketing positions, but no income still. Her final option was something called Project Share, which matched homeless but responsible people with elderly clients who were enfeebled and needed helpers. One afternoon, she took the bus an hour to San Leandro to meet a former chiropractor who greeted her by announcing she hadn't seen a doctor since 1953. She had also stopped throwing away food and no longer flushed the toilet. When my mom arrived, the woman offered her a dish of ice cream, which my mother ran her spoon around, afraid to eat it. The woman glared at her and the melting ice cream, obviously feeling insulted and asking increasingly mean-spirited questions. That match didn't work.

Mom sat in our living room and read aloud to me the descriptions of other seniors she might meet. *Hildegarde, 80, an intellectual—has limited eyesight and likes to be read to . . . Sue, 90, Alzheimer's, needs to be escorted to the bathroom at night . . . Sam, 74, Parkinson's, has his own car, but needs someone to drive it.*

When she was discouraged, I played classical music for her on the stereo because I couldn't think of anything else to do. With sighs, she explained to me how hard a worker she was in the office jobs she hadn't even wanted. She just wasn't a team player—she hoped that if she were professional enough, nice enough, her bosses would eventually have to be nice back. Someone named Candace had paid her five dollars an hour, but paid the janitor eight dollars an hour, and yelled at my mother when she offered advice. Law students got their résumés done, then sued her when she tried to get paid. Jared, another boss, stole her paycheck. Another set up an investment pool that turned out to be a pyramid scheme. Mom only found out when she came to work on payday to find all the equipment gone and the FBI asking questions. Paul was a physician who made her babysit a girl he'd gotten pregnant and performed an abortion on. She shook the list of Project Share candidates as she talked.

It was a moment transparent enough that I understood it. Here was a rogue's gallery of people who had already been cruel to her; here was a list of seniors who would be the same way. Why bother? She made an appointment to apply for food stamps. She had to throw away her only pair of sandals because they'd fallen apart.

Lindsay and I were tentative around each other. Mom tried to be as unobtrusive as possible but the fact of her was a constant reminder of something dark. Her troubles seemed to bend whatever environment she was in until it matched wherever she'd come from and wherever she was going next.

She wanted to be a good guest. She insisted on doing the dishes after dinner, working hard at the sink. After she closed the door to the study, Lindsay would go to the kitchen and do the dishes again to get the spaghetti sauce off of them while the television shows my mother watched beat against the walls at high volume. *America's Funniest Home Videos,* or *TV's Bloopers and Practical Jokes,* the canned laughter distorted into wails you could feel in the floor coming from what I no longer called Fifi's room.

A couple Lindsay and I knew were going away for a month. Their apartment would be empty. I asked if my mother could house-sit. I couldn't blame them if they said no. But then they said yes, and I wanted to fall on them with gratitude.

Telling my mother about the house-sitting was tense. Did I pitch it to her like this, perhaps? "You'll have a month to recoup. You can stretch out without us underfoot. It's a lovely space in a great neighborhood." I can still see her face intelligently sizing up the situation—the house was high in the Oakland Hills without access to public transportation. If she went there, it was a guarantee she wasn't going to find a job. If I suggested she go, it meant to her it was more important to me that she get out of my house than that she actually support herself.

With grace, she agreed the change in scenery would be nice. It only took part of the morning for her to insert her belongings back into the cardboard boxes she'd kept in the study. She taped them shut.

I drove my mother away from my house, the trunk and backseat overflowing with clothes and papers and knickknacks. She rode with her Rolodex in her lap, because she wasn't going to give up her sales leads.

We stopped at the Safeway on 51st, which had a huge parking lot that always seemed to bake in the sun. I was going to buy her a week's worth of groceries. But I didn't have much money. Brown rice and vegetables. Canned tuna. My mother saw yogurt was on sale, three for a dollar.

"I had no idea there were so many varieties," she said. "If I eat three a day, that should be enough." She stood in the dairy aisle for a good, long time, taking in all the flavors, asking a clerk what the difference between the white and the colored containers was. The colored ones were pre-stirred.

She counted out twenty-one yogurts, and looked to me for confirmation, and I said it was a good choice. But was she sure she didn't also want brown rice? Vegetables? She was ambivalent. There were some basic hygiene items, too, toothpaste, for instance. She didn't want to run up too much of a bill.

Walking with my mother through the aisles of the supermarket defined me in ways I still don't understand, because with every item she rejected as unnecessary, I was seeing her diminishment. She had gotten so much smaller than when she used to have a checking account and money in it. She was choosing now to be smaller still. She was tucking her legs into a steamer trunk, seeing with something like pleasure what a refined and uncomplaining appetite she had for a life that wouldn't be a bother to anyone as she tumbled back into chaos and its deep, familiar shelter.

As she was leaving my home, I was going to stand on the shoreline and wave. I started to see her receding as the twenty-one yogurt containers went into the plastic sacks that we carried into the parking lot.

When we were outside the Safeway, a homeless guy put his hand out. "Spare change? Be generous."

It took me by surprise. I laughed harder than I had in weeks. It was a cruel, stupid, heartless laugh, and I didn't even stop walking. I yelled over my shoulder, "You have no fucking idea." I remember my mother either smiling or grimacing. What did she think of me? Who did she identify with?

A couple of days later, I was sitting on the couch with Lindsay, who was slowly paging through a *Penthouse* magazine I'd bought to show her. There were photos of women I thought she would like. I rubbed her feet the way you would rub two sticks together, my eyes flicking toward any page she lingered over. I couldn't remember when we'd last had sex. Her eyes had that kind of cool appraisal that homed in right before her drive to fuck woke up, I thought.

The phone rang. Lindsay picked it up and said hello. She started talking to someone. She continued to turn the pages of the magazine, talking as if fully engaged to whoever it was. I couldn't interpret from her tone if it was a relative or one of her friends, and my inability to read her made me feel weak. I felt I was witnessing my own cuckolding. I began to tell myself it was Charles Blank on the phone. I pressed against the most sensitive part of her arch as if that would tether her to me. I was thinking, I will feel an inch beyond the tips of my fingers again. I will bring you back from outer space. That's how it works with us. We have a connection.

After she hung up, she looked at me. "Are you all right?"

"Sure."

She kissed my forehead, tossed the magazine to the couch, and went to make tea.

My mom was in her house-sit for a couple of weeks before she started having a problem. She'd had the landlord over for dinner and he'd made a crude pass at her, which she'd rejected, and since then he had been making her uncomfortable. I asked Lindsay if in the time we'd known our friends they'd ever mentioned their landlord. No. Lindsay said it was odd for him to both materialize and hit on my mother.

I said it was like her presence had contorted the place until it matched her world she'd brought with her.

Lindsay realized I didn't understand what was going on. "Your mother is trying to move back here."

A few days later, I got a phone call from Susie, who said my mother was exploring returning to England. This made sense to me—she should return to her family. But Susie wanted me to stop this, to kill it. My mother wanted to bring Daniel with her.

I almost said, "But Mom and Daniel broke up," but then I realized *of course, right*. They weren't broken up—they were apart. My mother was seeing a path to a friendly horizon and a cottage somewhere in which Daniel could start over again.

I called my mother to tell her she shouldn't take Daniel to England. She bristled. It wasn't any of my business. Why would I say something like that?

"He's a drug addict. He steals."

"Your relatives are drug addicts. They've stolen themselves many times. Don't get on your high horse about that." And then she said, "He's just fine when he's not around drugs. I've told Susie that."

"That's like telling her he's great—just keep him away from knives. He'll find knives if he wants to, Mom."

She said I didn't understand. I shouldn't be so critical about him. He spoke in tongues in his sleep. He'd had a hard life. He'd been jailed as a teenager and raped there. He'd been to many of the fifty states.

She was no closer to knowing where she could go. Oregon, where her sister Elizabeth lived? My mother didn't like this idea. She said, "Elizabeth is, well, you know."

Elizabeth was disorganized and friendly and chipper, and chaos followed her even more closely than it did my mother. She tended to spontaneously drive several hundred miles in a car filled with clothes and broken furniture and what she called gifts, but which no one wanted. I wasn't quite sure how many times she'd been married. At a picnic with my cousins, I once saw her running up the side of a hill naked, with a butterfly net, yelling at the summit, "Heigh ho, Glen! Heigh ho!" Of all the many sisters, Elizabeth was the one the rest could agree was impossible. I understood why my mother didn't want to live with her.

My mother said, "I keep telling Susie, it's so difficult when she and I are the only sane ones."

I had a huge straw cowboy hat that was tattered and ridiculous, the kind of thing that should have had holes cut in its brim for a donkey's ears. At parties I photographed friends in the hat. When writers did readings at Black Oak or Cody's, I'd bring the hat and ask if they minded posing with it on. So I photographed Jay McInerney, I. F. Stone, and Tama Janowitz wearing it, or holding it with confusion. It felt like a better trophy than an autograph.

When Don DeLillo came, I thought I should leave it at home. Same with David Leavitt. That time, I didn't trust myself, as if I might accidentally do something snide with it.

Leavitt read endearing material, however, and during the Q&A afterward, my hand shot up of its own accord, and he gave a very funny answer to my question: he *hated* that *Esquire* had called him the voice of a new, as-yet-unnamed generation. All he'd done was sell them an essay, and when it came out with that claim on it, he'd winced, and his friends had made fun of him ever since. I liked this answer.

While he signed books, an acquaintance of his talked about how his agent and publisher were worried about sales numbers. This was a strange thing to overhear, because I'd assumed that after you were declared the voice of a generation, you had nothing further to worry about. Publication—still an unimaginable distance away—was supposed to be some kind of finish line, but now I wasn't so sure.

I bought Lindsay and myself a present. A psychic astrologer read our charts. I'd visited first, and though the psychic was accurate about describing me, she couldn't quite grasp my relationship with Lindsay. She wasn't sure we'd known each other in previous lives. "If so, it wasn't as lovers. Maybe one of you was the other's patron? Or a mother and a son?"

I had two thoughts as my session ended. One was that she was wrong and this was a scam. The other was the opposite thought, that it was all accurate, which depressed me more. I wasn't prepared for a third possibility, which turned out to be the correct one.

The astrologer made audiotapes for us. Lindsay's tape begins with several long minutes of the astrologer getting only about half of it right. Maybe less. She could feel Lindsay's attention drifting. It struck her as strange, as she didn't tend to make spongy observations that may or may not fit. Then she showed Lindsay the information she copied down. Wrong birthday.

With the correct birthday information, she was immediately on track. She described Lindsay with great accuracy—funny, vibrating one-half second away from the world, a former femme fatale, fighting off the death-obsessed influence of her father, striving to go forward and do some sort of public work for the common good. The astrologer described this desire in depth, ecological remediation, and as I heard the tape, I thought, "Maybe, potentially, but—"

And then, on tape, Lindsay said that yes, she was interested in exactly that. She'd been thinking for months about going to grad school. This was news to me.

I had wanted a moment of magic and there it was, yanked from the clouds, a deep understanding of desires she'd never spoken, and it made me uneasy. I hadn't thought the magic would take the form of a stranger knowing Lindsay better than I did. But, annoyingly, that turns out to be how magic works sometimes.

After describing Lindsay's conflicts and desires and options, the astrologer turned back to our relationship. She still wasn't sure we'd known each other in a past life. She also thought I needed Lindsay more than she needed me. I don't remember what she said after that.

A few days later Lindsay and I went to a party where I talked to nobody but instead sat on the couch, petting a cat in my lap. I can't remember the house we were in or the time of day, just a small pair of spotlights on myself and on my girlfriend. I watched her interact with people, how she nodded and showed an interest in their lives. I knew I should be doing the same. She was learning how to say, "I'm going back to graduate school," and with every conversation she repeated it, I wanted her to tell me we were okay. I had a poetic or paranoid feeling that the more she talked about her future environmental career the more likely she was going to leave me. I was thinking, How did we get here? Weren't we a little more like myths once?

In late September I took my mom to the Greyhound bus station on San Pablo, an avenue wide enough to seem like a highway. It was deserted except for the homeless people the cops were rousting from the bushes. Mom found a shopping cart, and I helped her unload her cardboard boxes and her luggage from the car. She wheeled it into the station. I paid for her fare at the ticket window, and then I joined her on the platform.

Her trip to Oakland had failed. And here we were. I wasn't paying much attention to what she was saying because a bad reckoning was welling up in me. I was telling myself, "This is what my mother looked like on the day I gave up on her."

She was wearing running shoes and a plastic raincoat. Her hands were on the rim of a metal supermarket shopping cart, and her nails drummed without rhythm as she talked about what she would do next. Oregon had better programs for job training. She'd looked into it, and she qualified for something, she thought, but she could only get the details once she was a resident there. She would learn to deal with Elizabeth until she found a place of her own. She wasn't going back to Daniel, she said. That's when I realized, not for the first time, my mother believed everything she said, until the next thing she said.

They loaded her boxes into the bus. She had food for the trip. Before she got on board, I gave her the money in my wallet, fifteen dollars. It doesn't matter if we kissed or hugged goodbye, because I'd already said goodbye from whatever you would call the place my heart was.

Later I was sitting in my car, somewhere. I was thinking about Lindsay, to whom I had finally talked about how hard it was that she no longer wanted me. She had said, shrugging, "Celibacy gives me strength." I burst into tears, and then I stopped crying because I understood there was no point to it.

THE *BENSHI*

L INDSAY SAID, "I want to start trying to be the woman you wanted to marry." She'd been lost, the way people are after graduation, only she'd meandered now for almost five years.

The University of Colorado had an excellent ecological studies program. She studied for the necessary exams, did some volunteer work, and applied to grad school. If she got in, the plan was for us to move to Boulder in September 1990. I'd get a day job of some sort while I finished my new novel.

I'd written and rewritten *The Clown Joke*, which a few agents and editors had read the first fifty pages of. One had asked for the whole thing, and returned it in an untidy mess that I liked looking at. Her rejection note was extensive and heartfelt and suggested I try writing something more personal.

The book I was working on was deeply weird. I'd been having vivid dreams that took up several pages at a time in my journal. I was rarely in them; instead, they were the plots of impossible movies or novels. The dreams were lengthy, ornate, ugly, and three acts in structure. I generally woke up sweating and confused, and I would lie awake for a few moments wondering why I had dreamed about an existing novel—until it dawned on me that I'd created it myself. Astronauts struggled on the banks of rivers while flowers tried to strangle them. The court of a fairy-tale king backstabbed each other and conspired to insert needles under their skin in order to feel life more intensely. An older couple eroti-cally punished a younger one in infinite gardens behind ornate brick mansions. The dreams made no sense either as narrative or as emotional artifacts someone could follow in a surrealist sense.

In the spirit of following art wherever it goes, I began my mornings transcribing that night's dream, then bending my novel-in-progress in some direction that the dream suggested. I'd say it was like Calvino working with Tarot cards, only his book was good and mine, so far, was just *strange*.

In the afternoons I would read or go on long runs by myself, and in the evenings I would work on depositions, then return to my book. I read somewhere that you should name books that have no obvious title after something you love, so I called this *Bondage and Discipline*. The joke was that I was bound to the work, I was showing discipline by doing it. It wasn't a joke anyone asked the meaning of, because my friends had stopped reading my work.

I was walking in the hills of Oakland, past rich people's houses, and I was starting to sing a song to myself:

> A lack of grace
> How fucked the cost
> I once was found
> And now I'm lost

A familiar numbness was seeping into my day. It didn't feel like my perceptions had altered so much as they'd deepened, and I saw the lies the world was built on. It was like I'd uncovered a rock, which was an anchor for me, and it was no one else's rock but mine. No one could take this depression from me. It was an old friend without the warmth of friendship.

Oregon hadn't worked out for my mom. When she took her first pay-check to the bank, it turned out to be drawn on a dead man's account. She applied for Displaced Persons Emergency Relief for access to their job listings, then learned she would have to take a state-mandated six-week course in résumé writing and self-promotion before she could see them.

She moved into a trailer park owned by a one-eyed man with a Doberman so vicious the mailman refused to deliver letters there, so any mail coming to my mother was probably lost, she said. She thought people who owed her money might have chosen that moment to send it. A few weeks later, I heard she'd moved back in with Daniel.

I felt like an unseemly uncle discovered living in an attic. I wished I could see the future. I wanted to see a big X stamped where I was now, and a bigger one showing me that there was success ahead if only I kept plowing forward through what might have otherwise been insane. "For so long, I thought this project was crazy," I imagined saying to some interviewer, eventually, "but that was before this book succeeded so wildly." And then I wanted to punch myself in the face for thinking that.

At parties, when people asked me if I'd published anything, I said, "I'm not good enough yet," which I thought was at least self-loving. I collected rejection slips. I submitted to contests; *Mademoiselle* didn't reject me immediately.

I'd read about how, when silent film came to Japan, the Western editing techniques made no sense to audiences raised on Noh and Kabuki dramas. Neither did Western emotional expressions. So cinemas hired men to stand at the side of the screen and narrate what was going on. "Now there are Indians attacking the cabin. The father loves his daughter, and he is exclaiming to her with *love*"—because the emotions weren't apparent and had to be explained—"that he will defend her." Ironically the best *benshi* weren't the most accurate, but the ones who told the stories that seemed most resonant.

When I read this, my heart fell. At some point, Lindsay had stopped telling me how she felt. Instead, I would say to her, "Are you doing *this* because you feel *that*?" And she would say, "I don't know," so I would get more detailed about it. "I think you resent cooking for both of us and you're angry at me, but it's hard for you to say that," and she might say that sounded right to her, and I would feel like we'd made progress or that we were still close. But I'd become the relationship's *benshi*.

"Do you think you don't want sex because of what maybe happened when you were a kid? Do you think you should get therapy because of it?"

I'd become clingy. Lindsay wasn't used to seeing that side of me.

"Is it weak for me to need you?" I asked.

"I don't know," she said.

It's not that we argued. We didn't know how.

One evening, after her shower, applying lotion, she asked quietly, tentatively, if maybe I'd thought of sometime, you know, shoving her on the floor and just raping her. Being violent, ignoring whatever she said or did, just to shut her the hell up. But we were so far apart I couldn't imagine doing that without it coming from pure anger, and that frightened me.

I had a very dark thought. What if—and I could barely say this aloud—I hadn't been a soul mate dropped into her path by the forces of destiny and reincarnation and Tarot and all the supernatural realms, but a distraction?

And then I did another accounting: Heidi to Melanie to Cindy to Jess to Noelle to Lindsay, mostly overlapping, hardly a breath between them. That seemed like a problem.

Once Lindsay asked, in a question so well formed that I understood she'd been trying to phrase it for a while, "What if you end up being thirty and you're working in a café? Seriously, *thirty*?"

In February, she decided to accompany her mother to Egypt on a trip for a few weeks. This seemed like a great idea for both of us. "You'll get to miss me," she said.

A couple of days after she left, a thick envelope from the University of Colorado arrived—she'd been accepted. I left it on the kitchen butcher-block table, walking past it like it was a spring-loaded trap. That afternoon and evening, I became more uncomfortable, and when I woke up the next morning, I had a fever. *Is this me missing Lindsay?* I wondered. I pissed blood. I had a kidney stone.

The doctor suggested I piss through a strainer (I rather enjoyed doing that), because it was small enough to come out on its own. Until then, I would be in pain. One afternoon I was writhing on the couch when the phone rang. It was my mother. She started to talk. "The real estate thing fell through," she said, and I didn't know what she meant. Daniel had pawned her VCR. She'd tried to get a restraining order against him but the judge refused. Her current boss had paid himself a bonus and had stiffed her. "I don't think he intended to rip anyone off," she said quickly, "but he does have diabetes and I wonder if that can impair your judgment, but still it's so unfair, just when I'm getting my act together."

It was all one sentence, and it was hard for me to concentrate through the pain enough to hear her voice. I told her I was fine, I was fine, everything was fine, and after we hung up, I realized I was gushing sweat.

There was no one to check in on me. That felt normal.

What would I write if I had no time left? In pain, sweating, clutching at my side, drinking water to eventually flush the stone out, I wrote a scene in a living room in Corona del Mar in 1974. A slick con man meets a mother and son and begins tempting them to move to San Francisco.

Twelve hours of work straight. The mother takes on some bad boyfriends. The son, who is snide and ill-kempt, is abandoned when she moves to New York without him. It is cliché to say something is written in a fever, but courtesy of my kidney stone this novel really was written that way. The fever broke, and the kidney stone passed a few days before I finished the book. I wrote about seventy thousand words in eight days. It was raw, and I knew it needed a little rewriting, but there was something vital in it. I called it *The Man Behind the Curtain*.

When it was done, I carried it with me. I put it in front of me at the Thai place where I had lunch. I took it into Moe's Books, as if introducing it to family it would meet more lingeringly at a reunion to come. I felt like I was walking on railroad tracks, and the tracks had begun to sing a little. Lindsay couldn't come back soon enough—I'd rescued myself. This hadn't been a waste of time, it had been incubation.

One of those nights, I dreamed it was twenty years in the future. I was in an open contemporary kitchen with barstools and on one side a dining room and the other side a living room. Lindsay was making breakfast. She looked much the same, still hennaing her hair red, but she was dressed in a business suit and her face was fuller, and she had wrinkles under her eyes. A girl, thirteen, got a yogurt from the refrigerator. She looked almost exactly like a young version of Lindsay, but more awkward, all knees and elbows. She was talking. I couldn't concentrate on what she was saying. I blurted out "Suzannah" and as she looked at me comically, about to say something she'd said a thousand times before to me, I was awake.

I couldn't tell if this dream was cruel. I said to myself, even before I was fully conscious, "Don't give up."

When Lindsay came back from her trip, I gave her the manuscript. I explained that unlike whatever involuted dream story I'd been writing, this was urgent. I'd tapped into something new. She put it on her desk. Every day, I noticed that it was still there. Finally, I saw it in a manila folder on my work chair.

I asked her what she thought. With discomfort, she said she hadn't read it. She'd thought about it, but she couldn't bring herself to open it. "The thing is," she said slowly, "when you talk about your writing, you're starting to sound like your mom talking about her business opportunities."

It was a remarkably targeted kind of strike. I was livid. When I'm livid, my temperature drops. I almost whispered, "How dare you judge me."

She nodded. "Yeah. I wish I didn't. But I do."

It was already late August and Lindsay was moving to Boulder in September. The plan had been for us to go up at the same time, but that changed. It would take many maps and diagrams to find the source of the decision, because we were both very good at figuring out what the other person needed, then trying to bend ourselves to fit that, but the actual words came out of my mouth: she should go up first and I would stay in Oakland for a couple of months. I told her she needed to work on having compassion for the person she loved. She agreed.

We took down the watercolors and the music posters. She started saying goodbye to friends. I dismantled my shrine to writers my age who were published. She was changing how she did her makeup. I didn't understand how to talk with her or touch her. And then Charles Blank called.

He was going to be in the neighborhood. I was that day at my ebb. I was still sickly and pasty from the kidney stone, and confused about everything else. I was a mess.

What, I asked, did Lindsay plan on doing with him? She said they would go to a café for lunch, probably. Be gone an hour or two. I faced this impassively. It seemed like such irony, I decided my only course was to meet him and try to find flaws in him that Lindsay never would, because after he left, she probably would have fucked him and I would never know.

"When you move to Boulder," I said, "will you—"

"Yes."

"What?"

"You're about to ask me about therapy."

This was true. She was putting on that new makeup. She stopped, and looked from the mirror to me.

"The problem is, I've been thinking about it, and I don't think it happened."

"What didn't?"

"Anything."

I nodded.

When I laid eyes on Charles Blank, it was remarkable, because he showed up as advertised. Six foot five and cold and muscular and smooth, like a boa constrictor. He dressed the way I would have, if I looked like him and had money. He had a dead unblinking stare that was uncanny, in that it was like an ultraviolet, deep-space version of Lindsay's icy-blue eyes. He and Lindsay looked alike, which delivered a stab of jealousy that was strangely worse than the possibility of them sleeping together.

Then he started talking. "I know Julien Temple" was the first thing he said to me. He hadn't even said hello.

"Julien—"

"He directed *Absolute Beginners*." I didn't understand why he was telling me this. He pointed—I had the novel on a shelf. Charles had something to do with music video production and while Lindsay got ready to go, he named more people that he knew. I'd heard of some of them, and the ones I didn't know, he explained their importance. He mentioned how much he got paid, and how he didn't clean his own house or maintain the garden he had, but he paid people to do it. He told me how much he paid them, more than minimum wage, because he had money. He told me what kind of car he drove.

I'm not sure how I seemed to him. I remembered vaguely that long ago people had been intimidated by me. I wondered: Was *he* feeling insecure? Was I to him the man who had, even if only for a bit, won Lindsay? I wasn't feeling insecure at all; in fact, I was past that, as insecurity suggests you're afraid you can't hold on to something. I was already resigned to Lindsay giving herself to him.

There she was, in the hallway, purse in hand, between her boyfriend and the man who disrupted the love of all boyfriends, and she was unreadable to me. Fables of the impervious lover.

I saw them off, closed the door, watched from our living room window as they walked down the alley to the car. For a moment, I thought about putting "Cuyahoga" on, but there were multiple reasons I didn't, beyond how sad it would be for someone probably about to be cuckolded to try and ignite some remotely controlled sense of purpose or guilt or love in a woman who would never be swayed by sentimentality.

When she came back she didn't have much to say about their time out. It's quite possible nothing happened. I knew not to ask questions, because I didn't want to hear "I don't know."

There's only one moment left to mention before the move to Boulder. It might have been two or three in the morning. I was working late, having returned to the weird dream novel, because I didn't know what else to do.

Our loft bed meant you had to climb up a rough-hewn ladder before you'd see the books and ChapSticks and face lotions by Lindsay's side of the bed. I'd had a good work night, and my head was big with that momentary belief in myself when I peeled back the netting and put my hand on her hip. It was a gesture I made almost nightly, and she had in the last year taken to brushing it away in her sleep. Trying to seduce her had become like stealing apples off a tree.

She turned, opened herself a little. My palm seemed to dissolve as I brushed it across her skin. She was asleep still, but wherever I touched, her skin woke up with Yes. Every motion I made caused some need for more touching ignite in her. We were fucking, and she was now fully awake. I could feel her coming back into consciousness. She was weeping.

There were deep sobs like I'd never heard from her, sounds that were dark, animal keening, and yet her body kept encouraging me to go on. I'm sorry it all happened so fast. In a few moments, she came, but then she recoiled from me and pulled her hips away so I was no longer inside her and then she broke down into full, trembling, sloppy tears.

She wiped them off with her knuckles. I'd never seen her cry like this. She had promised me when we met that she never cried, and she'd kept her word until now. I hovered over us, a young couple uniting one last time, and a small mercy had been them sharing this last supernatural coupling that was part of their secret vocabulary, and it is now extinct. So sorry, so so sorry. It's over. We were sharing a story finally, but it was the story of our end, Camelot gone. I was telling it to myself now and she was, too, and that we agreed so silently made it worse.

Lindsay was making noises that weren't words yet, but she was trying. Finally, she said, "Sea turtles."

"What?"

"Sea turtles." She choked back more tears. "They see a plastic bag in the ocean and they think it's a jellyfish, and they eat it. And it kills them."

I'd heard about that. But I was confused.

"That's why I was crying," she said. "I started to feel sad when you touched me and I needed to think of something that would send me over the edge."

I kissed her eyes. I knew that her saying "sea turtles" was something I would repeat to myself. It would take a couple of drinks, but I would tell Owen, and eventually other friends I knew well enough, and they would know a fundamental sadness that didn't belong to me. After a month knowing me and maybe a long country drive, women who had never met Lindsay would hear me say "sea turtles," and they would understand the way things had fallen apart without need for further explanation.

A month later, I was at a party very late at night in San Francisco. I didn't want to be there, but my ride had on the spur of the moment decided to drop acid, and all the buses had stopped running, so there was no way for me to get home. They were showing Jane's Addiction videos on the ceiling. My voice was wrecked from the beginnings of laryngitis, again, and I'd had four cups of tea to soothe my throat. The tea turned out to be mushroom tea, so I was about to have an involuntary four to six hours of hallucinating.

I was lying on the concrete floor, looking at the ceiling, where they were now projecting a movie called *Greaser's Palace,* a surreal retelling of Christ's life set in the Old West. I was thinking, "Lindsay, you won't even deal with your life," and she felt like a coward to me. I would have to deal with my mom, whatever that meant, because I wasn't a coward, to show her how adults behaved. The whole time, I was shivering and spasming with the onset of the flu. I was feeling righteous self-pity.

Jean was there. She was still associated with the Berkeley Psychic Institute. She was still leading people through past lives. She crouched down and asked how I was.

I whispered: terrible. Lindsay was in Boulder. She'd been there less than a week before she broke it to me. She was seeing someone else. She was already in love. She promised to write me a letter explaining why she'd ended it, but weeks had gone by. She was throwing herself into a relationship, and was that what I'd been to her, too? It hadn't been fate that made her leave Paul for me—it had been convenience. My emotions were on the outside of my body. Plus, I added, I was taking a mushroom trip I didn't want.

Jean had experience with bad trips, and she gave me some advice about surviving the next few hours. Find some ascorbic acid, like I was treating a cold. Actually, that worked better for acid, but at least I should know it would be over eventually. Tomorrow would be better.

"Sorry about Lindsay," she said.

Sharply, because I couldn't help myself, like it was something Jean had done, I said, "I thought she and I had a contract."

She shrugged. "Yeah, those things never work."

SCORPIO

IT WAS SIX MONTHS LATER. I was going through a phase where I was especially mean. This was in my motorcycle days, when I had a blue BMW R100/7. I spent two hours a day at the gym rowing with my Walkman on, playing the Pixies at an unhealthy volume. My form was excellent, I was relentless and I was eager to find women to be awful to. As soon as I could stop crying. I was pale, my hair was long, and the light in my eyes was gone. People tended to advise women they knew to stay away. There should have been police tape around me.

My friend Kirsten was getting married, and there was a wedding reception. She had known me for too long, and thought I was harmless. She had introduced me to a few girls. The reception was friendly, the June Berkeley light made everyone seem like they were dressed in white, and I'd planned to just come and go, but Darcy was there. Apparently I'd seen her before.

She was small, like Audrey Hepburn, and hazel-eyed, and she wore strangely tailored clothing made from bizarre combinations of fabrics—though I know I'm remembering it wrong, I think of her wearing nylon and feathers, cotton and latex, wool batting fringed with cake frosting.

Darcy held a glass of champagne, and another, and another. A great deal of the conversation was about whether we'd met before. She insisted we had, and during the party, she kept coming up to me, listing dates and places I thought she was making up, then leaving me in annoyance, which I found charming. Right before Halloween 1988, she'd passed me on Shattuck Avenue but I hadn't said hi. Rose Street, August 1986, she'd been talking to Vincent, and I'd come up and said something to him about soccer players. Things like that, which as they piled up seemed like a funny ploy to keep talking.

As I was leaving, she came with me to my motorcycle, and stood on her toes to be kissed goodbye. She kissed me again, and again, and again, pushing her jaw against my stubble. "That feels good," she said. "Don't leave yet. Wow, I feel that."

She had gotten a wisdom tooth pulled a month before, and the dentist had sliced a nerve, leaving her unable to talk at first. Sensation had started to return, but she still slurred her words and people always thought she was drunk.

"Oh. Are you drunk now?"

"No."

She was.

She didn't want to let me go, and eventually I left on my own, while she stood on the sidewalk, touching her fingers to her face as if pressing against me might have given it definition.

Single friends are, to married people, like fantasy football leagues, and Kirsten thought Darcy would be interesting for me. "But be careful."

"She should be careful of me," I said.

"No," Kirsten said, "I'm pretty sure you should be careful of her." Darcy was bright and funny and a confidante, easy to tell secrets with, but she had angles to her. Years before, Kirsten used to have a nemesis named Inga. Inga was the thorn in her side. Inga was her Moriarty. She was German and she always wore black and she never smiled. For a year, Inga had been at parties, flirting with the men, saying rude things to the women, and—thankfully—leaving early. Sometimes with someone else's boyfriend. Kirsten had never even seen her, and yet Inga had been spreading lies, some of them about her.

Kirsten told me this, and then looked at me expectantly. "You don't know where this is going?" She said she'd complained to Darcy about Inga, and Darcy said, "Oops. That's me."

Kirsten had laughed. No way. Inga was German. She spoke fluent German at parties, sometimes to other German people, sometimes just to exclude clueless frat boys who addressed her in English. Darcy confessed that she was fluent in German, and spoke with a Ripuarian accent. When she was Inga, she wore a wig. She said that sometimes she was Paisley, and she was Irish, but Kirsten wouldn't have seen her then, because Paisley only hit on girls.

The women I have fallen for have little in common except high-functioning rationality. I like women who have been through dark alleys, but who have survived because of their backbone. Always, when it comes to paying bills or recounting how they got a speeding ticket just once, they are reliable.

I'd recently slept with as many women as I could, which was made difficult because I still tended to collapse into fits of weeping three nights out of five. By the time I met Darcy, I was dating a woman named Colleen, who in turn was dating someone else, who was married. Colleen had made it clear that she would drop her man if and only if I was interested in commitment. It was an arms race of a relationship. Colleen was clever and rode a better motorcycle than mine, but there was something vulnerable and sexy in Darcy I wanted to touch.

A week or so after the wedding, thinking about that lisp and the kiss against my chin, I took Darcy out. She hadn't been on too many motorcycles before, which made me seem more exotic than I was. We rode through the hills of North Beach. Occasionally she would point toward an apartment and tell me who lived there, and what terrible things they'd done.

We went to a bar. She'd had a bad break-up with a German guy named Hans. "I'm trying not to drink," she said.

I bought her a Guinness, which she drank through a straw, eyes on me the whole time.

She said, "You bought me a drink."

"Yes."

"After I just told you I'm not drinking."

I nodded.

"How sad." She thought for a moment. "What's your sign?"

"Aries."

"All the Aries I know are rapists." She drained the rest of her beer, then stared at me expectantly, like: "So, what are you going to do about that?"

An hour later, we were back at her house, trying to be quiet in the way people with roommates are always failing to be quiet, and she said she didn't fuck on a first date while I undressed her.

She whispered, "Oops."

Nude, Darcy's body seemed to glow, not brightly, but from sorrow. Her slumped posture, the way she could hardly meet my eye, was an aphrodisiac for me. She was tiny and fragile and seemed relieved to know what was about to happen, and at the same time disappointed that this was happening again.

"Boys are awful," she said. A moment later she said, "Because they never know how to make me come."

That was a challenge. I held her arms behind her back. Both wrists fit in one of my hands. She responded by relaxing into full relief at a stranger having understood her.

We had another date, which consisted of her showing up at my place. I was poor, and couldn't take her out to dinner. She was unemployed and she had time on her hands. She drove a rust-colored diesel Peugeot the size of a fishing boat. She carried in her chaotic rice-sack-and-sisal purse a videotape which she demanded we watch, *Betty Blue*. It was her favorite movie, she said, and she tried to watch some of it every day. It was a French film about a crazy woman who needed to fuck a lot. After we walked back downstairs, she shoved me against my garage, bit me, said, "I hate you," and drove off.

She kept insisting we'd met at Rose Street. But when she described the place, it felt like a perversion of what I'd thought of it. To her, it was just another group of people who thought highly of themselves and their relationships. After I tried to insist that no, it was a place where people actually were a little larger-than-life, she said, "I kissed Vincent." And this was before Hannah had even left, she said. While Vincent was insisting he had some kind of moral backbone, she continued, he was making out secretly with girls. She said it triumphantly, like she was pointing out roaches in a diner I'd loved. Also: maybe it was a lie.

She was dating a few other people now, but she'd—well, she hadn't really broken up with them so much as started to ignore their phone calls. The last was a man named Erik. "He tries to keep up but he's not on my level."

"What does that mean?"

"He believes everything I tell him."

On the third date, she and I were grinding, clothed, on my futon, and she said, "I have to tell you my rule. If you fuck me three times you have to marry me."

I found this amusing.

Afterward, she said, "Oops."

Darcy said, "You realize I'm bad, don't you?"

"You're not bad."

She smiled patiently. "I'm pretty bad. I'm really mean sometimes but I'm lucky, and at least I always have people to talk to in airports."

When she was on the phone, she sometimes opened the dictionary and tried to use words from that page in conversation to see if the person noticed she kept using words beginning with "ro—".

She asked to read my stories while I made dinner. I walked back into the bedroom to ask her something. Her jeans were undone, and she was masturbating while reading. As if waking up from a daydream, she said, "Oh, hi." She explained, "When I look at art I get excited erotically. It's like making a new friend. That's how I feel when I'm reading your stories." As we ate dinner, she kept coming back to the stories, with approval. But she warned I had a big ego. "Not that you think you're great. It has to do with taking up space. You take up a lot of space. You need help with that."

She wanted to see old pictures of me. I did that unveiling of my life, without actually feeling much. Here's when we were rich. Here's me in San Francisco. Here's me at Thacher. Here's my mother, who has become someone I don't know how to deal with. This is Lindsay, whom I'd loved.

"Tell me about Hans," I said, and she ignored me.

She went back to an old photo taken in my childhood bedroom. Me, my mother, and an infant whom I didn't recognize.

"That's me," Darcy said. I laughed, but she was shaking her head at me like I'd just let her down. "No, seriously, that's me." She wasn't talking about the baby. Instead, she pointed at the wall of my bedroom, the collage of posters from the Balboa Island hippie emporium.

My mother had cut them up so that, for instance, the bassist from the Banana Splits, all Day-Glo cartoon, was superimposed over a Denison's Chili advertisement. And right behind my bed, there was Dennis Hopper on his motorcycle, with balloons now behind him. Very small, and actually impossible to see in the photograph, was a child's hand reaching for the balloons. And yet Darcy had seen it.

"There," Darcy said. "That's my hand."

Her parents had a poster company back when she was a kid. One of the posters was her and her brother and a huge array of balloons. And there it was, behind me in the photograph. As a child I'd unknowingly fallen asleep every night with a little piece of Darcy in my room.

It could be magic. I wasn't sure about things like that.

I was waiting for her to calm down. She was capable of having long, complicated, normal conversations with strangers, but the things she said to me were becoming like a series of tests with multiple choice answers, any of which could suddenly be wrong, and it was like the testing agency was run by magpies.

"What do you think?" she asked once.

"About?"

"Uh-huh."

"About what?"

"Uh-huh."

"No, about what?"

"Uh-huh."

"What do I think about what?"

She nodded. Not only did she want an answer, but she wouldn't answer my question or tell me what her question was.

Finally, she said, as if this answered anything, "It depends."

"On?"

"It depends."

"In the sense of what? Sometimes but not other times?"

"Is that what 'it depends' means?"

I stared at her with a sickly feeling of antagonism. The charm of her forty-five-degree answers had worn off and I'd woken up in the middle of a game I didn't particularly like. "One day you're not going to answer me and it'll be over."

"I guess it's over," she said, and was up and out of bed. She was out the door with a slam that made the air in the room pucker. I heard her car drive away.

Maybe five minutes later, I heard her car driving back. She ran up the stairs, threw her bag on the floor, and said, "You don't love me." She stripped off her clothes, and while she was on top of me, with each downstroke of her hips, she chanted, "He doesn't even love me, he doesn't even love me," until she came.

It's hard for me to account for what my response was to any of this. "Two parts Holly Golightly, one part strychnine," I said, often, like that explained anything. I felt pretty much nothing at any given time, except in rare moments where it penetrated through the layers of bark that had grown over me.

Once, my mother called while Darcy was there, studying me quietly. After I hung up, Darcy said it was like I'd left the room. It made her sad to think I was doing something that flattened me out. She herself had a great relationship with her parents. She seemed to talk to everyone in her family at least once a day. She asked her mother for advice, she and her sister called to triangulate the advice they'd gotten from their mother. Her father was hilarious and loving and a bully whose approval I could see her embracing.

She wondered why we never visited my mother. I started explaining by asking Darcy how her childhood was. All I got at first was a slow shake of her head. Her mouth was like a line segment.

"Sharing stories isn't something you trade back and forth," she said. "Most people do, but not you," she said. "You bleed people for information, analyzing them until there's nothing left."

"That's not what I do."

"It's exactly what you do."

Did she know something I didn't? I didn't trust my mother, but this was a new person to recount evidence to, and perhaps come up with a new conclusion. I told her about the bonds I'd signed over to my mother that she'd never repaid. I knew the money wasn't important, but at least I knew how to count it.

I told Darcy about Daniel eating Lindsay's Valentine candy. She said, "Of course he was a junkie. Junkies love candy. Everyone knows that. It's not like Lindsay was an oracle or something. You still love her."

"The story's not about Lindsay."

"Every story is about Lindsay."

My fingertips were like plastic when I touched Darcy. I never read her mind. For a brief period I'd thought I knew how my life was going to go, and now I didn't. When Darcy said something awful, I took it as a challenge to actually *feel*. My depression was now a part of me as much as my crooked nose and my urge to write. It was a part that Darcy couldn't touch. I read a line in a book about Picasso at eighty, "His face had lost the capacity for joy," and I felt that described me, like a medal pinned to my chest.

I wondered what it was like to be angry. I tentatively tried yelling at Darcy now, as it seemed to me that even a reasonable person would get angry at her sometimes. As I yelled whatever it was, I was thinking, "This is what yelling is like and it's awful."

The effect on her was immediate. She apologized. She became docile. There was a hot, simmering silence between us, just as unfinished and sickly as the yelling had been. What was it like to feel a revelation? Did anger lead anywhere?

I told her how Daniel and my mother had met. The eviction, the scummy part of town, the mattress. Her letting him smoke crack while they drove. And then I waited.

"Oh, come on," Darcy said. "Lindsay would have done the same thing."

"What?"

"That 'Oh, I'm so psychic, we have a connection, we're so mysterious' bitch would have sucked their dicks, too, and you know it." The look that came with this was angry and dry-eyed.

After a few seconds ticked by, I said something. I said, "I love you."

She said, "Why?"

It was actually a great question. I don't think anyone had ever said anything so mean to me. What she'd said was from a place in the spectrum so far past "bitchy" and into the ultraviolet of nihilism that I don't think we have a word for it. But I *felt* something. It was like a signal from a galaxy so far away it was only theorized about, but it was an actual feeling, and so I loved her.

. . .

My job summarizing depositions was drying up. I was being replaced by software. I kept telling interviewers of the future that no matter how bleak my current situation was, I had faith in myself as a writer, so much faith that I never made fallback plans, like getting a reliable job. This was a bad idea.

I won a local fiction contest. (Darcy raced to my house upon hearing the news, took off her clothes, and cried out, "You're my James Joyce," which made me love her more.) There was nothing phenomenal in my progression—I'd been getting a little bit better every time I sat down to write. But agents still didn't like any of the novels (I'd finished three of them) I was sending out. I was still in a hole. I needed money.

I worried that the story I'd published might have been a fluke. I asked Darcy, "What if this is the end for me?"

She hugged me. "Baby, this isn't even the beginning."

Part of me wants this thought to linger: alongside her abrasiveness, Darcy was supportive and often loving. I'd like to say there was a reason why I stayed for four years, and I'd say "it wasn't so bad." But that would echo intolerably. It reminded me of my mother crying to me over the phone not to judge Daniel, that there were good times, I had to believe there were good times, didn't I believe her?

THE UNDERTOAD

HERE IS THE PHONE RINGING. It could happen anytime. I was frightened by the sound, because I never knew what was going to happen if my mother was calling.

Mom once said that she and Daniel were driving down to Oakland, and they would come see me and Darcy. I told her no. I told her that Daniel was not welcome at my house. She was startled, and she said that I was being unfair, and I said that might be true, but I felt unsafe. She couldn't understand why. I explained that she said he wanted to kill me. She said that he was just feeling threatened. I told her I felt threatened sometimes but managed to not say I wanted to kill anyone. She paused for a good, long time, maybe a minute of silence on the phone, and said she wouldn't be speaking to me again anytime soon, and she hung up.

Then she called a month later as if nothing had happened. And called again and again. Sometimes she asked about my writing. Sometimes she said she and I would both write great books about our lives, a mother and son, writing. She was proud of me for continuing to write even if I needed to get a desk job. "When we come down," she would say, and I would say, "Mom, I'll see you but not Daniel," and she would ask me why, and then the conversation would go the way I've said, and she wouldn't call for a week or a month.

Sometimes she would try a different tack. I would receive parcels. Candy. A wicker scoop used for fishing in ponds. Part of a gum ball machine. Books. A brick of cheese that had been cut open and resealed with duct tape. The ruffled shirts and polyester suits from a short, fat, dead man's storage locker.

"When we get on our feet, you should come visit," Mom said. They lived in and around Las Vegas, then Oregon, I think in San Diego again, and definitely near Sacramento, sometimes in rentals, sometimes in shady arrangements I didn't ask for details on. For some weeks they lived in what I think was a survivalist's compound in the desert, leaving abruptly. My mother sent me the first few pages of a short story about it that foreshadowed an appalling event, but the story was unfinished.

I'll never know what happened between them on a daily basis. My mother lied to me. I don't know how much. When they were anyplace for more than a week or two, her descriptions of the places became more enchanted and perfumed. Come stay on a cot, she said, or there was a sleeping bag for me, or a bed for me and Darcy, or they were saving for a deposit so we could have a room for ourselves. Daniel would get a catering job or cook at a restaurant until his meth use got him fired.

My mother told me it wasn't his fault. He'd grown up unloved. His mother was irresponsible and cold, flinty, and self-centered.

Darcy nodded when she heard that. "Daniel is your mother's good son," she said.

That was incisive. He was a compulsive gambler at bingo and the state lottery, using my mother's money, then his, to buy fifty Scratcher tickets at a time. He called her a fucking bitch. He was the good son.

I was completely out of money. On the first of the month, July 1992, I paid half my rent and, lying to my landlord, promised to have the rest by the fifteenth. I had no prospects.

I applied at a temp agency, which turned out to be problematic. My hair was unruly and long, which meant I needed a haircut, but my motorcycle was also out of gas. Luckily, the couch I'd bought at a thrift store turned out to have a couple of dollars in change under the cushions, but that was everything I had. I put some gel in my hair and a dollar's worth of gas into my tank, and rode to the agency.

The test showed I typed seventy words a minute, and because one method of procrastination for me was to delve into the guts of MS Word to see what strange features might make my manuscripts look interesting, I was an "advanced word processor." But I knew nothing about spreadsheets and my suit had come from a thrift store, so the agency pondered sending me only to places where "professional attire" wasn't required.

If I could go to work somewhere that day, I would have a small paycheck by the weekend, which I would put toward my rent. They ran a credit check on me, to see if I could be bonded, and found a note from the Internal Revenue Service. Apparently when I had worked as a short order cook in Las Vegas, I hadn't paid taxes on my income.

The woman reported this to me, and looked up to see if I had an explanation. People had good explanations all the time.

"I've never worked in Las Vegas."

"It's right here."

I looked. There it was, my Social Security number, right next to Daniel's name. He had used my card, which he'd apparently stolen the same day he'd eaten Lindsay's Valentine's candy, to defraud the government of some income tax.

When you don't know what a normal parent is, you tend to not react within the range of behavior that, say, a potential employer would recognize. So I was naive when I said, as if this was a reasonable explanation, "That's my mother's boyfriend."

The woman blinked at me. "Pardon?"

I kept going. I said he was a junkie, they probably lived in their bus then, and I'd never visited them even though my mom wanted us to pretend we were a family. I can't tell you why I talked so much. This wasn't just naive now—it was information that no one would ever professionally need to know.

But another thing about how I grew up is that I frequently find I'm not alone. The woman said, "I have a mom like that." She gave me the address of a place that needed help that afternoon.

I did well enough there to get hired at another place, and then another. It wasn't much, but this is how I started getting a regular paycheck.

· · ·

Darcy and I moved in together. I was hoping my friends would talk me out of it. They didn't.

She wanted to work in film. She immediately got a series of local production assistant jobs on Bay Area shoots. She turned out to be fantastic at coordinating complex projects. She never forgot a task or dawdled when dawdling was forbidden. She worked twelve or sixteen hours easily and her weird and angular sense of humor made her fit in. Every job recommended her for the next shoot. At cast parties, the more approachable stars told me I was lucky to have her. She said, "The right people trust me and the rest are frightened."

She was the first person I was close to who was different privately than in public. The closer you were to Darcy, the meaner she was.

I have problems with anger, I thought. *I'm learning by being with her. This anger is good for me.*

I retired the first three novels I had in circulation with agents, as the pages of the manuscripts were too dirty, advertising how often they'd been sent out. I started writing a new book. I'd read a few recent first novels by men my age who were either better writers than I was, or luckier and better connected, that had been published to acclaim. Maybe it was just a coincidence, but each of them had the same sneaky way of letting us know how sensitive his protagonist was: his mother had died. This enraged me. I started writing a novel called *My Dead Mom*.

It was about a bad writer named Glen David Gold who is struck mute when hit by a lightning bolt that also kills his mother. I couldn't tell if it was good, but as I wrote, it started generating its own gravity and rules. I had ideas that made me laugh about what was going to happen in ten or twenty or a hundred pages.

At the time, my mother and Daniel were living in a cabin near the Sierra foothills. Daniel's drug habit had gotten out of hand. He was violent and he was stealing money from her. She made a series of phone calls to me over a couple of weeks, whispered, hand over the receiver. She'd stood up to him. He'd left her. He came back, promising to get clean.

I couldn't keep up with the shifts in her situation, but I know how it ended. He seems to have had a break from reality and, isolated in that cabin, finally tried to kill my mother. She called the cops. Daniel pulled a knife on them.

My mother called me late that night, frantic, telling me the story in full as I was lying in bed, staring at the ceiling. She was horrified, out-raged, in a panic she needed me to understand. I was detached, listening to a soap opera update and hoping the story would end with the cops killing him.

Unfortunately, they showed restraint, disarming Daniel and sending him to a mental hospital. Mom continued to tell me of Daniel's journey into the hospital with the same breathless panic, there were guards, he was being arrested, and I realized that this was the horror she needed to communicate, not the assault, but that Daniel had been taken away from her.

My mother moved into a women's shelter, took a job assembling TV dinner trays, and later lived with a woman whose children were trying to have her declared incompetent so they would inherit their share of their father's estate.

Mom had a therapist. She hadn't had a therapist in years. She told him—and then told me she'd told him—that one of her main problems was that I didn't like Daniel. The therapist asked what was at the root of that. She said, "Glen doesn't like Daniel because he ate some of his girlfriend's Valentine's candy."

If there was still a rhetorician in me, a smug one that wanted to pin my mother's wings to the page above a Latin appellation, I'd end that story right there. It would be a cruel story, and I could dust my hands together like a villain. Her story continues, though. The therapist said, "If I were your son, I'd hate Daniel, too."

My mother told me this and didn't pause after finishing it, as this was her proof the therapist was against her. This, she explained, angry now at the world, and me, and feeling righteous, was why she was leaving the shelter and returning to Daniel.

The chronology, never easy to follow, tangles here to impenetrability. Daniel left the hospital, reunited with my mother, they quarreled again, he fled to San Diego on a drug binge. She took him in again, he promised to give up drugs, he returned to the hospital, where he was put on complete disability. The government would pay Daniel six hundred dollars a month, plus all of his medical bills.

During the physical, the doctors discovered Daniel was HIV positive.

This was a death sentence. For him, but not my mother, apparently—she said that they had stopped the physical part of their relationship some time before.

I began to feel relief, but it was clouded over by wondering how much damage Daniel could do before his life ended. My mother was too canny to ask me to come up, or to say they would visit again. Instead, over a few weeks, she dropped broad hints about how much Daniel had changed since he'd given up the meth. He was motivated, he worked hard. She no longer had to hide her purse. What she was actually saying: these were his final days and she saw a sunset in which everyone would be friends.

I finished my manuscript. I had however burned out my circle of friends, who had read multiple drafts of my first three not particularly good novels.

A friend knew a literary agent and got him to agree to read *My Dead Mom*. A couple of days later, my phone rang. The agent had just started reading it. He thought it was brilliant. He asked if we could meet at the end of the week. I said, *Sure, sure, of course,* and agreed to the time and place he suggested. I'd been down similar roads before so I tried not to get my hopes up, even as I still got my hopes up.

The night before our meeting, he called again. "I finished reading your book," he said slowly. "But I still want to meet with you." This reset my expectations.

In person, he was caffeinated and trim and quick with verbal jabs. When he figured out that I could take criticism, he took my manuscript from his satchel, and he put it into three piles, the first forty pages, the next seventy, and the final two hundred. He brought his palm down on each of them in quick order, and said, "Great, Good, Crap. What happened?"

This was the nicest thing anyone had said about my work in months. He explained that I'd begun a great plot line, but I'd gotten in the way of it. I was too goddamn clever. I abandoned my setup to show off. Had I thought about applying to writing programs? Iowa? UC Irvine? Use the first forty pages of *My Dead Mom* for my application. He said they were good enough to show my promise and flawed enough to show I could learn something.

He asked me how old I was.

"Thirty."

"Ah, congratulations."

"Why?"

"You wanted to write the great American novel before you were thirty. You failed. You're free," he said.

THE PUT-DOWN ARTIST

A FEW DAYS AFTER DARCY'S BIRTHDAY, a package showed up, a crate of mandarin oranges from my mom. Some of them were molding, but many weren't. Darcy thought it was a nice gesture.

I called Mom to thank her. She told me about Daniel's new meds and how happy he was to see a mental health film about manic depression because it labeled him so accurately. He was on antipsychotics, anti-allergy pills, and AZT, and no one knew what the interactions would do. A month later, he couldn't get out of bed, but then he could, and he was doing well. A month after that, his legs were paralyzed and there was some kind of mass growing in his intestines. He was supposed to die at any minute. He stopped taking his meds and he felt better.

Another month went by. The doctors said he had terminal cancer but then a month later they weren't sure. He seemed to be getting better. He was off drugs. Mom said he was a different person, or rather he was the person he should have been, the bright and kind one who had surfaced from underneath all the drugs.

I wasn't interested in seeing him, still. But I had a nagging thought that maybe I wasn't giving him credit. People did redeem themselves. When I compared my mother and Daniel to me and Darcy, they did seem like the happier couple.

They had a setup that sounded as if it suited them well. My mother had taken a job managing a mini-storage. Daniel was wheeling and dealing at the local swap meet. They took over the lien sales held when mini-storage customers failed to pay their bills. Daniel was a born auctioneer, and the townspeople loved talking to my mother, whose accent lent the operation a touch of class.

They had a secondhand place stocked with items from the mini-storage or local estate sales or Sunday swap meets. They lived in a trailer that was cluttered and cozy and that had a garden in back where they'd planted tomatoes. Daniel bought and sold furniture. He fixed up the house, played bingo in church, and had started panning for gold. He had a society of other gold panners and Big Spin fans to trade theories of luck with.

He started collecting interesting rocks that he found on his long walks in the countryside. My mother bought him modeling paints. He painted funny faces on the ones with the most evocative shapes. On my thirtieth birthday, I received two rocks, one painted like a wolf and the other like a medicine man.

I also received an audiotape called "Missy Sings Happy Birthday." Daniel had rescued a shaggy, squat orange dog I thought looked like a Butterball turkey. He and my mother knew nothing of her past except that whenever they opened a newspaper, Missy tried to hide. Missy tolerated my mother, barked at everyone else, and focused her attention on Daniel as if he were the sun. He fed her meat from his plate and every night after dinner, he said, "Missy, where's your dolly?" And Missy would bring him a little doll, and they would play catch. Daniel loved to sing, and when Missy heard him, she tried to sing along. Hence the birthday tape.

I hated the dog. Violently. I made fun of how she looked, only I called her "it." Every photograph I received, every anecdote I heard just focused my hatred. It was an ugly dog. It barked. They couldn't even come up with a name that different than the kitten Daniel had probably strangled. It was a little like thunderheads finally breaching when I thought, "This dog doesn't prove a fucking thing." Then I realized it wasn't the dog's fault. I wasn't being fair.

In summer 1994, I relented and agreed to visit. Darcy and I drove to their town, four or five parched blocks sliced by the freeway an hour past Sacramento. When we pulled up, Mom ran to a banner she'd hung, "Welcome Glen and Darcy," and we took turns posing in front of it.

We had a tour, my mother showing us their setup with pride and overt fear that I might not approve. Here was the mini-storage, here a typical unit. A tour of the trailer, the garden I'd heard so much about, staked tomato plants ripe in the sun. And gifts for me, books Mom thought I might like. Clothing she hoped Darcy would find worthwhile.

She introduced us to her boss, who told us what a fine woman she was. Then the firemen, the owners of the deli, the bookstore, the antique store. When people drove by in pickup trucks, she waved them down to introduce them to me, her son, Glen, the writer, here's Darcy, his girlfriend, she's involved in film.

At a certain moment, Mom took Darcy somewhere to show her something that didn't actually matter. Daniel and I had some time alone. He told me how happy my mother looked today. He talked about how the cure for AIDS was coming. He showed me the lottery ticket he'd bought that said "spin-spin-spin," meaning he'd get to be on TV and might get a chance to spin the big wheel for millions. "If anyone's gonna win the Big Spin, it's me. I've got that kind of luck."

He was sober. He was chatty but not in his old drugged, hostile way. He loped through words and sentences and paragraphs in a monotone, slurring through details to get to the punch line about what good deals he'd gotten or how much he loved my mother. Love is the Answer. I can't claim I liked him but I could at least start to see him. He did love my mother. He was trying to be better.

"All that speed, that was me trying to self-medicate. The first time I took what the doctors gave me for the bipolar, I could understand people for the first time, like everything in my brain slowed down enough to make sense."

When exactly fifteen minutes had passed, my mother reappeared with Darcy. We all stood outside the trailer, my mother pointing out the unusual things Daniel had brought to decorate. Daniel said, "I keep telling her, 'Babe, with me every day is Christmas.' I told her that when we met. She didn't believe me."

This reminded me. I'd brought a gift. I gave him a tiny geode I'd bought for his rock collection. He looked at it with interest. Then he tossed it over his shoulder. It bounced into the gravel. "Yeah," he said, "thanks, but I don't collect those anymore."

The next day my mother wanted to go for a drive in the countryside. Because it was so hot, we stopped for drinks every hour or so at a gas station, where Daniel would each time buy a fistful of lottery tickets. He wanted to pan for gold. As my mother drove along the blacktop, Daniel turned backward, cigarette in hand, to tell me stories of friends who had struck it rich. One of them had some family heirlooms he would never sell, but Daniel thought this was a lie, because he was "really, really Jewish." He knew to the ounce the weight of the major nuggets dug out of the hills, and as he continued to talk, repeating whole phrases, whole paragraphs, whole speeches, whole statements of how the world was and how it should be, how he was going to win and win big, I stopped being able to follow what he was saying.

My mother had been maintaining a fiction, that Daniel, off drugs, was a different person than Daniel on drugs. But there, in the car, cigarette smoke stinging my eyes, I was feeling the effort of pretending he'd become normal.

Daniel was focusing his flat brown eyes on me, and it was like someone had adjusted the knob on a radio, and the signal was coming in clear: he was angry. "You have this way of staring at people. It makes 'em seem stupid."

This hung in the air. I couldn't remember what he'd been saying before. My mother drove. I didn't dare break eye contact with Daniel.

"It's like you're trying to intimidate people, like you think you're smarter than them. You make people feel stupid."

His fists were balled on the backrest. I thought of all the times he'd beaten guys up, or been beaten himself. He laid into me, repeating himself until something else caught his attention—another gas station with lottery tickets, something—and he forgot about me.

An hour later, we were walking on the banks of a broad, slow-moving river. Chest-high weeds burned brown were on either side of the path and insects made a humming sound like electricity. Daniel was telling the funniest joke he knew. It was about an old black couple packing for their second honeymoon, and Daniel did all the voices, in all octaves from deep bass sharecropper to shrieking pickaninny. The joke ended, and the punch line was so nightmarishly racist I had no response. Daniel said, "You want to be a writer, right?"

"Yeah."

"You want to write screenplays?"

"Sure."

"I've got a screenplay idea for you."

My mother lodged a feeble protest. She knew what was coming. If she has seemed absent, I've captured it just right. Weeks later, when I told her I wasn't visiting again, I said, "Daniel is dangerous, Mom. He was going to hit me when he said I made him feel stupid."

"He was just feeling threatened."

"He's still a religious fanatic."

"What do you mean?"

"When he talked about hell?"

"I don't remember that."

We were pushing through weeds, back toward the car, as Daniel told me the greatest screenplay ever written would be about an angel who blows one note on a trumpet, and it knocks down a house. Just one note, so loud it makes all the houses of the world cave in. It's Gabriel's trumpet and it means the end of the world is coming and Jesus will return to the earth and all the sinners will go to hell and paradise will come. Revelation was Daniel's favorite book of the Bible. He hadn't read it but knew what was in it.

He said he'd fasted when he was a tour guide at the Grand Canyon. He'd fasted to have religious experiences and he had fasted so long he had seen hell. "I saw the lake of fire. I saw hell, I really did! It wasn't just a vision, it was the truth, God showed it to me! You know what they have in hell? I saw it! In one place there's one guy just punching another guy in the face over and over again"—he smashed one fist into his open palm, *bam bam bam*—"just beating him for all of eternity! And that's not the worst part of it."

There was no way to stop him. He was too excited, he was on a topic he knew more about than we did, and with the weeds so tall, the day so hot, the cigarette smell so choking, I felt claustrophobic as he continued.

"The worst part is for perverts. I saw it. There's a place God showed me for the perverts, where one guy buttfucks another guy"—here he put his hands out as if gripping a saddle, and he thrust his hips back and forth—"for eternity. One guy buttfucking another forever, for all of eternity."

A couple of hours later, in the late afternoon, we were back at the mini-storage. Daniel's mood had blackened since the drive. He chain-smoked now, every gesture with his cigarette *furious*. He was ignoring Darcy. He was telling me the same stories for the second, or the third, or the fourth time, but he seemed to be squinting more while he talked, eyes searching my face. I had taken stock of all that he said, and all that he was, and found it lacking. He talked as if his best stories could make me see the real him, the one that was worthwhile, if only I took another look. And then when the stories came around the last time, they did so with force, a list of all the things I had ignored. They were his complaint against me.

I gave our regrets. We had to leave. I blamed allergies and no one was fooled. What did I feel inside? Nothing.

Before we left, Daniel wanted me to help him with an errand. He had to carry a table from the mini-storage to the antique store owned by an old woman nearby. It would take five minutes. Now I started to feel something creeping up. I was afraid to be alone with him again.

He and I walked to the mini-storage together. I was quiet. He told me he didn't believe I had allergies, that sickness was all in the mind. He said that when I was little I'd soiled myself and that when I'd learned to speak, I'd told my mother her brain was slow. "You're a real put-down artist, aren't you," he said, and I knew my mother had shared this with him, a story between lovers. I was their enemy in common.

A glass tabletop, thick and heavy, was stored under blankets. We picked it up together and carried it out of storage, down a flight of stairs outside, and we crossed the street with it, bringing it up a wooden walkway that led to the antique store. The store was three or four rooms packed with furniture, shelves of Depression glass, stacks of *Collier's* magazines and sheet music, walls of framed landscape prints. The proprietress, about seventy-five years old, sat in an easy chair that had long ago molded to her shape. Daniel knew where she wanted the table, and after we set it down, I dusted off my hands, ready to leave.

"Before you go, say hello to Dennis," Daniel said. He pointed to a doorway leading to another room.

I had no idea who Dennis was. There was a sign over the doorway, "Dennis's Room," and I could hear odd noises, like applause, and I heard a quick chirp or two as if in response. I wondered if Dennis was a bird.

Beyond the doorway was another room of antiques and bargains, and in the center was a hospital bed, and next to the bed was a television tuned to an afternoon talk show. Dennis was in the bed, positioned to see the TV and any visitors who came in. He was so deformed it was hard to tell where the different parts of his body were. My impression was of a misshapen head, almost hairless, eyes unfocused, and a lump of a body concealed by pajamas with cowboys on them. His arms were like broken twigs, shiny and dark in places like cooked chicken.

A hand-lettered sign next to the bed read, "Hi, My Name Is Dennis and I Like Visitors." It went on to list his favorite programs (*Wheel of Fortune* and *The Price Is Right*) and said that although he was probably blind and deaf (no one really knew), you should always come in and say "Hi." I don't remember my reaction. I hope I at least said "Hi." But I was mostly dumbfounded. Who expects to find this when browsing for antiques? I have a memory of his caretaker coming in and making me put my fingers into Dennis's moist fist and feeling his grip.

But that didn't happen. The memory is something my mind created. It's like a dream that I forced into being, a metaphor. Mother, the good broken son, and me.

A few weeks after our visit, Daniel began to lose weight. He had skin problems. Digestion problems. He was taking seventeen pills a day. At one point he was so constipated he could not walk. He had CAT scans, MRIs, blood tests, psychiatric workups, experimental therapies. He was not the crystal-wearing, positive-thinking, relaxing-technique kind of sick man. He chain-smoked. He ate meat and potatoes, drank two or three six-packs of Coca-Cola a day. He ran up over a hundred thousand dollars in medical bills.

My mother reported these developments in phone calls of waxing and waning dread, for no matter the prognosis, Daniel always recovered from whatever was about to kill him, the way a cartoon character gets up after being hit by an anvil. He was indestructible.

Darcy had progressed as far as she could in local film production. She wanted to move to Los Angeles with me. I reacted to this the way I did when she said she wanted to marry me, with enthusiastic statements that sounded almost exactly like agreement. We always argued after I agreed with her, and I told her she was unfair, et cetera. I was the same person I'd been with Noelle, only older and more depressed.

One of my caveats was brilliant. Moving to Los Angeles was automatically good for her career, but not necessarily mine. I'd written a script that had about as much ambiguous traction as my novels did— basically none—but the idea of being a screenwriter wasn't bad. Still, I didn't want to be yet another guy moving to Los Angeles in hopes of getting the attention of Tim Burton's personal trainer. I wanted to have a good reason to be there. I would move down if I was accepted into the UC Irvine Creative Writing MFA program. Darcy agreed—I should definitely apply, and I did, not emphasizing that roughly three hundred people applied every year for one of their six spaces.

I had a job at a nonprofit. It was a commune of PhDs with government grants. I was the worst kind of office staff, the unacknowledged writer with four novels in my desk drawer who answered phones with a "May I help you?" that made each of those four words sound like its own snap judgment. There was little work to do (we had multiple NIH contracts with overlapping sums designated for office support). My supervisor, a sweet and tiny French woman, self-published chapbooks of poetry. She sprayed one with lavender before giving me a copy, and every day, she asked if I'd yet been accepted to UC Irvine.

My many bosses were scared of me. When I look at photographs, I understand why. I was thirty-one, and I'd won one local fiction contest about two years beforehand. When my supervisor walked by and whispered, "I hope you're using our quiet time to work on your novels," it broke my heart a little. The troubles on my face read like confidence, and I think that to her I looked like someone who would succeed.

The phone rang one afternoon. It was Darcy. "You got in," she said. By this, she meant I'd gotten into UC Irvine. They'd called the house, and she'd talked to them. I asked her to repeat the conversation, which was pretty simple. They wanted to know if I'd come be a student there.

This didn't seem likely. I wasn't even excited, as I was sure there was a caveat. I'd had so many almost-but-not-quites from agents and editors that I asked her for their phone number. I called and asked the department secretary if I'd really gotten in, or if this was some kind of cruel hoax. She laughed and said that was the best response she'd heard yet.

We had a very brief conversation in which I said that of course I accepted, and she told me the names and locations of the students who had already confirmed. I wrote them down. Aimee Bender (Los Angeles). Phil Hay (Los Angeles). Alice Sebold (New York). Brando Skyhorse (Los Angeles).

After I got off the phone, I looked at the names. Long ago, I'd mythologized the potential in my friends at Thacher or the bookstore or Rose Street. I tried not to imbue those names with extra grace or lightning. But I put a star next to Alice Sebold's name. It looked special to me, like we might be friends, but I'd been burned before by believing such things. To cover up, I wrote beside it, "I think she wears Agnes B," which was a code to me—I liked agnès b. clothing. I also felt a mild disappointment and embarrassment, sorry to learn the program had fallen into such straits that they were admitting me.

CHRISTMAS

DANIEL HAD AN ANEURYSM and went into a coma. The doctors said that even if he survived, there had been so much brain damage that everything you'd call "consciousness" was wiped out, along with all chance of voluntary movement. At least, that's what they thought for now. They'd been wrong about him before.

The reports happened so rapidly I had trouble believing the situation was real. It didn't seem possible he could go from functioning to incapacitated with a snap of the fingers. I was fairly sure this was a false alarm. Still, I visited.

It was 106 degrees. The few streets in Mom's town were all deserted. I walked from the trailer to the general store to buy a soda. I saw, two streets away, the town minister—jeans, boots, straw hat—walking slowly toward the fire station. To pay the bills, he also did something for the railroad that involved standing by the tracks for hours with a walkie-talkie, waiting.

When we ran into each other, we said hello and then he took on a thousand-yard stare. He was going to tell me something instructive. Fixing me with watery blue eyes, he said he'd talked with Daniel many times. He said Daniel got riled up about the Book of Revelation, and he

used to tell him, "Easy, Daniel, easy." He said the whole town was praying for him, and he looked at me as if testing whether I believed him.

There were many awkward pauses in a conversation that couldn't
have lasted more than two minutes.

"God has a plan," the minister said to me. "It's not for us to question
it. He won't take Daniel one second too early or too late."

I do not have a poker face. It was obvious I was just tolerating this
sympathy, and that I held different opinions about God and Daniel.
So the minister told me a story. His own mother had Parkinson's disease and had been in a hospital bed for five years. For the last two, she
had been fed through a tube in her stomach. But God hadn't taken her
away yet.

I asked, "Does she know what's going on?"

"It's hard to say. She has Alzheimer's, too. But the important part is,
it's brought the rest of us much closer to God."

He said it sincerely, openly, and he waited for his story to soothe
me. When he realized I was not soothed, he poked his tongue into his
lower lip.

"Glen, are you a Christian?"

"Jew."

He jerked—literally jerked—like I'd given him an electric shock.
He'd thought he'd had me in a theological corner and now he didn't.
Then he recovered, slowly put on a grin and offered me his hand.

"Well," he said, "eventually, we'll both see what's what."

I walked up the dusty street. I was disturbed. Maybe Daniel's religion
meant he was truly struggling with being a good man. Coming the
opposite way was my mother's closest neighbor, a woman who had
steely eyes and a short, efficient way of laughing. I told her about the
minister's comments about praying.

She said, "Sure, a lot of us are praying for Daniel." She whispered,
"We're praying for him to die."

I was in the van with my mother. We were going to the hospital. Mom
was saying, "Part of this is difficult for me. The way Daniel ... what
brought it on ..." My mother sometimes revealed startling information

to me when she was driving. I knew when it was coming because of a shift in her expression. She looked at the road as if she were paying strict attention to something she would have to later describe to the authorities who guard eternity. Her diction, circumspect. I had already learned that when she was fishing for words, I wouldn't want to hear them.

"When I found him," she said.

"You don't have to tell me."

"He was lying on the bed."

"You don't have to tell me. I don't want to know."

She looked from the road to me and back. She didn't tell me.

Missy was moping around the trailer, or the store, waiting for a voice that never called her. No whistles or exhortations to sing. After dinner, my mother said, "Missy, where's your dolly?" and Missy looked at her as if wondering whether Mom thought she was an idiot or something.

In the emergency room waiting area, my mother talked about the last time she'd seen Daniel at the store. They'd fought. He had gone home. She knew something was wrong when Missy came back, acting strangely, so she went to the trailer and found him. She called the paramedics but she "fixed him up" first. They had led separate lives sexually since long before he tested positive . . . and she was grateful that he never put it in her face . . . he was always discreet . . . but this time . . . so, when she found him—

I stopped her.

Daniel's mother appeared. I have a vague memory of a small, determined woman with dyed black hair who seemed used to taking charge of chaotic situations. My mother disliked her because she hadn't been there for Daniel through much of his life. Apparently she had only come now after learning that, should Daniel survive, SSI would pay thirty-five hundred dollars a month to a full-time caregiver. As a registered nurse, she would do well if the court awarded her custody.

He was in the intensive care ward. My mother, Daniel's mother, and

I went to the foot of his bed, where he lay nude under a sheet that covered him to his navel. His hair had been shaven by his right temple and a cone-shaped monitor had been inserted under his scalp, wires running to a machine by his side. There were electrodes on his chest, on either side of an amateur Playboy bunny tattoo.

He didn't look asleep. His face was straining, as if he had become paralyzed mid-flinch. Because I felt embarrassed to look at him, I looked away. There was a mirror by him, under which my mother had put a dozen PayDay candy bars, his favorite. She had taped to the mirror a piece of paper that read "Love is the Answer."

I looked at the machines. One breathed for him fourteen times a minute. Another monitored heart and brain activity. There were three IV bags, with potassium, saline, and morphine. A bag at the end of the bed was half-filled with urine.

My mother and his mother were talking to him. It was a strange competition between them. Who could make him come back? I read his charts. I couldn't find where it said he was HIV positive. I looked straight at him. I tried to feel glad that he was almost dead, but all I could feel was a cheated kind of emptiness. His head was lolling, his legs were braced in some unnatural position, frequently changed to keep the blood from pooling. His penis was outlined in a hump under the sheet. His privacy had already died.

Because Daniel's mother was a nurse, she knew how to make him do something eerie.

"Daniel. Daniel? Daniel? Daniel!" When she got it just right, demanding an answer, his brain monitor started pumping out square waves and he jerked and his eyes opened. Spasmodic twitching in his arms; then he flopped back onto the bed.

His eyes had met mine. I had seen him see me.

My mother, unnerved and now insecure, announced that when she had brought him a small, stuffed dog and told him it was Missy, he had done the same thing.

This disturbed me. "I thought his arms and legs were paralyzed."

"He might recover," his mother said.

I was horrified. If there was any chance for Daniel to come back, he would. He would make a partial recovery and my mother would fight tooth and claw to be his full-time nurse for the next twenty years.

Daniel's mother said we should all talk to him, to bring him out of the coma. She lectured him in a nurse's voice, telling him to be a good boy and that she loved him. Then my mother took over, telling him Missy was here and needed someone to play with her dolly. The store needed to open. He'd bought the winning lottery ticket. There was no response, and my mother looked like she was feeling inadequate.

They wanted me to talk to him. While they consulted with a doctor, I looked at the shaved part of his head, the tattoo, the clench to the brow that had only deepened when his mother called him back.

I said, "Daniel, you're going to live forever."

On the way back from the hospital, Mom stopped for ice cream, which we ate in the baking fall afternoon shadows. She brought up Daniel's terrible mother, then fell silent.

She asked me if she'd ever taught me to do certain things, bits of common sense and wisdom that she couldn't remember if she imparted. "Did I ever teach you to dry between your toes after you get out of the shower?"

"That explains the mushrooms," I said.

She looked puzzled.

"Between my toes."

She laughed. I did, too. I'm not sure we were laughing the same way but maybe we were.

A week after he went into his coma, Daniel was taken off his respirator. The doctors felt he wasn't strong enough to breathe on his own and that death would be almost instantaneous. Disconnecting the machine was a humanitarian gesture.

My mother called me to report with pride that Daniel immediately started breathing by himself. It was possible he would recover. One of my mother's neighbors called me to say it was the only thing the town was talking about. Why was this nice woman so in love with this awful man?

· · ·

At three o'clock one morning my mother woke up to see Daniel standing at the foot of the bed. He dissolved as she became fully awake. She called the hospital. He'd had a second aneurysm and a stroke, and had died.

She called me, sobbing her heart out. She kept telling me there had been good times, that she wouldn't have stayed if there weren't good times.

Later, she put out a flyer thanking the community for their help. She talked about how special Daniel was, and made sure to write *Love is the Answer*. It was a touching, heartfelt, effective piece of writing.

At the time, I was dismantling my life in Oakland. Darcy and I were looking at apartments in Long Beach, which was halfway between her potential jobs in Hollywood and mine in Irvine. Before we even started to pack, even when we were just having her family over for the first of many goodbyes, my eye would wander over our belongings and I would mentally separate out what was hers from what was mine. I envisioned the unpredictable impact of landing in a new city, and I wondered what could happen that would break us up.

I had watched a woman in love with a person who didn't deserve it, not even slightly, talk herself into staying because they were soul mates. It was something no one else could understand, by the exclusivity of love's design. To the end my mother believed she and Daniel had a psychic connection—that appearance at the end of the bed was no hallucination to her.

I had thought I'd loved in opposition to how my mom loved, and yet this was disturbingly familiar to me. Mom was so grief-stricken for weeks that I called my friend Norma to help her. Norma, a counselor for battered women, had been a prostitute and a heroin addict and had seen everything. Mom and Norma talked, and afterward, Norma called me back. My mother had told her I wasn't supportive, I looked down on her, she blamed me for deserting her. I can't say that was easy to hear, but it was by then an old story.

"Your mom was upset by something else. You didn't want to hear what Daniel was doing when he had his aneurysm."

"That's right."

"Well—she told me," Norma said.

I thought about this. "Not just masturbating, right?"

"No. There's more."

"And it's bad?"

Norma, who once bit a man's finger off when he was trying to kill her, had a metal plate in her head from when another guy caved in her skull. She said this was pretty bad.

Darcy was dying to know. She bet it had something to do with the dog. I put her on the phone with Norma. I went out on the balcony and listened to traffic. A few minutes later, Darcy came out, eyes wide. She asked me if I wanted to know what Norma had told her. I said no. For most of the night, she tried to bait me into asking. She couldn't believe I didn't want to know.

REVELATION

THE GHOST IN YOU

WHEN I WAS TWELVE, I went for the weekend to Lake Tahoe with my mother and some of her more responsible friends. A couple of the men and I took a bait bucket of crawdads into a small fishing boat just before dawn. We motored out onto the lake, and we cut the engine and we sat still in the darkness.

A few minutes later the sun was rising. It illuminated the sapphire blue of the lake, which is famous for its glass-flat tranquility. But then, not so far away, I saw multiple humps on the back of a fish that broke the surface. We all stared, because the displacement was so odd. The fish was leaving a wake. The wake got longer as something looking like a long slender back with fins rode upward. We were looking at something whose length was hard to understand.

It was just the current, my companions thought. They were accomplished fishermen, and they were a little puzzled by what they were seeing. And then a moment later, the humps appeared again, only more distinctly. We weren't looking just at water moving—within the shimmer of water was a row of darker, defined spines and then, flapping into the air, a tail. There was a thirty-foot animal near our ten-foot boat, but there was still some argument among the adults about it. Were we really seeing it? Or did we just want to see a mystery?

Then it dove under the surface, heading in our direction. The sun was high enough that I could see the blue water beneath us, and then something eel-like approaching. As it passed under us, I could see its form get thicker, then taper, and then it was gone.

The adults saw that, too. Over the course of the morning, we saw it once or twice more, sort of—one or the other of us pointed at a ripple or a wake but I can't swear something was still there.

I didn't believe in the Loch Ness Monster. As much as I wanted to believe in things that made the world a more magical place—ESP and ghosts, for instance—the evidence I'd read in my Fortean books seemed pretty cheesy, like Bigfoot, which I also didn't believe in. But we'd just seen something here that I couldn't explain.

Someone mentioned that since ancient times there had been stories of a lake monster here. Tahoe was deep and no one knew what was really at its bottom. Maybe it was an unknown dinosaur previously thought extinct. By the time we came back to land, I was bubbling over with excitement—I had to tell the folks who had slept in about this.

When I started talking I was betrayed immediately. The men who'd been with me smiled when asked to corroborate what I was saying. Well, they said, it was dark. And of course one of them had taken mushrooms the night before, so what had happened was, he'd seen something first and then convinced me I'd seen it. Also, I was looking for something to write about. Ha ha ha. Everyone now: Ha ha ha.

I came away from that angry. It hadn't happened that way. Some people didn't like to admit they'd seen something that made no sense. They needed to discount it. I came away with two facts: I didn't believe in lake monsters; I'd seen a lake monster. I now had the ability to believe two contrary things at once. That served me well. Also, I learned the lesson beyond that lesson, which is that people are frightened by what they know they've seen.

At the same time that Daniel was dying, I pitched an idea to a local newspaper for their Halloween issue. I would try a few different psychic activities and explain the results, no doubt comic, to their readers. I looked for ghosts, which flushed out charming stories from a hotel and a bookstore. I had a decades-old article from *Playboy* that I'd saved, folded many times, about how to astral project. It was a multistep process, and it would take at least several weeks to give it a good try, the article explained, so I had to be patient.

The first night I prepared for it by fasting after lunch. At bedtime I wore comfortably loose pajamas and I dozed off imagining myself floating several feet above my own body.

I was in a hotel room with Lindsay. We could not touch fast enough. I tore off her clothes, feeling the snap of her bra strap as I yanked it off her shoulder. It got nasty—I bent her over so her shoulders were to the bed, and noted how the skin and muscles on her back stretched. But also she was miserable. She wanted a fuck to fix it. I hesitated, and my rational brain kicked in, the rest unfolding with the same urgency as if I were watching a soap bubble drift toward a needle.

"Where have you gone?"

"Fuck me," she said.

"No." I said, "Where have you gone?"

She said, "I'm getting married. His name is Jack. He's a good man but I'm frightened. I'm making a mistake. Call me."

"If you're frightened, you call *me*. You have my number."

"Call me on a Thursday night. He's not home then."

"No. I won't rescue you. Call me."

"Please call me."

"You can call me on Thursday." And then, pop, I was awake.

My heart was pounding and I felt irritated and invaded. More than anything else, I was angry.

Thursday was long enough off that I had time to think. I told the story of that experience to everyone I knew except Darcy. I told my friends, male and female, I told people at work. I told the most rational, skeptical PhD at my job, and like everyone else she melted. "You have to call her."

"Why?"

"This is the most romantic thing I've ever heard—call her."

"I'm not sure it's real."

"All you described about what passed between you, and that doesn't seem real?"

"Well, I kind of believe two things at once," and I explained how I felt about lake monsters. "I might just be making this up. We wanted to feel special, and that connection might have just been two pretentious assholes agreeing on their imaginary worldview."

"Call her, Glen."

I didn't want to. It felt unfair. At some point I'd become the needy one in the relationship. I'd been the *benshi,* and I now knew that every time I'd tried to explain how she was feeling, I'd been depriving her of actually saying it. If I called it felt like I'd still be pursuing her. Lindsay could call me. If it was real, and not just my needy brain making something up.

That Thursday, Darcy wasn't home, so I had the place to myself. There was a time she'd been home every night, but we were drifting apart a bit, or she was just working late and I was pretending it meant we were drifting. I made dinner and I was aware at all moments of where the phone was. I tested it—I had a dial tone.

I turned on the stereo. I had three records to play. First, I put on the second movement of Vivaldi's Concerto in D Minor. I played it all the way through, recalling—or trying to recall—how I'd seen Lindsay centuries ago while hearing this for the first time. But it was like trying to will a match head alight. Then I put on "When Tomorrow Comes," and I thought about how she'd once promised to be here forever. It was hard not to feel pathetic. I started to put on "Cuyahoga," took it off, reconsidered, put it on. I played it once all the way through. I tried not to think too hard. The song ended, and "Hyena" began. I took it off, put it into its sleeve, filed the record away, and finished eating my dinner.

Six months later, I heard from friends that she was married to a man named Jack.

THE WHORE OF IRVINE

AFTER DANIEL DIED, the drama in my mother's life seemed to subside. She was sixty years old, and regardless of how closely she tended to skate toward the edge, she knew when to pull back. Her life became a little boring. She scraped by with the secondhand business. She didn't have Daniel's gift for making deals, but she wasn't bad at it. For a while she had her own billboard.

She dated, too. She told me she missed sex a little, so she went out with men, but nothing serious. One was a deadbeat dad. His son was born without a rectum. Another was in his eighties and dying of throat cancer. When Mom wished him a Merry Christmas, he burst into tears. Another man flew his own small plane, but she thought he was too much of a daredevil. On an evening she refused to go up with him, he crashed. He survived, running away from the plane, covered in gasoline, into downed power lines, and setting himself on fire. He lingered for weeks before he died.

But those were situations that she observed from a distance. Mom told me she was fine on her own. When men got too close, all she had to do was say Daniel had died of AIDS. She liked doing this. When a new dentist opened his office there, he asked my mother to be his first patient, free. She told him not to ruin his practice before it started.

She wasn't entirely alone, though. Missy liked how my mother cooked for her, pampered her, played with her doll. My mother had never owned a dog before, but soon they were inseparable. When they went to the park together, Mom teased her, crying, "Squirrel-y, Missy, where's the squirrel-y?" and Missy went crazy. They really were a good team.

Missy loved my mother. My mother loved Missy. Both of them loved Daniel but they were getting along okay. And that is where, if this were a film of her life, I would slowly close the iris, a sepia-tone vignette fading with a little grace into an ending for her. Her life wasn't over, but my part in it was, because I finally had an answer as to how I felt about my mother. Two different truths at once: I wished her well. I no longer loved her.

That happened in part because of Dr. Franklin D. Baum, MD. He has hovered invisibly over this story in that I was his patient in psychoanalysis from the age of four and a half until I was nine. He was a pioneer of child psychiatry. He had a kind, wide face with inquisitive eyes behind enormous black-framed glasses. He had the wavy chunk of white hair common to geniuses and philosophers. When I was a child there was a book on his shelf called *The Wolf Man* that I was disappointed to learn from him wasn't about a real wolf man.

I saw him four times a week (later three times a week) for reasons that do not entirely make sense. My parents had each been helped in their late twenties by psychiatry. I was, as I have described, a sensitive child. Insomnia, a weird imagination, encopresis, temper tantrums, getting bullied in school, rage, and a lot of churning anxiety. My parents regarded my brain like the control center of a nuclear reactor with some alarming dials and switches and they hoped Dr. Baum might have the operator's manual.

Those all sound like reasons for therapy, but they're only why I thought I was there. The real reason I was in psychoanalysis at the age of four and a half is that something was *wrong*. There was a tension in our house, invisible and dangerous, like a wire stretched across a hallway.

I benefited from those sessions, in that I liked knowing how a mind worked. At six and seven and eight years old, I talked to adults about the conflict I had between id and superego in a way that was disturbing but a little cute. I learned about repression and transference and projection, perhaps with more expertise than you'd think, because I had a partner to talk to. My mother was also Dr. Baum's patient. She went in the morning and I went in the afternoon.

Her therapy, I was told, was to help her deal with her migraines. Even at the time, my mother joked about this. She was a woman in Southern California with migraines and a therapist and a Mercedes and a house with a swimming pool. She was a type. It was ironic, she said, because that was so obviously not her.

Even at the time, I was suspicious of her therapy. I asked if they had candlelit breakfast sessions. When Dad took longer trips to Chicago, Dr. Baum asked me if I felt I had to be the man of the house with my father gone.

I said, "No, why, do you?"

"You have a way with zingers," Dr. Baum said to me.

This was how I learned about the Oedipus complex, and I was annoyed to learn that I was unnerved by their relationship because I secretly wanted to sleep with her.

I didn't resist this, because I had just recently found out there were bones in my hand. In other words, there were certain things common to all hands, including my own, and so there had to be things common to all psyches. If science insisted on it, and boxed me in by saying that to deny it was, well, denial, then I wouldn't deny it but embrace it. I asked him if I just admitted that my developing self wanted to sleep with my mother, would all those queasy-making feelings about him go away?

I didn't trust him. As my parents' marriage dissolved, my mother did what she called "breaking" with Dr. Baum, in anger at what she felt was manipulative behavior (he told her that if I ended therapy, I would become a drug addict). She stopped seeing him, I stopped seeing him, and shortly after, we moved to San Francisco.

For years I rarely thought of Dr. Baum. I had a vague feeling that therapy wasn't a real science. If I told someone that I'd been in psychoanalysis until I was nine years old, people assumed I misremembered, and if I added that my mother was also his patient, I was told I had to be wrong about that, too. It made no sense.

. . .

When my mother was living with me and Lindsay, I asked her about her odd choices, and she told me, as I have mentioned, of her terrible upbringing by a father who didn't want her, of the many ways the world treated her poorly.

"When your father was traveling, I took a lover," she said, and I knew who it was. "He opened me up as a woman," she continued, and I think she said more in that vein but everything after the involuntary visuals that accompanied "he opened me up as a woman" was lost in the resulting riptide of my stomach trying to turn itself inside out. As soon as I was able to hear more, my mother was saying that my father was inept, but this man gave her her first orgasm.

"It was Dr. Baum," I said.

"Oh, no," she said. "No, no, no." Startled I would even think that. And she named instead a friend of my father's whose marriage had been over in every way but actual divorce. "They were swingers," she explained. "Or I thought it was both of them. He was, at least. He gave me herpes," and then there was more again, but I heard it like the static you hear in between the frequencies of radio stations.

How I reacted to hearing all at once about her first orgasm, her herpes, and how she cheated on my father reminded me of World War I movie footage of a strong man showing how he could withstand being hit by cannon balls. I knew what his grimace meant as he was mouthing the silent words, "I'm fine."

Then, years later, I had a long conversation with a friend of hers whose relationship with her had fallen apart. She wanted me to know one thing specifically. "Your mother was never the same after her affair with that psychiatrist."

I interrupted her, "Which psychiatrist?" She'd known several, socially, in San Francisco.

"Her psychiatrist."

I couldn't remember if my mother had continued therapy in San Francisco. "Someone she knew?"

"The one in Newport Beach. Your psychiatrist. Whatever his name was."

I need to be specific here. After the conversation was over I lay down on the floor and I hissed: *You bastard, you bastard, you bastard,* so many times the syllables lost their literal meaning and became instead much older than myself, a chant maybe or a Greek tragedy's strophe, without translation. Then I wrote down everything I could remember of what she had said. My mother had absolutely, positively told her that she'd slept with Dr. Baum.

It should have been settled for me. My mother had slept with my psychiatrist—her psychiatrist. But I was reminded of how patting down a cowlick only works for so long, and before much time had passed it was like the hair was beginning to stand up again. My mother was lying. Either to me or to her old friend.

It could have stayed there, open-ended. You can make a life with unanswered questions.

During my second semester at UC Irvine, I enrolled in a memoir-writing class with Geoffrey Wolff, whose book *The Duke of Deception* unraveled the past of his con man father. Wolff encouraged us to go deep, and so one evening while my girlfriend took a shower, I wrote the beginning pages of this volume, and, as I've mentioned, I tried to throw them away.

After Alice told me to keep going, I wrote without much effort or emotion. I managed about ten thousand words. It read like I was presenting a diorama of horrors whose victims screamed through thick museum glass. But it was beautiful in a cold, mechanical way, so I was satisfied with it.

But I kept coming back to Alice's initial question: how did it make me feel? It annoyed me that I didn't know the answer.

Being a graduate student meant I was entitled to eight free therapy sessions with a graduate student in psychology, in my case a woman slightly younger than me. Carrie was fresh to her profession, smart, alert, and fascinated by why I was there.

I didn't come in presenting my question about the memoir. Instead, I explained that I wanted to talk about my heart. Was it a problem that I was in love?

I'm not sure Carrie had ever wondered if this could be a problem for someone, but I explained that I had once been in love with Darcy, and that had winked out instantly. And before that, I had been in love with Lindsay, and before that Melanie (I hadn't had time to fall in love with Jess or Cindy, but eventually I would have tried). And before that Noelle, and Heidi. Further, I went from relationship to relationship without a gap in between. And now I was in love with Alice. Was I setting myself up to repeat my old problems?

Carrie asked about how it had ended with Darcy. I explained that right after the first semester had started, she was walking down the staircase of my father's house, and she tripped. She was holding a bottle, and when she fell, she drove a piece of glass through the meat of her palm. At the emergency room we learned she had almost severed a tendon.

Darcy decided to convalesce back at her parents' house for a few weeks. This left me and Alice to start getting to know each other.

Carrie asked if it was like letting go of one hand, panicking, and then grabbing at another, which I thought was a smart and familiar question. I explained that no, I'd fallen out of love with Darcy long before, but was so terrified of her anger that I hadn't broken up with her. Without her around, it was like having white noise removed from my life. I could hear myself think again.

Then why was I with Alice, she asked.

I asked her if she'd ever noticed the piped-in music in Irvine? It seemed to come through invisible speakers, and you could barely hear it. Carrie wasn't sure if she had, so I explained.

Corona del Mar, where I'd grown up, was near Irvine. I knew some secrets about the place. Irvine was a planned community, and since it was planned in 1965, the idea behind every decision was to prevent riots and insurrection. So the campus and community were made to be containable, predictable, safe, and boring.

On my first day back in town since I'd left Setting Sun Drive twenty years before, I asked my classmates if they'd noticed you couldn't walk directly into any of the university's buildings—you had to go up or down stairs, and around corners, and all the windows were slits, to deter rioters from storming the buildings. The design had worked better than they could have imagined in that the students here were famous for being docile. They were the children of Asian immigrants, born-again Christians whose most rebellious streak was skateboarding, but only in the officially sanctioned skating zones. The students I taught freshman composition to were so polite I felt that forcing them to answer questions was like ripening fruit by hitting it with a brick.

In short, no one had noticed how odd the building entryways were, except Alice. Of all the graduate students I talked to, only she had taught college before. Ten years in New York City, freshman composition, just like we were teaching now. Only she'd been doing it with students who were slightly less docile, you might say. She had a New York knowingness, like Leonard Michaels, but without the attitude. This was why the staff here already deferred to her, and she deferred right back to them, because she didn't want to stick out more than she already did.

So that, I explained to my therapist, was one reason I liked her. She had experience and authority on her side. But there was something deeper than that, and it had to do with the imbecilic food court that had arisen in place of a student center.

The first time I had lunch with my classmates at the food court, I was showing off how much I knew about the area. There was no student center because they didn't want a place where rioters could congregate. So instead, this tame series of courtyards contained retail shops. Alice had already noticed how it was different from New York. She didn't mean the obvious stuff. Not just how clean it was here. Nor how pleasant the weather. Nor how hard it was to read someone's economic or class status. No, this place was really different, disturbingly.

"Like what?"

"We're outside. Why is there music?"

I almost said, "What music?" But I knew what she meant—it was just so obvious that I wasn't paying attention. There were hidden speakers playing safe, no-lyrics jazzy arrangements of songs that had never even had much of an identity when they were in vogue twenty years ago. I couldn't explain why. This was, now that she'd pointed it out, weird.

I wanted to read Alice's fiction because I suspected it was probably smart. I read her first submissions a few weeks later, and her work was annoyingly good. It was funny and cynical and forgiving of characters' weaknesses. This admiration didn't go the other way: when she first read my work, she thought it was too clever. I hated not being able to impress her easily.

Most of our classmates were in their twenties. Alice and I were in our thirties, and each of us had failed novels hidden in boxes. We'd each gotten handwritten rejection notes and been finalists in contests, and felt success was tantalizingly close often enough that we were, if not cynical, *informed*. When I looked across the workshop table, I saw a fellow commando who wasn't going to let a moment of training go to waste.

Alice said, "I like you because you seem calm, but inside you have this tension and anxiety."

"You mean I remind you of you."

"Yup."

We tried not to get involved with each other, in part because I was still technically with Darcy, but also because we were both cautious. Alice was especially cautious.

Breaking up with Darcy was messy. She and I had rented an apartment together but she'd never quite moved in. One afternoon, Alice volunteered to help me segregate Darcy's stuff, which she turned out to be proficient at. "I'm good in a crisis," she said, which wasn't exactly an explanation of her past. In two hours, all of Darcy's belongings were in a neat, squared-off stack in the living room, all of my stuff was elsewhere ("You don't want her to fuck with it," Alice explained), and I kept asking, "Why are you so good in a crisis?"

She just shook her head. "I'm not ready to tell you my thing."

Like I've said, you aren't an adult until it takes more than one date to tell your life story. Alice and I had a few trips to Starbucks, a few sakes at sushi bars, before she'd caught up on the tales of what made me. Not told in any particular order, but in a serpentine way that I hoped would encourage her to talk about herself. She responded to many anecdotes with a quiet, "You have an eight-hundred-pound mother to deal with."

For over a month, regardless of how many openings I gave her, she didn't talk about her own past, beyond, "New York. Teaching. Ten years." She said that it was a relief to be in a new place where no one knew "her thing." What thing? She still wasn't ready to tell me.

When she did, finally, at a touristy diner in Long Beach, she said it without amendments: beaten and raped at knifepoint, on a mound of broken glass. She testified against the guy at trial and then her roommate was raped.

So there we sat, a man with an eight-hundred-pound mother, and a woman who'd been raped. We were like a couple of U.S. marshals who'd just shown each other their trauma badges. I said what she'd just laid out was so much more intense than anything I'd been through. She said it wasn't a contest.

"Sometimes," she said a little later, "you find someone you realize you can share—"

"Oh, shut up!" I yelled, and then after a second, she burst out laughing as hard as I'd ever heard anyone laugh.

A few weeks later, she and I were having lunch in the student center area. It was packed with students again, fresh-faced, obedient kids buying ramen bowls in this clean, safe, temperate place. The music was playing, as ever.

Alice looked beyond me. "It's the whore." She was too subtle to gesture, but she directed me with her eyes. She knew how to indicate without anyone else noticing, but I tended to wear big muddy boots when I was trying to see.

Here were five hundred students churning around in white shorts and clean expensive T-shirts, sunglasses and TUMI book bags. It could not have been a more prosperous or naive environment. But there, walking in the crowd, was a whore.

I can't guess how old she was. Her skin was sun-damaged and dehydrated. Her jaw jutted unnaturally. She was slinging a heavy purse over her shoulder. She wore a red, spangly top and a distressing amount of makeup. She was somewhere between hobbling and marching on her heels toward the ladies' room.

No one else saw her. But Alice and I were there long enough for the woman to come out and walk again unnoticed through the crowd. No one reacted. She didn't draw a single student's glance. It was like she was invisible to most people.

I couldn't account for this. What was a whore doing in Irvine? Of course—she was doing what she would be doing *anywhere*. Apparently it wasn't all about obeying rules here. But why wasn't anyone else able to see her? Alice was in that moment my inspiration for noticing what was right in front of my eyes.

This was a long story to tell in therapy. But at the end, my therapist nodded. Alice saw things. Which I needed help with. It wasn't bad, was it, Carrie asked, falling in love with someone who heard the music and asked why it was there? Someone who saw the whore and didn't need to ask why the whore was there?

I said it was like having a guide to the secrets of all the world and what monstrous text lay underneath. Also, I said, Alice had amazing green eyes and was a great kisser.

Relationships can be the easiest place to freely make the same damned mistake over and over. Or to break free. I felt like I was asking the right questions now. I had shit to deal with. So did Alice. We were doing it separately, but it was helpful to have a friend who understood the mission.

As my announced reason for being in her office seemed to be resolved, Carrie's approach shifted from active listening. She said what I was telling her was a little more unusual than talking to undergraduates who missed home. She was curious what else I might want to discuss. Her program allowed her to extend therapy for one client per year if she thought it would be fruitful. Obviously I had some life experience to process. Was there anything I wanted to explore?

I didn't hesitate. Of course there was. "Your program? One of the founders was Franklin Baum. He was my psychiatrist. And my mother's. And it's possible he was sleeping with her."

"Pardon?" She needed me to explain that. More than once.

I was saying that Dr. Baum, who lived nearby, who was part of her school's theoretical framework, might be a sexual predator. I saw some uncertainty cross her face. I'd told her about my upbringing, my mom, Daniel's death, and yet this was the first thing I'd said that made her stumble.

She said that we surely had more to work with, and she asked if I was okay. This made me laugh. Of *course* I was okay. I'd been okay for thirty-two years. I asked if *she* was okay, and she said she would probably be eating some chocolate later. As I left, I felt honored, in that my problems had sent her to comfort food, and that meant I was stronger than she was.

Afterward I told Alice what had happened. She said my therapy was over. I had just gotten fired. I explained that no, I wasn't fired. Hadn't she heard about my sessions being extended? In response Alice gave me the kind, sad look you give a good student whose work has been based on the textbook.

When I went back the next week, Carrie had brochures. They were about patients' rights, and how having a therapist seduce you was wrong, and there was a board you should report that to. I remember her explaining this while nodding, trying to get me to nod with her. She was wrapping up our therapy. She told me that it had been good to see me make such progress, please keep in touch, goodbye.

Alice had called it. I was asking a graduate student to help investigate the possible misconduct—based on twenty-five-year-old hearsay related by the son of a strange woman who had already denied making the claim—of the pillar of her own institution. This outweighed how fascinating my problems were.

Which I understood. Being fired made me feel like a hard case. My problems are bigger than any of you can handle, I thought, except Alice. I loved her a little bit more now.

Dr. Baum was in the phone book. I called him.

THE MAN BEHIND THE CURTAIN

WHEN HE ANSWERED, I couldn't focus on what he was saying, because his voice was the same as it had been twenty-five years before. He remembered me immediately. Clients called as adults. He didn't even need to ask why I was coming back. We made an appointment to meet again. "You need to double-check your memories," he said with a purr.

I don't mean to make you further distrust him by saying how soft and careful his voice was. He was a professional and this was his professional persona. His voice means nothing.

I went to his house looking at every detail for confirmation of what I knew for sure, and for some sight or sound that would unveil memories, even banal ones. Ranch house, patient entrance to the left, a little tranquil garden to the side, office inside with leather couch, chairs, toys, and *The Wolf Man* among other books on the shelf, just where it had been in 1972.

The house was on a street high above Newport Beach. The first thing I asked him was about his backyard, which apparently ended in a cliff side. I'd never seen it, as its approach was on the side of the house he lived in, not for patients to see.

He chuckled while confirming a fairly complicated memory. During the 1969 rains, which coincided with my first few weeks of therapy, the soil had started to erode. His lawn had started to collapse into the bay, dramatically. It had been on the news. So, yes, he said, I remembered that correctly.

And now? It was fine now. It had been fine for years. He looked at me quietly.

It's too formal to say I had a plan. I felt that this was going to help me answer the question of why my mother was the way she was. Not with a diagnosis, but with the professional impressions of someone who'd once wondered the same thing. I was aware Dr. Baum had a template for returning patients. He asked me questions about the outcomes of my life (no, I wasn't married; yes, I was fulfilled, generally speaking), but offering little unless I asked.

Then he asked about my mother. I was reluctant to spill much yet. I was interested what he might say without decades of subsequent events to influence him.

He asked, "Do you remember why you were here?"

I overexplained, because he kept looking at me gently, and as a kind of encore returned to one of my greatest hits, saying Mom still hadn't forgiven me for saying, "Mommy's brain is slow."

"Yes. You said many pithy things then." This wasn't exactly sympathy.

"She tends to call me a 'real put-down artist' because of that."

After a longer silence, he continued, "Your mother didn't know how to be a parent. She wanted not a son, but a companion." He shrugged. I should pause here long enough to include the silence that followed, creaks in the house.

There was a little more, but not much. He encouraged me to have sympathy for her, as she'd had a hard childhood. I said I knew about it. He nodded.

I'm not sure how I ended up leaving so quickly. Twenty minutes, maybe a half-hour of stops-and-starts. Right before I left, I handed him a draft of the memoir I'd written about my mother and Daniel. At the time it felt both like we'd had a full accounting and yet I was aware on my motorcycle ride home that I'd been hustled on a conveyor belt through the attractions like a patron at the Haunted Mansion. I hadn't confronted him. We'd made arrangements for me to return in a week, to see if I remembered further things I wanted to talk about.

．．．

When I came back, the atmosphere was remarkably different. I knocked; he told me to come in, but he hadn't left his desk. He was hunched over sheets of paper, reading them with a face unlike what I'd seen from him before. He looked ashen. He was reading my memoir.

"Is this all true?" he asked eventually. He tidied the manuscript up with hands that were actually shaking. I took in the cause and effect of that—what I'd written had done that. I had never seen him look distressed before, and I hadn't known it was possible.

When you're a therapist, he said, you hope for positive outcomes for your patients. That her therapy had failed so miserably made him feel awful. It was clear his experiment hadn't been useful.

It took a moment for me to catch up with that. When I did, at least one word he'd said was confusing.

"Experiment?"

"I took your mother on as a patient as part of your own therapy."

"I thought you were seeing her for her migraines."

"That was an aspect of it. But *you* were my patient. She was part of your problem, and I hoped if I could treat her, it would help you." I was confused, and it showed. He said, "You were manifesting her symptoms."

He said this evenly, as if it was the conclusion of a persuasive argument. I shook my head—I didn't understand.

"I'm sorry," he said. "I wasn't planning on talking about your mother today, but I'm deeply affected by this." He asked me further about her current life, and he interrupted me several times with a strange sensation of heat coming from him.

"Charming," he said, which was not a name I'd used in the memoir. I hadn't said it to him today. He'd remembered it on his own, twenty years after the fact. "Peter Charming."

"Yeah."

"She deserted the marriage for Charming. She deserted therapy—*me*. She deserted *me* for Charming. I guess his influence over her was stronger than mine."

I nodded. *See this. Remember,* I was thinking. It is a sign of the elasticity behind my sense of how the world works that I was unsure if it was troubling that a psychiatrist would say that.

Dr. Baum said, "You know, he said he was a trained psychologist?" This, I filed with "attorney" and everything else Peter was supposed to be. Dr. Baum looked at me. "I don't think he was a mental health professional," he said.

"Oh, but he was."

A pause. "In the sense that he was a psychopath who preyed off of people?"

"Right."

He asked, "Do you talk to her?"

"Funny you should ask. I did, yesterday."

"Who called whom?"

"She called me."

He ran his fingernail across the edge at the corner of the first page of my memoir. "She'll try to move in with you."

"My girlfriend said the same thing."

"Sometimes women know women." I could see him trying to decide how to add something. He said my essay was a frighteningly accurate portrait of her. I had well described her "magical thinking," a concept I hadn't heard of before, and which I needed him to explain, because it just simply sounded as transparent as the oxygen my mother breathed. It also described my old relationship with Lindsay. And maybe much else in my life. So there my mom and I were, united by worldview.

"Your mother has post-traumatic stress disorder from her childhood." He explained that she was continuously drawn to re-creating the trauma of her life on the edge. It was the only way she felt comfortable. This was only going to continue, he said. "Your mother's life has been a tragedy." He was evaluating me now. "As a therapist, when I read this, I was left with one question. What about you?"

"Me?"

"I see you've nearly written a therapeutic history of your mother, and yet, emotionally, you're almost entirely absent. The question is how did you cope?"

He was a good therapist; he had put the answer into the question: distance. I reacted now with pride. I was so objective and such a good journalist now I could hear anything he said without flinching, I thought. But he didn't seem to be complimenting me.

It was ironic, Dr. Baum said (and when I heard how he drew the word out I realized that my mother had probably adopted it from him), that I had omitted myself, in that I was the center of my mother's world. More so than most mothers, he said.

"Your mother's affection for you was problematic," he finally said.

"How so?"

He answered by saying, "You cannot imagine the horrors of her childhood," which I didn't think was an answer.

"I know."

"You don't. Not the mother, not the father. The rest of it." He reached for a file. It was mine. He'd pulled it for reference. He hadn't planned on showing it to me. Inside were my intake papers from 1969.

He directed me down the page, to a section showing a statement someone had typed into a small box. Mother says that her own mother locked her in a closet with servicemen at age seven so that she would "get in trouble the way her mother had."

A closet. I remembered my strobe light.

Dr. Baum then said that my mother had been repeatedly raped as a child. He provided more details, but I was starting to have a problem. I sat there in his office, but I was also nine years old, on the back porch, looking for Kohoutek. Dim objects, deep space. My father glances toward the house, where my mother is inside, somewhere, alone, having a migraine. We always secretly knew that there's a dim, huge, monstrous planet exercising gravity.

"The rapes were only some of it," Dr. Baum said. "It was a house of horrors. She never really escaped it." He then added, skipping the other steps in this proof, "Your mother looked upon you with the feelings one usually reserved for a lover." He paused. "Or a father. She also gave you the same authority as one gives a father, looking to you for approval."

I was thinking of the portrait of George that had lived in our house. I didn't know where it was now, but the way I used to talk to it when I was young made some kind of sense. When enough time had gone by, however, I said, "I never trusted you."

"That would be appropriate," he replied.

"I used to stay in here for hours, playing games of gin rummy or pick-up sticks with you, and I promised myself I wouldn't tell you anything. I thought you were sleeping with her."

"Of course. We even talked about that then." He made a small gesture with steepled hands, as if he was carrying one intangible thought from one place to another. "Your mother had very strong sexual feelings for you. It was inappropriate."

"Her friend said you were sleeping with her."

"Which friend?"

I named her. He knew the name. She was one of the responsible ones.

I could see, not for the first time, something shaking around, one loose moth just out of reach. "There may," he said, "have been fantasies."

That was the end of his sentence. He was looking through me with a face that forty or so years of practice had perfected. The passive voice was brilliant. The conversation continued in a brief circle, me bringing up, in different ways, that he might have slept with her; him conceding that regardless of what he said now, I'd never know. He added that no therapist would ever admit to sleeping with a patient—it would be suicidal.

Then, something happened that made me, even me, understand how far into the woods the conversation had gone. He returned to a previous topic, "You were my patient. She wasn't."

"She was."

"Technically. But remember I was only seeing her as an adjunct to your therapy, Daniel. I thought if I could help her with her issues, it would help you."

I still didn't get it, and I was startled, but he continued:

"You infantilized yourself as a child to cope with your mother's issues. It was the only way to deal with that anxiety, Daniel. She wanted to treat you not as a son but a lover."

I felt fortunate that I was used to not feeling anything. I said, "My name is Glen."

He blinked. "What did I call you?"

"Daniel."

"I have a patient named Daniel," he responded.

"My mother's boyfriend, the one you were reading about just now, was named Daniel."

"Where?"

I pointed out his name.

He looked back at the pages. "So he was."

I said he had to understand why that slip was weird. While telling me about my mother's attraction to me he'd called me by my mother's boyfriend's name. The guy who I'd called "the good son" in the essay. That was one hell of a mistake.

He nodded.

We sat there in nontherapeutic silence, me reading how red his face was. I knew less than when I'd walked in.

The rest of that conversation was brief. We agreed this was the last time I would see him.

I walked out of his office, trying to memorize the way the bamboo and pebbles were supposed to provide a Zen experience.

I was sitting on my motorcycle, and I was putting my helmet on. I looked at his house. I was shaking. I thought, "Mother*fucker*," and then I got angry at myself when I laughed.

I never rode when upset, and so I just sat at the curb, breathing slowly. I thought about the house's backyard on the cliff side. I would never know what it looked like, and so I would have to use my imagination. I pictured the heavy rains of 1969 and the land collapsing, the storm for the history books followed by so many years of stability that people didn't know it had even happened. This didn't soothe me.

I'd gotten confused over time. For some reason I'd thought that knowing whether they had slept together would be the missing piece that explained my mother. But that was a simplification that didn't do her or the world she traveled in any justice.

In the years since then I've checked in on Dr. Baum. He's given up his license. A friend who knows how to interpret the language of bureaucracy said it was probably due to Alzheimer's. When I realized this meant his memories were gone, it was like the Sphinx disappearing into a sandstorm.

An image I can't shake, a crumbling yard high over tidal wetlands with danger signs plastered to a fatigued chain-link fence, soil eroding with the forces of time, wind exposing whatever bones are back there. It's a thin metaphor, embarrassing in its insistence. It means part of me still believes there will be an answer. This will be part of my imagination as long as I'm around. It turns out growing up means accepting ambiguity. It's a lesson I don't like.

FASTER THAN FIRE OR WATER

For years I didn't write this memoir because I was unsure of myself. I was waiting for a specific perception to cascade down and surround me and I was hoping it would feel like radiance. *Oh now I understand why my mother did that.* I was waiting for the moment I would be a slightly better person. Only recently did I understand this meant I was waiting to become a person who agreed with my mom. That was for most of my life the definition of a good son.

When I was a freshman in college my psychology text had a pair of photographs: What happens when you give a baby monkey a warm cloth puppet as a mother? He clings to her. What if you give him a cold mother made of wire? The same: he clings to her. I teared up. Not because my mother was a wire mother—she wasn't—but because the monkey's situation was *obvious*.

I am infinitely secure, in the sense that I have created my own security, not to mention my own infinity, as best I can. But I am missing parts that I think other people have. When I was six or seven, playing in the swimming pool, eyes closed, I would say, "Marco?" and there was tension in my throat, the faint, irrational experience of suspecting I had, by closing my eyes and *trusting*, accidentally thrown off the veil that hides the silence we came out of, revealing myself to be alone in the universe. I live in that moment. I am alone. As are we all, but I see it more plainly than I should.

I am the firstborn son of a firstborn son, I am left-handed, half-Jewish, half-European, an Aries with Scorpio rising, smart, born to every advantage in life. When I am not thinking clearly enough, I believe I control the universe, because that impossibility is carved into me. It's like a scar. To say I don't smacks of weakness, not lucidity. And this isn't because I think I am so powerful, but because I regret I'm too weak to save my mother.

My mom is smart enough to say that she never asked for saving. All those times she said you create your own reality, she hedged her bets with a little irony but—ironically—she was right. She did create her own reality.

If you were to ask my mother what she thinks of me, she would say she's proud of me. I'm a put-down artist. She loves me completely and I am spiteful and I am bitter. She wonders if I still play my flute. (I played the flute in 1973.)

She would tell you I am heartless, arrogant, and spoiled. I didn't invite her to my wedding, which is true. I show my pets more consideration than I show her. I view her as an inconvenience. I'm condescending, judgmental, cold, distant, and will never be a good writer because I lack compassion. I have stolen elements from her life, used them in fiction, and shown her nothing but ingratitude in response.

Nothing you read here will change any of that. I know she feels like this because she wrote an email recently outlining all the ways I've let her down as a son. I didn't read it, but had someone read it to me, and I watched the hands of a clock move as she read. It lasted a little over seventeen minutes.

At one point I burst into laughter, and it wasn't an insane laugh. I realized this was the unexpected sequel to the story she'd written when I was still a child, *My Mother's Lovers—and Other Reasons I'm Valedictorian!* Here was another fantasy about the person I was, only it, again, quickly slid into being about her.

I have empathy for my mom, but I guess she sees, towering over that, how I really do judge her, in the sense that I look at the evidence she's left behind. When I think of my mother, I see a landscape of payment-due storage units, immolated friendships, bankruptcies, double-wide trailers illuminated by sheriff's deputies' flashlights, flies buzzing over kitchen counters with government-issued tubs of ketchup and relish standing open like interrupted surgeries. I see electrical outlets over-loaded with octopus plugs, cords frayed and alarmingly warm to the touch, and in the darkness an old solid-state television with its volume turned up to the maximum, the program casting abrupt blue illumi-nation on chipped chrome dress racks on which hang outfits from many generations that smell of someone else's sweat, exhumed clothes people thought had vanished long ago. I see yellowing multilevel mar-keting brochures with notations made in pen around the bonus struc-ture, fluorescent lights shining on manila files bundled and standing in empty cubicles like abandoned public housing, dead plants choked with impacted roots, Styrofoam coffee cups and fast-food meals flat-tened under the wheels of town cars with bald tires and missing hub-caps fleeing down the interstate in the middle of the night. And on the other side of that, there's my mom, pulse racing, alive, barely, again.

The destruction my mother has brought onto herself is so much larger than how it impacted me. My mother has very carefully, day by day, decision by decision, ruined her own life. She has just as carefully never been destroyed, knowing with the cunning of an aristocrat when exactly to pull her troops back from the border. She's a survivor.

As I heard the email unfolding the story of how I was a traitor, I real-ized there was never going to be an end to the carefully inflicted dam-age. My mother was torturing the person I came into this world loving the most. There was nothing I could do and I was angry about that in every way you can imagine. So I laughed, like a man thrown clear of the wreckage. With that laugh, something in me went free.

Sleeping has never been easy for me. I tend to work at night. I procras-tinate. One midnight, calling it research, I sorted through a five-gallon tub of photographs. I found my infancy, childhood, adolescence, and young adulthood. I also found a flimsy four-by-six-inch spiral-bound booklet with thin red covers on which the word "Snapshots" was hot pressed. It was a thrifty kind of purchase you could have made in a drugstore in 1968, filling in pictures that you glued to cardboard and protected with little plastic sleeves.

The album contained photographs my mother had taken in an attempt to explain her American life to her family back in England. She'd made a copy for each of several sisters, and kept one for herself. Sitting on the floor of my office, I wondered what my earliest memory unsupported by a snapshot actually was. And that night, falling asleep, I drowned.

It's not that I *dreamed* I drowned. Instead, maybe ten minutes after I closed my eyes, I startled awake because I was suffocating. I could see, refracted by currents, distant daylight above me. I was too far from the surface. My lungs were full of water. There was no time for a last thought. I felt my limbs thrash and the sensation leach out of them. There was a useless fight, gray threads piling in at the edges of my vision, and then I lost the battle. Whatever I was, was gone.

I woke up from this, not quite all the way, and then upon my falling asleep it happened again. And again. And again. There were small variations—never in the feeling itself, which was always suffocating terror, but in my understanding of the way death will end me. There was never time for metaphor or resolution, sad little methods (I realized) of trying to distance death enough to lessen its authority.

I couldn't talk to death. I couldn't contain it with an analogy. Instead, I felt sensations of smothering, thrashing, and a few seconds of fighting, long enough to turn animal but too short for narration and then my life was snuffed out.

In between, my most vivid feeling was loneliness. Alice was next to me, but she was asleep and she was in her own dreams, not mine. I was alone, as I had ever been. The regret it came with was devastating. I had loved people, feeling that in my final moments I could surely take comfort in having loved. But there was no room for this as I drowned.

My cat Teddy was on the bed and I tried like hell to make his weight on my legs mean I had a connection to make my ending less awful. It didn't work. I drowned every time I dozed off. It didn't get easier. Around four a.m., I could sleep for a couple of hours.

The following night, it happened the same way.

What was I supposed to learn from this? That second night, I fought and lost as before, and then when it happened again a few minutes later,

I changed the approach of my death, a rhythm I recognized from Eastern philosophy. I tried to relax, and to accept the loss. Perhaps inevitability was a blessing. I died better. I felt a little triumph, as if taking a punch particularly well. Which gave me a shabby happiness. Then, dying a third time, pure acceptance, and I have to admit, impatience. By the fifth or sixth repeat that night, I could no longer hold on to the feeling of surrender, as it was like submitting to an occupying force that doesn't care about your acceptance, as it's simply going to destroy you again and again for no particular reason.

Was this what eternity would be like?

I thought of hospice patients who reached upward. I wondered if they were doing so not because they were reaching for something but because it was the posture of acceptance, as they were being taken from their bodies and into something beyond comprehension. The full terror of that phrase, *beyond comprehension,* resonated with me. What if it's not oblivion, nor an afterlife, but something our brains genuinely can't recognize, something actually beyond terror? The enormity of dying is beyond comprehension.

Analogy is what sets us apart from the animals. But in the same way that dogs can never understand where we go when we leave the house without them, we cannot grasp the process of dying. Death is immune to analogy.

I had a glimpse. In weak translation, it was like being a dim light without form, without senses, without voice, without breath, without control, without the ability to communicate, suspended in a void that was not going to end. All those "withouts" are meant to say that we have no words for the stream-of-consciousness that gibbers in a stew of itself, and only itself, in what could make up eternity.

Oh, I thought, *this is what they mean by hopelessness.*

There was no further place to go, philosophically or spiritually. I was done.

Then I fell asleep and I drowned again.

Alice was sympathetic. She thought it made sense I'd be tangling with death, given what I was writing about. She wondered: if I fell into this void with the sense of the general benevolence of the universe, then what I was describing was actually *joy* beyond comprehension.

As I lay in bed that night I thought that death couldn't be punishment. I didn't believe that whatever poured us into these bodies in the first place followed that up with an eternity of pain and suffering. There was something inexplicably liberating awaiting me after my consciousness finally seeped away. This was the full understanding I was meant to have, I grasped this. I went back to sleep. I was exhausted.

I felt joy. Which stopped nothing, because I drowned again.

I leaned into it. It killed me, just as painfully and mercilessly as before. I was sick of trying to do this with grace or acceptance. I just fucking wanted to stop dying.

I made a mistake—using pharmaceuticals to sleep gave me hangovers, so I signed up for legal marijuana. Rather than smoke it, I decided to try eating some. There seemed to be no effect, so I ate more an hour later, a rookie move.

About four hours after that, I sprang awake with a complete sentence suspended before my open eyes: THERE IS A METAL DEMON PUTTING THOUGHTS IN MY HEAD.

I had never thought this before, and had enough wherewithal to recall that the only difference between now and the rest of my life was the marijuana chocolate I'd digested. The Internet told me there was a thing called "marijuana-induced psychosis," and it lasted four to five hours, and then it left without after-effect.

I wrote as much as I could, recognizing flashes here and there of how the more disturbed members of my family must think. I was relieved to realize that madness and creative impulse aren't the same thing. Madness is disorganized and demoralizing and even in my few hours of trying to negotiate conflicting flashy paranoid thoughts, I felt terribly sad for how much effort empirical thought takes, as every bit of evidence is equally likely, and conspirators are whispering in your ear.

I had nothing better to do, certainly not sleep, so I went back to my old photographs. As a child I had smiled almost every time the shutter snapped. I loved being photographed so very much that I ruined most shots by performing—putting stuffed animals on my head, mock-strangling myself. There was a shot of me on my fifth birthday with my grandparents. I'm wearing a shirt my mother had sewn letters onto:

GLEN THE GREAT. In case that message isn't clear enough, I'm pointing to the shirt with the index fingers of both hands. How long had it taken my mother to select those letters and iron them on herself? I wonder what she had thought while she was doing it. That I'd said, "Mommy's brain is slow"?

I opened the small Instamatic album my mother had made. A documentation of the cornucopia that moving to America had given her. Barcelona loungers, Danish Modern rosewood wall unit, electric stove, dishwasher, my father's darkroom, her new Mercury Cougar. It was quite a haul, and my father hadn't even taken Certron public yet. We were still middle-class.

What could my relatives in England have thought of this? By the time "Tennis Club" showed up they must have dismissed her as a posh showoff who had forgotten her beginnings and who thought she was better than everyone else when all she wanted to do was suggest that they, too, could have this.

A photograph was badly pasted in; I straightened it. Me, on a diving board. It's the only photograph in which I'm not quite smiling. I'm uneasy.

I felt chills between my shoulder blades.

Sometimes there is no metaphor. Instead, it's just flat-coated truth trying to get out of a crate. I wasn't using analogy. I was sending myself a message. My first memory is of drowning.

When I was about two years old, I took swim lessons at a public pool a few minutes by freeway from our house. The prevailing theory then was "sink or swim," which meant that once I had been changed into trunks, a man I'd never seen before would toss me into the swimming pool. I was supposed to start swimming, but I didn't. Instead, I sank to the bottom and had to be dragged out.

My vision of shifting light overhead and my lungs filling with water weren't dreams, but memories. Fished up, on the concrete beside the pool, I hacked and coughed out all the water in my lungs, terrified and weeping. He was angry with me. He yelled. I have always associated the smell of bleach with failure and weakness, and this was the smell of the changing room my mother led me back into.

The next week, we returned. I was thrown into the pool again. And I started to drown again. The week after that, according to my mom, I started crying when we got to the pool, and she had to pry me out of the car. She felt guilty, but she thought she was doing the right thing. Once again, I sank and had to be rescued.

The week after that, when I spotted a water tower by the freeway that meant we were heading to the pool, I started bawling my head off, she says, and we never went back again. She told me the story many times—not the drowning part, but how heartsick she felt when she realized she was punishing a baby. Why did she take me back? The same authority that had told her how to raise a baby was explaining to her that I would learn, eventually, and I would be stronger for it.

Her guilt in telling me of those moments is as strong as cologne. She feels like what she did was unforgivable. The idea she was following the professional advice of the day is something she dismisses. It's almost what Eichmann said, in her eyes. It's where she feels like a bad mother. She thinks that I feel she's a bad mother.

I can almost see her seeing me. I can almost do the voice in her head. She thinks that my infant brain, all emotion and no reason, lashes out, when she was just trying to do the best she could. But that's not good enough (she thinks, and in turn she thinks I think that, too), there is no real excuse, and so, for reasons that she knows are not her fault, I launched into estrangement when I was two years old. It's unfair, she thinks, but part of her also understands me for becoming estranged. She deserves it, at the same time that she doesn't deserve it. I blame her, just like her father did. I'm unwilling to understand, and cannot be led to the truth because I find her unworthy. This is because she finds herself unworthy and knows that I, so much more powerful and condemning than herself, must not only agree but have cruel, enigmatic ways to demonstrate how she has come up short.

I went through that piercing of the onion while the sun was rising and my psychosis retreated. I was breaking a strange barrier by pretending I knew what my mother felt, and within that likely incorrect guess was her guessing, incorrectly, about how I felt. Russian dolls of narrative.

Twice in my life I have taken drugs that have left footprints along a pathway that were worth following when sober. The Ecstasy trip with Lindsay, and this one. They seemed to bookend something.

I don't hate my mom. Sometimes a parent does something thinking it's a good idea, and it isn't. And it leads the next generation into trauma, but it's not something intentionally inflicted. I needed to remember that, not to condemn my mother, but to let her go. I felt like the kink in a hose had shaken out. I didn't hate my mother and I also didn't love her. I felt something clearer and stranger.

There's a sentence I've heard from people who have difficult parents: they did the best they could. It's a sweet idea, especially if you want to get on that scenic road to forgiveness that's supposed to be how being an adult works. But I'm not so sure every parent does the best they can. I'm not even sure what that means.

My mother, like many parents, did something that traumatized me, and then, like many parents, she stopped doing it. But she gets into danger all the time. What I kept coming back to, working the question like wax in my hands, was this: why did my mom *stop* bringing me to that swimming pool?

People have asked me if my mother has been diagnosed with something. She hasn't. I'm polite when I hear them speculate about syndromes and disorders. The axes of the *Diagnostic and Statistical Manual* by which patients are quantified are a complex, evolving net which means to eventually catch all the different oddly colored fish in the sea of mental illness. But to me, if the diagnoses don't also come with a pill to fix them, they're only as helpful as astrology. You are forward and brash, you ignore others' opinions unless they reflect your own desires. You have Narcissistic Personality Disorder. Or you're an Aries. Either way, it diminishes. My mother is not her symptoms nor her sign.

The deeper question for me at one point was whether her behavior was the inexorable approach of a disease—in other words, was her leaning into punches the result of biology? This meant she was blameless. You don't blame a tuberculosis victim for falling sick. Or was her behavior her *choice*? If so, then she could always choose differently.

I came to different conclusions all the time. If my mother was mentally ill, she was doing the best she could. And just maybe there would be a therapy, a pill. If it was her choice to live this way, that meant she could have done things differently and she didn't, and it made me angry at her. But I also hoped she would eventually choose differently, because how could someone so smart and so worthwhile keep hurting herself?

Either way, much of my life I've unconsciously assumed there would be an explanation, and either way, my mother would get eventually better. Or that *I* would get better. What I mean is this: she has started promises with the phrase, "when my ship comes in," and I have wanted to believe there is a ship. And on that ship, deep within an unaccounted-for crate, between flats of tea and exquisite silks made for royalty, there is a box, and in that box, written on a slip of paper in a firm and compassionate hand, is the explanation of how my mother has behaved the best she could, even if this might mean I am a terrible son not to love her.

I imagined myself weeping, and thinking, "If only I had known, all this would have made sense." In other words, I have felt that when my mother's ship came in, it would confirm the story she has told throughout her life.

Here, dawn, weed wearing off, I am realizing there is no ship. My mother will never change. She thinks she loves me, and I believe that if you could biopsy her soul and put the resulting slide under a microscope, you would find that every fiber of her being does in fact love me. Which makes me sad, because her love is terrible.

My mother didn't keep bringing me to the swimming pool. Which meant she had the capacity to change. As I started to feel the truth of this, I felt that same sensation of water filling my nose. I sank into something, reluctantly. *My mother is the sum of her choices. She is what she does.*

I was out of a loop. I was no longer part of her. I could feel this before my brain kicked in and made words to describe it. It was strange, because I had imagined that there would be a word, like "anger" or "sorrow" or "happiness" written across some dark board that only I could read, but it wasn't like that. There weren't words, or interpretations, just the inarguable heaviness of a perspective having shifted. Once, 1974, age ten, in the back of a cab, I went into a tunnel of words, and here, now, I was out of the tunnel, a reveal of sky and air. I felt it, I felt everything, and I didn't need to talk about it, and even though the sun had come up, I went to bed finally and I slept soundly for the first time I could remember.

DIAMOND

MY MOTHER AND DANIEL were living in a van. I arranged to meet her alone in Corona del Mar, at Fashion Island, an outdoor mall near where she, my father, and I had once lived, back when we were rich. It was a grand place for champagne brunches, stores where the salesladies still wore real pearls and sold monogrammed silver tea services. Neither she nor I had been back in years, as we had no real business being there. It was just a coincidental meeting point for us.

I hadn't seen her in a year. She was having trouble walking in her shoes, which she'd found in a dumpster, and the ice cream cone I'd bought her dripped into her lap. She kept asking me when I was going to get married, when I was going to make her a grandmother, if I wanted to get in on her multilevel marketing scheme, if I wanted to learn to be a paralegal.

We walked slowly past the expensive stores. When I was a child, I had loved going into Russo's Pets to see their two-headed snake. And it was still there, now stuffed and in a diorama kept in back. This was where we'd gotten Leo. She asked if I remembered that. I told her I did.

My mother mentioned, not for the first time, a story she'd heard when she first came to America. A woman was trapped in her car when trying to drive in a flood. The waters came up, and up, and she drowned.

But when they found her the next day, her hands were sticking up out of the river, and in them was her baby, whom she had held up even after she drowned. My mother said that when she first heard that story, she felt bad about herself, because she knew she could never live up to that woman's heroism. But that changed when she was pregnant. Once she had a baby, she knew that she could do that for me. Her love was that deep.

She looked at the toddlers on the playground. She reminisced about how patient I was with children who weren't as smart as I was. "You'd be good at sales," she said.

The kids were darting behind a wall of colored glass, primary color blocks that distorted their reflections. There was a koi pond with huge square river rocks below our feet, and I had a fleeting perception of the children and the fish in motion, the clarity of water and the filter of glass being somehow one and the same to me.

I knew that after Mom left she would go with Daniel, who might kill her. I was going to hug her goodbye. In the crowd, I saw children, dozens of children, startling in their simple needs. My mother saw deposed princes, unjustly accused doctors, inventors who need money to fight the patent office. When she looked my way, she saw through a kaleidoscope.

My mother, I thought at the time, was trapped in a fantasy, unable to tell the difference between the Mighty Oz and the Man Behind the Curtain. I think that before that day, if you had asked me, I would have said I loved my mother, and I hoped things were looking up for her, and they probably would, as soon as the lawsuit was over, as soon as the landlord got his blood money. After that day, I would tell you it was like seeing the koi below our feet. Clear as water. And later, much later, I would tell you I felt sad for her. My mother has lived with a fiercely intelligent enemy determined to almost destroy, but not quite, the life of her host, and anyone who gets close enough will sense the long shadows near the sweet woman who always looks so concerned. *Mom, that thing you tried to escape? It's you. I am so sorry.*

It was getting late, I said. She agreed. We were at the base of the hill on top of which our old house on Setting Sun Drive stood. People who were still millionaires lived there. Neither of us looked that way. What would we have said?

Mom always has an eye for the next venture. What she spotted now was a jewelry store she used to shop in. There was a sign in the window: "Ask about our contest. Details inside." She wanted to go in for a minute before we said goodbye.

The store had dropped from its former days into something starved and humiliated. There were bright orange SALE! signs over most of the merchandise. The owner, red-eyed, broken veins in his nose, asked if he could help us.

"My son and I came in about your contest."

He walked us to the end of the counter. Ten diamonds, half a carat each, rested on a black velvet backing board. "Nine of these are cubic zirconium," he said to my mother. "If you can guess which is a real diamond, you get fifty dollars off any purchase of two hundred dollars or more."

I thanked him. I was tired. I thought we were ready to leave.

But my mother said, "Diamond," pointing at one particular stone.

The owner smiled. "That's right. That's the diamond. You're the winner."

ACKNOWLEDGMENTS

People rarely ask if historical fiction is autobiographical. This has allowed that genre to be a good tent for showcasing my impulse to rewrite events from my life in accordance with my worldview. I haven't used that muscle in this book.

Nonetheless, if you appear here, you probably remember things differently than I do. After he read a draft, I asked my dad if he wanted this book to provide more nuance, and he said, "I don't do nuance."

Which is a shame. While I was interviewing him, I mentioned the Fabergé chess set and its place as a metaphor in this story for the riches that had passed from our lives, valuables that—

"It wasn't a Fabergé," he said.

I said, "Wait—what?"

He explained that at the time of the auction, he wasn't that sophisticated about who Fabergé was. But he'd convinced himself that it was Fabergé's because he wanted it to be true.

This abruptly made it an entirely different but equally good metaphor.

"It was contemporary. It was a collectible," he said, pronouncing the word like it was a kind of luncheon meat.

"I thought it was incredibly valuable."

"Expensive, but not valuable."

So, regardless of what he claims, I'm saying there are nuances. There are things I didn't know.

I've seen memoir writers account for the distortions in their narratives. My own issue is cause and effect. I have tried, by saying that one thing happened, and then another thing happened because of it, to make sense out of some chaos. My mother bailed out the man who stole her jewelry. Peter Charming showed up at our door with a rubber tree plant as an apology. But was it for the infraction I've outlined here or for something else? It's possible I have organized some events so they'll make sense. If I were to console myself for that (and I'm not sure I should), I'd add that this is a pathology which did not start with, and certainly doesn't singularly apply to, the written part of my life.

I first wrote a small section of this during a memoir workshop taught by Geoffrey Wolff at UC Irvine in 1996. After class, Wolff patiently explained to me that my mother hadn't really found the diamond. I will never forget the series of emotions that crossed his face when I said, "Wait, are you sure?" That's when the door opened. Thank you, Geoffrey.

You are correct: "Nicolas et in Arcadia ego" isn't the name of the painting. Saturn actually takes twenty-nine years and then some to get around the sun. Some of the addresses are approximations. Miriam actually was pretty. "Camelot gone" is Richard Brautigan's phrase. Sherman Day Thacher wasn't the first person to say "there's something about the outside of a horse that's good for the inside of a boy"—but he did say it eventually. In *Fantastic Four 51*, the Negative Zone was still called "Subspace." I have tried to find reference for my father's insistence that a character in the daily *Los Angeles Times* version of the Asterix strip was named "Ropus Dopus," but I've come up empty. Xander Cameron made an observation about Thacher and Athens that I've adapted here. Amy Gerstler said, "Fear is a civilizing influence," an observation so excellent I've put it in two books.

I gave up on this project as impossible several times, and several times unexpected grace gave it new life. Thank you to Alice Sebold for taking the pages out of the trash; *Zyzzyva* for publishing an early version of the "2709 Setting Sun Drive" chapter; the Squaw Valley Community of Writers for asking me to give a lecture about memoir; Rob Spillman for shoving me in front of Vivian Gornick's *The Situation and the Story;* Diana Miller for happening to telephone me while I was walking in circles around my manuscript in anticipation of throwing it away, again. Each of these resulted in the resurrection of what I'd thought was beyond comprehension.

People to whom I complained along the way: Ben Acker, Steve Adams, Lisa Alvarez, Aimee Bender, Amber Benson, James Bierman, Carolyn Birnbaum, Ben Blacker, Diane Bourdo, Gavin Bryars, JoŸ Butler, Ron Carlson, Tim Caron, Bill Charman, Howard Chaykin, Mark Childress, Laura Cogan, Tom Cole, Bernard Cooper (everyone should read *Truth Serum*), Jeffrey Cranor, Shawn Cuddy, Rob Delaney, Lynne Dixon, Amanda Eichstaedt (listen to *Bakersfield and Beyond* on KWMR), Maria Farrell, Joseph Fink, Matt Fraction (finally, a part of the book he'll like), Dagmar Frinta, Sina Grace, Judith Grossman, Michelle Henning, Eli Horowitz, Sean Howe, Jan Iverson, Brady KaŸ, Evan Karp, Hope Larson, Michelle Latiolais, Felix Lu, Joen Madonna, Paul Madonna, Maggie Malone, Patrick McDonnell, Maria MocŸacz, Katie Moody, Judith Moore, David M'Rahi, Violaine M'Rahi, Kirsten Neilsen, Vix Nolan von Throuple, Karen O'Connell, Lexi Olian, JoŸ Parish, Alison Powell, JoŸ Raeside, SeanMichael Rau, Kit Reed, Adam Rogers, Diana Schutz, Julia Scott, Gail Seneca, Matt Shakman, Jon Shestack, Paul F. Tompkins (who is now legally required to admire this book), Andrew Tonkavich, Oscar Villalon, Barb Wagner, Matt Wagner, Karen Wessel (nice try!), Wally Wolodarsky, and Vanilla Ya-Ya. Some of these names might be desserts.

Supportive institutions: ALOUD, Babylon Salon, CSULB, East Bay Express, the Hammer Museum, Greenlight Books, The Grotto, KWMR, MacDowell Colony, Manx Museum, Marin Sun Farms, Quiet Lightning, Pints & Prose, the *San Francisco Bay Guardian,* Why There Are Words, Writers with Drinks, the Corporation of Yaddo, and my family (you know who you are).

This book is now complete: Susan Golomb & Writers House; Diana Miller, Betsy Sallee, Jessica Purcell, Danielle Plafsky, Sonny Mehta, & Knopf; Carole Welch, Jenny Campbell, Fleur Clarke, & Hodder.

Animals I Have Known: Coco, George, Charlie, Max, Bogie. We are all brothers under the skin.

Berry/Buck/Mills/Stipe: Guys, I'm so sorry.

David Leavitt: Also very sorry.

Unicorn: Sara Shay

I yam what I yam.